THE THERAPEUTIC RELATIONSHIP

THE THERAPEUTIC RELATIONSHIP

PERSPECTIVES AND THEMES

EDITED BY

SHEILA HAUGH

AND

STEPHEN PAUL

PCCS BOOKS
Ross-on-Wye

First published in 2008
Reprinted in 2008

PCCS BOOKS Ltd
2 Cropper Row
Alton Road
Ross-on-Wye
Herefordshire
HR9 5LA
UK
Tel +44 (0)1989 763 900
www.pccs-books.co.uk

The Therapeutic Relationship: Perspectives and themes

A CIP catalogue record for this book is available from the British Library

ISBN 978 1 906254 04 9

Cover design by Old Dog Graphics
Printed by Athenæum Press, Gateshead, UK

DEDICATIONS

To my parents, Pat and John Haugh, and my husband, Patrick Baker. No longer here, much loved and profoundly mourned.

Sheila Haugh

To my mother, Joan, my wife, Kathy, and my daughter, Rosie, with heartfelt appreciation.

Steve Paul

ACKNOWLEDGEMENTS

The enthusiasm for the topic of this book was born from working with many people across different orientations for over twenty years. In particular, my colleagues Alison Hall, Kate Kent, Kay McFarlane, Steve Paul and Geoff Pelham in the Centre for Psychological Therapies at Leeds Metropolitan University, during the past four years.

Sheila Haugh

I wish to acknowledge the contribution of Petruska Clarkson to the development of understanding in relation to both the therapeutic relationship and group work. I also wish to acknowledge the influence of my many colleagues and clients over thirty years of practice. Thank you to my family, particularly Kathy and Rosie, for their patience and support during the writing of this book.

Stephen Paul

CONTENTS

CHAPTER 1

THE THERAPEUTIC RELATIONSHIP
BACKGROUND AND CONTEXT

STEPHEN PAUL
SHEILA HAUGH

More and more theorists, researchers and practitioners are becoming aware of the centrality of the relationship in therapy. In this book, we will explore the place of the therapeutic relationship in all the current major traditions; significant developments in these approaches; those aspects of the therapeutic relationship that do not fit into a 'schools' model, and consider the future for practice.

As we survey the profession of counselling and psychotherapy at the beginning of the twenty-first century, it is clear that the field has mushroomed in growth in recent years. Although the roots of the theory and practice of counselling and psychotherapy go back hundreds of years, from Persian practice in the eighth century to the advent of moral therapy in the eighteenth century, it was in the twentieth century that orientations within the discipline started to become established. Most references define the word 'psychotherapy' as coming from the Greek *psyche*, meaning spirit, soul, life or mind and *therapeía,* meaning healing. The term 'counselling' had been used previously to refer to vocational guidance (Parsons, 1909) and it was Carl Rogers who first used the term to describe his (and others') work with distressed people. This use of the word 'counselling' by Rogers was a pragmatic response to the American psychiatric profession. Although a psychologist, Rogers was not allowed to call himself a psychotherapist by virtue of the fact that he did not have a medical degree and so, in their eyes, was a 'lay' practitioner. Indeed, it was not until 1988 that the American Psychoanalytic Association admitted non-medically qualified practitioners to their ranks, despite the fact that Sigmund Freud, the founder of psychoanalysis, had always supported the idea of lay practitioners (1927).

Freud, as well as being the architect of psychoanalysis, can be regarded as one of the great forebears of psychological therapy. His formulation of the id, the ego and the superego, and his hypothesis of the unconscious, laid the groundwork and infrastructure for the development of psychoanalysis and indeed, many other orientations. Traditionally, the therapist analysed the client (or 'patient' as the client was called) and there was little emphasis on the interpersonal relationship.[1] From the early work of Freud, four traditions have developed which are commonly called 'forces', and within any force there may be a range of specific schools of therapy.

---

1. This is not to ignore the concepts of transference and countertransference. However, these notions, in most formulations, were understood to be giving information about the patient's unconscious processes rather than the therapeutic relationship per se. (See Howard, this volume.)

THE FOUR FORCES

The first force of *psychoanalytic*[2] psychology focuses on the dynamics between the conscious and unconscious parts of the self and relations with the outer/social world. The analyst, with an understanding of the dynamics of the mind, could, when appropriate, offer an interpretation of the patient's material, bring the unconscious to consciousness (Mitchell & Black, 1995). In this way, a Freudian therapist typically analysed the patient and functioned in an expert role. Freud's ideas influenced the work of many psychologists, among them Adler, Assagioli, Bowlby, Fairbairn, Guntrip, Jung, Klein and Rank. Through these theorists and practitioners, Freud's work was instrumental in developing many of the analytic/dynamic approaches to therapy. In recent years, within the psychoanalytical tradition, there has been an increasing emphasis on interpersonal relations in the therapeutic process.

The second force, *behaviourism*, developed out of social learning theory influenced by the work of Skinner, Watson and others (Baum, 2005). Rather than an interest in bringing unconscious material into awareness, as with psychoanalytical practice, the focus for the behaviourist was on changing behaviour. Beck, Ellis and others developed a range of approaches in this area, and in the last thirty years there has been a developing emphasis on cognition and its effect on behaviour. The field has more recently expanded to include cognitive therapy, cognitive-behavioural therapy and other approaches working with cognition. In this model, the therapist is seen more as a trainer, and their role as one of an educator.

Humanistic psychology, the third force, also called existential-humanistic psychology, has developed from divergent roots. Born in the optimistic post-war years of the 1940s and 1950s, particularly in America, humanistic psychology is interested in the subjective reality of the individual, focusing on individual responsibility and self-determination. The approach builds from a tradition of phenomenology, whereby the focus lies in the experience and perception of a person (rather than a notion of the unconscious or working only with behaviour). Abraham Maslow and Carl Rogers brought to the fore the notion of self-actualisation (Maslow) and the actualising tendency (Rogers). These concepts were in sharp contrast to the psychoanalytical ideas that human beings were driven to adapt to unconscious conflicts, and the behaviourist notion that human behaviour can be explained as conditioned responses or reflexes and the habits formed from those responses and reflexes. People such as Bugental, Laing, Perls and Rogers contributed to the development of widely differing orientations within the humanistic tradition. Bugental and Laing, for example, were key people in the development of existential therapy, a body of therapy that located the individual in the context of their life setting and with an emphasis on living authentically within life's limitations. Perls and Rogers on the other hand, placed the focus more clearly on the potential of the individual to actualise all their capacities in relationship to themselves and others. The

---

2. Some describe behaviourism as the first force and psychoanalysis as the second force. We have selected the more common usage. Nevertheless, this shows how little in the field of psychology can be stated as fact.

therapist was typically engaged in helping the client take responsibility for their situation and operated more as a catalyst for growth.

Finally, and most recently, has been the development of the fourth force in psychology, that of the *transpersonal*. Transpersonal psychologists consider humanistic psychology to be missing some essential part of the human experience, something they described variously as the spiritual, transcendent or beyond the personal. Seeing all the previous forces in psychology as limiting in their view of the full experience of being human, this psychology takes a much wider and explicitly holistic view of the individual. Some theorists, originally associated with the other forces, have been instrumental in the development of this approach, for example Assagioli and Jung, whilst others, including Grof, Vaughan and Walsh (Hastings, 1999), have developed specialised approaches to human development. A holistic development of the client may include an explicit role in guiding a person to what may be termed higher or transcendental states of development.

In the last twenty years, there has also been the development of a range of interpersonal and relational approaches. These approaches have sought to focus on human relations and the therapeutic relationship and have moved away from a traditional school-based approach. This had led to developments in eclectic and integrative ways of working with approaches typically focused on the application of interventions from a variety of models.

There is currently a myriad of approaches to counselling and psychotherapy – some have estimated there to be over 400 varieties of psychotherapies (see Corsini & Wedding, 2008). To add to this complexity, within the four forces, established schools are often characterised by slight nuances that differentiate them from each other, and Corsini and Wedding suggest that the barriers between the schools are becoming more and more permeable. Current research and meta-studies reflect this permeability in that there is no clear evidence that any one approach is better than any other (cf. Lambert, 2004, Stiles et al., 2006). Recent research has further indicated that the therapeutic relationship itself may be more instrumental in the process of therapeutic change in the client than any model of therapy or use of techniques or interventions. Lambert, Bergin and Garfield (2004), in their reviews of research in psychotherapy, suggest that the long-term dominance of the major schools of theory is over and that what might be called 'an eclectic position' has taken precedence.

THE THERAPEUTIC RELATIONSHIP: THEMES AND PERSPECTIVES

At its simplest, the therapeutic relationship is nothing more than the relationship between the client and therapist and, at first glance, this might be an adequate definition. But, as ever, the devil is in the detail. We are not referring to just any relationship: we are thinking about a relationship that is of benefit to at least one member of the therapeutic encounter – possibly both. We are thinking about a relationship that is healing, that is restorative. Some practitioners in some settings, ourselves included, would hope that such a relationship be growthful – something beyond curative and remedial. Thus, the demands made of this relationship are high. It goes without saying that each relationship is unique – each person in the relationship is unique. It perhaps also goes without saying that even within the different orientations, each practitioner will bring different nuances to their approach, a different understanding of the same concepts, a unique implementation of their theory in practice.

The original idea for this book was formed (by Stephen Paul) as a result of collaboration with a team of practitioners and academics working across orientations. For both of us, the creative challenges of describing, developing and, not least, living the therapeutic relationship in such an environment, led to the impetus to produce this book. With this in mind, the following considerations guided us in the commissioning of chapters.

• The therapeutic relationship is central to all therapy, and the relationship has many different dimensions (or different levels).

The one common theme in all therapeutic theory and practice, regardless of orientation, is the interaction or encounter between client and therapist. This interaction is the ground for all aspects of the therapy. Different theories conceptualise this encounter in different ways. At the same time, virtually all models accept the centrality and the dimensions of the relationship, and that both client and therapist create those dimensions (see Lambert, 2004). We have been interested in developing understanding and clarity on how the dimensions of the therapeutic relationship are conceptualised across different orientations.

• Evidence points to the relationship, not the theory, as fundamental.

There is evidence that the core model of the therapist has less influence on outcome than the relationship between the client and the therapist. Research has further identified generic factors that work across all approaches (ibid.). Bringing together descriptions of the way in which the relationship is conceptualised might help us to understand the elements of the relationship that are common, and perhaps therefore fundamental, to all orientations. This might go some way in providing the practitioner with a solid foundation for their work, embedded in ideas that promote a therapeutic relationship rather than ideas entombed in an ideology.

• Much training, practice and theorising is focused on a particular body of theory with little crossover of ideas.

The main approaches to counselling and psychotherapy continue to operate with a bunker-like approach, with distinctive philosophies, languages and concepts, and there is little serious interaction between these schools.[3] Whilst we are not necessarily interested in trying to synthesise these approaches in the first instance, it is clear that we are all trying to describe the same phenomena – the therapeutic relationship. It is also clear

---

3. We would include integrative approaches in this statement as they often rely on a psychoanalytical /psychodymanic model of the person and personality development.

that we are all trying to do the same thing: help (however we define that word) the client who has come to us with some level of distress or dis-ease. We wanted to draw together these descriptions to see if we could find commonalities that would aid theory and practice development.

• Many practitioners view themselves as trans-theoretical/integrative as they develop years of practice.

Feltham (1997) has noted the tendency for practitioners to train in one model and then to develop a wide range of expertise that fits their own needs for practice. In some cases, this has led to a more generic eclecticism and a move away from schools. It is also clear that experienced therapists across modalities are more alike in practice than inexperienced therapists within the same model, even if they do not consider themselves trans-theoretical or integrative. This suggests to us that as counsellors and therapists become less reliant on 'external' theory and more reliant on their immediate interaction with a client, there are some key and fundamental notions being lived in the meeting with the client. Bringing a number of perspectives and themes together might help us more easily identify these cross-orientation similarities.

• Focus on the client, not the theory.

The focus for change is clearly on the client, with the theoretical model informing an understanding of the processes. Increasingly, research has reflected this in an emphasis on exploring what the factors are that determine positive change in therapy rather than on therapeutic, school-based outcomes.

• Therapists often marginalise issues of power and culture.

Traditionally, issues of diversity, power and anti-oppressive practice were not considered central to practice. At the very best, they were thought of as something that needed to be considered in *addition* to theory and practice training rather than being seen as *pivotal* to the counselling relationship. In the last five to ten years, we are happy to note that this omission is being addressed, at least to some extent. Ironically, in our experience, the developing interest in the authentic encounter between client and therapist has, led some to assert, for example, that they do not physically see a person's colour/sex/physical abilities/age. In this example, we have used physically obvious aspects of a person. This dynamic can also happen for those aspects of a person's lived experience that may not be so immediately obvious, such as ethnicity, sexuality or class. We believe that approaches to practice which ignore such dimensions are limited and counterproductive, adding to a person's (the client's) distress. Thus, we wanted to draw out clear statements from the different orientations and approaches on how they might conceptualise this aspect of the therapeutic relationship.

• The therapeutic relationship is expressed in a myriad of ways, verbally and non-verbally and takes place in a myriad of settings.

The professionalisation of an encounter that seeks, for the most part, to remedy intimate personal pain may result in distancing the therapist from the client. Issues such as love, touch and intimacy may be central to the human encounter, but they risk being filtered out of the therapeutic relationship. Additionally, the place and context of therapy will determine the nature of both the process and content of therapy. These are both areas we felt worthy of attention.

• Increasingly, much current training now focuses more extensively on the relationship itself.

Training in counselling and psychotherapy has moved more explicitly towards a focus on interpersonal and relational factors. The emphasis for practice and review is on the relationship and extrapolating that out to theory. It seemed timely to reflect this tendency in a collection of writings whereby practitioners were asked to consider their orientation and interests specifically in the light of the therapeutic relationship.

• Many texts have been written to fulfil academic and scholarly requirements.

It has been our experience that these texts are often seated within a particular school of therapy and exclude wider exploration and contexts. We believe a more straightforward text, accessible to and readable for all practitioners be they trainee, lay or professional, is required.

An accompanying notion to all the above is that there is little substantive difference between counselling and psychotherapy and indeed, to some degree, between the whole range of what are now often called 'psychological therapies'. For some practitioners, how they engage in the therapy session may differ if it is called counselling or psychotherapy, but this may have as much to do with the context and the setting itself as with any particular ideological stance on the differences. For other practitioners, we have heard it argued that counselling is short-term, issue-based work, whilst psychotherapy is long-term and based on personality change. We have also heard it argued that psychotherapists usually train longer than counsellors and that their training involves longer therapy for themselves; this, so the argument goes, means that a psychotherapist can work more effectively with more deeply distressed clients. We are not convinced by these arguments for a number of reasons – not least as there is scant evidence for any of these assertions other than, 'it was good for me'. For the purposes of this book, the terms 'therapy', 'counselling' and 'psychotherapy' may be considered interchangeable unless explicitly differentiated by individual authors.

This book aims to:

• spell out clearly how different models view the relationship and its place in therapeutic change
• highlight modern developments and trends in each model
• identify commonalities and differences in different approaches
• help the practitioner understand different approaches and clarify their own approach

- illustrate how different models work with power and diversity
- consider those aspects of the therapeutic relationship that transcend the schools of psychotherapy.

As editors, we wanted to explore how the major schools in the four different forces in psychology conceptualise what we believe to be the context for change: the therapeutic relationship. We wanted to be able to identify current thinking in each approach and to explore other important areas that we believe might be influential in an understanding of the therapeutic relationship.

The book falls into two sections, and whilst it is possible to read each section and indeed chapter in its own right, we expect readers will find many of the themes and perspectives illuminating and challenging. It is only in this way that the commonalities and differences can be fully appreciated. It will be the way we can identify what aspects of the therapeutic relationship go beyond individual models.

PERSPECTIVES ON THE THERAPEUTIC RELATIONSHIP

In this section of the book, key practitioners in each of the main traditions outline and explore the concept of the therapeutic relationship in their approach. Aside from the two chapters on research, authors were invited to consider the following areas:

- The background to the particular approach: a summary of key developments, philosophical and historical antecedents and key elements of the theory

- The position of therapist and client in therapy: the conceptualisation of the client–therapist relationship, the therapist's stance to the work and the development of the therapeutic relationship.

- Psychological factors in the relationship: how the approach determines therapeutic change and psychological dynamics in the relationship.

- Therapeutic interventions: what the therapist does and does not do in therapy and a consideration of process and content factors.

- Cultural contexts, power and conceptualisation of individual differences: how the approach conceptualises the relationship in relation to culture, power and diversity, and an exploration of the place of power in the relationship.

- Strengths and weaknesses: how this approach helps our understanding of the therapeutic relationship and a consideration of deficits in theory and practice.

- Research evidence: what studies have actually found.

- New developments: a consideration of the approach both in theory and practice, and divergences from core theory.

The two chapters on research follow a different format. Our chapter, 'The relationship not the therapy? What the research tells us', gives an overview on the research into the therapeutic relationship and Jerold Bozarth and Noriko Motomasa critique the paradigms of research more generally.

THEMES IN THE THERAPEUTIC RELATIONSHIP

For this section of the book, we invited authors to explore what may be important and, in some areas, neglected aspects of the therapeutic relationship. Authors were invited to write about their area of interest and expertise with particular reference to the therapeutic relationship. There are other areas that we would have liked to include but, as ever, space has its limitations. Whilst the inclusion of the topics betrays the interest of us, the editors, the fact that something might be missing should not be understood to mean that we believe the topics included are the only ones of interest.

In conclusion, the theme that runs through the book is each author's commitment to the therapeutic relationship and their willingness to share their ideas with others. We hope that this exploration of the dimensions of the therapeutic relationship will enable the reader to develop their own understanding of the complexities of the therapeutic encounter.

REFERENCES

Baum, WM (2005) *Understanding Behaviorism: Behavior, culture and evolution.* Oxford: Blackwell.

Corsini, RJ & Wedding, D (2008) *Current Psychotherapies* (8th edn). Belmont, CA: Thomson Wadsworth.

Feltham, C (1997) Challenging the core theoretical model. *Counselling, 8* (2), 121–5.

Freud, S (1927) The question of lay analysis. In J Strachey *The Standard Edition of the Complete Psychological Works of Sigmund Freud, Vol. XX (1925–1926).* London: Hogarth Press.

Hastings, R (1999) Transpersonal psychology: The fourth force. In D Moss (Ed) *Humanistic and Transpersonal Psychology* (pp. 192–208). Westport, CT: Greenwood Press.

Lambert, MJ (2004) (Ed) *Bergin & Garfield's Handbook of Psychotherapy and Behavior Change* (5th edn). New York: John Wiley & Sons.

Lambert, MJ, Bergin AE & Garfield SL (2004) Introduction and historical overview. In MJ Lambert (Ed) *Bergin & Garfield's Handbook of Psychotherapy and Behavior Change* (5th edn) (pp. 3–15). New York: John Wiley & Sons.

Mitchell, SA & Black, MJ (1995) *Freud and Beyond.* New York: Basic Books.

Parsons, F (1909) *Choosing a Vocation.* Boston, MA: Houghton Mifflin.

Stiles, WB, Barkham, M, Twigg, E & Mellor-Clark, J (2006) Effectiveness of cognitive-behavioural, person-centred and psychodynamic therapies as practised in UK National Health Service settings. *Psychological Medicine, 36,* 555–66.

Chapter 2

THE RELATIONSHIP, NOT THE THERAPY?
WHAT THE RESEARCH TELLS US

Stephen Paul

Sheila Haugh

Many, if not most, therapists have been attracted to working in the psychological therapies because of their wish to work meaningfully with people. This desire to help another person in the therapeutic encounter has fuelled the passion of many. There is also a great deal of interest in the relational and interpersonal aspects of therapeutic practice at this time. A body of writing and practice development has rapidly grown as schools of therapy review their core theories and practice. Historically, there have not been many practitioner-researchers in psychotherapy and counselling, particularly in the UK. Indeed, it seems that many practitioners have had limited interest in research matters. To compound this situation, for those practitioners with little or no background in research, the concepts and methods can appear opaque, full of seemingly meaningless numbers and with questionable conclusions. Nevertheless, there is no doubt that the effectiveness of psychological therapies needs to be proven. The era when an entire therapy modality can be classified as a 'pseudoscience' (an approach with no empirical verifiability) as Popper called psychoanalysis (1962) is no longer acceptable, particularly in an era of limited resources.

In this chapter, we will review the research into psychotherapy over several decades, establish what the research might tell us, consider implications for practice, and we will also consider the future of research into psychotherapy. A further aim will be to consider the difficulties associated with the status of the research, asking the question 'how much does it tell us in relation to psychotherapy generally?' For the purpose of clarifying discussion in this chapter, evaluation of what may be called, psychotherapy, counselling, psychological therapies, and like terms, are considered similarly: we are using the terms generically. Typically, in some studies, the concept of 'patient' may be used; in this chapter we use the word 'client'.

BACKGROUND

Research in the talking therapies has proliferated in recent years (Freedheim, 1992, Lambert, Bergin & Garfield, 2004). Early Freudian research into 'the importance of early-life experiences, repressed conflict and unconscious motivation' (Lambert, Bergin & Garfield, 2004: 3) was followed by the empirical studies of Rogers (Rogers & Dymond,

1954). This was part of the scene-setting for the quantitative research of psychological therapies more generally. Early comparative studies (Luborsky, Singer & Luborsky, 1975) noted that all therapies were variably successful. The notion of the Dodo effect (from *Alice's Adventures in Wonderland*) was realised in psychotherapy: 'All shall be winners and all shall have prizes'. To this day, when one examines the relative differences in psychotherapy outcomes, the Dodo effect is still apparent across orientations (Luborsky et al., 2002). Even comparative studies exploring what therapy works for what condition are not conclusive in determining categorically any outright winners (see Roth & Fonagy, 2004). Many researchers are of the opinion that comparative studies of the schools of therapy will not assist us in deciding which school is the best in working with a particular client group.

Methodological issues and controversy over which therapy works best have, to some degree, been addressed by the use of meta-analyses in the reviews of primary research (Lambert & Ogles, 2004). Such studies employ systematic and objective methods to evaluate, compare and review many different studies. The key findings in psychotherapy research are often the result of meta-analyses of hundreds of studies. This goes some way to help remedy problems of poor methodology and the bias of researchers. Although it may be a surprise to some readers, given the generally accepted notion that research is 'objective', therapist bias is significant. Lambert (2002) comments that:

> Whilst statistically significant differences can sometimes be found favouring the superiority of one treatment over another, these differences are not so large that their practical effects are noteworthy. Furthermore, approximately two-thirds of the observed small differences between psychotherapies in outcome can be attributed to investigator allegiance. (p. 20)

The importance of the therapeutic relationship in research should not be underestimated. Orlinsky, Grawe and Parks (1994), in a meta-analysis of research, noted that the power of the therapeutic relationship was reflected in more than 1,000 studies. They identified key criteria, such as therapist credibility, skill, collaborativeness, empathic understanding, affirmation of the client and attention to the client's affective experience as associated with positive outcomes. They further indicated the following as the most important determinants of outcome:

- The quality of patients' participation in therapy as the most important determinant.
- The therapeutic bond, especially as determined by the client.
- The therapist's contribution, especially through 'empathic, affirmative, collaborative and self-congruent engagement' (Orlinsky, Grawe & Parks, 1994: 361) with the client.
- The skilful application of potent interventions.

They note these determinants 'can be considered *facts* established by 40+ years of research' (ibid.: 361–2).

WHICH MODEL WORKS BEST

Over most of the last century, different schools considered themselves more effective than others. Much of the literature and research focused on an endeavour to prove one particular school's efficacy over another. In recent years, research studies (Beutler et al., 2004) have indicated that whilst there may be marginal gains for one approach in one study, overall, there is little to separate one from another. Some researchers go further, for example Wampold (2001) in his meta-analysis of decades of therapy, states that there is no significant difference of measure in outcome between approaches. Wampold identifies the following factors that do affect outcomes:

1. General effects: common factors that underlie all psychotherapies – 70%.

2. Specific effects: particular aspects linked to a specific model – 8%.

3. Unexplained variability: most likely linked to client differences – 22%.

Wampold's findings indicate model-related effects to be very small (8%). He concludes that there is little evidence for a model of therapy based on specific treatment ingredients (i.e. specific techniques or interventions). On the other hand, there is strong evidence for a contextual model based on therapeutic setting and the client's presenting problem linked to common factors. Wampold's findings suggest that the current favouring of cognitive behavioural therapy (CBT) may be unfounded or unjustifiable in some contexts. He reports that the distinctive/specific ingredients of CBT for the treatment of depression and anxiety are not demonstrably responsible themselves for any successful outcome in these conditions. Wampold further reports that adherence to treatment protocol and manuals is not reliably associated with successful outcomes. Some studies suggest that there is even significant therapist variability within any model (see Malik et al., 2003). Malik's (2003) study further suggests that even a highly manualised cognitive therapy programme is undertaken according to the inner belief systems of the therapist. Some practitioners of cognitive therapy could not be distinguished from psychodynamic or experiential therapists.

A significant British study carried out by the British National Health Service (NHS) compared the outcomes of 1,309 individuals who received cognitive behavioural therapy (CBT), person-centred therapy (PCT) and psychodynamic therapy (PDT) at one of 58 NHS Primary and Secondary Care sites in the UK during a three-year period. This was using the Clinical Outcomes in Routine Evaluation-Outcome Measure (CORE-OM). Researchers compared outcomes of six groups: three treated with CBT, PCT or PDT only, and three treated with one of these, plus one additional approach (e.g. integrative, supportive, art therapy). All six groups averaged marked improvement (Stiles et al., 2006). The results indicate these three treatment approaches, practised routinely in NHS settings, were consistent with previous findings that different approaches tend to have equivalent outcomes. Furthermore, there is no evidence to suggest that a non-school-based approach is, in itself, likely to be any more successful than a particular treatment approach (Miller et al., 2005).

Miller et al. (2004) propose that the focus of therapeutic learning should be on developing the therapist and his/her practice rather than on the model. They note:

> Significant improvements in client retention and outcome have been shown where therapists have feedback on the client's experience of the alliance and progress in treatment. Rather than evidence-based practice, therapists tailor their work through practice-based evidence. (p. 2)

At the same time, research also indicates that training psychological therapists to focus on the therapeutic alliance per se has not proven more successful (Horvath, 2001).

Stratton suggests that the question 'which therapy works best?' has a 'long history of relative failure in mental health' (2007: 84). He is critical of this 'competitive outcome question' (ibid.) and proposes that the question be re-formulated to 'can we help our clients resolve their psychological distress by working with them on their contexts and relationships?' (ibid.: 90). This conceptualisation of the question would go some way in helping to redefine the focus of research to those areas that could be stated as being across orientations, as we will see below.

COMMON FACTORS

More and more researchers are considering what may be called 'common factors' in the therapeutic process. These are factors and variables across models which can be more objectively measured and can, therefore, be linked to outcome. Lambert (1992), after extensive reviews of practice in therapy, identifies four common factors:

1. *Extratherapeutic Change:* those factors that are part of the client's personal life out of therapy (such as family, work and social support) and that aid recovery regardless of participation in psychological therapy.

2. *Hope/Expectancy:* this is sometimes called a 'placebo effect': improvement that results from the client's knowledge that she/he is being treated and from the belief that therapy will 'work' (see below for a critique of the placebo effect).

3. *Model or Technique:* those factors unique to particular therapies (homework tasks, desensitisation etc).

4. *Therapeutic Relationship:* this covers all variables that are found in therapy, regardless of the therapist's theoretical orientation such as empathy, warmth, and acceptance.

In further developments in their research, Asay and Lambert (1999) differentiated the importance of these, which were each given a percentage of relevance to the successful outcome of therapy:[1]

---

1. Our thanks to Rosie Paul for her technological expertise in helping us with the diagram opposite.

Factors Related to Positive Outcome in Therapy
(after Asay & Lambert, 1999)

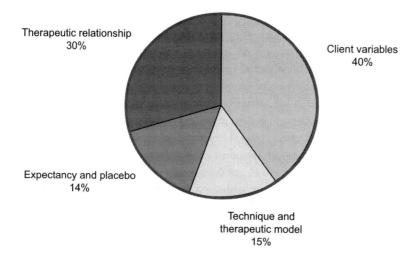

Therapeutic relationship
30%

Client variables
40%

Expectancy and placebo
14%

Technique and
therapeutic model
15%

Different reviewers differ on the quantitative weighting to the relationship and the importance of therapeutic relationship as a variable. Lambert (1992) gives a figure of thirty per cent; Andrews (2000) eighty per cent and Beutler et al. (2004) give a figure of seventeen per cent. Researchers clearly need to refine methodologies in order to be able to more equitably determine the importance. Taking these differences into account, overall, the therapeutic relationship is clearly considered the most important in-therapy factor. Even in technique-based programmes, the therapeutic alliance enhances positive outcomes (Barber et al., 1999). Given the weight of research findings on the importance of common factors, as opposed to model-specific linked outcomes, there is a strong argument for a different approach from a purely model-based approach to psychotherapeutic practice. More attention may need to be considered in relation to client–therapist suitability and/or therapist knowledge, expertise and speciality.

THE RELATIONSHIP AS A THERAPEUTIC ALLIANCE

In considering the therapeutic relationship, it is to be noted that various terms are used which globally cover the range of variables which are considered by researchers. For example, psychodynamic practitioners considered the therapeutic or working alliance. Others have used concepts such as the global alliance, the therapeutic bond, the therapist–client relationship and vice versa. Whilst, technically, such concepts may have unique shades of difference, reviewers tend to consider these relationship factors as one field of study (see Bozarth and Motomasa, this volume, for a critique of this position). Most theoretical definitions of the therapeutic relationship have three common factors:

1. The collaborative nature of the relationship
2. The affective bond between therapist and client
3. The client and therapist's ability to agree on treatment goals and tasks (see Bordin, 1979; Gaston, 1990)

Post-1990, process-outcome research has tended to focus on these areas.

Orlinksy, Rønnestad and Willutzki (2004), in their analysis of research since 1992, which built on the work of Orlinsky, Grawe and Parks (1994), note that no other area of process-outcome research has attracted more attention, both in terms of general relationship characteristics and specific relational factors, than what they call the therapeutic bond (Orlinsky et al., 2004). They note that 'global bonding characteristics' (p. 345) are robustly significant in relation to a successful outcome in psychotherapy. They considered 56 studies pre-1992 and 53 post-1992. They concluded that global alliance is consistently related to positive outcome. Martin, Garske and Davis (2000) in a meta-analysis of 79 studies conclude that the therapeutic relationship is consistently related to outcome regardless of a range of possible variables, including the type of treatment. Orlinksy et al. (2004) note that this virtually confirms statistical significance: that is, this is proven beyond doubt. A further 62 studies reviewed by Orlinsky et al. (2004), conducted across a wide range of modalities, including cognitive-behavioural, psychodynamic, interpersonal and integrative approaches (both group and individual), note a consistent association between positive outcomes and the contributions of the therapist when rated by their clients. At the same time, external raters noted some negative findings indicating that clients may rate therapy more positively overall when their personal outcomes are good.

Safran and Muran (2006) also explore the place that the therapeutic alliance is given in therapy and conclude there is significant evidence to assert it is central to therapy. They are not alone in this conclusion and many professional bodies concur. The American Psychological Association (APA), for example, stated 'the cumulative research convincingly shows that the therapy relationship is crucial to outcome' (Steering Committee of the American Psychological Association's Division 29 Task Force on Empirically Supported Therapy Relationships, 2002: p. 443). More recently, Bentall et al. (in submission), the team involved in a large-scale Study of Cognitive Realignment Therapy in Early Schizophrenia (SoCRATES) research, reported results from a randomised controlled trial (RCT) which showed that the therapeutic alliance accounted for the treatment effect in both CBT and 'supportive counselling' (SC) in groups of people with a range of diagnosed schizophrenic disorders. This study originally had SC as a control group, but when no significant difference between the treatment (CBT) and control could be found, they pooled the data and, using innovative statistical procedures, showed that improvements over treatment as usual were due to the therapeutic alliance. We can comfortably assert, therefore, the centrality of the therapeutic relationship to positive outcomes in therapy.

THERAPEUTIC CONDITIONS

Currently, there is much less focus on the original three conditions that arose out of Rogers' pioneering research. Virtually all schools accept these as fundamental in the forming of a working alliance in therapy. Sanders and Cooper (2006) suggest that the body of research indicates that the therapist variables of empathy, genuineness and positive regard are:

> probably not necessary and sufficient for *all* clients to achieve positive therapeutic change; but a strong correlation seems to exist between levels of empathy and therapeutic outcomes. Positive regard and congruence also show some correlation with clients' levels of improvement. (p. 108)

Asay and Lambert (1999) further found that therapists' facilitative skills are central to the formation of positive therapeutic relationships and contribute significantly to positive outcomes: therapist facilitativeness is now considered a more important area to study, certainly in terms of outcome. Lambert and Ogles state that the therapeutic 'alliance is seen as a necessary, but not sufficient, condition for personality change' (2004: 174).

What researchers mean by therapeutic relationship is much more complex than conceptualisations of empathy, congruence and unconditional positive regard. The movement away from orientation-based research and the associated theoretical debates means there is less core model-based conflict in the field. This can only be a positive factor in enabling us to discover what works in therapy.

SPECIFIC RELATIONSHIP FACTORS

Orlinksy et al. (2004) in their review of over 2,500 studies in process-outcome research have distilled a number of key relationship factors which have been considered by researchers. These are:

- the positive engagement in therapy by client and/or therapist
- the interactive coordination – the ability of both parties to work together on the therapeutic task
- rapport or empathic communication
- affective attitude, the communication of positive regard in the relationship
- experiential congruence, what we call here 'relational congruence' – the development of a common understanding of what is happening in the relationship.

POSITIVE ENGAGEMENT IN THERAPY

Orlinsky et al. (2004) note that 52 studies indicate that clients who viewed their therapist as positively engaged and credible had better outcomes. Sixty-six studies noted the same outcomes in relation to client engagement in therapy. There is little evidence of or research into joint client–therapist investment at this time.

INTERACTIVE COORDINATION

Whilst there is limited evidence here, favourable outcomes are more likely where clients view their therapist as more collaborative than directive. There is also a link between clients' relational style and therapy outcome. Where there is a good therapeutic relationship there is increased goal and task agreement between client and therapist (Bordin's (1979) concept of goals, bonds and tasks as components of a working alliance is supported here).

RAPPORT

There is now almost universal acceptance of the place of therapist's empathic understanding in relationship to success (Bohart et al., 2002). Clients' ratings of therapist empathy are directly linked to outcome. There is very little evidence that links therapists' self-reporting of high levels of empathy to favourable outcomes. There has been almost no research on a client's empathic understanding in therapy, which is a real deficit in our understanding of the therapeutic relationship. Orlinsky et al. (2004) note that if therapy is to be truly considered relational, rather than therapist-led, more research is needed in this area. Sadly there is little recent evidence on communicative rapport, or mutual empathic communication, between client and therapist, although 17 studies up to 1984 all show consistent linkage of high levels of communicative rapport to positive outcomes.

AFFECTIVE ATTITUDE

Many studies link therapist positive regard toward the client to successful outcome in psychotherapy. Thirty-six studies link client positive regard toward the therapist to successful outcomes. Twenty-six studies link reciprocal positive regard to successful outcome. Clearly, therefore, positive regard is an important factor in successful therapy.

RELATIONAL CONGRUENCE

This is a relatively new area of study. Research (Kivlinghan & Arthur, 2000) indicates that where therapist and client move towards an experience of the 'same relational reality' (Orlinsky et al., 2004: 354) there is a positive relation to successful outcome.

PHASES OF THE RELATIONSHIP

Recent research considers the relationship as a fluid dynamic process which goes through stages. In relation to outcome there are important factors to consider. Studies indicate that early gains in therapy strengthen the relationship, which then leads to a favourable outcome (Beutler et al., 2004). Other studies have directly determined that the better the relationship in its early stages – before any change in reported symptoms – the better the long-term benefit (see Weerasekera et al., 2001). Other research has clearly indicated that early positive ratings of the alliance are 'significant predictors of final treatment outcome' (Bachelor & Horvath, 1999: 139). Furthermore, evidence indicates that developing early positive alliance is a better indicator of outcome than the development in middle or later stages of therapy (Horvath & Symonds, 1991).

Some researchers suggest that a strong bond in the first phase of therapy allows for the challenges and exploration of negative feelings in the mid-stage which may not have been possible otherwise. Safran et al., (2001) for example, indicate the egalitarian, non-defensive working through of ruptures in the therapeutic alliance with clients is proven to lead to positive outcomes. Therapists need to be mindful of clients' fear of challenging the expert, and the deference (Rennie, 1994) of the client to the therapist.

SEX, AGE AND RACE

This whole area suffers from a paucity of research. Beutler et al., (2004) identify only ten studies since 1990. There appears to be no link between the therapist's sex and outcome, including drop out. Similarly, age is not considered an area of research importance and there are no studies of worth up to 2003. Beck (1988) found that therapists who were more than ten years younger than their clients had the poorest outcomes. The Department of Health (DH) (2001: 29) cites individual reviews that refer to sex and age but these are more related to particular diagnostic conditions and therapy groups than specific relational factors.

There is a significant body of literature which discusses issues such as cultural compatibility or multicultural competence in counselling and psychotherapy. However Beutler et al. (2004) report only 11 studies between 1990 and 2000 that consider ethnic/racial matching of therapist and client. The DH (2001) cites two reviews that are concerned with specific relationship factors: one indicates improved outcome in ethnically matched client–therapist pairs in short-term dynamic therapy and the other has found no effect of ethnicity on outcome (p. 29). The extremely limited number of studies does not enable any clear findings to emerge overall and it is obvious that more research is needed in this area.

CURRENT PRACTICE CONTEXTS

Mace and Moorey (2001) note that, whilst research still supports the contention that all therapies are equal in outcome, some are being considered more equal than others by funding and commissioning bodies. Furthermore, there is a reliance on the 'gold standard' of research, randomised controlled trials (RCTs), in the study of the talking therapies. The essential aspect of RCTs is 'the random assignment of [clients] to different conditions of treatment' (Shadish, Cook & Campbell, 2002, cited in Leichsenring & Rabung, 2007: 127). Pointing out that there are variations within RCTs, Leichsenring and Rabung identify a number of criticisms of this approach to research including:

- the suggestion that RCTs are not sufficiently representative of clinical practice. Therefore, the outcome of such research does not necessarily mean the same results will happen under usual clinical conditions

- there is emphasis on symptoms and disorders and not on the individual
- in clinical practice, clients often present with a number of different psychological difficulties. RCTs, with their use of treatment manuals, do not allow for multimorbid clients
- the manuals and 'randomised control conditions [are] hardly applicable to long-term psychotherapy lasting several years'
- there is a profound difficulty with the notion of the placebo effect (non-specific or common-factor controls) in psychotherapy. Leichsenring and Rabung state that 'placebo effects in psychotherapy are, in the end, psychotherapeutic effects'
- often, the size of the research groups is not large enough to meet its own criteria of being random (ibid.: 128).

This gold standard of a medical model of research may not be quite so useful for research into psychotherapy. Indeed they may be too general or inappropriate for the study of human pain and suffering. Orlinsky et al. (2004) argue that rather than considering any one approach to research into psychotherapy as the gold standard, 'a genuinely scientific understanding of psychotherapy demands the judicious and critical integration of results arrived at by varied methods' (p. 331).

Whilst RCTs may be effective in determining the efficacy, or not, of a pharmaceutical product, at the same time medical practitioners fiercely defend their right to retain clinical judgement in their practice and note the unique profile of each of their patients (Wessely, 2001). The clinical and professional opinion of the medical practitioner is the final arbiter for determining the best treatment. The UK Department of Health's report, *Treatment of Choice in Psychological Therapies and Counselling* (2001), in presenting guidelines for the choice of psychological therapies, also states, 'Clinicians retain clinical freedom to refer for therapies not recommended in this guideline if they believe there are good reasons to do so' (p. 41). As in medicine, the most significant way forward may lie in the development of generalist practitioners who refer people experiencing more complex or severe mental-health problems on to more skilled and experienced therapists in these areas (DH, 2001: 36). The focus will not be on model or school of therapy but the expertise of the therapist.

The medicalisation of the talking therapies and the emphasis on diagnosis is problematic. Consider the classic 'Schizophrenia Study' (Rosenhan, 1973), where researchers presented themselves to a variety of medical settings in the USA. They reported with the same set of symptoms and were diagnosed and treated in widely differing ways. Coupled with the focus on diagnosis rather than problem formulation and the assignation of diagnosis-based treatment, we are faced with serious challenges that need to be met. In the current health climate, cost is often the first consideration. Medical practitioners are limited to a range of medicines they are allowed to prescribe in the NHS, whilst they may wish to prescribe other more effective and more expensive options. This restriction seems to be paralleled in counselling and psychotherapy with the proliferation of brief/short-term counselling and therapy, usually meaning six sessions. This is particularly worrying as research indicates that less than eight sessions is 'unlikely to be optimally effective for most moderate … mental health problems' (DH: 35). Indeed, the DH suggests that 16 or more sessions are needed for 'symptomatic relief' and longer therapy for 'lasting change in social and personality functioning' (ibid.).

SUMMARY

In this chapter, we have undertaken a thorough review of relevant literature. We have been particularly grateful for the masterly and accomplished work of Bergin and Garfield (1994) and Lambert (2004) who have compiled the definitive overviews of research in the field. We make no attempt to understate their contribution to the material in this review.

Key themes have emerged:

- There is no evidence that any approach or manualised treatment is significantly better than any other. A small element of success is linked to the model of therapy or treatment used and successful outcome.
- There is evidence to suggest that an approach to therapy responsive to the presenting needs of individuals will be more fruitful in the future than a school or model-based approach.
- The relationship is the most significant in-therapy factor as related to positive outcomes.
- Common factors have emerged across approaches that are intrinsic to success in therapy.
- It is accepted, beyond doubt, that the therapeutic conditions originally developed by Rogers (1957) (and variously described) are important factors in the success of all approaches.
- Specific key factors that have proven effective in the therapeutic relationship are:
    1. Positive engagement in therapy
    2. Interactive coordination
    3. Rapport
    4. Positive regard or rapport
    5. Relational congruence

    More consideration of these factors is needed, particularly the interactive or reciprocal elements, which may guide us to further understanding of best practice.
- Evidence suggests that creating a good early therapeutic relationship augurs well for outcome, as does the ability to work through interpersonal issues.

We have also identified some difficulties with some of the research itself. There are areas that need further investigation; for the example, the influence of ethnicity, gender and age (and this list is not exhaustive). There is an over-reliance, particularly in the UK health services, on RCTs, which may not actually help answer the question of what best helps clients. Notwithstanding these caveats, the importance of the therapeutic relationship is clear and irrefutable.

REFERENCES

Andrews, HB (2000) The myth of the scientist-practitioner: A reply to R King (1998) and N King and Ollendick (1998). *Australian Psychologist, 35*, 60–3.

Asay, TP & Lambert, MJ (1999) The empirical case for the common factors in therapy: Quantitative findings. In MA Hubble, BL Duncan & SD Miller (Eds) *The Heart and Soul of Change: What works in therapy* (pp. 33–56). Washington, DC: American Psychological Association.

Bachelor, A & Horvath, A (1999) The therapeutic relationship. In MA Hubble, BL Duncan & SD Miller (Eds) *The Heart and Soul of Change: What works in therapy* (pp. 133–78). Washington, DC: American Psychological Association.

Barber, JP, Luborsky, L, Crits-Christoph, P, Thase, ME, Weiss, R, Frank, A et al. (1999) Therapeutic alliance as a predictor of outcome in treatment of cocaine dependence. *Psychotherapy Research, 9*, 54–73.

Beck, DF (1988) *Counselor Characteristics: How they affect outcomes.* Milwaukee, WI: Family Service Association of America.

Bentall, RP, Dunn, G, Tarrier, N, Haddock, G, Kinderman, P, Kingdon, D, Drake, R, Lewis, S & the SoCRATES Study Group (in submission). 'The influence of therapeutic alliance on the effects of psychological treatment on symptomatic outcome in early schizophrenia patients.'

Bergin, AE & Garfield, SL (1994) (Eds) *Handbook of Psychotherapy and Behaviour Change* (4th edn). New York: John Wiley & Sons.

Beutler, LE, Malik, M, Alimohamed, S, Harwood, TM, Talebi, H, Noble, S & Wong, E (2004) Therapist variables. In MJ Lambert (2004) (Ed) *Bergin and Garfield's Handbook of Psychotherapy and Behavior Change* (5th edn) (pp. 227–306). New York: John Wiley & Sons.

Bohart, A, Elliott, R, Greenberg, LS & Watson, JC (2002) Empathy. In J Norcross & M Lambert (Eds) *Psychotherapy Relationships that Work* (pp. 89–108). Oxford: Oxford University Press.

Bordin, ES (1979) The generalizability of the psychoanalytic concept of the working alliance. *Psychotherapy, 16*, 252–60.

Department of Health (2001) *Treatment Choice in Psychological Therapies and Counselling. Evidence-based clinical practice guidelines.* London: Department of Health.

Freedheim, DK (1992) *History of Psychotherapy.* Washington, DC: American Psychological Association.

Gaston, L (1990) The concept of the alliance and its role in psychotherapy: Theoretical and empirical considerations. *Psychotherapy, 27*, 143–53

Horvath, AO (2001) The alliance. *Psychotherapy, 38*, 365–72.

Horvath, AO & Symonds, BD (1991) Relation between working alliance and outcome in psychotherapy: A meta-analysis. *Journal of Counseling Psychology, 38* (2), 139–49.

Kivlighan, DM & Arthur, EG (2000) Convergence in client and counselor recall of important session events. *Journal of Counselling Psychology, 47*, 79–84.

Lambert, MJ (1992) Implications of outcome research for psychotherapy integration. In C Norcross & MR Goldfried (Eds) *Handbook of Psychotherapy Integration* (pp. 94–129). New York: Basic Books.

Lambert, MJ (2002) Research summary on the therapeutic relationship and psychotherapy outcome. In JC Norcross (Ed) *Psychotherapy Relationships that Work: Therapist contributions and responsiveness to patients* (pp. 17–32). Oxford: Oxford University Press.

Lambert, MJ (2004) *Bergin and Garfield's Handbook of Psychotherapy and Behavior Change* (5th edn). New York: John Wiley & Sons.

Lambert, MJ, Bergin, AE & Garfield, SL (2004) Introduction and historical overview. In MJ Lambert (Ed) *Bergin and Garfield's Handbook of Psychotherapy and Behavior Change* (5th edn) (pp. 3–15). New York: John Wiley & Sons.

Lambert, MJ & Ogles, BM (2004) The efficacy and effectiveness of psychotherapy. In MJ Lambert (Ed) *Bergin and Garfield's Handbook of Psychotherapy and Behavior Change* (5th edn) (pp. 139–93). New York: John Wiley & Sons.

Leichsenring, F & Rabung, S (2007) The role of efficacy vs. effectiveness research in evaluating psychotherapy. *Mental Health and Learning Disabilities: Research and practice. Special issue. 4,* (2), 125–43.

Luborsky, L, Rosenthal, R, Diguer, L, Andrusyna, TP, Berman, JS, Levitt, JT et al. (2002) The Dodo bird verdict is alive and well – mostly. *Clinical Psychology: Science and practice, 9* (1), 2–12.

Luborsky, L, Singer, B & Luborsky, E (1975) Comparative studies of psychotherapies: Is it true that 'Everybody has won and all must have prizes'? *Archives of General Psychiatry, 32,* 995–1008.

Mace, C & Moorey, S (2001) Evidence in psychotherapy: A difficult balance. In C Mace, S Moorey & B Roberts *Evidence in the Psychological Therapies* (pp. 1–11). Hove: Brunner-Routledge.

Malik, ML, Beutler, LE, Gallagher-Thompson, D, Thompson, L & Alimohamed, S (2003) Are all cognitive therapies alike? A comparison of cognitive and non-cognitive therapy process and implications for the application of empirically supported treatments (ESTs). *Journal of Consulting and Clinical Psychology, 71,* 150–8.

Martin, DJ, Garske, JP & Davis, MK (2000) Relation of the therapeutic alliance with outcome and other variables: A meta-analytic review. *Journal of Counseling and Clinical Psychology, 68* (3), 438–50.

Miller, SD, Duncan, BL & Hubbard, MA (2004) Beyond integration: The triumph of outcome over process in clinical practice. *Psychotherapy in Australia, 10* (2), 2–19.

Miller, SD, Duncan, BL & Hubbard, MA (2005). Outcome-informed clinical work. In JC Norcross & MR Goldfried (Eds) *Handbook of Psychotherapy Integration* (2nd edn) (pp. 84–102). New York: Oxford University Press.

Orlinsky, DE, Grawe, K & Parks, BK (1994) Process and outcome in psychotherapy: Noch einmal. In AE Bergin & SL Garfield (Eds) *Handbook of Psychotherapy and Behavior Change* (4th edn) (pp. 270–376). New York: John Wiley & Sons.

Orlinksy, DE, Rønnestad, MH & Willutzki, U (2004) Fifty years of psychotherapy process-outcome research: Continuity and change. In MJ Lambert (Ed), *Bergin and Garfield's Handbook of Psychotherapy and Behavior Change* (5th edn) (pp. 307–89). New York: John Wiley & Sons.

Popper, KR (1962) *Conjectures and Refutations.* New York: Basic Books.

Rennie, DL (1994) Clients' deference in psychotherapy. *Journal of Counseling Psychology, 41* (4), 427–37.

Rogers, CR (1957) The necessary and sufficient conditions of therapeutic personality change. *Journal of Consulting Psychology, 21,* 95–103. Reprinted in H Kirschenbaum & VL Henderson (Eds) (1990) *The Carl Rogers Reader* (pp. 219–35). London: Constable.

Rogers, CR & Dymond, RF (1954) (Eds) *Psychotherapy and Personality Change*. Chicago: University of Chicago Press.

Rosenhan, DL (1973) On being sane in insane places. *Science, 179,* 250–8.

Roth, A & Fonagy, P (2004) *What Works for Whom? A critical review of psychotherapy research*. New York: Guilford Press.

Safran, JD & Muran, J (2006) Has the concept of the alliance outlived its usefulness? *Psychotherapy, 43,* 286–91.

Safran, JD, Muran, JC, Wallner Samstag, L & Stevens, C (2001) Repairing therapeutic alliance ruptures. *Psychotherapy, 38,* 406–12.

Sanders, P & Cooper, M (2006) Research into person-centred counselling. In P Sanders (2006) *The Person-Centred Counselling Primer* (pp. 102–8). Ross-on-Wye: PCCS Books.

Steering Committee of the American Psychological Associations (2002) Empirically supported therapy relationships: Conclusions and recommendations of the Division 29 task force. In J Norcross & M Lambert (Eds) *Psychotherapy Relationships that Work* (pp. 441–3). Oxford: Oxford University Press

Stiles, WB, Barkham, M, Twigg, E, Mellor-Clark. J & Cooper, M (2006) Effectiveness of cognitive-behavioural, person-centred and psychodynamic therapies as practised in UK National Health Service settings. *Psychological Medicine, 36,* 555–66.

Stratton, P (2007) Formulating research questions that are relevant to psychotherapy. *Mental Health and Learning Disabilities: Research and practice. Special issue, 4,* (2) 83–97.

Wampold, BE (2001) *The Great Psychotherapy Debate*. Mahwah, NJ: Lawrence Erlbaum.

Weerasekera, P, Linder, B, Greenberg, L & Watson, J (2001) The working alliance in client-centered and process-experiential therapy of depression. *Psychotherapy Research, 11,* 221–33.

Wessely, S (2001) Randomised goal trials: The gold standard. In C Mace, S Moorey & B Roberts (2001) *Evidence in the Psychological Therapies* (pp. 46–60). Hove: Brunner-Routledge.

CHAPTER 3

PSYCHOANALYTIC PSYCHOTHERAPY

PAM HOWARD

We are never so defenceless against suffering as when we love, never so forlornly unhappy as when we have lost our love object or its love.
(Sigmund Freud, 1930: 80)

BACKGROUND TO THE APPROACH

The work of psychoanalysis and its derivative, psychoanalytic psychotherapy, is largely concerned with love. Specifically, it seeks to bring about an exploration of the client's own unique way of loving or as Sigmund Freud famously stated, 'his specific method for conducting his erotic life' (1912: 98). It is his[1] particular way of conducting his intimate, relational and erotic life which is thought to be at the root of the client's suffering. The interplay between love and suffering, therefore, is at the very heart of the psychoanalytic therapeutic relationship.

Psychoanalytic practice began with the work of Sigmund Freud at the end of the nineteenth century. Many of the underpinning principles which guide the psychoanalytic therapeutic relationship can be attributed to Freud and his immense legacy. However, the profession has developed in profound and important ways since Freud's time and a chapter such as this would not be complete without an examination of the contributions of Melanie Klein, Wilfred Bion, and Donald Winnicott, to name but a few. It is generally understood that psychoanalytic practice is a 'broad church' – practitioners vary in their style and approach – and much controversy and debate has taken place regarding which of us are the genuine inheritors of Freud. Nevertheless, there are fundamental principles which we all share and it is these that this chapter aims to address. These fundamental principles could be said to include the belief in, and privileging of, unconscious material; the notion of intrapsychic conflict and its corresponding defence mechanisms; resistance to insight; and the centrality of the Oedipus complex to the formation of the personality. It is the therapeutic exploration of these, through the examination of the transference/countertransference relationship, which distinguishes psychoanalytic work.

---

1. For the purposes of clarity, and for no other reason, the masculine personal pronoun will be used to refer to the client/patient and the feminine for the psychotherapist throughout the text.

Underpinning all these fundamental principles is the belief in the centrality of the formative nature of infancy in the adult personality. Psychoanalytic theory is characterised by a series of accounts of how the human infant comes to be who he is. These accounts differ in both their conceptualisations of the self and emphasis of what stages of development are crucial, but all share a belief in the formative nature of our experiences of early relationships. Intrapsychic conflict and its corresponding defence mechanisms arise out of the need to protect ourselves against the suffering to be found in our intimate relationships. In order to protect ourselves against suffering in infancy, we engage in what might be called 'distortions of love'. These distortions may be thought of as a means of protecting ourselves against feelings of envy, jealousy, rejection, abandonment, or the terror of annihilation, and lead to the infant developing his own unique way of relating to others. His mode of relating, therefore, seeks to balance the need to gain the love of those upon whom he depends with the need to protect himself from suffering. Paradoxically for most clients who find themselves in psychoanalytic psychotherapy, these distortions, which were originally designed to mitigate suffering, are now, in adulthood, at the heart of their distress. What distinguishes psychoanalytic work from other therapies is the belief that the client is not capable *on his own* of gaining understanding of these distortions and developing new, more empowering, ways of loving. In other words, the process of distortion is *unconscious*.

The systematic study of the unconscious for therapeutic purposes began with the work of Sigmund Freud. Freud and Breuer's writings of the work they carried out with 'hysterical clients' (*Studies on Hysteria*, 1895) movingly chronicle Freud's early insights into the relational world of young, affluent Viennese women. Freud and Breuer display a willingness and capacity to think laterally around the origins of the debilitating symptoms experienced by these young women. As intimate conversations are held between physician and client regarding the origins of symptoms, Freud claims, something magical occurs: the symptoms change or disappear. They suggest to us, therefore, that through conversation alone, through the 'talking cure', the client's experience of his symptoms is altered and alleviated. This work is largely centred around the notion of 'remembering'; through uncovering troubled and traumatic memories, symptoms would alter or disappear. The hysteric '*suffers mainly from reminiscences*', argued Freud (1895: 6), and it was through this work that he became convinced of the existence of '*powerful mental processes which nevertheless remained hidden from the consciousness of man*' (1925: 17, italics added).

From thereon in, we see a Freud who is dedicated to the understanding of how this 'powerful mental process' manifests itself in our everyday life and the part that it plays in the management of our emotional and erotic lives. With the publication of *The Interpretation of Dreams* in 1900, the centrality of the unconscious in Freud's work is established and it is in this work that we begin to see an outline for the 'mechanisms' of distortion which govern the human psyche. As a means of defence against suffering, material of a disturbing affectual nature is repressed and rendered unconscious. Dreams, argued Freud, are distorted communications of unconscious conflict which seek to be expressed and resolved. As the expression of such material is distressing and anxiety-provoking, we distort it in order to make it palatable to our conscious mind. The dream, therefore, is the compromise between prohibition and expression.

These principles were applied by Freud to the understanding of the 'symptoms' which his clients exhibited. Seen in this light, symptoms can be understood as distorted expressions of unconscious conflict experienced by the individual. This has become a key principle underpinning all psychoanalytic work: the cause of our clients' distress is often to be understood as the solution they have found to an unresolved infantile unconscious conflict. Depression, for example, is not the problem per se (although it is undoubtedly the cause of suffering) but can be thought of as the solution the client has found to managing intolerable intrapsychic conflict.

We distort our thoughts, our desires and our memories in order to alleviate psychic suffering and protect ourselves from punishment, judgement and excommunication by others. The Freudian human being is one who is inherently split: his structural model of the mind reflects three internal psychic agencies which play out their power struggles in the sphere of the individual's relationships. The *ego, id* and *superego*, presented by Freud in his brilliant paper, 'The Ego and the Id' (1923), provide a framework for understanding both the love distortions referred to earlier and the dream as compromise. The ego, as the bearer of reality, battles to gain control over, on the one hand, the ruthless id which seeks pleasure and satisfaction of instinctual drives and, on the other, the punishing, judgemental superego which represents the internalised authoritative parental figures. These need to be balanced by the demands placed on the individual by the external world. The demands of these three forces – the id, the superego, and the external world – are often in contradiction, and intrapsychic conflict is managed by inhibiting, repressing and distorting both our inner desires and our responses to external demands.

The origin of the unique manner in which these competing and often contradictory psychic forces play out their power struggles is to be found in Freud's concept of the Oedipus complex. There are many popularised and simplistic accounts of the Oedipus complex that loosely translate into children desiring the parent of the opposite sex and fearing punishment for these incestuous wishes. Contemporary psychoanalytic practice, however, sees the Oedipus complex as being the manner in which the infant conceptualises his place in the social networks within which he was formed. The Oedipal dimension is one where the child has to learn, for example, that his mother's love is not exclusive to him and that he must share loved ones with others. Furthermore, he will be excluded both from the parental couple and from the loving relationship between a parent and other siblings. These will give rise to unbearable feelings of envy, jealousy and rivalry, yet acting on these feelings will have consequences and give rise to the fear of punishment. Thus, the internalisation of prohibition, with its subsequent formation of the superego, provides the cornerstone for the child's entry into culture.

It is the negotiation of the Oedipus complex that provides the central structure around which the individual forms. It informs our relationship to our gendered identity, our unique relationship to authority, and provokes the development of our defences against envy, jealousy, and rivalry. Above all, however, Freud believed it informed our own specific method for 'conducting our erotic life' (Freud, 1912: 98) or, in other words, our unique way of loving.

Freud's structural model of the mind, which is still central to all psychoanalytic work today, translates into an individual who is riddled with ambivalence: the psychoanalytic client is deeply and unconsciously invested in his symptom. His symptom, as we saw earlier, is the best solution he has found to intolerable intrapsychic conflict. It follows that the psychoanalytic client arrives in the practitioner's consulting room asking for change but unconsciously working hard towards retaining the status quo:

> The resistance accompanies the treatment step-by-step. Every single association, every act of the person under treatment must reckon with the resistance and represents a compromise between the forces that are striving towards recovery and the opposing ones. (Freud, 1912: 103)

The client will find a number ways of sabotaging the work and thus impeding the gaining of fresh insight. Freud spoke of this as clients' resistance to 'remembering'. Freud's hysteric resisted remembering as an attempt to keep distress at bay. Therapeutic resistance can be thought of as the client's wish not to know, not to remember, that which causes pain and anxiety. The therapeutic process, which is designed to bring about new personal knowledge, can be expected to engender the client's resistance from the start. It follows that the closer the therapeutic work comes to uncovering unconscious material, the greater the resistance that will be expressed. The work of the resistance will often be played out within the realm of the therapeutic relationship and can be thought of as the point where the client withdraws from actively contributing to the therapeutic work. Resistance may take the form of the client missing sessions, arriving late, ceasing to contribute material to the therapy, feeling unable to think, dismissing their distress, flights into ill health, the compulsion to repeat, or aggressive or eroticised feelings towards the therapist. We will return to this later as we discuss the notion of transference and countertransference.

We have seen that, for Freud, the Oedipus complex constituted the cornerstone for psychoanalysis and the fundamental structure underpinning the adult's personality. He placed its onset and resolution as taking place somewhere between three and five years of age. As a result, classic Freudian psychoanalysis privileged experience formulated during this stage of development. Post-Freudian psychoanalysts became interested in the development which occurred earlier in the infant's life. Significantly, Melanie Klein focused on the infant's very early psychic development and her project can be seen as one which aimed to explore what could be called the 'pre-Oedipal' phase. Klein's work was dedicated to shedding light on the psychic life of very young infants and theorised that they were inherently relational. The infant is born with a fledgling ego, argues Klein, which is 'object-relating' from the outset. The baby is consumed with feelings of both love and hate towards her mother and envies and resents her seemingly magical powers to provide and to frustrate. The 'good' mother (breast) and 'bad' mother (breast) in the infant's fantasy are perceived as separate beings and the infant manages his difficult feelings of envy, frustration and terror of dependency by mechanisms of projective identification, projection, and introjection (see Klein, 1957). Over time, if the relational conditions are favourable, the infant is able to integrate the good and bad objects and perceive the mother as whole. This gives rise to feelings of guilt for the hatred which has been expressed towards the bad object and the infant seeks to make reparation – to make sense of the way in which she impacts others and the potential consequences of her actions. Klein's work shifted the emphasis of psychoanalytic exploration to much earlier in life and paved the way for other psychoanalytic thinkers and the creation of the 'object relations school' as characterised by the work of Donald Winnicott, Ronald Fairbairn, Wilfred Bion, John Bowlby and Harry Guntrip, amongst others.

Contemporary British psychoanalysis has been heavily influenced by the object relations school. The psychoanalytic 'object' refers both to the infant's external relationships and his internal representations of those relationships. This represents a move away from Freud's essentially 'intrapsychic' structural model to one which was essentially intersubjective and focused on the infant–mother relationship. Winnicott, Bion, Fairbairn, and later, Guntrip, have all focused on the manner in which the early infant– mother relationship acts as conduit for the psychological birth of the infant. The core tenet of these theorists, who differ in important ways, centres on the capacity of this primary relationship to facilitate or arrest the emotional development of the infant. Winnicott famously stated that there was 'no such thing as a baby' (Winnicott, 1964: 88) – only a baby and his mother. The 'good enough' early environment, he argued, enables the infant to manage his psychic separation from his mother in a manner which is tolerable and keeps anxiety at a minimum. The attuned mother meet her baby's needs in such a way that he is allowed the experience of 'creating' himself whilst his needs are, on the whole, being met. In time, as the infant's fledgling ego becomes stronger and more robust, he can begin to tolerate greater levels of 'impingements' from the environment and these allow him to negotiate what Winnicott called the 'me' and the 'not-me' (1964: 45).

Wilfred Bion (1970) in turn, conceptualised the mother's function as one of 'container' for the infant's unmetabolised and chaotic emotional experience. Largely through the mechanism of projective identification, the mother receives and 'contains' her infant's raw affectual material and anxiety, which he calls 'beta-elements'. By being capable of receiving these, containing them and 'translating' them for the infant, the mother is able to return this intolerable material to the baby in a form that is digestible and manageable for him. This is what Bion called the 'alpha function'. Through the experience of being contained, the infant can begin, over time, to learn to think for himself, to understand his emotional experience and to regulate his inner world.

NEW DEVELOPMENTS IN THE APPROACH

Yet another account of early infant development is Bowlby's well-known theories on attachment (1969), which were initially influential in the development of the object relations school but were subsequently discredited and branded *un-psychoanalytic*. During recent years, however, research from the fields of neuroscience and neuropsychology has brought about a return to theory and the creation of a new field: 'neuropsychoanalysis'. Writers like Peter Fonagy and Allan Schore are examples of contemporary psychoanalytic thinkers who are actively engaged in this interdisciplinary project. Central to the work of neuropsychoanalysis is the notion of an attachment couple whose function is to facilitate the infant's capacity to regulate his affectual world. There are important implications for the function of the psychodynamic therapeutic relationship stemming from this work. Fonagy has argued that the psychotherapist could be said to be 'lending' her client her subjectivity in order to provide the intersubjective space in which the client can reorganise his self-regulatory functions (Fonagy, 1996, cited in Green, 2003: 120).

We have seen how the psychoanalytic tradition privileges early relationships (whether pre-Oedipal or Oedipal) in the course of the individual's development and places them at the core of identity and suffering. It follows, therefore, that the most obvious and potent tool available to the psychoanalytic psychotherapist is the relationship between herself and her client. It is to the dynamic of this relationship that Freud ascribed the term the 'transference'. The 'transference' relates to the manner in which the client will act out, or repeat, towards the therapist aspects of earlier, formative love relationships. In other words, the distortions of love referred to earlier will manifest themselves in the way in which the client engages and attaches to the person of the therapist.

POSITION OF THERAPIST AND CLIENT

Early in his work, Freud became convinced of the power of the transference as an analytic tool. The analyst, argued Freud, must be alert to the manner in which that which cannot be remembered by the client is repeated, or acted out, in the therapeutic relationship. In his paper 'Observations on Transference-Love' (1915b) Freud argues that transference phenomena relate to aspects of the client's suffering that cannot be remembered. Instead, they are repeated or 'acted out' within the framework of the therapeutic relationship. Intense feelings of love, desire, anger and hostility directed towards the person of the therapist can be seen as manifestations of the client's unconscious relational conflicts. They are intensified, argued Freud, as the therapy progresses, as an attempt to sabotage the work of 'remembering' material of a distressing and disturbing nature. Initially, therefore, psychoanalytic practice conceptualised the transference as a 'resistance' to therapeutic work. Freud advocated a position where the therapist opens up a space to think about and explore the symbolic meaning of what is being played out between therapist and client. For Freud, the importance of not transgressing professional boundaries and entering into personal love relations with clients was not simply motivated by ethical reasons (although these were important to him) but also by clinical ones. If the therapist were to respond to advances from the client, states Freud, the client would succeed in repeating what ought to have been remembered and the therapy would fail in its aim to relieve the client's distress (Freud, 1915). Resistance to remembering motivates the client to play out with the therapist aspects of her unique way of 'conducting her erotic life' and provides the therapist with an opening for exploring the nature of his client's suffering.

Freud's interest in the wish to repeat rather than remember, to act out rather than to work through, was the starting point in the conceptualisation of the transference relationship. Throughout his early work, Freud often makes reference to our 'compulsion to repeat'. In what is arguably his seminal text, *Beyond the Pleasure Principle* (1920), Freud explores this phenomenon in depth and argues that we are destined to repeat unconscious emotional experiences which relate to trauma, unresolved psychic conflicts, anguish and anxiety. He speculates that we repeat these experiences in an attempt to master the unresolved conflict or trauma. The compulsion to repeat, therefore, became established as a phenomenon of the transferential client–therapist relationship. The client repeats both because he does not wish to remember and because he is compelled to do so as an attempt at mastery of unresolved, traumatic or distressing unresolved unconscious conflicts.

THERAPEUTIC INTERVENTIONS AND OTHER PSYCHOLOGICAL FACTORS IN THE RELATIONSHIP

Freud's assertion of the centrality of the transference in therapeutic work has remained the fundamental principle of the psychoanalytic therapeutic relationship to date. However, since Freud, the parameters of the transferential relationship have been redefined in significant ways.

The 1950s saw a flourish of interest in the therapeutic value of what is commonly known as the therapist's 'countertransference'. Post-Kleinian writers such as Paula Heimann and Harold Searles presented influential, classic texts which argued for the therapist's use of her countertransference as key to the understanding of the psychoanalytic psychotherapeutic relationship. Heimann's 'On Counter-Transference' (1950) articulates the therapeutic value in the therapist's use of her own feelings to inform her interventions and to gain insight into the transferential material. The analyst who 'ignores or stifles' (Heimann, 1950: 81) her feelings, she argues, risks making poor and mechanical interventions which do not address the unconscious communications from the client. It is through recognising our own internal affective states during our work with clients that we will enter the intersubjective unconscious sphere where the transference relationship is being played out.

Psychoanalytic practice places a great emphasis on the psychotherapist's own analysis or personal therapy. In present times, psychoanalytic psychotherapists engage in long and intensive personal therapies during their training years. With the emphasis on countertransference, the aim for personal therapy is not to create an individual free from unconscious conflict who can engage in 'interpreting' others as an intellectual endeavour. Instead, the point of personal therapy is to enable the psychotherapist to learn to recognise her own internal affective states and *to think about them*. In other words, to recognise intense feelings in herself and learn to contain and explore them in a way which allows for the integration of thinking and feeling – to metabolise experience rather than to be simply flooded by it.

29

Harold Searles' beautiful paper 'Oedipal Love in the Counter-Transference' (1959) speaks of the emotional experience engendered in the psychotherapist as a response to entering the client's Oedipal story. As the client repeats his Oedipal drama with the psychotherapist, she too must play her part in the play. She must allow herself to be moved, to receive the (unconscious) invitations from the client and to engage in the emotional experience together – not simply to intellectualise in an effort to understand. However, this comes with an essential caveat: what is necessary is to analyse these emotional transactions between client and therapist, rather than to enact them in an overt way. As Freud argued, to do so would be to succumb to repeating rather than remembering, to acting out rather than working through.

One of the traits which characterises the psychoanalytic psychotherapist is her caution against self-disclosure. What is at stake in psychoanalytic psychotherapy is the understanding of emotional experience as it is transacted between the two people in the room. A helpful distinction can be made between the lending of one's subjectivity, as suggested by Fonagy (1996, cited in Green, 2003), and the disclosing of facts about one's personal life and history. The former consists of a willingness to be impacted, pushed and pulled by the client's story and to be an active participant in the emotional relationship. As argued by Winnicott in his paper, 'Hate in the Counter-Transference' (1949), there may be exceptional moments when it is of therapeutic value to the client for the therapist's internal affective states to be disclosed. Disclosing aspects of one's own personal life outside the consulting room, by contrast, is to distort and collude with the client's unconscious wish to resist, to take the material out of the room, to change the focus on to that of the person of the therapist.

It is largely for this reason that the psychoanalytic psychotherapist pays particular attention to the area of boundaries. If the area of primary interest (the work) centres around an exploration of the client's own unique way of loving, their own way of 'conducting their erotic life', the psychotherapist is concerned to provide conditions within their therapeutic relationship optimal to enabling this material to be available for their mutual exploration. Contractual agreements around certain boundary issues – payment, timings of sessions, out of session contact, cancellations, holidays, etc. – provide a clear backdrop against which the client's 'distortions' can be mutually seen and explored. It is precisely in relation to the client's response to these boundary issues that transferential material will be most readily accessible. Adherence to time boundaries, to the consistency in the frequency of the sessions, to the rules applied to out-of-session contact, aims to provide a holding and containing environment in which the client's compulsion to repeat can be allowed to happen. This provides a new and unique opportunity to work through the conflict together with the therapist in the confines of a boundaried psychoanalytic relationship. The work, therefore, *is* the relationship and it is through the management of the transference that the therapeutic work takes place.

The therapist is 'listening-out' for unconscious communication in the stories of the client. These may take place, for example, through dreams or slips of the tongue in an otherwise ordered narrative. Material which is deemed important enough to bring to the therapeutic encounter, in whatever form, is considered potential communication of unconscious conflict. It is for this reason that the psychoanalytic psychotherapist typically does not 'start' the sessions but rather encourages her client to open the sessions with whatever he chooses to bring. The unconscious will find 'derivates' in the client's conscious narrative through which to give voice to repressed material. The contemporary psychodynamic field of communicative psychotherapy focuses almost exclusively on all the client's content as representing derivative unconscious material (for example, see Langs, 1992; Smith, 1991).

Seen in this light, 'interpretation' takes on a new meaning: the therapist directs the attention of the client to whatever she believes represents manifestations of unconscious material, either in the narrative or in the relationship between them. By doing this, she is encouraging the client towards overcoming his own resistance to 'knowing' himself – and towards remembering what he wishes to forget. The focus is therefore on aiding the process of overcoming resistance rather than interpreting the 'real' meaning of the slip, the dream, or the experience. The real value of an interpretation is seen in its potential to open up connections, associations, new thoughts, new ideas, rather than in its capacity to close down meaning to the 'right answer'. For such reconnections between unconscious and conscious material to take place, the client must overcome his own resistance and make those connections for himself.

The careful managing of the transferential–countertransferential relationship is what determines how successful the therapeutic dyad will be at reconstituting these broken links; at overcoming resistance and remembering what one wants to forget, and working it through within the confines of the safe and boundaried relationship between psychotherapist and client. In the end, it is by working through unconscious conflicts within the unique therapeutic relationship that the client may reorganise his internal world and gain the potential to engage in new and more satisfying ways of loving and being loved.

STRENGTHS AND WEAKNESSES

Due to its immense influence in a variety of clinical and academic spheres, psychoanalysis (and psychoanalytic terminology) has become popularised in the Western world. Much of its vocabulary has entered our day-to-day language and we often see (mis)representations of it in the media and the arts. This has, it could be said, often led to gross misrepresentations and reductionists caricatures of the cold, distant analyst, who interprets wildly and in a patronising manner. To be fair, it could be argued that psychoanalysis has not engaged effectively with this public perception (and has often fuelled it) and consequently, these exaggerated and distorted portrayals have been allowed to flourish.

It has proved difficult to summarise the strengths and weaknesses of psychoanalytic psychotherapy as, in the end, its effectiveness or otherwise is bound up with the unique skill of the practitioner and her ability to enter and maintain a containing therapeutic relationship. At its best, however, psychoanalytic practice allows clients to explore and gain insight into the roots of their distress. The cause of suffering, as opposed to its symptoms, is the object of joint inquiry between client and therapist and through this endeavour, new meaning and ultimately, new choices are available to be made in the individual's relational world.

In the psychoanalytic therapeutic relationship, the positive as well as the negative/ hostile feelings between the two partners are named and voiced and this often provides the opportunity, often for the first time, to rework the client's relationship to conflict, aggression and authority. Equally, the boundaried nature of the contract can make for a containing, holding and stable environment during times of anxiety and loss. All the above, however, are highly dependent on the skill and capacity of the practitioner to manage the transferential relationship.

CULTURAL CONTEXTS, POWER AND CONCEPTUALISATIONS OF INDIVIDUAL DIFFERENCES

The primary critique of psychoanalysis has been aimed at the notion of the unconscious and its tension in relation to individual autonomy. The privileging of unconscious communication, it is argued, leaves the individual at the mercy of the practitioner's subjective interpretations. Should he disagree with her, then she will perceive this as evidence of his 'resistance' to fresh understanding. One can easily see how this type of model is open to the abuse of power by the practitioner. Whilst, undoubtedly, this type of poor practice takes place in certain quarters, it is based on a misconception of the project of contemporary psychoanalysis. The reality of engaging with and experiencing a successful psychoanalytic therapeutic relationship is that the transactions which are observed are explored with much subtlety and tentativeness. The project is one of joint collaborative curiosity about unconscious processes transacting between the two people in the room. The psychoanalytic practitioner does not shy away from the obvious asymmetry in the relationship, yet seeks to bring herself, and her therapeutic skills, to this joint inquiry.

The history of psychoanalysis is full of controversy over the manner in which it has theorised what might be called 'individual differences'. Notions of gender, sexuality, culture and ethnicity have been, and continue to be, hotly debated within the profession. Historical psychoanalytic claims to the 'universality' of its accounts have meant that it has often been perceived as placing significant emphasis on the cross-cultural dimensions of therapeutic relationships. Equally, the privileging of normative developmental stories, such as the Oedipus complex, has exposed a significant lack of understanding in the areas of human sexuality and gender-identity development. Ironically, however, by its very essence, psychoanalysis provides us with the framework from which to engage in the complex exploration of individual differences. Notions of primacy of subjective experience, of the construction of identity (including gendered and sexual identity), and psychic bisexuality (Freud, 1905), all allow for the deconstruction of a unitary 'normal' developmental trajectory. The work of French psychoanalyst, Jacques Lacan, in particular, has provided the framework for psychoanalytic explorations of culture and the social upon the developmental of the individual (see Lacan, 1966).

RESEARCH EVIDENCE

The link between practice and research has always been a central one in the development of psychoanalytic theory and practice. As Freud famously quoted in 'The Question of Lay Analysis':

> In psycho-analysis there has existed from the very first an inseparable bond between cure and research. Knowledge brought therapeutic success. It was impossible to treat a patient without learning something new. (1927: 255)

To review research to date would not be an accomplishable task within the confines of this chapter. Tensions regarding epistemological and methodological assumptions regarding psychoanalysis have been rife for as long as the modality has existed. Currently, there is much debate regarding whether research studies should focus on outcome or process studies. In the current state of play, there can be no doubt that the literature suggests that psychotherapy in general, and psychodynamic psychotherapy in particular, is effective (Bergin & Garfield, 1994; Roth & Fonagy, 2004). A critical review of these books will reveal that short-term psychodynamic psychotherapy is effective with particular clinical groups, such as those suffering from depression, post-traumatic stress disorder, personality disorders, psychotherapy with children and older people, to name but a few. Equally, many peer-reviewed journals, such as *Psychoanalytic Inquiry*, devote much of their content to the publication and debate of current psychodynamic and psycho-analytically orientated research. Furthermore, research is flourishing in the interdisciplinary work being carried out by neuropsychoanalysts, who are bringing new findings from neuroscience and integrating these with metapsychological models developed from practice. In this author's opinion, this constitutes the most interesting and important area of current psychoanalytic research. For examples of such work, the reader could be directed to the work of, amongst others, Antonio Damasio, Sue Gerdhart, Allan Schore, and Mark Solms. The journal *Neuro-Psychoanalysis* is a rich source of much of this material.

SUMMARY

The summarising of what constitutes the psychoanalytic therapeutic relationship can but be an imperfect project. Defining it in any definitive way could be seen to be a deeply anti-psychoanalytic endeavour as, in the end, living, interpreting and relating to others is profoundly idiosyncratic. As such, some ideas have been omitted and some privileged, and the author's own 'distortions' of psychoanalytic thinking will be evident. However, if psychoanalysis teaches us anything, it teaches us that to be helpful to others, to be available to offer therapeutic work, we must not strive for some 'objective' truth about ourselves and others, but instead struggle to make meaning out of complex, multiple and often conflicting stories.

REFERENCES

Bergin, AE & Garfield, SL (1994) (Eds) *Handbook of Psychotherapy and Behavior Change* (4th edn). New York: Wiley.

Bion, WR (1970) *Attention and Interpretation: A scientific approach to insight in psychoanalysis and groups.* New York: Wiley.

Bowlby, J (1969) *Attachment* (2nd edn). *Attachment and Loss (Vol. 1).* New York: Basic Books.

Freud, S (1895) Studies on hysteria. In J Strachey *The Standard Edition of the Complete Psychological Works of Sigmund Freud, Vol. II (1893–1895)* (pp. 253–305). London: Hogarth Press.

Freud, S (1900) Interpretation of dreams. In J Strachey *The Standard Edition of the Complete Psychological Works of Sigmund Freud, Vol. IV (1893–1895) The interpretation of dreams (First part)* (pp. ix–627). London: Hogarth Press.

Freud, S (1905) The three essays on the theory of sexuality. In J Stracey *The Standard Edition of the Complete Psychological Works of Sigmund Freud, Vol. VII (years)* (pp. 123–246). London: Hogarth Press

Freud, S (1912) The dynamics of transference. In J Strachey *The Standard Edition of the Complete Psychological Works of Sigmund Freud, Vol. XII (1911–1913): The case of Schreber, papers on technique and other works,* (pp. 97–108). London: Hogarth Press.

Freud, S (1915) Observations on transference-love (Further recommendations on the technique of psychoanalysis III). In J Strachey *The Standard Edition of the Complete Psychological Works of Sigmund Freud, Vol. XII (1911–1913): The case of Schreber, papers on technique and other works* (pp. 157–71). London: Hogarth Press.

Freud, S (1920) Beyond the pleasure principle. In J Strachey *The Standard Edition of the Complete Psychological Works of Sigmund Freud, Vol. XVIII (1920–1922): Beyond the pleasure principle, group psychology and other works* (pp. 1–64). London: Hogarth Press.

Freud, S (1923) The ego and the id. In J Strachey *The Standard Edition of the Complete Psychological Works of Sigmund Freud, Vol. XIX (1923–1925): The Ego and the Id and other works* (pp. 1–66). London: Hogarth Press.

Freud, S (1927) The question of lay analysis. In J Strachey *The Standard Edition of the Complete Psychological Works of Sigmund Freud, Vol. XX (1925–1926): An autobiographical study, inhibitions, symptoms and anxiety. The question of lay analysis and other works* (pp. 1–292). London: Hogarth Press.

Freud, S (1930) Civilization and its discontents. In J Strachey *The Standard Edition of the Complete Psychological Works of Sigmund Freud, Vol. XXI (1927–1931) The future of an illusion, civilization and its discontents, and other works* (pp. 57–146). London: Hogarth Press.

Green, V (Ed) (2003) *Emotional Development in Psychoanalysis, Attachment and Neuroscience: Creating connections.* London: Brunner-Routledge.

Guntrip, H (1995) *Personality Structure and Human Interaction.* London: Karnac Books.

Heimann, P (1950) On counter-transference. *International Journal of Psycho-Analysis, 31,* 81–4.

Klein, M (1957) (1988) *Envy and Gratitude.* London: Virago Press.

Lacan, J (1966) *Ecrits: A selection.* London: Routledge.

Langs, R (1992) *A Clinical Workbook for Psychotherapists.* London: Karnac Books.

Roth, A & Fonagy, P (2004) *What Works for Whom? A critical review of psychotherapy research.* New York: Guilford Press.

Searles, HF (1959) Oedipal love in the counter-transference. *International Journal of Psycho-Analysis. 40,* 180–90.

Smith, DL (1991) *Hidden Conversations: An introduction to communicative psychoanalysis*. London: Routledge.

Winnicott, DW (1949) Hate in the counter-transference. *International Journal of Psycho-Analysis, 30*, 69–74.

Winnicott, DW (1964) *The Child, the Family and the Outside World*. Harmondsworth: Penguin.

CHAPTER 4

A PERSON-CENTRED PERSPECTIVE[1]

SHEILA HAUGH

BACKGROUND TO THE APPROACH

The driving force behind the development of person-centred counselling (therapy or psychotherapy – the terms are used interchangeably in this chapter) was the desire of Carl Rogers, the originator of the approach, to find ways of practising a therapy that actually helped his patients. Working in the Child Study Department of the Rochester Society for the Prevention of Cruelty to Children (1928–1940), Rogers found that the methods he had been trained in (traditional child-guidance methods which were, at that point, based on psychoanalytical philosophies) 'did not work very well' (Raskin & Rogers, 1995: 155). Like all other theories of counselling/therapy, a theory and practice called 'person-centred counselling' and 'client-centred therapy' did not spring fully formed from Rogers' head one afternoon. The precursors of Rogers' more fully formed theory (1951, 1957a, 1959) could be seen as early as 1939 in his book *The Clinical Treatment of the Problem Child*. Further, and again like all other theorists, there were many influences on his ideas, in particular, John Dewey, Karen Horney, Otto Rank and Jessie Taft. For example, Rogers acknowledges Horney as an influence on the development of person-centred theory, at that point known as non-directive therapy (Rogers, 1942: 28), and it is clear that one of Rogers' most fundamental notions, that of the actualising tendency (see below), had at least some of its seeds in Horney's concept of a person's 'urge to grow throughout life, [including] the constructive tendency to heal oneself' (Rubins, 1978: 153).

Rogers himself was clear on the philosophical and historical background to his developing approach, locating it in its academic, social and philosophical milieu.

> [C]lient-centred therapy has been influenced by psychology as it has developed in the United States, with its genius for operational definitions, for objective measurement, its insistence upon scientific method and the necessity of submitting all hypotheses to a process of objective verification or disproof ... it has also been indebted to Gestalt psychology, with its emphasis upon the wholeness and the inter-relatedness of the cluster of

---

1. This paper is dedicated to Tony Merry and Barbara Brodley who are both deeply missed.

phenomena which we think of as the individual. Some of its roots stretch out even further into the educational and social and political philosophy which is at the heart of our American culture ... Thus client-centered therapy has drawn, both consciously and unconsciously, upon many of the current streams of clinical, scientific, and philosophical thought which are present in our culture. (1951: 4–5)

More generally, at the same time as Rogers was developing his theory of therapeutic personality development, there was also evolving what became known as the third force in psychology – humanistic psychology. Describing it like this might give the impression that these developments – Rogers' theories, the influence of the academic, social and philosophical milieu and humanistic psychology – were separate, unconnected events. Such an impression would be unrepresentative, although Rogers has been described as one of the founders of humanistic psychology (along with Abraham Maslow and Gordon Alport), and it would be erroneous to try to isolate these events from each other. Rogers deeply influenced the emergence of humanistic psychology, which in turn influenced the psychological zeitgeist more generally, which in turn was a catalyst for the development of humanistic psychology, which in turn influenced Rogers. Thus, no one event can be said to have had more prominence on the development of what became known as person-centred counselling and psychotherapy. Rogers' work, originally developed from a therapeutic approach, and following on from his theory of interpersonal relationships (Rogers, 1959), was also seen to have applications in other areas, particularly education (Rogers, 1983), and became known as 'the person-centred approach'. This is an umbrella term for a number of applications of Rogers' theory, of which counselling and psychotherapy is just one.

Initially described as 'non-directive therapy' (Rogers, 1942), person-centred counselling/psychotherapy has over the last 65 years developed into three distinct schools: client-centred therapy (often described as 'classical'), focusing-orientated therapy and experiential person-centred therapy. Pete Sanders (2004: x) describes these three schools thus:

- Classical client-centred therapy – the 'original' approach, the starting point of it all, as described in Carl Rogers' early writings.
- Focusing – springing from the work of Eugene Gendlin, Carl Rogers' close colleague.
- Experiential therapy – developments which embrace ideas from both Rogers and Gendlin, infused with cognitive psychology and Gestalt Therapy.

Sanders also introduces the possibility that there are two further 'tribes' (Warner, 2000) in the person-centred nation (Sanders, 2004): existential therapies and integrative person-centred therapy. He notes that some people may take issue with the inclusion of these approaches under the auspices of the person-centred approach, as existential therapy is not person-centred, and integrative therapy is not a specific approach but more a method (ibid.: x). He proposes that the inclusion of existential therapies is justified, as Rogers was 'clearly influenced by existential writers', although this point is debatable[2] (ibid.). The inclusion of integrative person-centred therapy is proposed, as 'many practitioners integrate many elements of their experience into the therapeutic moment', and is a way of 'approaching therapy from a person-centred base of values, philosophy and theory' (ibid.).

Whether or not these different groups are all part of a person-centred approach to therapy is a debate that continues in the present day. The greatest point of divergence between them concerns how a theoretical attitude of non-directivity can be maintained in the practice of a therapy that focuses a client on some aspect of their experiencing (focusing and experiential approaches). Some theorists maintain that all these approaches fall under the umbrella of person-centred therapy (see Warner, 2000), whilst others see them as distinctly different approaches (Brodley, 2006). This chapter presents the ideas from a classical perspective.

FUNDAMENTAL PREMISE OF PERSON-CENTRED THERAPY

The key element of client-centred/person-centred therapy is the notion of the actualising tendency. This is the directional 'tendency in all forms of organic life to develop more complex organisation, the fulfilment of potential and, in human beings, the actualisation of the self "in ways which serve to maintain or enhance the organism" (Rogers, 1959: 196)' (Tudor & Merry, 2002: 2). Another key element is the concept of the formative tendency (Rogers, 1951, 1980; Neville, 2007). This is a tendency that Rogers proposed was true of the whole universe – a universe that is always 'building and creating' (Rogers, 1980: 126); the universe is continually developing new and more complex systems and, within that, the human organism developing new and more complex systems – the actualising tendency. Rogers (1963) proposed the actualising tendency as the only motivational force in human beings, and suggested that we 'have an inherent tendency to develop all [our] capacities in ways that serve to maintain or enhance the organism' (Rogers & Sanford, 1989: 1491). Further, 'this tendency is a reliable one, which, when free to operate, moves human beings toward what is termed growth, maturity, and life enrichment' (ibid.). If the formative tendency describes the movement of the universe and the actualising tendency describes the tendency of the whole organism, it is the notion of the self-actualising tendency that describes the tendency of the organism toward the development and maintenance of the (psychological) self-concept.[3]

---

2. Notwithstanding Rogers' references to Kierkegaard (Coulson & Rogers, 1968; Rogers 1957b, 1972), when asked about the influence of existential philosophy on his thinking, Rogers replied that existentialists were people 'who discovered the same sort of things I have, who have gone beyond what I've gone through in a number of significant ways. *But I didn't feel as though I was being introduced to a new field*' (Evans, 1975: 70, italics added).

3. Rogers used the term 'self-concept' to denote the subjective view of the person from within themselves. He uses the term 'self-structure' to denote that this was an objective view of the person. As the term self-concept is the most widely understood, I will restrict myself to this usage.

The self-concept develops in the child as she or he comes to differentiate between what is and what is not part of his or her being. The way the self-concept develops depends very much on the level of unconditional positive regard a child receives whilst growing up, particularly from significant people in their world (Rogers, 1959). Feelings, thoughts and behaviours that are positively accepted by significant others are integrated into the self-concept and are available to awareness. Those thoughts, feelings and behaviours that are not accepted (however subtly) are restricted to awareness through the dynamic of denial and distortion. For example, if I have learnt that I will not be loved and accepted if I shout a lot, then my desire (and perhaps need) to shout will either be completely unknown to me (denial) or changed into something else, such as feeling sick, perhaps (distortion). In these circumstances, I would be described as having developed a condition of worth (Rogers, 1959). In this instance, the condition of worth is that I will be loved if (a) I don't shout and (b) (even better) I don't want to shout. The self-concept, then, is made up of those aspects of my experiencing that are available to my awareness and those aspects of my experiencing that, because of conditions of worth (and there are usually many) are denied or distorted in my awareness. Consequently, 'the path of therapy is … the dissolving of conditions of worth, the achievement of a self which is *congruent* with experience' (Rogers, 1959: 226).

POSITION OF THE CLIENT AND THERAPIST

Given the phenomenological nature of person-centred counselling, meaning that the only expert on what is going on for a person is the person themselves, and the premise of the actualising tendency, it (almost) goes without saying that it is the client who is the expert in the therapeutic relationship. The outcome of this position is the belief that the client is the expert with respect to both the content and the process of the therapeutic relationship, a notion that is, in practice, as radical today as it was when Rogers first proposed the idea (see Kirschenbaum, 2007: 105–50). Furthermore, the implications of this stance are far reaching insofar as it includes both the practical arrangements for therapy (for example, do we meet once or twice a week or once or twice a month – for an hour, two hours or even ten minutes?), and the content of the sessions themselves (a client can speak of the here and now, or of past experiences and feelings, for example: this choice is entirely theirs). An often-quoted statement of Rogers makes explicit the attitude implicit in conceptualising the position of the client in this way: 'It is the client who knows what hurts, what directions to go, what problems are crucial, what experiences have been deeply buried' (1961: 11–12).

Rogers' theory of therapy rests on the presence of the actualising tendency. This resource can be tapped only if 'a definable climate of facilitative psychological attitudes can be provided' (Rogers, 1986: 197). This climate is generally understood to be made up of empathy, congruence and unconditional positive regard (UPR). However, these attitudes were only part of the picture for Rogers. In fact, he suggested that there are six conditions that are necessary and sufficient for therapeutic personality change. These are:

1. that two persons are in *contact*;
2. that the first person, whom we shall term 'the client', is in a state of *incongruence*, being *vulnerable* or *anxious*;
3. that the second person, whom we shall term 'the therapist', is *congruent* in the *relationship*;
4. that the therapist is *experiencing unconditional positive regard toward* the client;
5. that the therapist is *experiencing* an *empathic* understanding of the client's *internal frame of reference*;
6. that the client *perceives*, at least to a minimal degree, conditions 4 and 5, the *unconditional positive regard* of the therapist for him [sic], and the *empathic* understanding of the therapist. (Rogers, 1959: 213)

In short, the position of the therapist is that of providing a facilitative psychological environment so that the actualising tendency of the client may be nurtured in respect of the maintenance and enhancement of their experiencing. This will lead to therapeutic personality change (Rogers, 1959). The phenomenological nature of the person-centred approach informs us that the person-centred practitioner is *only* interested in trying to fully enter the world of their client (the phenomenological stance). For Rogers, two people being in contact simply meant that 'each makes a perceived or subceived[4] difference in the experiential field of the other' (ibid.: 207). In other words, some change would be experienced in each person's phenomenological field when they are together.

PSYCHOLOGICAL FACTORS IN THE RELATIONSHIP

In one-to-one therapy, there are two people in the relationship both bringing their own histories, current concerns, future aspirations and fears to the encounter. Congruence in the therapist means being open to all he or she (the therapist) is experiencing. This (hopefully) includes genuine feelings of empathy and UPR, as well as an awareness of his or her own limitations and difficulties, and feelings that may be traditionally considered 'anti-therapeutic' (for example, not feeling UPR). To put it another way, whilst we assume that a client has conditions of worth and, therefore, areas of incongruence, this is also true of the therapist. It is expected that the therapist is able to be open in and to the relationship (congruence), and thus open to all that the client may be. In essence, this means having fewer conditions of worth than the client does in this particular relationship.

Rogers hypothesised that when a client perceives, at least to a minimal degree, the genuine empathy and UPR of the therapist, a process of personality change will take place. This is often known as Rogers' seven stages of process, though it is more accurately described as a process conception of psychotherapy (Rogers, 1961: 125–59). Rogers

---

4. *Subception* means 'discrimination without awareness' (Tudor & Merry, 2002); i.e. the person 'may not be consciously aware of [the] impact' (Rogers, 1957a: 96).

was clear that breaking the process of psychotherapy down into seven stages was somewhat arbitrary, stressing that the process should be seen being on a continuum (ibid.: 131). Briefly described, there is a change from immobility and rigidity of personality and processing to flexibility in the person's way of being: from someone who sees all problems as being external to themselves (if indeed they perceive having any problems in the first place), with little apparent ability to reflect on their experiencing, to someone who 'sees life more as a process than something fixed' (Merry, 1995: 58).

The person at the seventh stage of Rogers' process conceptualisation is synonymous with his notion of the 'fully functioning person' and is someone whose '... self- experiences are accurately symbolized, and are included in the self-concept in [an] accurately symbolized form ... the state is one of congruence of self and experience' (Rogers, 1959: 206). The fully functioning person is supremely healthy from a psychological perspective. According to Rogers, this is a person who is 'more able to experience all his [sic] feelings ... he is his own sifter of evidence and more open to evidence from all sources' (Rogers, 1961: 191–2). The point to be emphasised is that the notion of the fully functioning person is a person who is in *process* rather than someone who is at a static end point and has 'actualised'; a person who is fully open to their experiencing in any one moment.

THERAPEUTIC INTERVENTIONS

In this model, the practitioner is not interested and sees no sense in directing the content or process of the client's deliberations. In fact, the therapist would deem such activities as evidence of a lack of empathy on their part. This is inexorably linked to the notion of the actualising tendency. The therapist trusts, deeply and with conviction, that this force is present; that as a person comes to believe and trust the relationship being offered, a relationship where they are understood and accepted, the actualising tendency will be the motivational force that impels a person in a direction toward psychological health. No matter how bizarre or unclear a person's way of being might seem; no matter how they may be 'using' counselling, the conviction is held that this is the healthiest way for the person to be in the world, as they experience it in this moment. At heart, the client–therapist relationship is seen as one that is collaborative, with the therapist accompanying the client on their therapeutic journey. The therapist does not, at any point, presume they know more than the client about the client's process or how the counselling might develop. The therapist only assumes that, if they can provide a psychologically safe environment, then therapeutic personality change will ensue. So, it follows that therapeutic interventions are best characterised as an empathic understanding process (Brodley, 2000) rather than interventions. Implicitly, and occasionally explicitly, empathic responses involve checking that I have understood the client's meaning and that have I caught all the nuances of that meaning (Rogers, 1951); as well as checking my understanding, if my responses are accurate enough, they also communicate UPR. The paradox of the empathic understanding process, where responses are often expressed verbally, is that they communicate UPR *non*-verbally. At the same time as communicating empathy and checking understanding, these responses also subtly disclose the non-judgemental attitude of the therapist. The therapist does not announce, does not need to announce, that they are acceptant and trusting of the client's process. Rather, empathic following responses are a behavioural manifestation of acceptance.

Person-centred therapy makes a heavy demand on the therapist, as these attitudes of empathy and UPR need to be truly genuine, a part of the therapist's philosophy and value system. In this context, being genuine, or congruent, means that all the experiencing (emotional and cognitive) of the therapist is available to their awareness without denial or distortion. The danger in the therapeutic relationship does not so much lie in the fact that, in this moment, I might not feel accepting of the client; the danger occurs if I am *not aware* that I am feeling judgemental, for these are the times the client will subceive this dynamic – thus undermining their experience of the attitude of UPR. It is not even necessary that I share these feelings with a client, though on rare occasions I might. It is necessary that I am congruent with my experiencing. This is why it is important that a supportive environment, for example, good supervision, is available to the therapist themselves to enable them to explore those aspects of their experiencing that are distorted and/or denied to their awareness.

Whilst the person-centred therapist is most concerned that his or her attitudes of empathy and UPR are genuine, the talent of the therapist also lies in his or her ability to communicate these attitudes to the other person. If there are skills or expertise to be associated with person-centred therapy, it is those of communicating empathy and UPR. I might be the most empathic person in the world and I might be authentically accepting of the person in front of me but, if I cannot communicate this, there is little point in my being there. Most, though not all (see Bozarth, 1984/2001; Keys, 2003) communication in counselling and therapy, as described here, is verbal. It may seem somewhat paradoxical to consider an approach 'so founded upon relationships' in terms of skills (Tolan, 2003: ix). Nevertheless, both the development and communication of attitudes of empathy, congruence, and UPR need to be of the highest priority in the training for person-centred therapists. Having developed the ability to *be* empathic (experiencing), we then need to develop the ability to *respond* empathically (communication) (ibid.: 19–20). Having developed our own awareness (congruence), we then need to develop the discrimination of when we share that awareness explicitly (communication). Having developed a genuine attitude of UPR (usually in tandem with empathic understanding), we need to develop ways to show our respectfulness and our prizing (communication).

CULTURAL CONTEXTS, POWER AND CONCEPTUALISATION OF INDIVIDUAL DIFFERENCES

As with most therapies in the UK today, person-centred counselling/psychotherapy evolved from within a white, Western paradigm – and the most recognised and well-known proponent was an American white man. This does not necessarily mean that the theory and practice is inevitably fatally flawed in some way. Nevertheless, notice needs to be taken of how these facts might show themselves in the theory and practice. For example, person-centred theory has traditionally placed the concept of the self at the centre of its hypothesis; psychological healing and growth comes about as the individual 'undoes' conditions of worth, and becomes more congruent with their organismic experiencing; experiencing becomes spontaneous and fluid rather than fixed and rigid. As a product of an individualistic view, and in common with most other psychotherapeutic approaches in the West, it is hardly surprising that this idea of the self as central should be found in person-centred theory. At the same time, deeply embedded in Rogers' theories runs the assertion that it is in relationships (of a certain emotional tone) where human beings flourish, from where the cure for psychological hurt, damage and distress comes.

Given the notion that it is the client, not the therapist, who is the expert in the relationship, it should be clear, theoretically at least, that the power in the relationship lies with the client. The therapist's sole intention is to understand and experience, as deeply as possible, the world of the other as they experience it. This intention leads quite naturally to a position of non-directivity. Non-directivity is not practised because it is a 'person-centred way of working'. A non-directive stance is the natural outcome of implementing the necessary and sufficient conditions for therapeutic personality change (Grant, 2002, describes this as 'principled non-directivity'). However, it would be deeply naïve to believe that non-directivity is the equivalent of non-influence. Leslie Greenberg describes this phenomena well when he writes, '… non-influence *is impossible*; the intention to try consciously *not* to influence what a person decides or chooses, however, *is possible*' (2004: 54). At the same time, whilst having the intention not to influence, therapists need to remember that they have a role of power (that is, therapy as an institution), may have societal power (for example, with reference to their ethnicity and/or gender), and will bring to the therapeutic encounter their own experiences of power and powerlessness (historical power) (Proctor, 2006). For the person-centred therapist, training, supervision and continuing professional development will include the ongoing development of congruence; in this context, on how their role and their societal and historical power impacts on their relationship with the client.

It is clear that some individual characteristics are based on the context of our lives – for example, our ethnicity, gender, sexuality, physical abilities or class. Traditionally, person-centred theory has not concerned itself overmuch with the question of individual difference in the same manner as perhaps can be seen in more psychodynamically orientated theories. Some individual characteristics are seen as dependent on the experience of UPR that an infant has received from significant carers. Someone who has received optimal UPR will be a 'fully functioning' person (Rogers, 1959). Thus, human beings are conceptualised as process-orientated rather than as having a fixed set of characteristics. When the six conditions are present, person-centred psychotherapy facilitates the reconnection between the actualising tendency and the self-actualising tendency through the dissolution of conditions of worth. When this happens, human beings are able to become their *'potentialities'* (Rogers, 1961: 351).

STRENGTHS AND WEAKNESSES

Perhaps the greatest strength of person-centred counselling and psychotherapy has been its attention to the therapeutic relationship. From his earliest writing, Rogers was concerned with the intimate meeting between the client and counsellor in a way that had not been approached before. This is not to devalue the work of predecessors such as Horney, Taft and Rank, but Rogers, in presenting the six conditions, hypothesised that the relationship *is* the curative factor in and of itself, and this interest has been maintained and developed for over 60 years. The deep concern with the relationship continues to be the focus for many person-centred practitioners and theorists across the tribes of the approach (e.g. Mearns & Cooper 2005; Schmid 2006) and places person-centred counselling and psychotherapy at the forefront of a theory of therapeutic practice.

This interest in the relationship has, at times, been to the detriment of the development of theories in areas such as the genesis of psychological distress (other than the development of conditions of worth). The premise of the approach rests on the notion of the actualising tendency, and the necessity and sufficiency of the six conditions for therapeutic personality change. In this context, a knowledge of the origins of psychological distress is not necessary in the moment of the therapeutic encounter. The diagnostic categories are, at best, simply a description of symptoms of dis-ease (see Bentall, 2003, for an in-depth critique of diagnosis generally). At their worst, these descriptions come to define the client and compound the specificity myth: the idea that there are 'specific treatments for particular disabilities' (Bozarth, 1998: 164). On the other hand, there is room to develop a person-centred perspective on different areas of human experiencing, for example, psychotic episodes, that take an explicitly process-orientated perspective rather than relying on notions formulated from other approaches (Warner, 2005; Haugh, in press).

A development of such theories would also be a response to those critiques that challenge the view of psychological disturbance propounded by the person-centred approach. These critiques suggest that the theory separates and isolates the individual from society. This stance results in the assumption that psychological disturbances are the result of an individual's personal history rather than having any connection with their social context (poverty and oppression for example) (see Waterhouse, 1993; Hill, 2004). Khatidja Chantler has challenged the approach to avoid the 'pitfall of reducing the political to the personal' (2006: 52). This position reflects a misunderstanding of the development of conditions of worth – conditions that are always developed in relationships, including a relationship to the wider community. At the same time, they also point to a serious omission in person-centred theory in Western countries: the omission of challenging its own white, Western and patriarchal heritage. The exploration of this heritage has become an area of investigation and study and is proving to be a challenging and fruitful area of development (see Proctor et al., 2006).

In terms of practice, the greatest strength and weakness of person-centred therapy depends on the abilities and talents of individual practitioners. This is perhaps the approach that makes the greatest demands on therapists – they have only themselves to offer in the relationship. There are no techniques, no interventions that can be planned ahead in supervision; there are no tools or strategies that can be brought into play if the going gets tough. As noted above, the only skills that the person-centred therapist requires are those of being able to communicate empathy and UPR and to learn to discriminate as to when to share their experiencing (congruence). The rest relies on the robustness of the therapist and their ability to meet the client with openness, truthfulness and profound understanding.

RESEARCH EVIDENCE

Notwithstanding the fact that Rogers was the first to publish research on the outcome of psychotherapy as early as the 1950s (Rogers & Dymond, 1954), Elliott, Greenberg and Lietaer, writing in 2004, pointed out that 50 per cent of the studies in their extensive review had appeared in the previous ten years. In this examination of experiential approaches to psychotherapy, Elliott et al. (2004) concluded that the body of evidence reviewed 'strongly supports the effectiveness of experiential-humanistic therapies' (ibid.: 510). Separating the research pertinent to classical person-centred counselling from the research into the more experiential forms of psychotherapy (process-experiential, person-centred counselling and gestalt counselling) needs to be undertaken if we are attempting to fully understand what studies show. For an in-depth review of Elliott et al. the interested reader is directed to Cooper et al. (2008), *Widening and Increasing Access to Psychological Therapies.* An overview of current research is offered by Sanders and Cooper. Their summary is as follows:

- For most clients, person-centred therapy brings about significant levels of psychological improvement, most clearly demonstrated in clients with mild to moderate depression, and those who are dealing with specific life issues.

- After thousands of studies, there is no convincing evidence that person-centred therapy is less (or more) effective than other established forms of psychotherapy, whether in general or in relation to specific psychological problems.

- Empathy, positive regard and congruence are probably not necessary for *all* clients to achieve positive therapeutic change; but a strong correlation seems to exist between levels of empathy and therapeutic outcomes; and positive regard and congruence also show some correlation with clients' level of improvement (Sanders & Cooper, 2006: 108).

Elliott et al. report of studies showing that a 24-month follow-up of post-treatment outcome for people diagnosed with schizophrenia showed 'CC [client-centred] therapy was substantially better than CB [cognitive-behavioural therapy]' (2004: 516).

NEW DEVELOPMENTS IN THE APPROACH

The death of Rogers in 1987 gave rise to a period of time where the development of client-centred theory seemed to become moribund, and there was little or no interaction between the different groupings within the person-centred approach. Over the last ten to fifteen years this situation has changed quite dramatically and there have been many new developments. For example:

- In 1994 Garry Prouty published *Theoretical Evolutions in Person-Centered/Experiential Therapy: Applications to schizophrenic and retarded psychoses.* The book detailed Prouty's approach in working with people experiencing florid psychotic symptoms which he called Pre-Therapy. Prouty (2001), describing his approach as an 'integrated empathic attitude' (p. 157), outlines psychological contact on three levels: contact reflections, contact functions and contact behaviours – contact behaviours being a measurement of the improvement in contact (Prouty, 2002: 15). This work is being continued and developed by a number of people (see Prouty, Van Werde & Pörtner, 2002; Sommerbeck, 2003; Van Werde & Prouty, 2007).

- It is clear that some people, some of the time, experience themselves in different ways. This can be as simple as feeling and/or behaving differently in different situations (at home or at work, for example) or it may be an experience of more profound differences (for example, dissociated process). Dave Mearns and Brian Thorne (2000) have suggested the concept of *configurations of self* to explain this phenomenon from a person-centred perspective. They are attempting to describe, in theoretical terms, the way in which people experience these different parts within themselves. The concept of the plural self (i.e the idea that we are not just one self but a number of selves) is neither new nor peculiar to person-centred theory. Mearns (2002) develops this idea 'in order to transform [Rogers' theory] from its earlier "unitary" nature into "dialogical" form' (p. 14) (see Cooper et al., 2004; Mearns & Schmid, 2006). Mearns and Cooper have also been developing the concept of 'working at relational depth' (2005), in an effort to continue this development of a '*dialogical* approach to person-centred therapy' (p. xiii).

- As noted above, person-centred theory has concentrated more on the exploration of the therapeutic relationship than developing specific theories related to psychological dis-ease. A notable exception to this has been the work of Margaret Warner who has been developing a concept of 'difficult processes' (2005), specifically fragile process, dissociated process and psychotic process (2007). This notion is built on a view of psychological dis-ease that is process-orientated rather than the static approach of traditional explanations for mental health problems. Latterly, she has proposed a 'process-sensitive model of psychopathology' (ibid.: 161). This is an attempt to 'go beyond those [understandings] of traditional diagnostic categories' (ibid.: 162) and maintains the concept of the relationship as fundamental to the alleviation of dis-ease.

- The publication of the series of books, *Rogers' Therapeutic Conditions: Evolution, theory and practice* (Wyatt, 2001; Haugh & Merry, 2001; Bozarth & Wilkins, 2001; Wyatt & Sanders, 2002), brought together a body of literature regarding the therapeutic conditions that encompassed seminal papers past and present. This series re-established Rogers' therapeutic conditions as necessary (and perhaps sufficient) and promoted a new era of theoretical exploration.

This list is not exhaustive and no doubt reflects those developments that particularly caught this writer's imagination. It is indicative of the vibrancy of the person-centred approach today that these new developments have all taken place (or at least been reported on and published) within the last thirteen years.

SUMMARY

This chapter has attempted to give a brief overview of person-centred therapy history, theory and practice. There will be omissions that another person-centred theorist and practitioner may not have made, just as there will be inclusions that someone else might not have incorporated. I hope I have been able to give the reader who wishes to follow an interest in this approach some useful references and I also hope that the reader who knows something of the approach has found something of interest to them as well. As we move into the twenty-first century, the vibrancy of person-centred therapy is undiminished, as evidenced by theory development and research. The commitment to the relationship between the client and therapist is likewise undiminished, being the ground of all our work.

REFERENCES

Bentall, RP (2003) *Madness Explained.* London: Penguin.

Bozarth, JD (1984/2001) Beyond reflection: Emergent modes of empathy. In RF Levant & JM Shlien (Eds) *Client-Centered Therapy and the Person-Centered Approach* (pp. 59–75). New York: Praeger. Reprinted in S Haugh & T Merry (Eds) (2001) *Rogers' Therapeutic Conditions: Evolution, theory and practice. Vol 2: Empathy* (pp. 131–43). Ross-on-Wye: PCCS Books.

Bozarth, JD (1998) *Person-Centred Therapy: A revolutionary paradigm.* Ross-on-Wye: PCCS Books.

Bozarth, JD & Wilkins, P (Eds) (2001) *Rogers' Therapeutic Conditions: Evolution, theory and practice. Vol 3: Unconditional positive regard.* Ross-on-Wye: PCCS Books.

Brodley, B (2000) The therapeutic clinical interview: Guidelines for beginning practice. In T Merry (Ed) *Person-Centred Practice. The BAPCA Reader* (pp. 103–9). Ross-on-Wye: PCCS Books.

Brodley, B (2006) Non-directivity in client-centered therapy. *Person-Centered and Experiential Psychotherapies, 5* (1), 36–52.

Chantler, K (2006) Rethinking person-centred therapy. In G Proctor, M Cooper, P Sanders & B Malcolm (Eds) *Politicizing the Person-Centred Approach. An agenda for social change* (pp. 44–54). Ross-on-Wye: PCCS Books.

Cooper, M, McLeod, J, Elliott, R, Mearns, D, Hilton, J, McGinnis, S, et al. (2008) Widening and increasing access to psychological therapies. Proposed intervention: Person-centred/experiential psychotherapy and counselling. Glasgow, Strathclyde University. Available from <http://www.strath.ac.uk/Departments/counsunit/docs/policy_Psychological _Therapies.pdf>. [Accessed 24 February 2008]

Cooper, M, Mearns, D, Stiles, WB, Warner, M & Elliott, R (2004) Developing self-pluralistic perspectives within the person-centred and experiential approaches: A round-table dialogue. *Person-Centered and Experiential Psychotherapies, 3* (3), 176–91.

Coulson, WR and Rogers, CR (Eds) (1968) *Man and the Science of Man.* Columbus, OH: Charles E. Merrill.

Elliott, R, Greenberg, LS & Lietaer, G (2004) Research on experiential psychotherapies. In MJ Lambert (2004) *Bergin & Garfield's Handbook of Psychotherapy and Behavior Change* (pp. 493–539). New York: John Wiley & Sons.

Evans, RI (1975) *Carl Rogers: The man and his ideas.* New York: Dutton.

Grant, B (2002) Principled and instrumental nondirectiveness in person-centered and client-centered therapy. In D Cain (Ed) *Classics in the Person-Centered Approach* (pp. 371–7). Ross-on-Wye: PCCS Books.

Greenberg, LS (2004) Being and doing: Person-centeredness, process guidance and differential treatment. *Person-Centered and Experiential Psychotherapies, 3* (1), 52–64.

Haugh, S (in press) A person-centred approach to loss and bereavement. In J Tolan & P Wilkins *Person-Centred Practice: Understanding and and working with reactions to life events.* London: Sage.

Haugh, S & Merry, T (Eds) (2001) *Rogers' Therapeutic Conditions: Evolution, theory and practice. Vol 2: Empathy.* Ross-on-Wye: PCCS Books.

Hill, M (2004) Woman-centred practice. In G Proctor & MB Napier (Eds) *Encountering Feminism: Intersections between feminism and the person-centred approach* (pp. 221–33). Ross-on-Wye: PCCS Books.

Keys, S (Ed) (2003) *Idiosyncratic Person-Centred Therapy.* Ross-on-Wye: PCCS Books.

Kirschenbaum, H (2007) *The Life and Works of Carl Rogers.* Ross-on-Wye: PCCS Books.

Mearns, D (2002) Further theoretical propositions in regard to self theory within person-centered therapy. *Person-Centered and Experiential Psychotherapies, 1* (1&2), 14–27.

Mearns, D & Cooper, M (2005) *Working at Relational Depth in Counselling and Psychotherapy.* London: Sage.

Mearns, D & Schmid, P (2006) Being-with and being-counter: Person-centered psychotherapy as an in-depth co-creative process of personalization. *Person-Centered and Experiential Psychotherapies, 5* (3), 174–90.

Mearns, D & Thorne, B (2000) *Person-Centred Therapy Today.* London: Sage.

Merry, T (1995) *Invitation to Person-Centred Psychology.* London: Whurr. Republished in 2006 Ross-on-Wye: PCCS Books.

Neville, B (2007) What kind of universe? Whitehead and transformative process. *Person-Centered and Experiential Psychotherapies, 6* (4), 271–85.

Proctor, G (2006) Opium for the masses or help for those who least need it? In G Proctor, M Cooper, P Sanders & B Malcolm (Eds) (2006) *Politicizing the Person-Centred Approach: An agenda for social change* (pp. 66–79). Ross-on-Wye: PCCS Books.

Proctor, G, Cooper, M, Sanders, P & Malcolm, B (Eds) (2006) *Politicizing the Person-Centred Approach: An agenda for social change.* Ross-on-Wye: PCCS Books.

Prouty, G (1994) *Theoretical Evolutions in Person-Centered/Experiential Therapy: Applications to schizophrenic and retarded psychoses.* Westport, CT: Praeger.

Prouty, G (2001) A new mode of empathy: Empathic contact. In S Haugh & T Merry, T (Eds) *Rogers' Therapeutic Conditions: Evolution, theory and practice. Vol 2: Empathy* (pp. 155–62). Ross-on-Wye: PCCS Books.

Prouty, G (2002) The theory of Pre-Therapy. In G Prouty, D Van Werde & M Pörtner *Pre-Therapy: Reaching contact-impaired clients* (pp. 15–20). Ross-on-Wye: PCCS Books.

Prouty, G, Van Werde, D & Pörtner, M (2002) *Pre-Therapy: Reaching contact-impaired clients.* Ross-on-Wye: PCCS Books.

Raskin, NJ & Rogers, CR (1995) Person-centred therapy. In RJ Corsini & D Wedding (Eds) *Current Psychotherapies* (4th edn) (pp. 128–61). Itasca, IL: Peacock.

Rogers, CR (1939) *The Clinical Treatment of the Problem Child.* Boston: Houghton Mifflin.

Rogers, CR (1942) *Counseling and Psychotherapy.* Boston: Houghton Mifflin.

Rogers, CR (1951) *Client-Centered Therapy.* London: Constable.

Rogers, CR (1957a) The necessary and sufficient conditions of therapeutic personality change. *Journal of Consulting Psychology, 21 (2),* 95–103.

Rogers, CR (1957b) Personal thoughts on teaching and learning. *Merrill-Palmer Quarterly, Vol. 3.* Reprinted in H Kirschenbaum & VL Henderson (Eds) (1990) *The Carl Rogers Reader* (pp. 301–22). London: Constable.

Rogers, CR (1959) A theory of therapy, personality, and interpersonal relationships as developed in the client-centered framework. In S Koch (Ed) *A Psychology: A study of a science. Vol. 3: Formulations of the person and the social context* (pp. 184–256). New York: McGraw-Hill.

Rogers, CR (1961) *On Becoming a Person.* London: Constable.

Rogers, CR (1963) The actualizing tendency in relation to 'motives' and to consciousness. In MR Jones *Nebraska Symposium on Motivation: Current theory and research in motivation, Volume XI.* Lincoln, NE: University of Nebraska Press.

Rogers, CR (1972) *Becoming Partners: Marriage and its alternatives.* New York: Delacorte Press.

Rogers, CR (1980) *A Way of Being.* Boston: Houghton Mifflin.

Rogers, CR (1983) *Freedom to Learn for the Eighties.* Columbus, OH: Charles E. Merrill.

Rogers, CR (1986) Client-centered therapy. In IL Kutash & A Wolf (Eds) *Psychotherapist's Casebook* (pp. 197–208). San Fransisco, CA: Jossey-Bass.

Rogers, CR & Dymond, RF (Eds) (1954) *Psychotherapy and Personality Change.* Chicago, IL: University of Chicago Press.

Rogers, CR & Sanford, RC (1989) Client-centered psychotherapy. In HI Kaplan & BJ Sadock (Eds) *The Comprehensive Textbook of Psychiatry* (Vol 2, 5th edn) (pp. 1482–1501). Baltimore, MD: Williams & Wilkins.

Rubins, JL (1978) *Karen Horney.* London: Weiden & Nicolson.

Sanders, P (Ed) (2004) *The Tribes of the Person-Centred Nation.* Ross-on-Wye: PCCS Books.

Sanders, P (2006) *The Person-Centred Counselling Primer.* Ross-on-Wye: PCCS Books.

Sanders, P & Cooper, M (2006) Research into person-centred counselling. In P Sanders *The Person-Centred Counselling Primer* (pp. 102–8). Ross-on-Wye: PCCS Books.

Schmid, P (2006) The challenge of the other: Towards dialogical person-centered psychotherapy and counseling. *Person-Centered and Experiential Psychotherapies, 5 (4),* 240–54.

Sommerbeck, L (2003) *The Client-Centred Therapist in Psychiatric Contexts: A therapists' guide to the psychiatric landscape and its inhabitants.* Ross-on-Wye: PCCS Books.

Tolan, J (2003) *Skills in Person-Centred Counselling and Psychotherapy.* London: Sage.

Tudor, K & Merry, T (2002) *Dictionary of Person-Centred Psychology.* London: Whurr.

Van Werde, D & Prouty, G (2007) Pre-Therapy. In M Cooper, M O'Hara, PF Schmid & G Wyatt (2007) *The Handbook of Person-Centred Psychotherapy and Counselling* (pp. 237–50). Hampshire: Palgrave.

Warner, M (2000) Person-Centered Psychotherapy: One nation, many tribes. *Person-Centered Journal, 7* (1), 28–39.

Warner, M (2005) A person-centered view of human nature, wellness and psychopathology. In S Joseph & R Worsley (Eds) *Person-Centred Psychopathology: A positive psychology of mental health* (pp. 91–109). Ross-on-Wye: PCCS Books.

Warner, M (2007) Client incongruence and psychopathology. In M Cooper, M O'Hara, PF Schmid & G Wyatt (Eds) *The Handbook of Person-Centred Psychotherapy and Counselling* (pp. 154–67). Hampshire: Palgrave.

Waterhouse, RL (1993) 'Wild women don't have the blues': A feminist critique of 'person-centred' counselling and therapy. *Feminism & Psychology, 3* (1), 55–71.

Wyatt, G (Ed) (2001) *Rogers' Therapeutic Conditions: Evolution, theory and practice. Vol 1: Congruence.* Ross-on-Wye: PCCS Books.

Wyatt, G & Sanders, P (Eds) (2002) *Rogers' Therapeutic Conditions: Evolution, theory and practice. Vol 4: Contact and perception.* Ross-on-Wye: PCCS Books.

CHAPTER 5

THE EXISTENTIAL APPROACH

ERNESTO SPINELLI

BACKGROUND TO THE APPROACH

All psychotherapeutic theories are underpinned by philosophical assumptions and postulates, even if, in many cases, these remain implicit and covert to practitioners. Existential psychotherapy initially stands out from other approaches to psychotherapy precisely because it acknowledges explicitly and utilises overtly its foundational philosophical assumptions. At the same time, it is not so much *that* it is philosophically grounded but rather it is *the particular set of philosophical suppositions which it espouses* that distinguishes existential psychotherapy from the various current competing alternative models of psychotherapy.

As several authors have argued, the existential approach has no single founder or authoritative source (Yalom, 1980; Cooper, 2003). Rather, it is best understood as a 'rich tapestry' of intersecting practices which focus on the analysis of human existence from a set of shared foundational principles. Briefly summarised, the most pertinent of these to a discussion on the therapeutic relationship are:

A. THE INTER-RELATIONAL FOUNDATION OF HUMAN EXISTENCE

Stated succinctly, *the* pivotal idea proposed by existential thought argues that the baseline, or foundational condition, for all reflected experiences of being is *inter-relation*. As Merleau-Ponty expresses it: '*The world and I are within one another*' (Merleau-Ponty, 1962: 123). This view stands in contrast to the dominant 'dualism' that permeates Western thought and culture as a whole and contemporary psychotherapy in particular. The Western tendency to both divide – as in 'subject' and 'object' – and assume the primacy of one subdivided aspect – 'the objective' or 'the subjective'– over the other is reflected in the diverse range of contemporary psychotherapeutic models whose competing emphases perpetuate this stance.

As such, and as this chapter will seek to explicate, the emphasis placed by existential psychotherapy upon the therapeutic relationship itself is pivotal to the whole of the therapeutic enterprise not only because of what may be achieved through it but, far more significantly, because the relationship itself expresses and discloses inter-relational ways of being as they are being lived.

B. MEANING

Existential theory argues that humans are 'meaning-making' beings. We *interpret* the world via the human process of constructing meaning of those 'things' or events which impinge themselves upon our experience and with which we are in relation. Consequently, we are disturbed by the lack or loss of meaning; similarly, we can go to great lengths to avoid or deny those instances and experiences that challenge our most deeply fixed, rigid or *sedimented*, existing meanings – even to the extent of disowning, or dissociating from, those experiences that challenge that currently maintained meaning (Heidegger, 1962; Cohn, 2002; Spinelli, 2005).

At the same time, as several key existential theorists have highlighted, our attempts to make meaning of the world reveal that inter-relational foundation through which both 'subject' and 'object', or 'self' and 'other', are mutually and simultaneously made meaningful. Every instance of meaning not *only* constructs, or re-constructs, the object of our focus. Just as significantly, the focusing 'subject' is also simultaneously constructed or re-constructed in and through the act (Merleau-Ponty, 1962; Ihde, 1986; Spinelli, 2005). As such, an individual's experience of, and given meanings to, existence can no longer be considered in isolation or as aspects of distinctly separate and independent systems. Rather, these must be placed in an inevitable inter-relational context.

As a consequence of the above conclusion, our reflections on all aspects of human existence emerge as being subject to the constant flux of inter-relation rather than fixed or fully definable. In this sense, they remain uncertain, insofar as they always remain open to the possibility of novel definitions.

C. EXISTENTIAL ANXIETY

If the qualities, features and conditions of human existence cannot be fully 'captured' or shared, an inescapable 'openness' (and, in this sense, 'meaninglessness') of existence emerges. The inevitable unease and insecurity that arises when we attempt either to deny, or claim to have resolved, the inter-relational tension between the demand to 'know' existence, while at the same time experiencing its constant elusiveness, is experienced as *existential anxiety*.

As such, existential theory argues that anxiety necessarily permeates *all* reflective experience of our relations with self, others and the world in general. However, rather than being understood as *only or necessarily* a debilitating, disruptive or problematic presence that must be reduced or removed, the experience of anxiety can also be stimulating, can put us in touch with our sense of being alive, and is the source to all creative and original insight and decision-making.

As such, the dilemma of existential anxiety is not so much *that* it is, but rather *how* each of us 'lives with' it.

D. CHOICE

The existential idea of choice has often been misunderstood to suggest that we possess unlimited freedom to choose how and what 'to be' or 'to do'. This view is incorrect. The choices that we are free to make arise within an inter-relational context which *situates* our freedom to choose. Rather than being free to choose what we want, when we want it, we are rather free to choose our *response* to the contextual situation in which we find ourselves (May, 1981; Cohn, 1997). In this sense, as Sartre argued, it may be more accurate to state that we are *condemned* to choose (Sartre, 1956).

Human choice is interpretive, not at the event, or stimulus, level. And even then, the range of interpretations we might be able to generate is dependent upon an inter-relational temporal context – that is to say, when, where and how each of us 'is' within such contextual factors as time, culture and biology.

As can be ascertained, many of the problems that clients are likely to bring to psychotherapy arise from the unwillingness to choose the choices which are available rather than insist that other, unavailable, choices are an option. The difference between 'choosing that which is there for me' as opposed to deceiving myself that any imaginable choice option is available is both significant and profound at every level of our experience (Spinelli, 1997, 2005). Quite simply, we are our choices.

POSITION OF THERAPIST AND CLIENT

From the standpoint of existential psychotherapy, the therapeutic encounter is seen to be the 'microcosm' which both explores and expresses the 'macrocosm' of the client's currently-lived experience of the possibilities and limitations of inter-relational being in the world (Cohn, 1997; Spinelli, 1997, 2001; Strasser & Strasser, 1997).

THE CLIENT'S WAY OF BEING IN PSYCHOTHERAPY

Existential psychotherapy proposes that the conflicts and issues presented by clients arise from, and are expressions of, the wider overall 'way of being' adopted by the client. From this perspective, the client's problematic presenting symptoms or disturbances cannot be isolated, or considered on their own, as separate and distinct from the rest of the client's various 'ways of being'.

In this way, clients are encouraged to examine the various embodied attitudes, values, beliefs, choices or assumptions regarding what it means and how it is for them to exist in and engage with themselves, others and the world in general. The way the client 'is' in the psychotherapeutic relationship reveals his or her wider stance to the possibilities and limitations of existence. As such, the focus of the relationship is on the *client-as-present.*

While clients' typical ways of being at the start of therapy focus upon becoming 'other than as they are' through some means of externally directed therapeutic change, existential psychotherapists seek initially to focus clients on their presenting way of being *as it reveals itself in the therapeutic encounter.*

THE EXISTENTIAL PSYCHOTHERAPIST'S WAY OF BEING IN THERAPY

Within the therapeutic relationship, the existential psychotherapist is the other in the client's current experience of being. As this other, the therapist acts as both the representative of all others in the client's wider world relations and, just as importantly, is also the other who challenges the client's way of being toward others, as well as the client's perceived impact of others upon his or her way of being.

It is via the first, and crucial, step of 'staying with' and 'attuning oneself to' the client's current way of being – no matter how debilitating, restrictive, limiting, and irrational it may appear to be to the therapist (if not all others in the client's world, client included) – that the existential psychotherapist, *simply via this client-attuned presence,* begins to challenge profoundly the client's expectations regarding how others are, how others expect the client to be, and how the client expects others to be with him or her.

On reflection, it becomes evident that any hope of achieving this enterprise requires initially the therapist's openness to, and acceptance of, the client's presenting way of being. To adopt any other stance which emphasises a directive or manipulative change in the client's way of being, no matter how benevolent or concerned to ameliorate the client's distress, will only serve to allow the client to continue to avoid reflecting upon, and perhaps eventually owning, his or her way of being *as it is* rather than as he or she might want it to be.

In adopting this stance, existential psychotherapists avoid adopting the role of superior, objective instructor who distinguishes for the client those beliefs, attitudes and behaviours that are assumed to be 'unreal', 'false' and/or 'irrational' and who attempts to replace them with 'real', 'true' and/or 'rational' ones. Similarly, rather than present themselves as 'symptom removers', 'treatment providers', 'directive educators' or 'professional helpers', existential psychotherapists return psychotherapy to its original meaning: the attempt to 'stay with', 'stand beside' and 'accept the otherness of the being who is present' (Evans, 1981: xix).

To be willing and, at least in part, able to be open to the uncertainties of this form of encounter, existential psychotherapists should demonstrate suitable life experience that infuses their ability to express and acknowledge the humour, tragedy, wonder and absurdity of living, and to adopt an ongoing openness towards, and tolerance for, the different ways to 'be-in-the-world' that their clients express and embody.

Via such attempts on the part of the existential psychotherapist, clients are more likely to experience themselves as being heard and, in turn, may begin hearing themselves in a manner that is non-judgemental and accepting of the stance they maintain. This attitudinal shift promotes the possibility of clients' greater willingness and courage to confront the fixed, or sedimented, biases and assumptions they hold with regard to their relations with themselves, others and the world in general, and to consider how these sedimented stances may themselves have provoked their current problems in living.

PSYCHOLOGICAL FACTORS IN THE RELATIONSHIP

PSYCHOLOGICAL DYNAMICS

From an existential perspective, human existence reveals '*the total, indissoluble unity or interrelationship of the individual and his or her world ... In the truest sense, the person is viewed as having no existence apart from the world and the world as having no existence apart from persons*' (Valle & King, 1978: 7).

When applied to psychotherapy, existential theory approaches the question of human nature from the assumption that it is open-ended, and capable of an enormous range of experience (van Deurzen-Smith, 1988; Cohn, 1997). Such a view rejects the still-dominant tendency in psychotherapy to categorise or 'typologise' clients or which attempts to divide and reduce them in terms of various constituents or components. Instead, it aims to remain at a descriptive and open-ended level of analysis that simultaneously acknowledges both the uniqueness of each 'being-in-the-world' and the species-shared 'givens' of being human that set the invariant boundaries for the possibilities of each client's experience of existence.

Existential psychotherapists take the view that the great variety of unwanted and unpleasantly experienced 'symptoms' of which clients want to be cured are themselves consequential expressions of the client's attempts to deal with and make tolerable their experience of existential anxiety. As such, it is not the treatment of these symptoms that is central but, rather, it is the reconsideration of one's defensive stances toward existential anxiety that is the focus of existential psychotherapy. As Irvin Yalom has stated: 'Existential psychotherapy is a dynamic approach to therapy which focuses on concerns that are rooted in the individual's existence' (Yalom, 1980: 5).

Any attempt to remove, amend, or 're-shape' the disturbing symptoms without sufficiently exposing their relation to the client's wider way of being may well provoke for the client far greater degrees of tension and disturbance in living than were experienced prior to the therapeutic manipulation of the presenting disorder. In recognition of this possibility, existential psychotherapists attempt neither to isolate nor pathologise the client's presenting symptoms and disturbances in living. Nor do they take the amelioration or removal of such symptomatic tensions to be their primary task. Rather, together with the client, their attempt is to expose and consider these symptoms as inter-related expressions of the client's wider 'way of being' so that the implications of their maintenance, reduction or removal upon that 'way of being' can be considered and evaluated.

HOW EXISTENTIAL PSYCHOTHERAPY DETERMINES CHANGE

The existential psychotherapist's task is not one of seeking to impose a directive change in the lived inter-relational world of the client. Rather, it attempts to clarify that world so that its explicit, implicit, and fixed or sedimented assumptions, values, and beliefs can be re-examined and reconsidered inter-relationally. In turn, this attempt can reveal those disowned or dissociated experiences, thoughts, behaviours and affects that serve to maintain the client's current way of being, even if these are experienced as being problematic, undesirable or even seriously debilitating. This should not suggest that existential psychotherapy is antagonistic to the possibilities and benefits of change. Rather, it cautions therapists to bear in mind that the change solutions that are initiated by them can generate far greater distress and unease in living for the client than did the presenting problem.

In addition, existential theory argues that change in any *one* aspect or expression of a person's way of being will alter *the whole* of it. And, further, that in terms of our current understanding, it remains uncertain as to how subtle or radical, beneficial or detrimental, the impact of any given directed manipulation may be upon a particular client's current way of being.

Existential psychotherapy argues that the very process of assisting clients to 'stay still' will permit them to clarify and challenge their stance towards change. Paradoxically, it is via this investigative stillness that the benefits of 'therapeutic change' are more likely to occur.

THERAPEUTIC INTERVENTIONS

The focus upon a descriptive attunement toward the lived inter-relational world of the client leads existential psychotherapists to recognise that they are no longer able to be the detached objective observer/explorer/clarifier of some facets of their clients' lived experience. Rather, the encounter between therapist and client, while undeniably focused upon the client, is, nonetheless, mutually revelatory. For both client and therapist, the encounter permits a conscious reflection of 'this is what and how it is to be who I am being in this relation'.

THE ATTEMPT TO 'BE-WITH' AND 'BE-FOR' THE CLIENT

In their attempts at *being-with* the client, existential psychotherapists seek to give expression to their respect for, and acceptance of, their client's way of being as it presents itself in their current encounter.

In their attitude of *being-for* their clients, existential psychotherapists express their willingness to attempt a non-judgemental, descriptively focused entry into that way of being in order to disclose, together with their client, the underlying, often implicit and inadequately acknowledged, values, beliefs, assumptions, attitudinal stances and their accompanying affective and behavioural components which infuse and maintain it.

While neither the attempt to *be-with* or *be-for* the client can ever be fully achieved, and remains an aim or attempt rather than a fulfilment, nonetheless the undertaking may well provoke one of the biggest challenges that the client is likely to experience: Here is an 'other' (the therapist) who is not distorting, subverting, interpreting, amending, or seeking to impose a novel set of beliefs and values upon the client's currently adopted way of being but who, rather, is attempting to accept it as it presents itself in the immediacy of the inter-relational encounter.

FOUR INTER-RELATIONAL REALMS

There exist various structured forms of enquiry which assist existential psychotherapists in clarifying their clients' inter-relational ways of being. Some existential psychotherapists such as Emmy van Deurzen-Smith utilise a variation of Ludwig Binswanger's *dimensional relations* – the natural world with its physical, biological dimension (*the umwelt*); the everyday, public social relations each of us has with others (*the mitwelt*); the private and intimate relations each of us has with both ourselves and the significant others or significant meanings in our lives (*the eigenwelt*); and the person's relations to the ideals and aspirational aspects of living (*the uberwelt*) (Binswanger, 1963; van Deurzen-Smith, 1988).

A related, and more explicitly inter-relational approach toward such investigations has been suggested and developed by the present author in various papers and texts (Spinelli, 1994, 1997, 2001, 2005). This approach focuses upon four distinct *inter-relational realms*.

I-focused inquiry considers those views, statements, opinions, beliefs, demands, behavioural stances and affective feelings that express the client's experience of being him or herself in the current encounter with the therapist. *I-focused* inquiry attempts to describe and clarify 'my experience of being "myself" in any given relationship'. It asks, in effect, 'what do I tell myself about my current experience of being me in this encounter?'

You-focused inquiry considers those views, statements, opinions, beliefs, demands, behavioural stances and affective feelings that the client assumes exist for the other (the therapist) in the current encounter. *You-focused* inquiry attempts to describe and clarify 'my experience of "the other" being in relation with me'. It asks, in effect, 'what do I tell myself about the other's experience of being with me in any given encounter?'

We-focused inquiry concerns itself with the explication of those facets of currently lived experience that emerge from the immediacy of current experience *between* client and therapist and that come into being via the encounter itself. *We-focused* inquiry attempts to describe and clarify each participant's (i.e. the client's and the psychotherapist's) experience of 'us' being in relation with one another. In short, it asks each to consider 'what do I tell myself about the experience of being *us* being in relation with each other in this encounter?' The *We-focused realm of encounter* is characterised by its *immediacy* – it is concerned with, and expresses, that which is being experienced 'in the moment' of a person-to-person standpoint. As such, it expresses explicitly that inter-relational grounding that exists (and is more implicitly expressed) in the statements which emerge from *I-focused* and *You-focused* inquiry.

Finally, *They-focused* inquiry centres upon the client's experience of those who make up his or her wider world of 'others' (extending beyond the other who is the psychotherapist) and their experience of their own inter-relational realms in response to the client's current way of being and, as well, to the novel ways of being that have arisen as novel possibilities for the client through psychotherapy. In brief, it challenges the client to consider the various facets of inter-relations between the client and these others as the client imagines *they* experience and interpret them. Further, it challenges the client to consider the impact of his or her stance upon the inter-relations between one other or group of others and a different other or group of others.

The *They-focused realm of encounter* serves to extend the 'world-dimensions' of the therapeutic relationship. It is an explicit stance that can be adopted by existential psychotherapists to highlight the inter-relational dimensions of existence and to counter the more common psychotherapeutic tendency to consider the client in isolation, or out of inter-relational context. The exploration of this fourth relational realm is particularly significant when, through therapy, the client has reached a point of considering and making choices about new-found alternative 'ways to be'.

The exploration of all four realms of encounter via the therapeutic relationship itself bestows upon that relationship a lived experience of its being real and valid rather than merely substitutive, symbolic, or 'transferential'. Further, this focus serves to highlight the client's way of being both within the therapeutic relationship and, with regard to the client's wider world-relations. At times, the client's experience of being with the therapist parallels his or her world-relational experiences of being. Just as significantly, however, the client's experienced way of being with the therapist may well contrast with his or her wider world-relations and, in this way, serves to challenge both the sedimentations and dissociations concerning who and how 'I am expected or required to be (and not be) with others' or 'how others are expected or required to be (and not be) with me'.

WHAT THE EXISTENTIAL THERAPIST DOES OR DOES NOT DO

Rather than stress yet another standard technique or set of practices, existential psychotherapy argues that any over-emphasis on technique, or on practice in general, can be one of the main obstacles to understanding the client and, thus, to any truly long-lasting outcome of therapy. It is the basic view of existential psychotherapists that 'it is not the understanding that follows technique, but the technique that follows understanding' (Misiak & Sexton, 1973: 87).

The unorthodox and iconoclastic relational psychotherapist, Leslie Farber, stands as a major representative of this stance. Deeply influenced by Martin Buber's notion of the *interhuman* possibilities of dialogue (Schilpp & Friedman, 1967), Farber's intent was to shift the enterprise of psychotherapy away from a set of inflexible methodological conditions and towards a *morally derived attitude* expressive of a particular way of being with others. In this sense, Farber's meetings with his clients could 'be about' anything; their content did not truly matter. Instead, Farber's focus centred on *a way of talking* that led both therapist and client toward a 'truthful dialogue' with themselves and one another (Farber, 2000).

This notion of a 'truthful dialogue' has been further explicated by the philosopher, George Gadamer. Gadamer contrasted two types of dialogue: (a) that dialogue whose focus, intent and direction has been pre-set by at least one of the participants; and (b) that dialogue whose focus, intent and direction only emerges, or finds its own way, through the dialogue itself.

All dialogues, Gadamer acknowledged, have (or more accurately, *find*) a direction, but there exists a truthful quality to a dialogue that shapes its own form and focus that cannot be ascertained – or experienced – in a dialogue that is being actively directed toward a certain pre-set goal. One consequence of this, as Gadamer wrote, is that:

the way one word follows another, with the conversation taking its own twists and reaching its own conclusion, may well be conducted in some way, but the partners conversing are far less the leaders than the led. No one knows in advance what will 'come out' of such a conversation. (Gadamer, 1989: 383)

In general, this receptive stance toward the unforeseen possibilities of a human (and humane) dialogical engagement requires the abdication of such security that comes with assumptions such as 'doing it right', or directing change, or of 'the expert's' superiority of knowledge and status. Hopefully, it can now be understood that this proposed stance is not some perverse belittlement or rejection of more typical psychotherapeutic enterprises but is, rather, a necessary constituent for the possibility of truthful dialogue.

CULTURAL CONTEXTS, POWER AND DIVERSITY

In line with all of the above, the existential approach does not merely tolerate, but, more correctly, values and embraces the diversity of living as expressed in terms of culture, race, gender and sexual orientation. Concerned as much with the 'universals' of human experience as with individual uniqueness, existential thought and practice has been shown to be of particular value to the clarification of various psychological factors relevant to multi-cultural psychotherapy, whether across cultures or in work with minority cultures (van Deurzen-Smith, 1988; Eleftheriadou, 1994; Asmall, 1997; Vontress & Epp, 2001). Indeed, according to the psychotherapist, Zack Eleftheriadou, 'existential ... analysis transcends culture, because it delves into the basic beliefs and values of the client, and examines the client's fundamental ideas and assumptions about human existence' (Eleftheriadou, 1994: 31).

With regard to the ongoing debates concerning sexuality and sexual orientation, existential-phenomenological authors such as Maurice Merleau-Ponty (1962), Hans W. Cohn (1997), as well as the present author (Spinelli, 2001) have provided highly innovative contributions emphasising the inter-relational dimensions of embodied sexual being, as opposed to medically derived concerns of 'normal' and 'abnormal' sexual practices and typologies.

Further, the adoption of this model removes from psychotherapists much of their professional mystique, and a good deal of the power that comes with this (Spinelli, 1994). For example, existential psychotherapists have proposed that the problems of mental disturbances are principally rooted in socio-ethical bases expressive of intolerable inter-relationally derived anxieties rather than in organic disorders and diseases requiring medical forms of intervention. As various authors have argued, a medical language focused on illness, disease and disorder creates significant power imbalances in the relationship between therapist and client (Laing, 1960; Szasz, 1974; Pilgrim 2000).

59

STRENGTHS AND WEAKNESSES

It has been suggested that existential psychotherapy is most suitable for persons who experience themselves as alienated from the mores and demands of their society or who are at points of crisis, such as confronting death or experiencing meaninglessness and isolation, who have lost their sense of relatedness to themselves, 'significant others' and/ or to the world in general, or who are attempting to cope with sudden and dramatic changes in a variety of personal circumstances. Similarly, those who inhabit a foreign culture, or who are members of a minority group within a dominant culture and society, might find existential psychotherapy to be of particular value (van Deurzen-Smith, 1988).

In general, existential psychotherapy may be of greatest benefit to those clients who find themselves in various forms of transition and who are open to the challenge of grappling with complex and paradoxical issues. Clients who are open to an approach which is reflective, exploratory and deeply challenging will warm to this system. On the other hand, those seeking certainty, and who wish to use psychotherapy to drive towards a fixed outcome, may struggle with the ambiguity it embraces. *MASLOW*

Existential psychotherapy has sometimes been accused of over-emphasising a pernicious form of individualism that is thoughtless or empty of direction, and which elevates an extreme form of solipsism. Hopefully, this brief discussion has demonstrated that such views express a distortion of the most basic existential assumption: the inter-relatedness of being. As such, rather than foster an individualistic ethos that separates self from others, or the client from his or her life and work context, the existential approach is foremost among approaches in asserting the necessity to acknowledge and place oneself in an inter-relational context.

Overall, existential psychotherapy's emphasis on 'being qualities' and meaning exploration as opposed to the development and refinement of the psychotherapist's 'doing' skills and repertoire runs counter to current dominant assumptions and emphases within psychotherapy as a whole. Whether this divergence will eventually prove to be its greatest strength or weakness remains to be seen.

Even so, because of the overwhelming significance to existential psychotherapy of the therapeutic relationship itself, its potential strengths and weaknesses rest predominantly upon the therapist's ability to 'stay with' the client in the relationship as it presents itself. What this implies is that the existential psychotherapist must demonstrate the capacity to acknowledge and even embrace the insecurity and uncertainty that comes with the willingness to engage with the client *as he or she is being in the current encounter* rather than focus upon who the client may have been in the past or who he or she may be in the future. This focus may challenge many of the therapist's professional assumptions regarding the therapeutic enterprise itself and, as well, may challenge the therapist's own personal assumptions regarding 'the right' or appropriate ways to be. As such, if the primary emphasis given to the relationship itself may be seen as existential psychotherapy's greatest strength, this same emphasis may well highlight the therapist's lack of preparedness for, or willingness to adapt to the uncertain conditions and implications of inter-relation and, hence, expose the weaknesses not so much of the approach itself but of those who attempt to practise it.

RESEARCH EVIDENCE

What research evidence currently exists for the effectiveness of existential psychotherapy is undoubtedly limited. Reported outcomes from this approach include individuals being more congruent with their lived experience and, thereby, becoming clearer about who they are and who they are not; the accessing of skills for managing complexity, ambiguity and anxiety; and the enhancement of attitudes of self-responsibility and ownership of choice within an inter-relational context. Some preliminary verification of this assertion has emerged from the successful outcome studies of the *Soteria* project focused upon the existentially derived treatment of severe mental disturbances (Mosher, 2001).

In spite of the paucity of research data, it would be incorrect to conclude that existential psychotherapy is antagonistic to, or disinterested in, research concerned with either psychotherapeutic outcomes or process analyses. In fact, it has played a major role in the development of qualitatively focused approaches to research (Churchill & Wertz, 2001; Giorgi, 1985; Karlsson, 1993). At the same time, existential investigators' views of relevant and appropriate research stand in direct contrast to the currently dominant natural scientific viewpoint and its underlying assumptions, principally because the questions they pose and the methods they employ are grounded in a carefully articulated, but undeniably different, set of philosophical assumptions (Spinelli, 2005).

NEW DEVELOPMENTS

The great majority of contemporary models of psychotherapy have concluded on the basis of recurring research evidence that the therapeutic relationship itself appears to be *the* critical factor or variable determining beneficial outcomes (Mearns & Cooper, 2005). However, what might be the distinguishing characteristics of such a relationship that serve as key factors to any process of change remains uncertain. While psychotherapists tend to focus on particular skills or forms of interventions, research analyses of client statements centre upon various experiential factors, from which the client's experience of the way of being of the therapist emerges as pivotal (Spinelli, 1994; Sherwood, 2001). Such studies strongly support existential psychotherapy's foundational emphasis upon inter-relation. Further, they highlight the importance of those analyses that centre upon the means by which the way of being of both the client and the psychotherapist can be further explicated and expressed as critical psychotherapeutic factors. This area of investigation is one to which contemporary existential psychotherapy has much to offer.

This inter-relational shift in the focus of the therapeutic enterprise introduces a 'world-conscious' moral dimension to the arena of psychotherapy, the lack of which has been justifiably criticised by both 'insiders' and detractors of psychotherapy. The present author's current interests are focused upon the impact of such a re-focus upon the therapeutic relationship (Spinelli, 2001).

Finally, new developments in the approach have also centred upon time-limited forms of existential psychotherapy (Strasser & Strasser, 1997), and the extension of existential practice into the arenas of mediation and dispute resolution (Strasser & Randolph, 2004) and coaching (Spinelli & Horner, 2004).

DIVERGENCES FROM MAIN THEORY

Existential psychotherapy's focus upon the inter-relational grounding to all subjective experience challenges a persistent assumption held not only by most of psychotherapy but, just as significantly, by our culture in general. This is the view that the person is a self-contained unit, understandable within his or her own set of subjectively derived meanings and behaviours. The debate provoked by these two competing views is crucial: at its heart lie distinctly different ways of examining and understanding ourselves and the world.

From an inter-relational standpoint, the problems and concerns presented by clients can no longer be seen as being solely their own in any exclusively individualistic sense, in that they are not derived from some internal or intra-psychic set of conditions but, rather, exist at the inter-relational meeting point between each person and the world. Such a stance emphasises far-reaching challenges to our culture's, and hence psychotherapy's, dominant assumptions. For example, it suggests that:

> questions of choice, freedom and responsibility cannot be isolated or contained within some separate being (such as 'self' or 'other') ... Viewed in this way, no choice can be mine or yours alone, no experienced impact of choice can be separated in terms of 'my responsibility' versus 'your responsibility', no sense of personal freedom can truly avoid its interpersonal dimensions.
> (Spinelli, 2001: 16)

The implications of such a shift upon our understanding and working with the therapeutic relationship and upon the practice of psychotherapy as a whole are as plentiful as they are dramatic.

Nonetheless, the emphasis given to the therapeutic relationship by existential psychotherapy should, hopefully, have become clearer to the reader. How better to expose and examine inter-relational disturbances and tensions than via the existing relationship between client and therapist? Such a means of exploration permits an *experiential immediacy* to all discourse regarding the client's way of being with and relating to self, others and the world. It is this 'inter-relational turn', I believe, that provides existential psychotherapy with its distinctive characteristics and which infuses its significant critique of other approaches adopted within contemporary psychotherapy.

REFERENCES

Asmall, I (1997) Existentialism, existential psychotherapy and African philosophy. *Journal of the Society for Existential Analysis, 8* (2), 138–52.

Binswanger, L (1963) *Being-in-the-World: Selected papers of Ludwig Binswanger* (Trans J Needleman). New York: Harper Torchbooks.

Churchill, SD & Wertz, FJ (2001) An introduction to phenomenological research in psychology. In K Schneider, JFT Bugenthal & J Fraser Pierson (Eds) *The Handbook of Humanistic Psychology: Leading edges in theory, research and practice* (pp. 247–62). London: Sage.

Cohn, HW (1997) *Existential Thought and Therapeutic Practice.* London: Sage.

Cohn, HW (2002) *Heidegger and the Roots of Existential Therapy.* London: Continuum.

Cooper, M (2003) *Existential Therapies.* London: Sage.

Deurzen-Smith, E van (1988) *Existential Counselling in Practice.* London: Sage.

Eleftheriadou, Z (1994) *Gateways to Counselling: Transcultural counselling.* London: Central Publishing House.

Evans, RI (1981) *Dialogue with RD Laing.* New York: Praeger.

Farber, L (2000) *The Ways of the Will: Selected essays.* New York: Basic Books.

Gadamer, HG (1989) *Truth and Method* (2nd edn). London: Continuum.

Giorgi, A (1985) *Phenomenology and Psychological Research.* Pittsburgh, PA: Duquesne University Press.

Heidegger, M (1962) *Being and Time* (Trans J Macquarrie & E Robinson). New York: Harper & Row.

Ihde, D (1986) *Experimental Phenomenology: An introduction.* Albany, NY: State University of New York.

Karlsson, G (1993) *Psychological Qualitative Research from a Phenomenological Perspective.* Stockholm, Sweden: Almqvist & Wiksell International.

Laing, RD (1960) *The Divided Self.* Harmondsworth: Penguin.

May, R (1981) *Freedom and Destiny.* London: Norton.

Mearns, D & Cooper, M (2005) *Working at Relational Depth in Counselling and Psychotherapy.* London: Sage.

Merleau-Ponty, M (1962) *The Phenomenology of Perception* (Trans C Smith). London: Routledge & Kegan Paul.

Misiak, H & Sexton, VS (1973) *Phenomenological, Existential and Humanistic Psychologies: A historical survey.* New York: Grune & Stratton.

Mosher, L (2001) Treating madness without hospitals: Soteria and its success. In KJ Schneider, JFT Bugenthal & JF Pierson (Eds) *The Handbook of Humanistic Psychology* (pp. 389–402). London: Sage.

Pilgrim, D (2000) Psychiatric diagnosis: More questions than answers. *The Psychologist, 13* (6), 302–5.

Sartre, JP (1956) *Being and Nothingness: An essay on phenomenological ontology* (Trans H Barnes). London: Routledge.

Schilpp, P & Friedman, M (Eds) (1967) *The Philosophy of Martin Buber.* La Salle, IL: Open Court.

Sherwood, P (2001) Client experience in psychotherapy: What heals and what harms? *Indo-Pacific Journal of Phenomenology 2,* 1–24.

Spinelli, E (2006) *Demystifying Therapy.* London: Constable. (Republished 2006, Ross-on-Wye: PCCS Books.)

Spinelli, E (2006) *Tales of Un-Knowing: Therapeutic encounters from an existential perspective.* London: Duckworth. (Republished 2006, Ross-on-Wye: PCCS Books.)

Spinelli, E (2001) *The Mirror and the Hammer: Challenges to therapeutic orthodoxy.* London: Sage.

Spinelli, E (2005) *The Interpreted World: An introduction to phenomenological psychology* (2nd edn). London: Sage.

Spinelli, E & Horner, C (2004) An existential approach to coaching psychology, In S Palmer & A Whybrow (Eds) *Handbook of Coaching Psychology* (pp. 118–32). London: Routledge.

Strasser, F & Randolph, P (2004) *Mediation: A psychological insight into conflict resolution.* London: Continuum.

Strasser, F & Strasser, A (1997) *Existential Time-Limited Therapy: The wheel of existence.* Chichester: Wiley.

Szasz, T (1974) *The Myth of Mental Illness* (Revised edn). New York: Harper & Row.

Valle, RS & King, M (1978) *Existential-Phenomenological Alternatives for Psychology.* Oxford: Oxford University Press.

Vontress, CE & Epp, LR (2001) Existential cross-cultural counselling: When hearts and cultures share. In KJ Schneider, JFT Bugenthal & JF Pierson (Eds) *The Handbook of Humanistic Psychology* (pp. 371–87). London: Sage.

Yalom, I (1980) *Existential Psychotherapy.* New York: Basic Books.

CHAPTER 6

GESTALT THERAPY

TONI GILLIGAN

BACKGROUND TO THE APPROACH

In deciding what to include in this brief introduction to the theory of gestalt therapy, I have focused on those concepts that I believe cast most light on the gestalt therapy view of the therapeutic relationship. For comprehensive accounts of the theory, see Yontef (1993), Phillipson (2001), Woldt and Toman (2005), and of course, Perls, Hefferline and Goodman (1994).

Gestalt therapy theory was first formulated by Fritz and Laura Perls, and a group that gathered around them in New York in the late 1940s. This included Paul Goodman, a writer, social critic and political philosopher, who is credited with a significant part in the theoretical articulation of the ideas and practice of gestalt therapy. The Perls were both trained psychoanalysts who had fled Nazi Germany, going first to South Africa where they founded the South African Institute of Psychoanalysis, and then, post-war, to New York. Formative influences included phenomenology, existentialism, gestalt psychology, Friedlaender's philosophy of creative indifference, movement, theatre and dance and, centrally, psychoanalysis. Fritz Perls had been in analysis with, among others, Karen Horney and Wilhelm Reich. Laura was a student of Kurt Goldstein and Paul Tillich. In South Africa they were influenced by Smuts and his ideas of holism (Bowman, 2005). The first full account of gestalt therapy theory appeared in 1951 (Perls, Hefferline & Goodman, 1994). A new edition was published in 1994 and page numbers shown here refer to this edition. Gestalt therapy's philosophical basis is phenomenology; its scientifc theory is a field theory and its therapeutic relationship is of an existential dialogue (Yontef, 1993).

GESTALT THERAPY THEORY: A THEORY OF RELATIONSHIP

Gestalt therapy theory is a theory of relationship. It asserts that it is relationship – of the person in their environment – that comes first, and that our ideas of individuality and identity are abstractions, reflections on this experience. Perls, Hefferline and Goodman write in their opening paragraph: 'We speak of the organism contacting the environment, but it is the contact that is the simplest and first reality' (1994: 3). This is an application of phenomenology to the field of psychotherapy. The phenomenological school of philosophy argues that since we can only know our world through how it appears to us, what we can know of our world is always, from the first, a co-creation of how we meet our world, how we interpret it, and how our world presents itself to each of us as individuals: 'Man [sic] and world are first and foremost in relation; it is only subsequently, at the reflective level of logic that we divide them into separate entities' (Kearney, 1986: 13) and hence 'meaning is neither in the mind alone, nor in the world alone, but in the intentional relation between the two' (ibid.: 15).

From its roots in phenomenology come key principles of gestalt therapy, including the emphasis on here-and-now awareness, our understanding of responsibility and choice, and the method of phenomenological enquiry. The basis of what we know is our direct experience, which we then interpret. This direct experience is always immediate and cannot be fully described by my account of it. It is an embodied experience (Perls et al., 1994: 3); only subsequently do we break it up into thinking, feeling, movement. So in gestalt therapy the emphasis is on developing *awareness* of this direct experience. 'Full awareness is the process of being in vigilant contact with the most important events in the individual/environment field with full sensorimotor, emotional, cognitive and energetic support' (Yontef, 1993: 144). The key practice here is the phenomenological enquiry and experiment. The phenomenological position is that subject and object are inseparable; there is no subjectivity without an object and no object without an engaged subjectivity. In other words, experience is fully co-created by the experiencer and the experienced. It happens at 'precisely this experiential interface or midpoint' (Kearney, 1986: 13). Although I choose my world in the sense that I actively construe it and am therefore responsible for how I do so, I am equally chosen by it, in the sense that I am interpreting something, the nature of which I can never ultimately know. Crucially, this applies to my peopled world and not just my inanimate world.

THE ORGANISM-ENVIRONMENT FIELD

Gestalt therapy theory starts with this radical realignment, that relationship is the fundamental reality and our experience of individuality is secondary. It follows that the person can only be viewed in relation to his[1] environment. I literally do not exist except as part of my environment. This is not just in the sense that without air to breathe or gravity to keep me in one piece, I would die – although this is certainly true! – but if contact belongs neither to the person alone nor to the environment alone then what it is to be human is intrinsically part of a whole that includes the person and their environment. This is equally true of the person in her psychological existence, the world of action- and meaning-making. The nature of the person resides in the relationship of the organism and environment; is a function of the organism-environment field – or person-environment field.

This is a field theoretical view. A key assumption of field theories is that the elements of the subject studied – be they atoms, perceptions, people, meaning or actions – do not

1. I will use male and female personal pronouns alternately: in each case they should be read to include the other unless the meaning makes clear otherwise

exist separately and outside of each other. Instead their very nature is formed by their interaction with and relation to the other, and to the whole to which they belong (Bohm, 1980; Goldstein, 1995; Parlett, 2005).

The field is an everchanging web of relationships in which it is the relationship of different parts of the field that constitutes a particular 'reality'. A person, a rock, a nationality, for example, is a relationship, an emergent event (Hodges, 2003: 250). Each may have a stable equilibrium, for a moment or for an aeon, but each is always an event of continuing and continually renewing relationship. In gestalt therapy the field is phenomenal – formed by my construing of it and its forming of me. It is 'a field in which at least social-cultural, animal and physical factors interact … From this point of view, historical and cultural factors … are intrinsic to the way any problem is presented' (Perls et al., 1994: 4–5).

CONTACT AND WITHDRAWAL: THE PROCESS OF FIGURE FORMATION AND DESTRUCTION

Contact – the interaction of the person and their environment – happens at the boundary of the person and his environment, indeed it is the function of that boundary; it is a boundary of differentiation, the 'experiential interface' (Kearney, 1986: 13) which both joins and separates me and my environment: it belongs to both. Awareness is our experience of this contact. Gestalt therapy adapted from the gestalt psychologists and Goldstein (1995), the concept of figure/ground process (Kohler, 1969). We perceive wholes (gestalts), or figures against backgrounds. The figure is the relation between foreground and background, it is not something existing in the field but is a differentiation *of* the field. Further, we tend to 'complete' incomplete wholes (I simply do not perceive the broken circle except as a broken circle). Gestalt therapy theory argues that this fact of our perception – to perceive in wholes or figures – does not just apply to sensory perceptions, but equally to psycho-social events: meaning-making and actions. In addition, it took the tendency for the incomplete figure to complete as the basis for the process of contact-making or figure formation and destruction.

Something happens, simply in the nature of things, that creates a dis-equilibrium in the person-environment field. A need arises in the *organism* part of the field – thirst, loneliness, desire – or an event in the *environment* part – a fire alarm sounds, the deadline for this chapter approaches, a friend calls. As a result, some aspects of both myself and my environment begin to stand out and develop into a new figure. When fully formed, this leads to an exchange at the boundary, which satisfies the need or responds to the environmental demand. For example, I am restless, less and less able to concentrate on writing. When I pay attention to this, I become aware that I feel empty, and my friend keeps coming to mind. I fantasise conversations, all interest in writing lost, and eventually go to the phone and call her. My awareness of what is outside the act of phoning and beginning to speak is diminished – I experience myself in the act of speaking to my friend – so at the moment when the figure is most fully formed, is almost all of my experiential field, the figure includes me. Or rather, it includes those parts of me and of my environment involved in the contact – the phone against my ear, my friend's voice – and both myself and my environment are changed, I am no longer lonely. Conversation complete, I assimilate this nourishment, my desire for company ceases to stand out, that figure returns to the ground and the next begins to form (Perls et al.,1994; Phillipson, 2001: 42–5).

In this view of the interaction of the person and their environment, *self* is a process, the functioning of the boundary in the formation of figure and ground. It is the system of contacts: I experience self in contact more strongly when contact is greater, less strongly as contact reduces (Perls et al.; 1994; McLeod, 1993; Phillipson, 2001).

PROBLEMS AND THE PARADOXICAL THEORY OF CHANGE

Gestalt therapy argues that this process of figure formation and destruction is a self-regulating dynamic of the person-environment field (Perls et al., 1994: 7). That is, the dominant need of the person-environment field reliably comes to the fore organising the contacting process. In healthy functioning, this is characterised by clear, vivid differentiation of figure and ground, freely building energy and excitement as the figure emerges, and a spontaneity of commitment to the final contact. Of course, it is not always possible to attend immediately to the dominant need and sometimes the situation presents us with competing needs. Many times this has little significance; I stifle a cough in the theatre, or override my need to sleep in order to comfort my crying child. My attention to what I am doing is less focused, the figure less distinct, my commitment to it less as the second potential figure of interest competes. But it is good enough, the best that the field conditions, which include my prioritising, allow. Problems arise when the process of figure formation and destruction is chronically constrained. The child's fears have repeatedly been met with punishment or they have usually received attention only when quiet and compliant or when attuned to the parent. The child creatively adjusts, making the best contact that the environment and her resources allow, and this adjustment becomes chronic and fixed. When faced with similar situations she interprets the figure-ground stereotypically, a fixed gestalt, as though the situation is the same, and she responds stereotypically.

BOUNDARY MODIFICATIONS

Maintaining fixed gestalts involves modifications to the boundary process, such that differentiation of self and other is reduced, thus restricting awareness of the full potentialities of the person-environment field. This limits the ability to respond creatively as the new situation requires. Gestalt distinguishes six such modifications. These are not pathological in themselves: each, when employed with awareness, and depending on the situation, may be beneficial and indeed desirable.

- In *confluence*, the boundary of self and other is not experienced. When I cannot distinguish my needs from yours, I am confluent. I probably find it hard to say 'I' and use 'we' a lot. I may say 'it' is cold and wait for you to put on the fire!

- When I *introject* I take in, without discrimination, aspects of my environment (beliefs, values, behaviours, information) which I have not 'chewed' (meaning I differentiated between those aspects of my environment that I can assimilate, that support organismic self-regulation, and those that don't and which I therefore need to reject). *Very frequently* in life, introjection is useful. As a novice driver I learned 'mirror, indicate, pull out' by rote, and without questioning my instructor. For a while, I drove consciously following these instructions. In time, I was no longer aware of them as they became an assimilated part of my ground. Problems arise when my introjecting is outside of my awareness and therefore fixed, irrespective of circumstances.

- When I *project*, I attribute some aspects of my functioning to the environment. I reject and maintain outside of awareness, responses that are proscribed by my introjects, seeing them as emanating from outside myself. For example, I don't experience myself as having needs, while seeing others as making excessive demands on me.

- In *retroflecting*, the person splits his self in two. Instead of directing the energy of his contacting process to the environment, he attempts to find satisfaction in manipulating his self. So he does to himself rather than to another, or may do to the other what he wishes for himself. He may clench his jaw rather than be angry, or talk to himself rather than to another. Again, there are situations in which retroflecting is healthy: arguing with the policewoman issuing a ticket is not a good idea!

- When *deflecting*, I avoid awareness by turning aside from contact: I may ignore, or not hear, or change the subject, or go on at length, whilst saying little of purpose. I may feel I somehow don't get through to the other, or that they do not get through to me.

- Finally there is *egotism*. Here, at the point of full contact, instead of completing contact by allowing the spontaneity and surrender of 'I' engagement and exchange with my environment – with you – I analyse it! I talk about it, intellectualise and philosophise, thus remaining 'in control', unsatisfied and isolated.

POLARITIES AND DICHOTOMIES

We often construe our experiential field as split into competing, incompatible parts, or dichotomies: either/or, strong/weak, good/bad. Gestalt argues that the field is not organised in this diconnected way: that such apparent dichotomies are inescapably related, the two poles of one whole. Splitting our experience dichotomously is necessary to maintain unaware boundary modifications and is evident in either/or thinking and expressions. It is also evident in clients' aspirations to self-conquest, that is, attempts to motivate themselves to desired changes by following introjects 'shouldistically' (Yontef, 1993: 143).

Gestalt therapists believe that change comes about through recovery of the vibrancy and full potential of the process of figure formation and destruction. This requires recovering awareness of the direct experience of the situation with the concomitant owning of my choice and response-abilty in the contacting process. When for example I deflect, *I do that*. In other words the lived experience of my existence. Hence the *paradoxical theory of change*: change comes about when I become more fully who I am in this moment, not when I try to be who I am not (Beisser, 1970).

POSITION OF THE CLIENT AND THERAPIST

Inevitably then, the gestalt therapy view of the therapeutic relationship is that of an existential dialogue:

1. This situation of the therapy hour is new and unique and phenomenologically I cannot know it any better than my client.
2. Both I and my client are 'of the field'. I am part of my client's person-environment field as she is of mine. So as I create myself, I create her, and as she creates herself, she creates me.

Thus, I am obliged to the existential position that in order for both of us to be as fully 'self' as is possible – to allow the best possible figure to emerge – both my awareness and my client's are necessary and equally important. Not only must I respect my client's phenomenal world as I do my own, I need curiosity and the desire to know her in her otherness, and to make known my otherness. This is most usually identified as the *I–Thou relationship* of Buber (Hycner & Jacobs, 1995), though that is only one articulation of this existential conclusion. Another is Sartre's formulation of acting in good faith, accepting the existential reality that I choose myself and in so doing choose for mankind (1948: 29). And another is the gestalt therapy view of awareness, responsibility and the co-created field.

Gestalt therapy, then, considers that change comes about through this relationship (Yontef, 2005) through the becoming that is possible only in relationship.

PSYCHOLOGICAL FACTORS IN THE RELATIONSHIP

Psychological problems, then, are the consequence of impaired functioning at the contact boundary. In the present situation these fixed boundary modifications are what brings the client to therapy. However, they were originally the client's best possible resolution (figure) of the conflicting forces of the field, i.e. to protest in anger versus protection from disapproval or punishment. They were a creative, chosen solution and still represent the client's creative self-regulation. In each new situation where a need to protest arises, the process of figure formation and destruction is constrained by the boundary modifications, but it is not absent. Each time a need to protest arises it requires energy to interrupt the process. This interruption may be unaware, but it is present in the here-

and-now contacting process and in the pattern of boundary modifications in the person environment field. In other words it is present in how my client relates to me and I to her: for example how she is confluent with me, always agreeing, desensitised to her own experience. Or it might be present in how she projects on to me the envious critic or good mother and I may, in turn, be helpful or soothing. Since the person-environment field is biopsychosocial, these boundary modifications are present not only in conversation (content, metaphor, imagery, use of language) but also in posture, movement, the totality of the here-and-now contacting process of client and therapist.

THERAPEUTIC INTERVENTIONS

My aim as a gestalt therapist is to support the development of awareness: mine and my client's. Awareness is always of the present situation, so what is spoken of, however apparently 'there and then' arises from a present concern. I keep in mind that it is the process of the present situation to which I must pay attention and I do this through dialogue and phenomenological enquiry.

DIALOGUE

My client tells me of her tiredness. I listen carefully, clarifying my understanding with her, imagining what it must be like for her. This desire to really understand the client's phenomenal world is the aspect of existential dialogue called *inclusion*. Another client tells me how distressed and ashamed he is at his anger with his children. I feel moved and may tell him this or I may start to feel my attention wane and share this. In other words, I allow myself to be responsive, affected by my client. I offer my *presence*, and in so doing contribute my awareness of my part of co-creating our field, my *commitment* to dialogue.

PHENOMENOLOGICAL ENQUIRY AND EXPERIMENT

Bracketing, horizontalisation and describing are the basis of phenomenological enquiry (Spinelli, 1989: 16–19). I may ask my tired client what she is aware of – sensations, words, images, feelings – while feeling her tiredness here with me. In this small phenomenological enquiry, I ask her to *describe* what she experiences, rather than explain it. I may speculate about the causes of her tiredness: I hold these ideas lightly, *bracketing*, or setting aside my preconceptions and interpretations. As a phenomenologist I know I can never do that entirely, so how I understand this is in terms of non-attachment – I practise not knowing, as captured by Staemmler's phrase 'cultivated uncertainty' (1997: 45). I do not assume what is relevant or important, only that all is potentially relevant – this is the notion of *horizontalisation*.

I may also suggest phenomenological experiments. These arise from and in the spirit of dialogue and are designed to increase awareness; that is to increase the experience of owning and choosing in *this* moment in *this* situation. This may be by focusing ('stay with', 'what are you aware of now?') or 'owning' (what do you do by doing that?' or 'give a voice to'). I may invite my client to place his bullying employer on an empty chair and dialogue with him (his employer); I might suggest he develops and intensifies the movement I notice he makes when he does this. In this I aim to support his identification with how he is, to 'own' his felt impulses and feelings and to allow them to moblise his contact. He tells me he should have stood up for himself: I invite him to a dialogue between that introjected critic that says he should have stood up to the bully, and his felt reaction to that (this last is an example of a top-dog/under-dog, two-chair experiment).

CULTURAL CONTEXTS, POWER AND CONCEPTUALISATION OF INDIVIDUAL DIFFERENCES

It is difficult to do justice to the area of cultural contexts, power and the conceptualisation of individual differences in such limited space. I will limit myself to one or two observations that interest me from a gestalt therapy perspective. Power is a field function, meaning it is relational. Since therapist and client are involved as equals in the phenomenological investigation of their contact process (the process of horizontalisation), the therapist cannot have any claim to define or interpret the client's experience to or for them and, therefore, in this sense, client and therapist are of equal power in this situation. However, the field is phenomenal and clients frequently experience themselves as having less power than me – knowing less, needing more. If my client experiences herself as less powerful than me, I must ask myself what my part is in creating and maintaining that. A continuing commitment to dialogue is necessary.

However this is not enough. The issue of power intersects with issues of cultural difference and diversity which are also field phenomena. Both I and my client bring to the process of contact between us the ground that forms us: but the ground is not an homogeneous backcloth. It is structured by the assimilated and unassimilated assumptions and constructions that I and my client have developed over our lifetimes within our own particular culturally located situations. Even with an effort of will, and as a fully paid-up phenomenologist, I am rarely aware that I am interpreting my sense data in a pre-judged way: this is as true with the 'givens' of my cultural world. They are so much part of the assumptive fabric of my ground that I am usually not aware of them as assumptions. I remember my indignant disbelief and disorientation as a child when my Scottish cousins commented on my accent! I didn't have an accent – they did! In other words, I don't know what I don't know – I need to continually work to reveal my assumptions. If, for example, I consider one definition of power to be openness to the possibilities of the field, and my client's awareness of those possibilities are constrained in ways which I literally cannot perceive, then my client is likely to feel disempowered by my invitation to her to experiment with these possibiities. Additionally, I am part of the whole that creates and maintains the fixed differentiations and disadvantages of our society and our world. If I apply my gestalt therapy principles, I am enjoined to be politically aware and, I would argue, politically active.

STRENGTHS AND WEAKNESSESS

As befits a gestalt practitioner, I view strength and weakness as polarities. As a phenomenological psychotherapy, one strength is that there is a methodology for practising phenomenologically – the awareness experiment. Such experiments can be simple and very powerful in revealing to client and therapist important insights into the problems that clients experience. The strength of this methodology may also be a weakness, these experiments can be seen as a quick fix and, indeed, gestalt has been sometimes mistaken for a collection of such experiments. When these experiments are attempted in isolation, outside of the dialogical relationship and ungrounded in theory, they are usually ineffective. When used in this way they may become disguised interpretations which constrain, rather than support, phenomenological enquiry, or lead to deflection of the contact between client and therapist.

The role of experiment provides scope for the client and practitioner's creativity: experiments may involve whatever is to hand – art work, movement, music and voice. This is a strength in providing non-verbal avenues for dialogue and awareness work. However there is the risk of the practitioner mistaking their creative range for relating!

RESEARCH EVIDENCE

Gestalt therapists have been sceptical that research can usefully reflect and represent the practice of gestalt therapy without reducing it to techniques, or clients to symptoms. Notwithstanding this view, there is a significant body of research on gestalt therapy, well summarised in two recent review articles (Strumpfel, 2004; Wagner-Moore, 2004). This includes process research, seeking to identify and describe key processes in gestalt therapy. For example, identifying the role of increased emotional intensity in intrapersonal dialogue (two-chair) work (Greenberg, 1992; Greenberg & Watson, 1998).

Greenberg and his colleagues, in a series of studies, have investigated the microprocesses of two-chair and empty-chair work, and also compared the outcomes of such intrapersonal dialogues with other interventions, including cognitive problem solving (Greenberg, 1992). They showed, for example, that such work is effective in helping with (career) indecision and in marital conflicts. In the latter it was as effective as a cognitive problem-solving method, and on some measures superior to it (Johnson & Greenberg, 1985). Other process research summarised by Strumpfel points to the validity of the concept of the contact cycle (Strumpfel, 2004: 18).

Strumpfel reviews studies evaluating the efficacy of gestalt therapy in clinical practice, including with psychiatric patients, with substance misusers, psychosomatic problems and chronic pain. In all, the results indicate positive (and where measured), long-term effects from gestalt therapy. Several studies have examined the efficacy of gestalt therapy with people with depression and anxiety. These include two series that compare gestalt therapy with cognitive behavioural therapy. Both found that the two therapies produced similar treatment effects (Beutler et al., 1991; Mulder et al., 1994). Mulder et al. found gestalt and cognitive behavioural therapy equally effective as judged against a control group, with the gestalt group scoring better on the subjective evaluation of patients. Johnson and Smith (1997) compared gestalt empty-chair dialogues with systematic desensitisation (a behavioural treatment) and a no-treatment control, in the treatment of a simple phobia in a non-clinical population. Both treatment groups showed significant and equal improvement.

In summary, studies have shown that gestalt therapy is effective in a range of clinical issues and, when compared with other approaches, is as effective.

NEW DEVELOPMENTS IN THE APPROACH

Field theory is a complex set of ideas, and significant developments in gestalt therapy have included the application of field theoretical principles to clinical issues (Parlett, 1991, 2005). Currently, one such area is in relation to recent developments in the neurosciences. These developments provide confirmation of our field theoretical and holistic view of the person and, at the same time, offer challenges to theory and practice. For example, the question is posed as to whether the ability to self-regulate is impaired in those from severely abusive backgrounds, perhaps limiting the applicability of the paradoxical theory of change (Phillipson, 2006; Staemmler, 2006). If this is the case then how might gestalt therapy respond?

The aim of gestalt therapy is to support the development of contact possibilites through awareness work and dialogue. For some of our clients, their self-regulation is so tenuous that attempts to increase contact have the opposite effect. These are often clients described as having 'personality disorders'. I invite my client to notice what he is doing with his hand and he pulls it back sharply, as if burnt, apologising, ashamed; or I tell my client that I notice I am tensing my shoulders as she talks, and she reacts angrily, accusing me of blaming her for how I feel. The developing understanding of the phenomenal world of such clients, and their fixed interpersonal gestalts, has led to a developing understanding of how to differentiate clients for whom more active phenomenological experimentation, or self-disclosure on the part of the therapist, needs to wait until the client's self-support and the establishment of the therapeutic alliance mean these support contact rather than disrupt it (Greenberg, 2002; Yontef, 1993; Jacobs, 2003).

SUMMARY

The gestalt therapy view of the therapeutic relationship follows from its reconceptualisation of the individual as an emerging event of the biosociopsychological field. As a phenomenological and field theory, the therapeutic relationship is one of existential dialogue, the therapuetic practice one of phenomenological enquiry and experiment.

REFERENCES

Beisser, AR (1970) The paradoxical theory of change. In J Fagan & IL Shepherd (Eds) *Gestalt Therapy Now* (pp. 77–80). Palo Alto, CA: Science & Behaviour Books.

Beutler, L, Engle, D, Mohr, D, Daldrup, R, Bergan, J, Meredith, K & Merry, W (1991) Predictors of differential response to cognitive, expereriential, and self-directed psychotherapeutic procedures. *Journal of Consulting and Clinical Psychology, 59*, 2, 333–40.

Bohm, D (1980) *Wholeness and the Implicate Order.* London: Routledge.

Bowman, CE (2005) The history and development of gestalt therapy. In AL Woldt & SM Toman (Eds) *Gestalt Therapy: History, theory and practice.* London: Sage.

Goldstein, K (1995) *The Organism: A holistic approach to biology, derived from pathological data in man* (revised edn). New York: Zone Books.

Greenberg, E (2002) Love, admiration or safety: A system of gestalt diagnosis of borderline, narcissistic and schizoid adaptations that focuses on what is figure for the client. *Gestalt!* 6 (3), 393–405.

Greenberg, L (1992) Task analysis: Identifying components of intrapersonal conflict resolution. In SG Toukmanian & DL Rennie (Eds) *Psychotherapy Process Research: Paradigmatic and narrative approaches.* London: Sage.

Greenberg, L & Watson, J (1998) Experiential therapy of depression: Differential effects of client-centred relationship conditions and process-experiential interventions. *Psychotherapy Research, 8* (2), 210–24.

Hodges, C (2003) Creative process in gestalt group therapy. In M Spagnuolo Lobb & N Amendt-Lyon (Eds) *Creative License: The art of gestalt therapy.* New York: Springer-Verlag.

Hycner, R & Jacobs, L (1995) *The Healing Relationship in Gestalt Therapy.* Highland, NY: Gestalt Journal Press.

Jacobs, L (2003) Ethics of context and field: The practices of care, inclusion and dialogue. *British Gestalt Journal, 12* (2), 88–96.

Johnson, SM & Greenberg, LS (1985) Differential effects of experiential and problem solving interventions in resolving marital conflict. *Journal of Consulting and Clinical Psychology, 53*, 175–84.

Johnson, W & Smith, E (1997) Gestalt empty-chair dialogue versus systematic desensitization in the treatment of phobia. *Gestalt Review, 1* (2), 150–62.

Kearney, R (1986) *Modern Movements in European Philosophy.* Manchester: University of Manchester Press.

Kohler, W (1969) *The Task of Gestalt Psychology.* Princeton, NJ: Princeton University Press.

McLeod, L (1993) The self in gestalt therapy theory. *The British Gestalt Journal, 2* (1), 25–40.

Mulder, C, Emmelkamp, P, Antoni, M, Mulder, J, Sandfort, T & de Vries, M (1994) Cognitive behavioural and experiential group psychotherapy for asymptomatic HIV-infected homosexual men: A comparative study. *Psychosomatic Medicine, 3*, 271–88.

Parlett, M (1991) Reflections on field theory. *British Gestalt Journal, 1* (2), 69–81.

Parlett, M (2005) Contemporary gestalt therapy: Field theory. In AL Woldt & SM Toman (2005) (Eds) *Gestalt Therapy: History, theory, and practice.* London: Sage.

Perls, FS, Hefferline, RF & Goodman, P (1994) *Gestalt Therapy: Excitement and growth in the human personality* (revised edn). Highland, NY: Gestalt Journal Press. (Original work published 1951)

Phillipson, P (2001) *Self in Relation*. Highland, NY: Gestalt Journal Press.

Phillipson, P (2006) Field theory: Mirrors and reflections. *British Gestalt Journal,* 15 (2), 59–63.

Sartre, J-P (1948) *Existentialism and Humanism*. London: Methuen.

Spinelli, E (1989) *The Interpreted World*. London: Sage.

Staemmler, F-M (1997) Cultivated uncertainty: An attitude for gestalt therapists. *British Gestalt Journal,* 6 (1), 40–8.

Staemmler, F-M (2006) A Babylon confusion? On the uses of the term 'field'. *British Gestalt Journal,* 15 (2), 64–83.

Strumpfel, U (2004) Research on Gestalt psychotherapy. *International Gestalt Journal, 27* (1), 9–54.

Wagner-Moore, LE (2004) Gestalt therapy: Past, present, theory and research. *Psychotherapy: Theory, Research, Practice, Training, 41* (2), 180–9.

Woldt, AL & Toman, SM (Eds) (2005) *Gestalt Therapy: History, theory, and practice*. London: Sage.

Yontef, G (1993) *Awareness, Dialogue and Process: Essays on gestalt therapy*. Highland, NY: Gestalt Journal Press.

Yontef, G (2005) Gestalt therapy theory of change. In AL Woldt & SM Toman (2005) (Eds) *Gestalt Therapy: History, theory and practice*. London: Sage.

CHAPTER 7

TRANSACTIONAL ANALYSIS
A DIVERSITY OF RELATIONSHIPS

JANE WALFORD
ROBIN WALFORD

Transactional analysis (TA) is both theoretically and relationally rich in that it offers to the therapist a wide conceptual framework and a diversity of possibilities for therapeutic relating. The many different approaches enable the therapist to tailor the work according to the personality of the client, their desired outcome, the limitations set by organisational imperatives and their preferred styles. In this chapter we outline some of the major contributions to the different ways of viewing and using the therapeutic relationship within transactional analysis theory.

BACKGROUND TO THE APPROACH

From its beginnings in the 1950s, transactional analysis has emphasised the centrality of Eric Berne's philosophy. His goal was to demystify both the theory and the therapist. Berne's aim was to empower the client and facilitate the therapeutic relationship between the therapist and the client. He believed that human beings strive towards health and, given the right opportunities, will develop and grow. The word 'transactional' indicates that Berne's focus was directed towards understanding the relationship and how each person's life drama was played out through their relationships. Berne was clear that establishing a relationship was not, in itself, necessarily therapeutic. He believed that a *therapeutic* relationship didn't 'just happen' but required a specific treatment plan and diagnosis held within a clear theoretical framework.

> The professional therapist's job is to use his knowledge therapeutically; if the patient is to be cured by love, that should be left to a lover. When the patient recovers, the therapist should be able to say, 'My treatment helped nature,' and not, 'My love overcame it' – a statement which should be reserved for the patient's intimates.' (Berne, 1966: 63)

During his psychoanalytic training, Berne became impatient with analytic practice at the time, which maintained a cloak of mystery around the role of the therapist through the remote attitude of the therapist and the highly technical psychological language. It was from this stance that Berne (1966) developed the philosophy of TA:

- *People are OK.* Everyone has equal value and worth as a human being.
- *People can think.* We are able to think about and evaluate our experiences.
- *Decisions can be changed.* Because we can think, we can decide our own destiny within the boundaries of our culture and resources, and these decisions can be changed.

The two principles which support this philosophy are:

1. *Open communication.* Central to the relationship is clear and transparent communication by the therapist. Straightforward language is used in a way that is understandable and useable by the client, and sometimes aspects of the theory may be shared with the client to both empower them to play an equal part in the process of change and enable effective communication.

2. *Contractual method.* The principles of transactional analysis practice emphasise the need to gain the client's agreement at all stages of the therapeutic process. This ranges from an agreement about the business contract to an agreement about the ultimate goals of the work. This practice supports the equality of the relationship, avoids an imbalance of power and highlights the joint responsibility for the therapeutic work.

In addition to the above philosophy and principles, Berne's medical training meant that he incorporated a further principle:

- *Above all do no harm.* He recognised the power inherent in the role of the therapist and emphasised the responsibility of the practitioner to use their skill appropriately, thoughtfully and with care (Berne, 1966).

The philosophy and principles run as a central thread through all transactional analysis psychotherapy.

It is common to distinguish three distinct schools of transactional analysis theory, with an additional fourth school containing more recent developments. Each of these schools has a different emphasis in terms of therapeutic style, theoretical models and therapeutic techniques.

THE SCHOOLS OF TRANSACTIONAL ANALYSIS

CLASSICAL SCHOOL

The early TA theory developed by Berne (1957, 1961, 1964, 1966, 1972) incorporated concepts such as life script, transactions, ego states, strokes, games etc. and became known as the Classical School of TA. The focus in the relationship was to demystify both the therapist and the theory. This was done by enabling a transparent process between the client and therapist and making available the theory to the client with the use of everyday words of 1960s America to describe the theoretical concepts e.g. racket, games. Sometimes, aspects of the theory were taught to the client to enable and empower them to use their knowledge for their own healing.

Berne wrote that 'A striving for intimacy underlies the most intense and important operations' (Berne, 1963: 127). He later described recognition hunger, tactilehunger and contact hunger which underlie the motivation for relationship and connection with another. Using the theories and methods of the Classical School of TA the client becomes aware of his script decisions and how they have contributed to his current difficulties, makes a contract to change these behaviours and feel differently.

CATHEXIS SCHOOL

Jacqui Schiff and other members of the Cathexis Institute (Schiff et al., 1975) developed TA theory in order to work effectively with psychotic clients, using a technique called 'Reparenting'. The theorists' view was that many here-and-now problems are a result of poor parenting. This involved working with regressed clients to offer them a different experience of parent figures. Schiff's work proved very effective with some of her 'children' and resulted in some of the cured clients further developing the theory with Jacqui Schiff. This approach has also been found to be effective with non-psychotic clients whose upbringing has been deficient.

REDECISION SCHOOL

Robert and Mary Goulding (1988) combined TA theory with the approach and techniques of gestalt therapy. Redecision theory is based on the premise that the earliest decisions are held in the psyche as 'feelings' rather than as a 'thinking' decision. It is therefore necessary for the client to contact early feelings, to express them and make a new appropriate *redecision,* which will result in the client feeling, thinking and behaving differently.

ADDITIONS TO TA THEORY BEYOND THE THREE SCHOOLS

In more recent years a psychodynamic approach to TA has been developed which some call the fourth school of TA. It is often termed the Relational School and encompasses work from a variety of authors, (Erskine, 1993, 1997, 1998; Erskin, & Trautmann, 1993, 1996; Hargaden & Sills, 2002) each with their own emphasis on the use of the therapeutic relationship within a transactional analysis framework.

POSITION OF THE THERAPIST AND THE CLIENT

The ethos and approach of the Classical School is central to all expositions of TA. The emphasis is on acceptance and valuing of the client and an expectation that both therapist and client are responsible for their own responses and behaviour. Both the process and content of the way the client relates to the therapist are essential to understanding the relationship. After the development of a relational alliance, the client is helped to identify ways in which, in response to early life experience, they evade taking responsibility as an adult. As the client develops an awareness of those strategies they are supported in determining more appropriate and effective ways of relationship.

Berne suggested that before and in the first few minutes of meeting with a client the therapist should ask him or herself 'some fundamental questions about the real meaning of the therapeutic relationship' (Berne, 1966: 63–4); firstly, regarding the therapist: 'Why am I sitting in this room? Why am I not at home with my children? What will this hour contribute to my unfolding?' (ibid.). Then Berne suggested reflecting on the client and their motivations: 'Why are they here? Why are they not at home with their children and doing what their fancy dictates? Why did they choose psychotherapy as a solution? Why not religion, alcohol, drugs, crime, gambling? What will this hour contribute to their unfolding?' (ibid.).

He emphasised particular qualities necessary for an effective therapist and central to this was authenticity in the relationship. The qualities that need to be demonstrated by the therapist were identified by Pat Crossman (1966) in the three 'Ps' – permission, potency and protection.

1. *Permission.* The therapist offers through words and/or actions, messages that contradict the early negative messages from parent figures.

2. *Protection.* The client needs to be able to perceive the therapist as competent, effective and powerful enough to manage the negative consequences of contradicting the early parental commands.

3. *Potency.* The therapist needs to be perceived as having more authority than the internalised parent figure.

Using the reparenting approach of the Cathexis School of TA, the therapist is able to offer some level of reparative experience as the transferential parent figure e.g. nurturing or appropriate containment within the session. Inappropriate behaviour and passivity is confronted and appropriate behaviour and problem solving are affirmed. The relationship between therapist and client is not unlike that which exists between a parent and a growing child, with the obvious power imbalance. The equality of relationship is gained through a healthy, non-symbiotic adaptation to the therapist by the client, and by the therapist and client agreeing a contract for the work.

Redecision therapy emphasises personal responsibility and the client's commitment to their own process of change. It is not the therapist's task to take any of the responsibility for the client in making this decision, their role is simply to facilitate the client and provide a positive role model. The therapeutic relationship is therefore not emphasised in this model of therapy other than as an affirming witness to the changes and redecisions made by the client. The therapist does not step into transferential roles with the client, but instead instructs the client to put the transference where it belongs: with the parent figure. Transactional analyst, Judith Barr (1987), was the first TA author to focus on the therapeutic relationship. She states that 'The task of the therapeutic relationship is to create a delicate tapestry, the purpose of which is to "keep buoyant the life project of the evolving person" (Barr, 1987: 134). She also states that this tapestry is interwoven with two sets of threads: the foundation threads that represent the core relationship between the client's capacity to recruit, and the therapist's recruitability, and the woven threads that represent the various theoretical concepts and clinical techniques by which the therapist assesses, selects and provides the needed holding environment(s) to help the client evolve through one or more stages. There have been further significant developments in TA theory through the work of Erskine (1993, 1997; Erskine & Trautmann,1996) who describes relationships as providing the experience from which the configuration of a sense of self, of others, and of the quality of life emerge.

Hargaden and Sills (2002) have made a significant contribution to the theory of the therapeutic relationship in transactional analysis and they state that it is important that the therapist and client have a shared idea of why they are in the consulting room together, but they do not believe that it is necessary or desirable for the client to have a concrete, observable change as their goal, since having a goal can be restricting and preclude a journey of discovery.

PSYCHOLOGICAL FACTORS IN THE RELATIONSHIP

Berne states that the client will present his or her 'past experiences in coded form to the therapist, and the therapist's task is to decode and detoxify them, rectify distortions, and help the patient regroup the experience' (Berne, 1966: 242–3). Berne's view was that it is the therapist's job to 'cure' the client by making a systematic diagnosis of the client's problems and determining a treatment plan that would lead to the desired outcome as efficiently as possible. He suggested that the trained therapist could offer clients three clinical qualities that other non-trained helpers might not have: observation, equanimity and initiative (ibid.).

Erskine states:

> In a relationship therapy the concept of contact is the theoretical basis from which clinical interventions are derived ... A major goal of therapy, then, is to use the therapist–client relationship – the ability to create full contact in the present – as a stepping-stone to healthier relationships with other people and a satisfying sense of self. Through respect, kindness and contactful listening we establish a personal presence and allow for an interpersonal relationship that provides affirmation of the client's integrity. This respectfulness may best be described as a consistent invitation to interpersonal contact between client and therapist, with simultaneous support for the client to contact his or her internal experiences and receive an external recognition for those experiences. (Erskine, 1997: 77–8)

Hargaden and Sills 'locate the transferential relationship at the heart of the therapeutic work' (Hargaden & Sills, 2002: 115) and state that 'the extent to which a therapist is informed of her own truths and has understood and integrated her unconscious self will inform the value of her interventions' (ibid.: 116). They describe a number of different transferences that are present within the client–therapist relationship: *introjective transference* or early child longings, *projective transference* or defensive and splitting transferences, *transformational transference* or primitive affect.

Introjective transference. The client seeks to develop a symbiotic relationship with the therapist with the aim of meeting early unmet child needs. This unconscious striving results in mirror transference, idealising transference and twinship.

Projective transference. These transferences occur when the client projects a parent figure onto the therapist in order to work through unintegrated experiences. In a misattuned environment, the infant splits between good and bad. The projective transference is the client's mechanism for keeping a sense of self by projecting repressed internal conflict onto the therapist.

The parent's face. The client projects the mother's or father's face onto the therapist and then behaves towards the therapist as if they were the parent and attributes the therapist with the qualities and attitudes of the parent.

Good/bad splitting. Projection of the good self leads to idealising of the therapist who is seen as all things wonderful, but it is only a matter of time before the therapist falls from grace and represents the bad self of the client.

Transformational transference. In the process of projective identification (Ogden, 1982) the client induces a feeling state in the therapist that corresponds to a state that he is unable to experience for him/herself. The client splits off and disowns their vulnerable self. This split-off self is felt by the therapist who experiences the feelings as foreign and often powerful. The therapist is required to transform the transference by making it containable and meaningful. The therapist must hold it and manage it in a way that is different to the client's experience.

THERAPEUTIC INTERVENTIONS

This view of the task of the therapist led Berne (1966) to develop eight therapeutic operations: interrogation, specification, explanation, confrontation, confirmation, interpretation, illustration and crystallisation. These are divided into interventions and interpositions.

Interventions
Interrogation: Asking questions to elicit information from the client.
Specification: Fixes or highlights a point for the client.
Confrontation: Used to point out an inconsistency or incongruity.
Explanation: Used to strengthen the client's ability to think differently about a problem and function effectively in here-and-now reality using their Adult ego state.

Interpositions
Illustration: Anecdote, metaphor or simile used to reinforce or soften a confrontation.

Confirmation: Confirmation of a confrontation using further material produced by the client.

Interpretation: Used to decode the client's early experiences as held in their Child ego state.

Crystallisation: Statement of the client's position from the therapist to the client to facilitate the client being in a position where they can exercise an option to change.

Using a classical approach of transactional analysis the therapist's aim is to facilitate the client in separating out their adult 'here-and-now' thoughts, feelings and beliefs from those taken in (introjected) from parent figures or carried from childhood to enable problem solving and changes in behaviour.

Barr (1987) describes five relationship modes which refer to the form or expression of a relationship that impacts the therapeutic process:

The First Relationship – the original caretaking relationship and other significant primary relationships.

The Intrapsychic Relationship – refers to the internalisation by the client, not simply of the mothering person, but the entire first relationship, into the developing sense of self. The client therefore develops an internal image of what other people are like and of what relationship is like.

The Transference Relationship – refers to the externalisation of the intrapsychic relationship onto the outside world. The client projects his or her experience of relationship into the environment between self and others and the therapist therefore is not seen for who he or she really is, and the relationship is not seen for what it is, or has the potential to be.

The Developmentally Needed Relationship – enables the therapist to examine, understand and determine how to respond to the tasks the client needs to accomplish in order to resolve developmental gaps.

The Core Relationship – the relationship the client, as the person he or she really is in the here and now, has with the therapist, as the person the therapist really is in the present. The goal in establishing the core relationship is for the therapist to interact with the client to provide a new healthy experience of relationship and at the same time to take him or herself as a person into account.

Barr suggests that the relationship modes provide a way to systematically evaluate how to respond within the therapeutic relationship. Erskine and Trautmann (1996) emphasised the need to psychodynamically connect with the early child through Inquiry, Empathy, Attunement and Involvement.

INQUIRY

Erskine and Trautmann (1996) emphasise the importance of asking questions which expand the client's horizons and invites them to explore new or avoided territory. The process of inquiry is not linear but moves in harmony with the client's ever-increasing internal awareness and awareness of self in relationship. The goal of therapeutic inquiry is for the client and therapist together to discover and distinguish the functions of intrapsychic processes and defensive dynamics.

EMPATHY

Empathy is an introspective process whereby the therapist finds within themselves something akin to what is going on in the client. This is about being in the client's skin, neither total immersion in the client's feelings nor intellectual distance. It is the therapist's posture, gestures, voice tone, facial expressions, as well as their words that convey an empathic understanding.

ATTUNEMENT

Attunement goes beyond empathy, but starts with it. 'It is more than simply feeling what the client feels: it includes recognizing the client's experience and moving – cognitively, affectively and physically – so as to complement that experience in a contact-enhancing way' (Erskine &Trautmann, 1996: 319). Effective attunement requires that the therapist remains aware of the boundary between client and therapist as well as his or her own internal processes. The communication of attunement validates the client's needs and feelings and lays the foundation for repairing the failures of previous relationships. The process of attunement also includes responding to relational needs as they emerge in the therapeutic relationship. Erskine & Trautmann (1996) identified eight relational needs:

1. *Security* – the visceral experience of having our physical and emotional vulnerabilities protected. Attunement involves the empathic awareness of the other's need for security within the relationship, with a reciprocal response to that need.

2. *Validation, affirmation and significance within a relationship* – the need to have the other person validate the significance and function of our intrapsychic processes and the need to have all of our relational needs affirmed and accepted as natural.

3. *Acceptance by a stable, dependable and protective other person* – the need to look up to and rely on parent figures. The search for protection and acceptance may manifest as idealisation of the other as the much longed for parent. Attunement involves the therapist's recognition of the importance and necessity of idealising as an unconscious request for intrapsychic protection for the early child vulnerabilities (Child ego state) from an internal harsh and controlling parent figure (Parent ego state).

4. *Confirmation of personal experience* – the need to have experience confirmed through the desire to be in the presence of someone who understands because their experience is similar, and whose shared experience is confirming. The therapist provides attunement by revealing carefully selected personal experiences.

5. *Self-definition* – the relational need to know and express one's own uniqueness and to receive acceptance by the other. Therapeutic attunement occurs in the therapist's consistent support for the client's expression of identity. It requires the therapist's consistent presence, contact and respect, even in the face of disagreement.

6. *The need to have an impact on the other person* – attunement to the client's need occurs when the therapist allows him or herself to be emotionally impacted by the client, including when the client is critical of the therapist.

7. *The need to have the other initiate* – the reaching out to the other by the therapist in a way that acknowledges and validates the importance of the client in the relationship.

8. *The need to express love* – love may be expressed through gratitude, giving affection or doing something for the other person. The importance of the relational need to give love by the client, if overlooked, leads to a thwarting of the expression of self in relationship.

INVOLVEMENT

Therapeutic involvement that includes acknowledgement, validation, normalisation and presence diminishes internal defensive processes (Erskine & Trautmann, 1996).

1. *Acknowledgement* of the client by the therapist happens through attunement.

2. *Validation* makes a link between cause and effect and communicates to the client that their feelings, defences, behavioural patterns and ways of being in relationship are related to something significant from their past experience.

3. *Normalisation* is used to change the client's perception or definition of their internal experience or coping behaviours from a pathological perspective to a normal defensive reaction that many others would have if they encountered similar life experiences.

4. *Presence* is experienced by the client through the therapist's sustained, attuned responses to both verbal and non-verbal expressions of the client. Presence is an expression of the psychotherapist's full internal and external contact.

> Through the therapist's full presence, the transformational potential of a relationship-orientated psychotherapy is possible ... More than just verbal communication, presence is a communion between client and therapist. (Erskine & Trautmann, 1996: 326)

Hargaden and Sills (2002) promote the use of the empathic transaction to build a working alliance with the client and they develop Berne's therapeutic operations and rename them the 'empathic transactions': enquiry, specification, confrontation, explanation, illustration, confirmation, interpretation, holding and crystallisation.

Enquiry involves the therapist in exploring the client's phenomenology from a position of genuine enquiry – asking questions and promoting narrative. Hargaden and Sills also include in enquiry an 'invitation' to the client to share his or her experiences of the therapy.

Specification is used similarly to Berne's original intention – to fix something that the client has articulated in both the mind of the client and of the therapist. Hargaden and Sills describe specification as a type of accurate empathy which includes the therapist hearing what is under the surface of the client's awareness, which allows the client to feel heard and deeply understood.

Confrontation can be used as a powerful force for change, but Hargaden and Sills stress the need for sensitivity by the therapist and an awareness of the potential to shame the client.

Confirmation of the confrontation can be very useful if the client is able to hear it, and Hargaden and Sills suggest that it be based on previously attuned enquiry, acceptance and understanding by the therapist.

Explanation involves the therapist describing the dynamics of the client's experience to provide the client with 'not only an understanding of her needs and her phenomenological experiencing but also a context by which to understand the basis of those specific needs' (Hargaden & Sills, 2002: 124). Hargaden and Sills stress the importance of the collaborative process between therapist and client in the giving of explanations, so that it is sometimes the client who makes the intervention. They describe the therapist and client working together to make this transaction effective: the client helps the therapist to understand him or her and the therapist is involved with finding a voice for the Child ego state. 'In such a context interpretation can invoke within the patient a phenomenological shift that supports the integration of previously split-off affective states.' (ibid.: 125). 'For interpretation to be valuable, it is therapeutically more effective when the empathic resonance is maintained … We believe that understanding, which can include naming and voicing the meaning of the dynamics, is one of the deepest forms of empathy' (ibid.: 125–6).

Illustration is used in very much the same way as Berne (1966) suggested, drawing on stories, metaphors, analogy, imagery, jokes, fantasy to further the therapy. Hargaden and Sills suggest that it can be used as a specification, a form of accurate, advanced empathy, or a confrontation.

Holding is an addition made by Hargaden and Sills to Berne's original therapeutic operations and refers to 'an intervention aimed at doing no more than offer the steady containing presence of a non-judgemental therapist who is perceived as having the potency to offer the protection and permission needed.' (Hargaden & Sills, 2002: 127) *Holding* refers to a metaphorical holding within the space of the therapeutic relationship – not physical holding.

Crystallisation involves the therapist outlining their understanding of the options now available to the client. Hargaden and Sills point out that it is important that the client has been able to achieve an experience of integration with her 'self' in order to feel that such a statement of the therapist is true, and suggest that crystallisation is very much a co-created understanding that comes towards the end of therapy.

Hargaden and Sills (2002) link the use of the empathic transactions to each of the different transferences and in so doing create a relational transactional analysis psychotherapy.

CULTURAL CONTEXTS, POWER AND CONCEPTUALISATION OF INDIVIDUAL DIFFERENCES

Pearl Drego (1983) was one of the first TA theorists to identify the cultural dimension of the therapeutic relationship. She located this in the individual's Parent ego state and she termed it the Cultural Parent. Drego (1983) proposed that a significant influence in how individuals relate is the culture in which they were raised, and identified three dimensions of this culture:

Etiquette. These are culturally inherited beliefs: rules, customs, ideologies, moral codes; beliefs about life and death, good and evil, the ideal man and woman etc. She describes this as the Parent-type contents of thinking, behaving and valuing in a culture.

Technicalities. These are culturally-inherited ways of doing things: techniques, methods of production, skills, economic processes, organisations, political processes, etc. She describes this as the Adult-type contents of the actual organisation of the material and social dimensions in a culture.

Character. This comprises culturally inherited ways of acting out and experiencing love, hate, vengeance, distress, grief, hurt, happiness, birth, death, freedom, identity, hungers, freedoms, ways of sabotaging the culture etc. This includes socially programmed ways of handling biological needs, feelings and emotional expressions, especially relating to compliance and rebellion within a culture. She describes this as the Child-type contents of the emotional expression of a culture.

These dimensions of culture not only profoundly affect the identity and sense of self of the individual, but are significant in how relationships are formed with others. This level of understanding of the subtleties of culture results in the counsellor realising that the differences that they need to consider are much more diverse than colour, race, sexuality or gender, and are present in all relationships. The therapist, therefore, cannot assume that his or her cultural values are any more right (or wrong) than the client's. It is also important for the therapist to determine which aspects of the client's responses are part of their cultural inheritance and which are the influence of significant others. In light of the common initial, and often sustained, transferential response by the client onto the counsellor as being the 'Parent' and expert, it is apparent that the counsellor will not only take on aspects of the early transferential figures but also the culture in which those figures existed. Clearly, it is therefore essential for the TA therapist to understand as fully as possible the nature of their own and their client's cultural frame of reference and Cultural Parent in order to enable their client to address the appropriateness of the cultural influence on their life now, and to avoid unconsciously imposing their own cultural perspective on their client.

STRENGTHS AND WEAKNESSES

One of the greatest strengths of transactional analysis theory is the diversity of different approaches to therapeutic relating that are encompassed within the same model. The many ways of conceptualising the understanding of the relationship within TA theory, together with a wide variety of clinical approaches, brings the possibility of great flexibility in the therapist's practice with both the client and their problems. This allows for therapists with very different individual styles to practise transactional analysis counselling and psychotherapy, and also enables therapists to work with a broad cross-section of clients and personality styles within a TA framework. Vital to any humanistic approach is the centrality of the relationship in the therapeutic process. It is often profoundly healing for the client to experience a healthy relationship that is reparative, challenging and supportive, and transactional analysis does offer this possibility.

A potential disadvantage of such a wealth of different ways of thinking about and working with the therapeutic relationship might be a lack of clarity about what *is* the TA model of relationship, and possible confusion for the beginning practitioner who is searching for an identity as a transactional analysis therapist.

RESEARCH EVIDENCE

It is in this area that transactional analysis theory is at its weakest. Almost all developments in TA theory are based on observation, reflection and clinical experience, and very little has been subjected to the disciplines of research. Although TA practitioners know that their approach and style of therapeutic relating is successful, both from their own experience and from reports from their clients, this has not been evidenced by research studies. This deficit is currently being addressed by the European and International Transactional Analysis Associations and is a much needed area of growth for the model.

NEW DEVELOPMENTS IN THE APPROACH

Summers and Tudor (2000) propose a fundamentally different view of the therapeutic relationship in their model of co-creative transactional analysis. They outline three guiding principles:

1. *The principle of 'we'-ness:* The therapeutic relationship is more potent than the potency (or impotency) of the therapist or client alone. It provides a supportive theoretical framework that emphasises the 'we'-ness of the therapeutic relationship as the medium for human development and change. It also emphasises the cultural context of the individual and field.

2. *The principle of shared responsibility:* Co-creative transactional analysis emphasises the shared client–therapist responsibility for the therapeutic process, in contrast to traditional TA which emphasises the personal responsibility of the client, and integrative TA approaches which tend to emphasise the responsibility of the therapist. The healing aspects of relationship – for example, potency, permission, protection, support and challenge – are co-created and co-maintained by active contributions from both therapist and client. Summers and Tudor point out that shared responsibility is not the same as equal responsibility and that the therapist's particular contribution is his or her skill in facilitating and using this shared responsibility to promote awareness and development.

3. *The principle of present-centred development:* Co-creative transactional analysis emphasises the importance of present-centred human development rather than past-centred child development. Summers and Tudor view psychotherapy as an adult process of learning and healing with the therapeutic focus on supporting the client's here-and-now developmental direction. This reduces the possibility of inappropriate infantilising of adult clients.

Summers and Tudor propose that a TA model of the therapeutic relationship needs to be based on the analysis of transactions in the therapeutic relationship. There are two ways of relating: present-centred adult relating (between the Adult ego state of the therapist and the Adult ego state of the client) and past-centred co-transferential relating, with the addition of 'partial transferential transactions' which are the stepping stones between past- and present-centred relating. Co-transference relating creates familiar transferential themes, and present-centred relating allows for fresh meanings to emerge. Summers and Tudor give equal value to both ways of therapeutic relating and the movement between them. They describe the advantages of this model of therapeutic relating as follows:

• It names and emphasises the present-centred therapeutic relationship.
• It locates and equalises the partial transferential transactions, as both client and therapist may be experiencing the past in the present, and suggests that either the therapist or the client can initiate a shift from past- to present-centred relating.
• It emphasises the shared responsibility of both client and therapist for creating and maintaining a co-transferential relationship when engaged in past-centred relating.
• It describes therapeutic relationships by analysis of transactions between therapist and client.

Summers and Tudor suggest a series of self-supervision questions for the practitioner, based on a co-creative approach:

What patterns emerge between us?

How are we presently making sense of these patterns?

What are we each contributing to these patterns?

What happens if we create different meanings for the same patterns?

What happens if we do something different?

How do we make sense of different patterns that we co-create?

What ego states are we evoking and co-creating in each other?

Why are we creating these ego states at this point in time?

What else may be possible?

What version of reality might we (have we) been confirming?

How can we explore, acknowledge and choose between different realities?

What constructs are we using to define self and other?

How do these constructs support or limit us?

SUMMARY

It can be seen that transactional analysis theory offers a varied and sophisticated understanding of the nature of relationship. It is only through a diversity and breadth of understanding and approaches that we can begin to understand, and call the client–therapist relationship therapeutic.

REFERENCES

Barr, J (1987) The therapeutic relationship model: Perspectives on the core of the healing process. *Transactional Analysis Journal, 17,* 134–40.

Berne, E (1957) *A Layman's Guide to Psychotherapy and Psychoanalysis.* New York: Simon & Schuster.

Berne, E (1961) *Transactional Analysis Psychotherapy.* New York: Grove Press.

Berne, E (1963) *The Structure and Dynamics of Organizations and Groups.* New York: Grove Press.

Berne, E (1964) *Games People Play.* New York: Grove Press.

Berne, E (1966) *Principles of Group Treatment.* New York: Grove Press.

Berne, E (1972) *What Do You Say After You Say Hello?* New York: Grove Press.

Crossman, P (1966) Permission and protection, *TAB,* 5 (19), 152–4.

Drego, P (1983) The cultural parent. *Transactional Analysis Journal, 13,* 224–7.

Erskine, RG (1993) Inquiry, attunement and involvement in the psychotherapy of dissociation. *Transactional Analysis Journal, 23,* 184–90.

Erskine, RG (1997) *Theories and Methods of an Integrative Transactional Analysis: A volume of selected articles.* San Francisco, CA: TA Press.

Erskine, RG (1998) The therapeutic relationship, Integrating motivation and personality theories. *Transactional Analysis Journal, 28,* 132–41.

Erskine, RG & Trautmann, RL (1993) The process of integrative psychotherapy. In BR Loria (Ed) *The Boardwalk Papers: Selections from the 1993 Eastern Regional Transactional Analysis Conference.* Madison, WI: Omnipress.

Erskine, RG & Trautmann, RL (1996) Methods of an integrative psychotherapy. *Transactional Analysis Journal, 26,* 316–29.

Goulding, M & Goulding, R (1979) *Changing Lives through Redecision Therapy.* New York: Grove Press.

Goulding, M & Goulding, R (1980) *The Power is in the Patient.* San Francisco, CA: TA Press.

Hargaden, H & Sills, C (2002) *Transactional Analysis: A relational perspective.* Hove: Brunner-Routledge.

Ogden, T (1982) *Projective Identification and Psychotherapeutic Technique.* London: Karnac Books.

Schiff, JL, Schiff, AW, Mellor, K, Schiff, E, Schiff, S, Richman, D, et al. (1975) *The Cathexis Reader: Transactional treatment of psychosis.* New York: Harper & Rowe.

Summers, G & Tudor, K (2000) Co-creative transactional analysis. *Transactional Analysis Journal, 30,* 23–40.

CHAPTER 8

COGNITIVE BEHAVIOURAL DIMENSIONS OF THE THERAPEUTIC RELATIONSHIP

MIKE THOMAS

BACKGROUND TO THE APPROACH

The underlying principles which support Cognitive Behavioural Therapy (CBT) indicate that client problems have three components requiring therapeutic interventions: mood, cognition and behaviour. Alongside the view that these components should take the interventionist focus is another principle that the client and therapist work together as a team to overcome identified problems. The majority of CB therapists agree with Aaron Beck, the original clinician who popularised CBT from the late 1950s, that the goal of therapy is to modify thinking patterns. By 1976, Beck was proposing that dysfunctional thinking and its influence on mood and behaviour is found in all psychological disturbances. Realistic evaluation and then alteration to thinking produces improvements in corresponding mood and behaviours and, most importantly, a longer-lasting enhancement in overall psychological health. Others suggest that goals can assist the client to achieve greater self-esteem, better performance at work, or to gain more meaningful interpersonal relationships (Burns, 1989; Clarke & Fairburn, 2005). Its application across a number of clinical diagnoses and identified personal problems is one reason for its wide use in therapeutic practice. This is coupled with the pragmatism which promotes the view that therapy itself is aimed at relieving the mood, cognition or behavioural difficulties presented by the client. Beck states that CBT also aims to teach the client to modify underlying irrational beliefs so that there is demonstrable symptomatic relief.

In the late 1950s and throughout the 1960s Beck utilised his clinical observations with clinical studies to conclude that psychiatric disorders such as depression and anxiety were due to disordered thinking. This was demonstrated by his patients showing systematic biases in the way they interpreted their own experiences. Beck discovered that if he proposed different (and more likely) interpretations then the patient showed an immediate improvement in the presenting psychiatric symptoms. In the 1960s he went on to discover that teaching his patients to work on immediate and present problems caused most symptoms to disappear in 12 to 14 weeks. By the late twentieth century, Beck had consolidated his work into a psychotherapeutic model with its own theory of personality and its own set of therapeutic assumptions, goals and interventions. Beck is therefore the originator and proponent of CBT, but other models have also arisen which are close to his work (and often co-authored by Beck or involving colleagues he has worked with in clinical practice, see Beck, Emery & Greenberg, 1985). Albert Ellis' Rational-Emotive Therapy (1962) is perhaps the most well known, and there is also Arnold Lazarus' Multimodal Therapy (1987) and Meichenbaum's Clinical Behavioural Modification Model (1977).

CBT's history is entwined in the cultural and intellectual changes of the late twentieth century. During the 1960s, a major consideration for behaviourism (the then dominant model of psychotherapy) was its attempts to make the client–therapist relationships more democratic. According to Free (2000), this led to a general view that therapy was primarily an educational process. Behavioural techniques were enthusiastically applied in educational settings and then moved to therapeutic practice. Behaviourism quickly evolved into a more collaborative form of therapy with the client taking more responsibility for the process of therapy. The educational approach also emphasised that clients should be informed about behavioural prompts, reinforcements, contingencies, generalisation and extinction techniques. Subsequently, the model grew closer to cognitive work as the psychotherapy trend moved away from theoretical inferences about the unconscious. By the 1980s, Gelder (1989) was able to claim that CBT received so much interest because its technique involved working with both thoughts and feelings and therefore provided unification between behaviourism and the 'dynamic psychotherapies'. CBT was also considered to be more empirical in its ability to both provide a model and have that model exposed to evaluation through clinical trials.

Beck himself, whose original training was as a psychoanalyst, has claimed that he implemented behavioural techniques in his own practice in the 1960s and his theories achieved widespread acceptance amongst behaviourists at the time (Clark & Fairburn, 2005). Beck's work has grown to be the dominant clinical model in the UK. Later collaborators demonstrated that CBT can be applied across a range of psychological conditions and psychiatric diagnosis. Empirical studies show that CBT is both effective and efficient and a collaborative group of clinicians and researchers have spread the message throughout the last quarter of the century from their bases in Oxford and London. Beck, writing in Clark and Fairburn (2005), paid homage to the team led by Michael Gelder at Oxford (who worked with Beck, who in turn operated from his base at the Center for CBT, University of Pennsylvania). These included well-known CBT proponents such as David Clark, Christopher Fairburn, Keith Hawton, Adrian Wells and Paul Salkovskis. It was common practice for clinicians from both sides of the Atlantic to spend time at both Beck's and Gelder's centres and a profusion of published work has emerged from their joint endeavours. CBT is now practised across the world in areas that adopt Western approaches to therapeutic interventions.

POSITION OF THE THERAPIST AND CLIENT

CB therapists attach great import to the therapist–client relationship, not only because of the level of trust and confidence required to explore painful and distressing experiences, but also because of the logic that the clients' interpersonal difficulties will be reflected in the therapeutic relationship. The skilled therapist should know how to monitor the relationship and help the client to change any relevant negative assumptions. In 1995, Aaron Beck's daughter Judith (who dedicated her book on CBT to her father) stated that 'it is essential to start building trust and rapport with patients in the first session' (Beck, 1995). She went on to state that the therapist should express empathy and use communication techniques to convey commitment and understanding through tone of voice, use of words, expressions, posture, summarising, information-giving, questioning and reflection. Free (2000) discusses the need for the therapist to have good interpretation skills and be able to convey openness, interest in the client, authenticity and a belief in the treatment intervention, whilst Bennett-Levy (2006) focuses on self-reflection and self-referenced learning as a tool for training therapists.

In CBT, the good, experienced therapist should meet the following criteria, they should:

- have sound interpersonal skills
- have good communication skills coupled with sound knowledge of a range of assessment tools and their analysis
- utilise educational techniques
- understand treatment formulation
- be familiar with applying reflective models
- have knowledge and application of relevant clinical interventions
- use their skills to monitor and intervene in times of crisis for the client
- demonstrate warmth and sympathy for the client's predicament ('sympathy' meaning the characteristics of offering practical help and support)
- demonstrate the ability to care about and value each client as an individual
- utilise the skill to terminate the therapeutic relationship (closure skills).

Despite the reputation of CBT as an austere form of therapy, the CB therapist values the quality of the interpersonal relationship between themselves and the client. This relationship is necessary for the interventions to be successful.

PSYCHOLOGICAL FACTORS IN THE RELATIONSHIP

Cognitive behaviour therapy is a psychological intervention with particular emphasis (agreed assumptions) in the psychodynamic branch of psychology. Whilst CBT and cognitive psychology share a common view regarding perception, memory, retrieval and analysis, it has developed a view of the person which is different to the clearly disease- or injury-based neuropathological cognitive models. CBT is a counselling approach with a rigorous principle of developing a therapeutic relationship with individuals who have problems with autonomy, self-worth, socialisation and standard-setting due to underlying irrational beliefs acquired during early development. Underlying irrational beliefs support the individual's erroneous self-concepts which, in turn, support negative symptoms (e.g. depression, anxiety, obsessions, fear). The CBT model does not view mental health diagnoses as organic disease entities, but instead holds to the view that psychogenic problems are surmountable. Underlying irrational beliefs can be altered and negative symptoms can be reversed with therapeutic interventions based on working alongside individuals to enable them to think, feel or behave differently to their established patterns.

Another divergence from neurocognitive psychology is the stress CBT places on situational and environmental factors in contributing to mental health problems. CBT highlights these factors as powerful influences on mood, thinking and behaviour. Beck (2005) postulates that underlying irrational beliefs are trait-like personality attributes which are life long and impact on the individual's perception (their assumptions) of events. Mood, thinking and behaviours are seen as having equal interdependence, each component supporting the other two (due to their growth from the single-stemmed underlying irrational belief) which may produce overt problems in any one or more of these three areas. An individual can have a life – experiencing the storm, stress and joy of living – without developing the negative stress (distress) which leads to mental health problems. This is as long as their life situation or environment does not precipitate perceptual disturbances. Individuals can often have a hidden predisposition towards disease, pathological change or health conditions which remains latent unless triggered by environmental or situational conditions (the precipitating factors). This is as likely to be seen in genetically predisposing conditions (Type 1 diabetes for example, or certain cancers); in environmental predisposing conditions (asbestos in the workplace, for example, or background radiation); in situational conditions (Type 2 diabetes due to obesity); in memory triggers (post-traumatic episodes), or in a tendency to depression prevented by having a supportive, loving relationship (a breakdown in the relationship would be the precipitating factor to the development of depression). For cognitive behavioural therapists, the person's situational or environmental conditions are very important aspects for therapeutic assessments and interventions. Whilst not always mentioned as being of equal weight to the three components of mood, cognition and behaviour, it is clear that, for most people, their situational and environmental factors can be the precipitators for psychogenic problems, or important factors in maintaining (perpetuating factors) their negative perception of life experiences.

Within CBT, the reason for the import on predispositions (being precipitated and perpetuated by situational and environmental factors) is based on the views espoused by Beck, Freeman and Associates (1990) that when an underlying irrational belief is activated, it causes further interlinked effects. The underlying irrational belief appears to be quickly reactivated by subsequent precipitators which become more generalised, more distant from the original triggers and appears to have less relevance to the predisposing belief. Reactivation appears to cause the irrational beliefs to be more dominant over other schemas which may be more appropriate to effect positive change. Irrational beliefs also direct more of the person's energy into sustaining the beliefs, causing difficulties in apportioning resources to feelings, thoughts and behaviours that would alter irrational beliefs. Identifying situational and environmental factors following assessments will impact on the treatment formulation to be considered by the therapist and client. A reduction in situational or environmental triggers, whilst not always initially possible, is an obvious objective. This schema-deactivation is important because it frees energy for the client to develop new strategies, reduce the frequency of negative automatic thoughts, explore different perceptions and try out new behaviours and thoughts. By developing problem-solving abilities – internal techniques to inhibit negative automatic thoughts – and altering the analysis of retrieved memory and perceptions, the client will either change existing underlying irrational beliefs or produce other more appropriate underlying beliefs.

This emphasis on precipitating and perpetuating factors played a role in the development of Ellis' earlier work (1977) and widely followed the ABC approach to therapy. The model provides a simple example of the interrelationship between thinking, feeling and behaviour. *A* refers to the activating event, *B* to the beliefs associated with the event and *C* to the thinking, emotional and behavioural consequences. For example, if an individual with autonomy problems (requiring demonstrations of achievement in order to have feelings of self-worth) was turned down for promotion, then the conclusion of the interview panel would be the activating event. The individual may then believe they have failed a self-imposed test: that the panel could see their weakness, may even dislike their manner, personality, presentation or even fashion style. The emotional consequence may be depression, the behavioural consequences, a disinclination to apply for future promotions, and the cognition consequence, poor self-regard ('I'm not good enough').

In assessment, the therapist can use ABC as a formulation model supported by other measuring tools and interview. The therapist can then involve the client in planning the actual interventions.

THERAPEUTIC INTERVENTIONS

Cognitive Behavioural Therapy, as emphasised by Beck, is a structured therapy which modifies dysfunctional thinking and behaviour. The initial intervention (following assessment) is based on the therapist teaching the client to recognise their negative automatic thoughts (NATs) and to identify triggers for these negative thoughts, to evaluate their impact and to modify them in order to prevent negative symptoms and provide relief. (Beck (1983) refers to this phase as the surface level of intervention which deals with negative automatic thoughts.) Following successful interventions, the client is then supported to explore the underlying beliefs which prompt NATs. This intermediate phase of therapy allows clients to evaluate their beliefs in different ways so that they can then adjust their perception of particular experiences. At a deeper or more core level lie more fundamental beliefs (called schemata) which can be explored at later stages of the therapy. CBT at the schematic level is thought to enable clients to alter their self-perception and the world within which they exist, and it is this phase that Beck postulated would prevent future susceptibility to relapse.

Most CB therapists practise in this way, with interventions initially aimed at the present and most overt problems followed by work on the client's thinking, mood and behaviours. There is a widespread assumption, not yet supported by empirical evidence, that alterations in cognition, mood or behaviour produce changes in core beliefs at the schematic level.

The first responsibility for the therapist is to carry out a thorough assessment and detailed case history in order to identify the priority problems. There are a number of different measuring tools, with many assessing specific diagnosis. For example, depression and anxiety inventories; self-harm risk scales; hierarchical avoidance tests; social interaction lists; psychological symptom identification; exposure to fear scores; sleeping diaries; activities logs; food intake records, and so on. The therapist can also utilise structured questionnaires, memory tests, medical results, and structured or semi-structured interviews.

The therapist needs to be adept at not arriving at a prejudgement – as likely to occur with inexperienced and experienced therapists; with the inexperienced because they lack the knowledge to utilise the right assessment tool from the myriad in the tool box, and with the experienced because they fall into the trap of assuming that there is a precedent of clients with similar presentations and therefore other assessment tools are not used with a new client. In other words, the therapist falls into their own patterns of interventions and forgets to explore other tools and their uses.

The therapist carries out assessments to arrive at a theory regarding the relationship between the client's cognition, mood and behaviour. This is necessary in order to formulate a treatment intervention. Sometimes, the client presentation allows for easier formulation, as the client is actively seeking treatment for specific issues arising out of assessment and interviews. Formulation is an important therapeutic skill because it prevents the simplistic approach of erroneously treating only the symptoms. This is the first phase (the surface level of identifying negative automatic thoughts), and it should be followed by a pre-planned treatment modality tackling intermediate level assumptions.

Following the assessment phase of therapeutic intervention, problems are often presented by clients on two levels: the *perceived* problem, which can be demonstrated by the client as the most distressing (anxiety, depression, phobias, fears, sleep disturbances and so on), and the *underlying, intermediate* problems that cause the perceived problem. These underlying cognitions are often presented as irrational beliefs about the self, relationships with others or relationships with the world. All three components of mood, thinking and behaviour can demonstrate the irrational underlying assumptions made by the client. A principle of CBT is that negative mood states invariably involve negative automatic thoughts and, in general, this combination inhibits the energy required to explore solutions. In early sessions, the client will often describe their problems in their own words whilst the therapist's role is to reflect on the relationships at the intermediate levels between thinking, feeling and behaviour.

The client's world-view, expressed through the cognition component, is a very common presenting problem and, whilst often described by clients in terms of their worsening problem-solving abilities (poorer reaction time to understanding incoming data, flawed thinking, repetitive and obsessive thoughts, intrusive ideas and difficulties with language utilisation), the cognitive domain can also include mental imagery, memories, fantasies, dreams and nightmares.

The behavioural component can best be described as the individual's motor movements, verbal and non-verbal actions and psychological responses. These include direct avoidance behaviours, as well as palpitations, nausea, perspiring, sleep disturbances, loss of appetite, obsessive or compulsive behaviours, and crying. Verbal and non-verbal behaviours include self-expression, continual requests for reassurance, self-pity, self-hugging and auto-touching (for example, nail or lip biting).

The mood component can be articulated within the CBT application as *feelings* identified by clients. These are often negative emotions such as feelings of fear, anxiety and depression, hopelessness, self-loathing and distaste, but they can also be joy, love, security and so on. However, most treatment interventions involve tackling negative mood descriptors. Following intervention at the surface level working on negative automatic thoughts, the intermediate level follows and works on the assumptions held by the client in one of the three components. CB therapists accept the premise that a successful outcome in one of the three components has a beneficial effect on the other two components.

Fundamental beliefs (at the core or schema level) are viewed as lifelong, relatively fixed traits, which have a direct causal link to the development of mood and stress adaption. Any problems or deficits in a person's underlying beliefs are responsible for difficulties in the perception of the self and interaction with the world. This can be expressed by clients emphasising alternate hopes or choices ('if only ...') and direct verbal protestations ('I'm ugly'; 'other people don't like me'). Nevertheless, the CB therapist recognises that whatever mode of expression is presented by the client, the problems at the underlying, fundamental beliefs level produce the intermediate level assumptions, which in turn influence the negative automatic thoughts.

It is interesting to note that CB clinicians adopt a different view to schema theory than those offered by mainstream, non-clinical psychological theorists. As far back as 1932, Bartlett (cited in Groome et. al., 1999) proposed that the individual makes sense of incoming perceptual data by comparing the new data with knowledge previously held in the memory. The new information is compared through its defining characteristics until a match is found. The knowledge held in the memory to aid the matching analysis is referred to as schema, and is close to the earlier gestalt theory. (Gestalt theory suggests that the individual will add existing information to incoming data so that knowledge of what is perceived can be expanded.) Schema theory developed into the view that both perception and memory of perception can be changed to fit the view required by existing schemas. Each person makes sense of similar stimuli experienced by another from their own unique set of knowledge, experiences and memories and will therefore perceive things in a different way.

Both schema and gestalt theories are integral to the development of cognitive psychology. Whilst general psychology now emphasises perception within memory, attention, the visual field, language and computational models, the CBT application has centred on the relationship between cognition, mood and behaviour which are underlined by the individual's core beliefs.

CULTURAL CONTEXTS AND POWER

Inevitably, the issue of power occurs in any therapeutic relationship and CBT is no exception. The therapist should be trained and skilled in being transparent and explicit in presenting assessment tools and their results, in discussing case formulations and treatment regimes with clients and working with clients on what they (and not the therapist) see as their primary problems. CBT also requires client feedback to confirm issues around case formulations and to confirm that overt problems (such as negative automatic thought) are undergoing change. The therapist in turn helps the client to identify the components under scrutiny (cognition, mood or behaviour) and the immediate assumptions being challenged. The clients themselves are the only ones able to describe and present the underlying beliefs being explored, as well as the effects of alterations in their situation or environment. Without this feedback, therapy reverts to (outdated) behaviourism or therapist-based assumptions which, being unchallenged, lead to error-prone interventionism. In CBT, the therapeutic work is carried out within the general boundaries of the behavioural, cognitive or mood components, which in themselves help the client to have control of the therapeutic relationship, and certainly some control over its pace and direction.

CBT utilises therapeutic boundaries to help the client gain control of their identified stressors and the components in distress. This is why the therapeutic relationship is provided in a contractual form and why the therapist explains to the client the method of therapeutic intervention and the importance attached to feedback. The therapist also provides information on their own accountability – to their employing organisation, professional body and (to a high degree) their peer supervisor.

The basis of all therapeutic relationships, irrespective of the methodology, can be seen as one of trust between client and therapist, involving confidentiality, mutual sensitivity, the client's openness and feedback, and the therapist's expertise and transparency. There is a further responsibility on both sides to make time for each other, to hold discussions in an appropriate physical environment and for the therapist to care for and protect the vulnerable. The therapist also has a duty to adhere to a professional and ethical code, to maintain awareness of current developments and interventions, and to provide effective care. They should not abdicate the responsibility of ethical and cultural considerations; for example, the gender of the therapist when presented with a female victim of sexual assault or domestic abuse; the faith and beliefs of the therapist when presented with a client who follows deeply held faith rituals; the inclusion of an interpreter when presented with asylum seekers who have suffered great harm.

The therapeutic agreement or contract is an attempt to make explicit constraints in the use of power within the therapy process. The locus of control may often transfer from the client to the therapist in the very early stages of therapy, during the period of revelation and assessment. There is often a sense of relief expressed by clients as they unburden long-held assumptions and beliefs. However, by identifying the component (cognitive, behavioural and mood) that harbours the automatic thoughts, the client and therapist can begin the process of exploring different coping strategies. Thus, control in that area is passed back to the client. This shift of authority (from therapist back to client) and responsibility in dealing with the perceived problem within the component boundaries, not only alters the balance of power but also promotes client autonomy and self-trust. It is, therefore, an integral aspect of CBT that the feedback given by clients is used to highlight the control (and power) they are gaining over their perceived problems and their lessening reliance on the therapist. This regular reinforcement eventually leads to the termination of the therapeutic relationship as the therapist relinquishes power. The dominant principle in CBT of the therapist and client working together as a team (a principle which arose in response to the democratic movement in the 1960s) remains strong and helps to keep the issue of power at the forefront of CBT interventions.

WHAT STUDIES HAVE FOUND

A discussion on the cultural contexts and power within CBT cannot be fully undertaken without at least some reference to its popularity in present public-funded settings. Clinical effectiveness and resource efficiency are now firmly established as response mechanisms to public concern about government's spending practices (as demonstrated by NHS provision of talking therapies) but heavily influenced by guidelines published by the National Institute for Health and Clinical Excellence (NICE), which has produced a range of material stressing CBT as the recommended treatment therapy. For example, its guidelines on children and young people states that for those with mild depression, CBT should be offered for eight to twelve weeks. For severe depression, individual CBT (or interpersonal therapy or short-term family therapy) should be offered for a minimum of three months. These guidelines are being replicated across most mental health provision with CBT mentioned as a core intervention.

The issue of access and the NICE guidelines are in response to the wider application of CBT in a number of mental health settings. This has increased over the past few years. For example, Hawton et al. (1989) demonstrated the effectiveness of CBT with panic and generalised anxiety, phobias, obsession disorders, eating disorders, sexual dysfunctions, relationship problems, somatic problems and depression. A few years later, Haddock and Slade (1997) discussed the use of CBT with individuals experiencing psychotic disorders and, more recently, Murray and Cartwright-Hatton (2006) focused on child and adolescent mental health, whilst Free (2000) looked at CBT in group settings. Beck himself examined its application in personality disorders (Beck et al., 1990). Because CBT has demonstrated itself to be widely applicable and effective, it meets the first of two important requirements for public spending in the present health service. The ability of CBT to be effective has been shown in evidence-based studies which indicate that CBT provides a treatment effective in reducing client symptoms and consequent poor health, and results in a positive change in behaviour. This means the client requires less healthcare intervention, meeting the second public spending requirement: the efficiency of the therapy. CBT is relatively cost effective, particularly with its time-limit ethos of around eight to twelve sessions. This efficiency also makes it a therapy of choice for a number of independent healthcare providers. Free (2000) argues that it is an ethical responsibility for therapists to provide both effective and efficient therapy so that more people can access the treatment itself. CBT has demonstrated its dominance in these areas in recent times and is now being implemented within self-help groups as well as time-limited therapy.

STRENGTHS AND WEAKNESSES AND NEW DEVELOPMENTS IN THE APPROACH

New developments in cognitive behavioural therapy will be outside traditional mental health services. The clinical application of CBT will be more widespread with more emphasis on its use in supporting healthier lifestyles and general well-being. Within the government's public health agenda, for example, CBT could be used in programmes for smoking cessation, weight loss, exercise, nutrition, for rehabilitation or coping with cardiac conditions, arthritis and Type 1 diabetes, and more generally in schools and the community (perhaps with specific focus: home-based carers, relationships, work, careers or use of leisure time).

There are issues, however, that CBT needs to explore further, producing evidence for its effectiveness in these different settings. It needs to be compared with simple self-help guidance such as information and advice services. Even more difficult to implement is the evidence-based work which compares CBT with pharmacological treatments, although this is another development area, particularly for new CBT researchers.

Despite these new developments and the current tide of enthusiasm, cognitive behavioural therapy has other challenges for its implementation in healthcare. Its very popularity and applicability in so many general areas suggests that it may be subsumed as a therapeutic 'tool' within any form of counselling intervention from person-centred work to psychoanalysis. There is nothing wrong with this development, after all, CBT itself evolved in the 1960s by bringing cognitive and behavioural approaches together. Beck himself had been a practising psychoanalyst, and there are many CBT-related interventions currently being applied (i.e. Rational Emotive Therapy, psychoeducation, and brief therapy). It may be that CBT interventions are adopted in various phases of other therapies and that new practitioners drop CBT's theoretical view of personality development and apply other theories.

There is as yet no empirical evidence to clearly show underlying beliefs, and new work in neuropsychology and early childhood development may either support this premise or demonstrate that there is no evidence for it. The work on the three components of cognition, mood and behaviour indicate for CBT proponents that there *are* corresponding changes to irrational underlying beliefs, but how this works is not clear to date. CBT adherents assume there is a connection between underlying beliefs and the three components, but the difficulties in this area can be demonstrated by the ambiguity concerning whether irrational underlying beliefs actually change or are superseded by new, more rational beliefs. The jury is still out on this one.

Another corresponding area awaiting further research evidence is the work in the realms of schema itself. Ironically, as CBT becomes more adept at short bursts of therapy with its attendant cost efficiency, there may be less time to work with clients at the core level. Beck (1976) has stated that working with fundamental beliefs towards the end of therapy enables the individual to change themselves to an extent that makes them less susceptible to relapse. It is questionable whether future practitioners will have the time or resources to provide such schema work with partner clients. The rate of relapse and return rates for further treatments within CBT, as currently practised, also needs a more systematic assessment. It is not explicitly clear whether the therapist is actually working on negative automatic thoughts and the clients' assumptions at intermediate level (the three components and the situational/environmental factors). If there is a rising re-referral rate it may be due to therapists not working at core levels. This means that the client is actually just experiencing the same therapeutic intervention for a longer period without any beneficial effects. There is the risk that such individuals are classified as treatment resistant. Further work with clients experiencing chronic and enduring mental health problems requires more support from researchers and clinicians. Such work lies at the opposite spectrum of self-help and brief interventions. A comparative evaluation would not only provide useful data regarding schematic work but also the effectiveness of CBT over a longer time period.

Finally, the practice of maintenance therapy may be a useful companion to CBT interventions in chronic illnesses or long-term complex conditions and dual diagnosis. Maintenance therapy provides support in short sessions over a long period to individuals on a 'when required' basis. It is not offered as a long-term therapy but can be utilised for brief periods of illnesses or relapses, and uses CBT techniques for specific problems identified by the client. More work is required to evaluate the efficiency of maintenance therapy in conditions such as addiction, eating disorders, enduring mental health problems such as schizophrenia and bipolar disorders, chronic debilitating conditions and complex dual diagnosis.

Cognitive behavioural therapy is a counselling intervention with nearly half a century of empirical study supporting its application across a wide range of diagnosis and settings. It has a distinct body of theoretical assumptions supporting its clinical techniques and is shown to be an efficient and effective therapy. Its popularity has spread it beyond the clinical and educational environment in the last few years and it is now practised in both the workplace and social spheres such as sports and leisure. Its emphasis on learning and partnership is becoming more pronounced, and CBT may be utilised within or alongside person-centred and psychoanalytical approaches. In the future, as research develops, present therapeutic techniques may be integrated with other interventions by a multi-skilled therapist across a range of community environments.

REFERENCES

Bartlett, FC (1932) *Remembering.* Cambridge: Cambridge University Press.

Beck, AT (1976) *Cognitive Therapy and Emotional Disorders.* New York: International University Press Inc.

Beck, AT (1983) Cognitive therapy of depression: New perspectives. In PJ Clayton & JE Barrett (Eds) *Treatment of Depression: Old controversies and new approaches.* New York: Raven Press.

Beck, AT (2005) *Science and Practice of Cognitive Behavioural Therapy.* Oxford: Oxford University Press.

Beck, AT, Emery, G & Greenberg, RL (1985) *Anxiety Disorders and Phobias: Cognitive perspective.* New York: Basic Books.

Beck, AT, Freeman, A & Associates (1990) *Cognitive Therapy of Personality Disorders.* New York: Guilford Press.

Beck, JS (1995) *Cognitive Therapy: Basics and beyond.* New York: Guilford Press.

Bennett-Levy, J (2006) Therapist skills: A cognitive model of their acquisition and refinement. *Behavioural and Cognitive Therapy, 24* (1), 57–78.

Burns, DD (1989) Foreword. In JB Persons *Cognitive Therapy in Practice: A case formulation approach* (pp. vii–ix). New York: WW Norton & Co.

Clark, DM & Fairburn, CG (Eds) (2005) *Science and Practice of Cognitive Behavioural Therapy.* Oxford: Oxford University Press.

Ellis, A (1962) *Reason and Emotion in Psychotherapy.* New York: Lyle Stewart.

Ellis, A (1977) The basic clinical theory of rational-emotive therapy. In A Ellis & R Grieger (Eds) *Handbook of Rational-Emotive Therapy.* New York: Springer.

Free, ML (2000) *Cognitive Therapy in Groups.* Chichester: John Wiley & Sons Ltd.

Gelder, MG (1989) Foreword. In KJ Hawton, PM Salkovskis, J Kirk & DM Clarke (Eds) *Cognitive Behaviour Therapy for Psychiatric Problems: A practical guide* (pp. v–vi). Oxford: Oxford University Press.

Groome, D, Dewart, H, Esgate, A, Gurney, K, Kemp, R & Towell, N (1999) *An Introduction to Cognitive Psychology Processes and Disorders.* London: Psychology Press.

Haddock, G & Slade, PD (Eds) (1997) *Cognitive-Behavioural Interventions with Psychotic Disorders.* London: Routledge.

Hawton, KJ, Salkovskis, PM, Kirk, J & Clarke, DM (Eds) (1989) *Cognitive Behavioural Therapy for Psychiatric Problems: A practical guide.* Oxford: Oxford University Press.

Lazarus, A (1987) The multimodal approach with adult outpatients. In N Jacobsen (Ed) *Psychotherapists in Clinical Practice: Cognitive and behavioral perspectives* (pp. 286–326). New York: Guilford Press.

Meichenbaum, D (1977) *Cognitive Behavior Modification: An integrative approach.* New York: Plenum Press.

Murray, J & Cartwright-Hatton, S (2006) N.I.C.E. guidelines on treatment of depression in childhood and adolescence: Implications from a CBT perspective. *Behavioural and Cognitive Therapy, 34* (2), 129–37.

National Institute for Health and Clinical Excellence (2005) Depression in Children and Young People: Identification and management in primary, community and secondary care. Available from <http://www.nice.org.uk/guidance/index.jsp?action=byID&O=10970>

CHAPTER 9

THE RELATIONAL APPROACH

GEOFF PELHAM

BACKGROUND TO THE APPROACH

In the late twentieth century, there was a developing move away from the established unitary core model approaches to therapy as therapists sought to widen understanding of the therapeutic relationship (Paul & Pelham, 2000). The concept *relational* appeared in therapy literature in the 1980s and has increasingly appeared as an element of existing forms of therapy (e.g. Mackewn, 1997; Cornell & Hargaden, 2005; Mearns & Cooper, 2005) or as a form of therapy in itself (e.g. Paul & Pelham, 2000; DeYoung, 2003).

The central premise is: *it is through relationships that we become and maintain who we are, and it is through the therapeutic relationship that personal change can take place.*

This emergence of relational ideas has been described as a shift from 'one-person to two-person psychologies' (Mitchell, 1988: 5; Modell, 1984). One-person therapies view the person as entering the world 'pre-wired' with a fixed human nature that unfolds in an environment that either facilitates or distorts optimal growth. Such a view underpins the classical Freudian approach (with human nature based upon instincts of sex and aggression) and classical humanistic approaches (with human nature based upon self-actualisation). Two-person psychologies do not assume a fixed human nature; rather the self is formed in a matrix of close personal relations, in a process of co-creation of identities.

The relational challenge to classical Freudian psychoanalysis has a number of different sources. There are relational aspects in Freud's own work as, for example, his account of the formation of the superego (Freud, 1923). In the early days of psychoanalysis, relational ideas persistently reappeared, leading to the expulsion of many of Freud's closest colleagues, such as Adler, Rank and Ferenczi, as Freud was unable to tolerate deviations from his orthodoxy (Breger, 2000). In Britain from the 1930s onwards, the Object Relations School, including Klein, Winnicott, Fairbairn, Bion, Balint and Bowlby (attachment theory) radically transformed psychoanalysis (Greenberg & Mitchell, 1984) by introducing into the theory the importance of internal and external relations with others. Fairbairn put the challenge to classical psychoanalysis most starkly, saying that it is the desire for relationship, not drives of sex and aggression, which is at the heart of being human. Fairbairn quotes a statement by a patient that summed up the difference between classical and relational psychoanalysis: 'You're always talking about me wanting this and that desire satisfied, but what I really want is a father' (Fairbairn, 1952: 137).

In America, the challenge to Freud came from Harry Stack Sullivan (1953) who in the 1930s and 1940s developed a radically interpersonal psychoanalytic psychiatry, seeking to reformulate all concepts that referred to fixed processes and things inside the person (such as innate drives: id, ego, superego) into concepts based upon relations between people. Sullivan's approach, combined with the existential/Marxist ideas of Eric Fromm, form the basis for the flourishing contemporary interpersonal schools of psychodynamic therapy. In the 1980s, the relational theme was developed in new ways by Heinz Kohut's self-psychology, with the central concept of *self object*, focusing how the self is developed through relations with others. Kohut (1977) placed great emphasis on empathy in the therapeutic relationship, and careful exploration of this relationship led to the emergence of intersubjective theory (Storolow, Brandschaft & Atwood, 1987) in which the therapeutic relationship is described in terms of an *intersubjective field* created by both therapist and client. The first explicit references to relational approaches to psychotherapy emerged from psychoanalytic writers such as Stephen Mitchell in the 1980s.

Relational themes are important in humanistic therapies, again existing in tension with ideas of fixed human nature, particularly the notion of self-actualisation. In the client-centred approach, the initial exclusive focus in therapy on the internal world of the client, through unconditional positive regard and empathy (whereby the therapist as a person became as invisible as Freud's 'blank screen'), was transformed in a relational direction with the introduction of congruence (Lietaer, 1993). Gestalt has moved from the individualism of 'Perlsism' (Mackewn, 1997) to integrate the existential relational ideas of Buber's I–thou relationship, field theory, notions of dialogic relationship, as well as incorporating aspects of psychoanalytic self-psychology and intersubjectivity (Hycner & Jacobs, 1995). Relational strands in transactional analysis are described in Cornell and Hargaden (2005). Relational ideas have also provided the basis for theoretical integration across humanistic, existential and psychoanalytic approaches (Erskine, Moursund & Trautmann, 1999).

The relational themes in the various therapeutic approaches are supported by research in infant and child development. The work of Beebe and Lachmann (2002), Brazelton and Cramer (1991), Stern (1985) and many other authors, has shown in great detail the exquisite synchronicity of the interaction between infant and parents, and how the child's sense of self and manner of relating to others develops in the crucible of these early relationships.

Many different traditions have contributed to the notion of relational therapy. Amongst this variety there are common themes and concepts: relationship, relational patterns, co-creation, empathy, attunement dialogue, mutuality, interaction. The decisive step taken by relational theorists is to place the therapist into the therapeutic relationship, not as the incarnation of a particular method (e.g. the blank screen interpreting the client's free associations, or providing the core conditions) but as a full participant in co-creating the relationship. This step creates profound theoretical and clinical challenges (such as, how the therapist understands and accounts for their own contribution to the therapy?)

The notion of paradigm rather than approach is more appropriate to describe the position of relational concepts in contemporary therapy (Paul & Pelham, 2000). A paradigm (Kuhn, 1962) is not a unified theory, more a set of basic assumptions that allow for a variety of concepts and practices. Within the relational paradigm, differing positions have been taken on various aspects of the psychological development of the person and the implications of this for the therapeutic relationship (Clarkson, 1995; Mitchell, 1988, 1993, 1997, 2000). For example, from the psychoanalytic tradition, some writers (Winnicott, 1965; Kohut, 1984; Storolow & Lachmann, 1980) argue for a 'developmental arrest' position, i.e. that the growth of the client has been interrupted in childhood, and that the therapeutic task is to provide the facilitating environment that will address the deficit. This involves adapting the therapy to the growth needs of the client. A similar position is taken by therapists who explore the notion of 'relational needs' (Erskine et al., 1999). Other writers of an interpersonal stance, such as Levenson (1991) and Ehrenberg (1992) argue that the therapeutic relationship is co-created in the present moment by the client and therapist, and that therapeutic change comes through exploration of that relationship in the here and now.

Given the above, the account offered here is not *the* relational approach, rather a position within and drawing upon the resources of the relational paradigm. In this account, the primary human desire, as stated by Fairbairn, is for relationship with other people. The infant/young child develops their sense of self and the nature of relations with others through their experience with caregivers, relations that permeate to the very heart of their personality (Fraiberg, 1996; Stern, 1985).

The person organises their experience in ways that make sense of the world and their place in it, and provide ways of relating to others that meet the difficulties, dangers and opportunities of their world (described, for example, by Bowlby (1988) as forms of attachment). An important aspect of the self-organisation is the various means of protection from perceived threat to the sense of self and in relations with others (what Sullivan called 'security operations' (1953: 191) and Freud called – from an intrapsychic perspective – 'defence mechanisms'). The forms of self-organisation become central to personality and structure relations with self and other such that distinct patterns of relating develop that are carried into new relationships. A certain relational 'self-fulfilling prophecy' becomes apparent as familiar scenarios repeatedly emerge in a person's life. It is the difficulties in living that flow from a person's relational pattern that brings a person to therapy. These difficulties may be in the form of experiences of anxiety, depression, sense of loneliness and meaninglessness in life, or difficulties forming satisfying relations with others.

POSITION OF THERAPIST AND CLIENT

There are two interrelated aspects for the therapist to consider. The first aspect acknowledges the fundamental relational quality of meeting (as expressed, for example, in the work of Buber (1970) and other existential-humanistic writers). The challenge is to meet the client as a fellow human being (rather than a 'thing', e.g. a 'client' or a 'diagnosis') and offer a relationship that recognises and honours the other as a person. This recognition involves being respectful, honest, trustworthy, reliable, seeking an understanding of (empathy for) the client, and so forth. These qualities are attributes of good relating, whether as a therapist, teacher, friend or parent and, though fundamental, do not need to be transformed into something special that the therapist offers the client.

This position concurs with Peter Lomas (1994) who argues for the quality of 'ordinariness' (pp. 121–34) in the therapist's manner, rather than the therapist embodying a particular stance (neutrality, authenticity, dialogic). This 'ordinary' stance also includes the willingness, where appropriate, to share aspects of the therapist's experience. The message offered is something like: 'I recognise you as a fellow human being who has come with the hope of dealing with your problems in living, and I'll do my best to help you in this'.

The second aspect acknowledges that the client has come to a professional therapist and is indeed looking for that professional to offer something to help resolve current difficulties. This is an entirely reasonable position: the development of such expertise has been the reason for the therapist's extensive training. The therapist will encourage the client to explore the issues that brought him or her to therapy, with particular attention paid to areas of pain and conflict. The therapist will invite the client to go more deeply into their experience of difficulty, connecting with thoughts, fantasies, feelings and actions, and also noticing how the client seeks to protect himself from distress.

Whilst listening to and working with the client as described above, the therapist will also pay attention to the relational patterns that emerge in the client's material, relations internal to the client's psyche (such as self-criticism, management of feelings) and relations with others (such as anticipating criticism, desiring/fearing intimacy). These relational patterns can be complex – more like dramas, that catch the subtle relational tensions and conflicts of earlier family life (Mitchell, 1988) where the client is caught between competing and conflicting fears and desires. The therapist can draw attention to these patterns and then invite the client to explore them as they appear throughout their life.

For the client, the therapeutic relationship is, fundamentally, like any other relationship and can only be experienced in terms of familiar (familial) relational patterns. She or he will, then, enter and experience therapy in terms of these patterns, bringing the familiar hopes, fears, ways of managing the other, ways of protecting self, into this relationship (this is the relational meaning of the concept of transference).

The emergence of the client's forms of relating in the therapeutic relationship provides both the greatest opportunity for and the greatest challenge to the therapy. There is opportunity because the issues previously being discussed as located 'out there' in the world are now reappearing 'in here' with immediacy and emotional impact, providing the possibility for powerful therapeutic work. The challenge arises because these relational patterns are not communicated consciously and verbally but rather primarily, through unconscious communication and enactment (Casement, 1985), with the therapist perhaps being 'invited' to play the role of persons in the client's internal drama, or to experience what it is like to be the client in relation to these internal others.

The invitation to participate in the client's relational dramas can be experienced by the therapist as variously frightening, confusing, frustrating, exciting, anxiety-provoking, seductive, and so forth (the relational meaning of countertransference). It is here that the development of the therapist's self-awareness (through personal therapy, supervision, personal development groups, life experience) is absolutely crucial, as it is by this means that the therapist can recognise that her subjectivity is being drawn into the client's relational drama, and have an understanding of the interaction between the client's relational communications and her own internal world. Rather than enacting the drama, the therapist can invite the client to be curious as to what is happening in the relationship. There is the potential here for the client to experience something new and transforming if the familiar relational pattern is met not by the 'expected' response but by the therapist's desire to honestly and respectfully collaborate with the client as a fellow human being seeking to develop ways of relating to self and others that are more satisfying and fulfilling.

THERAPEUTIC INTERVENTIONS

The primary task of the therapist is to meet the client in a way that is, as much as possible, trustworthy, accepting, and so forth. The capacity to meet the client in this way depends to a large extent on the therapist's self-awareness of her own issues, anxieties and prejudices.

A further task is to assist the client to move more deeply into their experiences of difficulties in living, and to explore the relationships within which these difficulties were, and are, embedded. There is not a well-defined set of strategies or techniques for this task. The therapist can draw upon ways of working from across the spectrum of approaches to therapy. The primary consideration is clarity of intention for using a technique and also thoughtfulness about why it is being used now. For example, it sometimes happens that the therapist is drawn to using a technique ('doing something') to ward off anxiety in the relationship. In such circumstances, exploration of the anxiety is appropriate, whereas unreflective use of a technique is more of a 'security operation' (Sullivan, 1953) for the therapist and client. It must also be recognised that use of techniques has relational implications. For example, should the client's response to an invitation to engage in, say, empty-chair work or creative arts, be understood as a form of acquiescence, a desire to please the therapist, or excitement and curiosity engendered by the therapist's interest in the client? The offering and response to such an invitation by the therapist is never 'relationally neutral'.

The therapist is also listening for relational themes in the client's life and will seek to facilitate the client's exploration of these themes as they arose in early life, have reappeared or been transformed through life, and are significant in current relationships. The exploration of these themes as they appear in the therapeutic relationship is at the heart of the therapeutic process, as discussed above.

The relational approach offers a framework for practice, but its lack of specific directions for intervention is likely to generate some anxieties in the therapist in terms of 'what am I supposed to do now?' This is especially the case during training. The anxieties are likely to be exacerbated by the focus on the relationship as the heart of the therapeutic process, as the relational dynamics are often played out at an implicit, unconscious level, sometimes hard to grasp and frequently very challenging (a refrain from a Bob Dylan (1965) song catches some of the flavour of this experience: 'Because there's something going on but you don't know what it is …'). The holding and space for thinking offered by supervision is crucial in this form of therapy.

CULTURAL CONTEXTS, POWER AND CONCEPTUALISATION OF INDIVIDUAL DIFFERENCES

The client and therapist meet in a cultural context which shapes and informs their relationship. One important aspect of this context is that of *therapist as healer*. Frank and Frank (1993) in their comparative historical study of psychotherapy, explore this theme, viewing therapy as a practice that relates to traditions of healing across cultures. Central to healing is a belief in the power of the healer and the therapeutic procedures. The importance of this belief is recognised in accounts of the early years of psychotherapy (Caplan, 2001; Shorter, 1997), in accounts of the doctor–patient relationship (Shorter, 1991) and, in its more modern form, the extensive evidence of the role of placebo in medicine and therapy (Hubble, Duncan & Miller, 1999; Moerman, 2002). The archetypal figure of the therapist as healer may account for the many times that clients report some relief and hope through the sheer fact of meeting the therapist for the first time, before therapy has really started, and may also be a factor in what has been termed the 'power of the relationship' evident across therapies.

Terms like 'suggestion' or 'influence' have been used to account for the power of the healer. Though Freud's earliest work was steeped in suggestion through the use of hypnotism (Freud & Breuer, 1955), with the move to a 'one-person' psychology the possibility that the therapist influences the client became anathema to psychoanalysis. Similarly, humanistic therapists, with their belief that wisdom is to be found within the individual, were insistent that the therapist should not influence the client. Paradoxically, in what might be termed the return of the repressed, the power and influence of the leaders of these movements were elevated to cult-like status, with the capacity to transform peoples' lives.

The nature of the processes that come under the heading of influence and suggestion are not well understood, perhaps because they have been banished from consideration for many decades and overshadowed by a focus on differences in theory and technique. Relational therapies, which are based upon the mutuality and co-creation of the therapeutic relationship, must however, explore the issues of influence, not because it constitutes a problem but because it is an aspect of all relationships (including the family, education and politics).

One area where the issue of influence *is* addressed is in discussions of power in the therapeutic relationship. Within this context, influence is again viewed with suspicion, as it is recognised that clients can be susceptible to the influence of the therapist. Power is, however, an aspect of all relationships, and is not inherently good or bad. The refusal to exercise power can be as damaging as the abuse of power (Pitt-Aikens & Thomas-Ellis, 1990), as is evident in the lives of children whose caregivers have not set appropriate boundaries. A challenge for relational therapists is to know when and how to explicitly exercise power; for example, cautioning a client who is in a very vulnerable state about making major decisions that will significantly affect his life and the lives of others.

If the therapist knows the client is set on taking a course of action that is likely to be highly damaging to him or herself, or to others, should she step in and knowingly using her influence to interrupt the intended action? (Of course, ethical frameworks strongly suggest therapists should step in if there is likely to be serious harm.)

HOW THIS APPROACH HELPS OUR UNDERSTANDING OF THE THERAPEUTIC RELATIONSHIP

The relational approach has one defining assumption:

> Relations between people are the basis of social and individual life, and relational concepts are used to understand human life in all its complexity. (Paul & Pelham, 2000: iii)

The relational approach has shifted the focus from therapy as a process occurring between two separate individuals to a process that is co-constructed by therapist and client. This shift brings with it a sustained effort to understand relational processes in the development of the person and in the therapeutic relationship. Much of the extensive research into adult–child interaction has been explicitly within a relational perspective and has sought to apply the research findings to psychotherapy. Such research has deepened our understanding of concepts like intersubjectivity, co-creation, mutuality and reciprocity. It has demonstrated the processes whereby the caregiver influences the inner world of the child and in doing so helps form the inner landscape of the child (Stern, 1985). The research has also explored the reciprocal influence of the child on caregivers, including forms of implicit communication, such as tone and pitch of voice and non-verbal behaviour, by means of which the person comes to regulate their inner world and relations with others, including the therapist (Beebe & Lachmann, 2002).

Such research is very relevant to understanding the dynamics of the therapeutic relationship. For example, it contributes to understanding the power and importance of implicit communications as powerful channels of mutual influence and possible transformation. It also offers new ways of understanding the transference and countertransference, concepts which are still entangled with 'one-person' psychology (evidenced by the perennial question with regard to countertransference of 'which of these feelings belong to me, and which come from the client?' as if they can be parcelled out in this way). For example, Beebe and Lachmann (2002: 185–207) argue that relations between therapist and client can be understood in terms of 'self and other regulation'.

RESEARCH EVIDENCE

The relational approach is in full accord with research on child development, for example, in the literature on attachment (Karen, 1998) where the formation of patterns of relating are described, and the persistence of such patterns in later life explored. The detailed analysis of the development of the infant's subjectivity through relations with caregivers has been the focus of extensive research and explicitly linked to forms of psychotherapy in the relational tradition (Stern, 1985; Beebe & Lachmann, 2002).

Research on the effectiveness of therapy has robustly demonstrated that it is attributable to 'common factors' shared by various models and approaches to therapy (Asay & Lambert, 1999). On the basis of his review of the research literature, Lambert (1992: 97) concluded that improvement in therapy can be roughly attributed in the following way:

1. 40% to client variables and extra-therapeutic influences
2. 30% to the therapeutic relationship
3. 15% to expectancy and placebo effects
4. 15% to model-based techniques

Client variables, the most important 'common factor', include the quality of the client's involvement and investment in the therapy, their openness, motivation, reflexivity, resourcefulness, and so forth. From a relational perspective, this research underscores the importance of recognising that relationship involves the participation of at least two people, each contributing to the work, and it is an antidote to the assumption that the client is a somewhat passive recipient of the therapist's ministrations. The client is a proactive co-creator of the therapeutic relationship. Indeed research has shown how the client can actively seek to manage the content and direction of the work, including managing the therapist, when, from the client's perspective, the therapist has gone off track (Tallman & Bohart, 1999). The research also shows the importance of the resources and support available to the client in their everyday life (see below on the concept of *being-in-the-world*).

The research on the importance of the therapeutic relationship, expectancy and placebo (relevant to these discussions) provides valuable analysis of the many aspects of the relationship (such as empathy, self-disclosure, and impact of relational styles) relevant to the discussions above. Indeed, the results of further extensive reviews of research into the effectiveness of therapy under these headings (Hubble, Duncan & Miller, 1999) are fully compatible with a relational paradigm as a basis for psychotherapy.

DEFICITS IN THEORY

As discussed above, relational theory has pushed past the limits of 'one-person psychologies', developing 'two-person psychologies' that focus on the interaction of people – in particular, the interactions of close personal relations in the family. Theoretical priority is given to the relations between caregiver and child as the primary crucible in the formation of personality.

Relational theory is, in turn, limited in that social relations that go beyond two-person psychologies remain mostly beyond the scope of the theory. These wider social relations are not 'personal', rather they are impersonal in the sense that they have a historical and cultural existence beyond the relations between particular individuals and do, to some extent, condition the more intimate personal relations. For example, forms of religion, embodied in sacred texts, myths, buildings, rituals, rites, clothes, foods, behaviour and so forth, are a powerful source of identity and direction in life. At the same time, religion cannot be understood in purely personal terms, rather, such understanding requires concepts and perspectives that encompass wider historical and cultural dynamics.

The limitations of two-person psychologies become apparent in a number of important areas of psychotherapy theory and practice. For example, relations of class, gender, ethnicity, disability, sexuality and so forth are addressed under the headings of difference and diversity. These are terms that are devoid of a sense of systematically related social relations that powerfully affect people.

Relations of gender, for example, involve more than just 'difference' or 'diversity', rather they are constitutive of identities, and generate dynamics of inclusion and exclusion, repression, exploitation and so forth. Unable to adequately theoretically grasp these wider social relations, relational theory tends to reduce them to familiar 'two-person' terms. In this view, difference and diversity are problems situated in the particular relationship of therapist and client. The difficulties are created primarily by the therapist's personal limitations, i.e. her prejudice and lack of knowledge. If the therapist can work through her prejudices and become more knowledgeable, then the difficulties of difference and diversity can be overcome. The inadequacy of this formulation is signalled by the perpetual and pervasive fear in practitioners that they will 'get it wrong', that their prejudice will slip out in something they say or do, creating a sense of guilt and shame and perhaps leading to a complaint. It is clear that working through personal prejudice and developing knowledge is important, but acknowledgment is also required that these relations, whilst constitutive of identity, are generated in social and political relations wider than particular dyads or small groups.

The limited focus on close personal relations reappears in accounts of the sources and effectiveness of change in therapy. In theory and practice there is an implicit assumed equivalence between the source of problems in early life (close family relations) and the curative power of the close, intense personal experience of the therapeutic relationship. In this view, close personal relationships (first of all in the family and later in therapy) are both the source and the cure for difficulties in living. Again, aspects of life that cannot be encompassed in these 'two-person' terms (such as unemployment, financial hardship, crime, discrimination) are hard to adequately address. The significance and nature of these events tend to be understood in terms of the client's personal attitudes and reactions to them, as if changing the client's mind and behaviour can transform their impact on his life. The inadequacy of this formulation is signalled by the explanations offered as to why clients do not change aspects of their lives during therapy. Such explanations are usually couched in terms of either the client's personality and intra-psychic dynamics, or the inadequacies of the therapist and/or their method (hence the 'evidence-based practice' approach, as if the secrets of change lie in particular methodologies). Attention is rarely paid to the power of social relations outside the scope of influence of the therapeutic relationship to generate and maintain particular difficulties in living (Smail, 2001, 2005).

For example, there is a dramatic increase in the diagnosis of attention-deficit hyperactivity disorder (ADHD), symptoms of which include difficulties in attention span and behaviour. Explanations for ADHD are primarily in terms of biology (neurotransmitters) or the effect of close personal relations (inadequate parenting), with treatment either through medication or psychotherapy. Much research in psychotherapy on ADHD is about which approach is most effective (Roth & Fonagy, 2005), as if the correct 'dose' of the right therapy will cure the condition. Left out of the discussion is an adequate analysis of the social conditions that may generate and sustain ways of living described by ADHD. We live in a world where commerce is driven by slogans of having our desires met ever quicker: we should have what we want and we should have it now. Deferred gratification is a notion of a bygone age. Activities such as video/computer games, television and radio with multiple channels, internet and fast foods, indicate a lifestyle where attention span is ever reducing. It can be said that we live in an attention-deficit hyperactive society (DeGrandpre, 1999) and there is a resonance between the inner and outer worlds of people. Understanding and 'treatment' of ADHD will always be inadequate if the focus is primarily on the inner world with little attention to the culture in which it appears.

In summary, it could be said that relational theory is not relational enough. There has been a shift from one-person to two-person psychologies, but two-person psychology is in turn limited, as the real world involves social relations that are not reducible to close personal relations between people.

NEW DEVELOPMENTS IN THE APPROACH

Relational therapy, if it is to develop, needs to move beyond two-person psychology, to a theoretical base that grasps the totality of our social, relational existence. The existential philosophy of Heidegger offers the possibility of addressing this totality. The philosophy of Descartes has dominated Western thinking, including psychotherapy:

> Perhaps the most basic Cartesian assumption is that human life goes on 'inside', not 'outside'. There is a special sphere in which human existence takes place,

> which we may call the mind, the subject, consciousness, the ego or the self. Outside this 'subjective sphere', there are, or may be, 'external objects'.
> (Polt, 1999: 55)

Heidegger challenged this philosophy that creates a separation between mind and the external world and, in doing so, prioritises mind. He used the expression *Dasein* to refer to human beings. Dasein means *being-in-the-world*. Dasein is always/already 'dwelling' in the world. Our being comes through living/acting in the world that is already a totality of relations, meanings, identities and activities. From this perspective, being-in-the-world precedes and gives rise to our thinking, feeling and doing: there is no radical split between mind and the world, rather a constant interpenetration of these two aspects of being. Heidegger (1962) offers a detailed analysis of how even our most private thoughts and feelings are inextricably interwoven with the world we live in.

From this perspective, rather than a focus on 'the mind' (or psyche) as a distinct separate realm, the focus would be on our being-in-the-world, and the world-we-are-being-in. For example, relations of class, sexuality, gender, ethnicity and so forth *are our being* in all the complexity, possibilities, conflicts and contradictions of the world we are being in. The inner journey, familiar in therapy, also needs to be accompanied by an outer journey to understand the nature of the world we live in that has shaped us. Changing our being-in-the-world will not be just changing our mind but, rather, addressing our stance in the world and the world we live in.

SUMMARY

The relational paradigm has emerged in the past two decades, drawing upon the recognition of the importance of relationship in many different approaches to psychotherapy. The concept of 'relational' is now in common parlance across the range of therapies. It is an approach that invites exploration of the nature and dynamics of relationships and their importance in the development of the person, difficulties in living, and the therapeutic process. It is argued here that though a significant development on 'one-person' therapies, relational 'two-person' therapies are, in turn, limited by the horizon of close personal relation. The challenge, therefore, for all approaches that embrace a relational focus is to encompass wider social relations, with particular reference to race, class, sexuality, gender and disability.

REFERENCES

Asay, T & Lambert, P (1999) The empirical case for the common factors. In M Hubble, B Duncan & S Miller (Eds) *The Heart and Soul of Change* (pp. 33–55). Washington, DC: American Psychological Association.

Beebe, B & Lachmann, FM (2002) *Infant Research and Adult Treatment.* Hillsdale, NJ: The Analytic Press.

Bowlby, J (1988) *A Secure Base.* London: Routledge.

Brazelton, TB & Cramer, BG (1991) *The Earliest Relationship.* London: Karnac Books.

Breger, L (2000) *Freud: Darkness in the midst of vision.* New York: John Wiley & Sons.

Buber, M (1970) *I and Thou.* Edinburgh: T & T Clarke.

Caplan, E (2001) *Mindgames.* Berkeley, CA: University of California Press.

Casement, P (1985) *On Learning from the Patient.* London/New York: Tavistock Publications.

Clarkson, P (1995) *The Therapeutic Relationship.* London: Whurr.

Cornell, WF & Hargaden, H (Eds) (2005) *From Transactions to Relations: The emergence of a relational paradigm in transactional analysis.* Chadlington: Haddon Press.

DeGrandpre, RJ (1999) *Ritalin Nation.* New York: W W Norton & Co.

DeYoung, P (2003) *Relational Psychotherapy: A primer.* Hove: Brunner Routledge.

Dylan, B (1965) 'Ballad of a Thin Man': *Highway 61 Revisited.* New York: Columbia Studios.

Ehrenberg, D (1992) *The Intimate Edge.* New York: WW Norton & Co.

Erskine, RG, Moursund, JP & Trautmann, RL (1999) *Beyond Empathy: A therapy of contact-in-relationship.* London: Brunner-Mazel.

Fairbairn, RD (1952) *Psychoanalytic Studies of the Personality.* London: Routledge & Kegan Paul.

Fraiberg, SH (1996) *The Magic Years.* New York: Simon & Schuster.

Frank, J & Frank J (1993) *Persuasion and Healing.* Baltimore, MD: John Hopkins University Press.

Freud, S (1923) The Ego and the Id. *Standard Edition of the Complete Psychological Works of Sigmund Freud, XIV,* 237–58. London: Hogarth Press.

Freud, S & Breuer, J (1955) Studies in hysteria. *Standard Edition of the Complete Psychological Works of Sigmund Freud, XI.* London: Hogarth Press

Greenberg, J & Mitchell, SA (1983) *Object Relations in Psychoanalytic Theory.* Cambridge, MA: Harvard University Press.

Heidegger, M (1962) *Being and Time* (Trans J Macquarrie & E Robinson). Oxford: Blackwell Publishing.

Hubble, M, Duncan, B & Miller, S (1999) *The Heart and Soul of Change.* Washington, DC: American Psychological Association.

Hycner, R & Jacobs, L (1995) *The Healing Relationship in Gestalt Therapy: A dialogic/self.* New York: Gestalt Journal Press.

Karen, R (1998) *Becoming Attached.* Oxford: Oxford University Press.

Kohut, H (1977) *The Restoration of the Self.* New York: International Universities Press.

Kohut, H (1984) *How Does Analysis Cure?* Chicago, IL: University of Chicago Press.

Kuhn, TS (1962) *The Structure of Scientific Revolutions.* Chicago, IL: University of Chicago Press.

Lambert, MJ (1992) *Psychotherapy Outcome Research.* In JC Norcross & MR Goldfried (Eds) *Handbook of Psychotherapy Integration* (pp. 94–129). New York: Basic Books.

Levenson, E (1991) *The Purloined Self.* New York: William Alanson White Institute.

Lietaer, G (1993) Authenticity, congruence and transparency. In D Brazier (Ed) *Beyond Carl Rogers* (pp. 17–46). London: Constable.

Lomas, P (1994) *Cultivating Intuition: An introduction to psychotherapy.* Harmondsworth: Penguin Books.

Mackewn, J (1997) *Developing Gestalt Counselling.* London: Sage.

Mearns, D & Cooper, M (2005) *Working at Relational Depth in Counselling and Psychotherapy.* London: Sage.

Mitchell, S (1988) *Relational Concepts in Psychoanalysis.* Cambridge, MA: Harvard University Press.

Mitchell, S (1993) *Hope and Dread in Psychoanalysis.* New York: Basic Books.

Mitchell, S (1997) *Influence and Autonomy in Psychoanalysis.* Hillsdale, NJ: The Analytic Press.

Mitchell, S (2000) *Relationality: From attachment to intersubjectivity.* Hillsdale, NJ: The Analytic Press.

Modell, AH (1984) *Psychoanalysis in a New Context.* New York: International Universities Press.

Moerman, D (2002) *Meaning, Medicine and the 'Placebo Effect'.* Cambridge, MA: Cambridge University Press.

Paul, S & Pelham, G (2000) A relational approach to therapy. In S Palmer & R Woolfe (Eds) *Integrative and Eclectic Counselling and Psychotherapy* (pp. 110–26). London: Sage.

Pitt-Aikens, T & Thomas-Ellis, A (1990) *The Loss of Good Authority.* London: Penguin Books.

Polt, R (1999) *Heidegger.* London/New York: Routledge.

Roth, A & Fonagy, P (2005) *What Works for Whom?* New York: Guilford Press.

Shorter, E (1991) *Doctors and their Patients.* New Brunswick, NJ: Transaction Publishers.

Shorter, E (1997) *A History of Psychiatry.* New York: John Wiley & Sons.

Smail, D (2001) *The Nature of Unhappiness.* London: Robinson.

Smail, D (2005) *Power, Interest and Psychology: Elements of a social materialist understanding of distress.* Ross-on-Wye: PCCS Books.

Stern, DN (1985) *The Interpersonal World of the Infant.* New York: Basic Books.

Storolow, RD, Brandschaft, B & Atwood, GE (1987) *Psychoanalytic Treatment: An intersubjective approach.* Hillsdale, NJ: The Analytic Press.

Storolow, R & Lachmann F (1980) *Psychoanalysis of Developmental Arrests.* New York: International University Press.

Sullivan HS (1953) *The Interpersonal Theory of Psychiatry.* New York: Basic Books.

Tallman, K & Bohart, AC (1999) The client as a common factor: Clients as self-healers. In M Hubble, B Duncan & S Miller (Eds) *The Heart and Soul of Change* (pp. 91–132). Washington, DC: American Psychological Association.

Winnicott, D (1965) *The Maturational Process and the Facilitating Environment.* New York: International Universities Press.

CHAPTER 10

TRANSPERSONAL DIMENSIONS OF THE THERAPEUTIC RELATIONSHIP

JOHN SHIERS
STEPHEN PAUL

BACKGROUND TO THE APPROACH

The word *transpersonal* means beyond (or through) the personal. It refers to experiences in which there is an expansion beyond our ordinary sense of self and a feeling of connection to a larger, more meaningful reality. Religious or spiritual experience is often seen as central to the transpersonal agenda, although the transpersonal can also be about expanding our concern for (or our sense of identification with) other people, humankind, life, the planet or nature. (British Psychological Society, n.d.)

Transpersonal psychology as a specific modality originated in the USA. It grew from the collaboration of a group of primarily humanistic and existential psychological researchers and clinicians. They concluded that humanistic psychology (considered the 'third force' in psychology to distinguish it from psychoanalysis and behaviourism) had not addressed states of consciousness outside ordinary everyday experience. These include:

- peak experiences of beauty, awe, wonder, ecstasy
- creativity which emerges from self-actualised individuals
- altered states of consciousness occurring particularly in Eastern spiritual practices such as meditation and yoga
- the 'doors of perception' opened by psychedelic substances such as LSD, mescaline and peyote
- indigenous and tribal cultures, such Native American and Aboriginal, where human beings live in close connection to nature and feel intrinsically part of the process of life.

The *Journal of Transpersonal Psychology* was established in the USA in 1969. This was the first time the transpersonal name reached the wider professional and public domain. It was further consolidated when the Association for Transpersonal Psychology was formed in 1972. The term 'transpersonal' was, however, first used by William James at the turn of the twentieth century.[1] It was also prefigured in the work of Carl Jung [2] and by Roberto Assagioli in developing his psychosynthesis model.[3] Abraham Maslow, Victor Frankl, Anthony Sutich, Stanislav Grof and Michael Murphy were key figures in its foundation (Sutich, 1969; Hastings, 1999).

Michael Daniels identifies some of the key intellectual influences in the development of transpersonal psychology to be:

- William James (1986) in his groundbreaking work on paranormal experiences and the varieties of religious experience.

- Aldous Huxley (1942), from his investigations into consciousness expansion using mescaline and his presentation of the 'perennial philosophy'– the hidden unifying core – which he held was at the heart of all the world's spiritual traditions.

- Teilhard de Chardin, who developed a model of the evolution of consciousness, integrating biological science with Christian spirituality.

- Sri Aurobindo, who, based in India, created a spiritual philosophy called 'integral yoga', which placed the evolution of consciousness as the core purpose of the evolutionary process.

- Carl Jung, who introduced the concepts of the collective unconscious and archetypes, and sought to understand religious archetypes from a psychological perspective.

- Abraham Maslow (1968), through his studies of self-actualisation, peak experiences, self-transcendence and metamotivation.

- Stanislav Grof, through his carefully researched explorations in the 1950s and 60s of the healing transpersonal impact of working with non-ordinary states of consciousness induced by the clinical use of the drug LSD. In the 1970s, in collaboration with his wife Christina Grof, he developed a natural process of supporting non-ordinary states of consciousness called Holotropic Breathwork™ .

- Roberto Assagioli, the founder of psychosynthesis. Assagioli provided the first comprehensive model of psychological development from the Freudian unconscious to the humanistic emphasis on the immediacy of experience, to the Jungian and existential search for meaning and individuation, to the transpersonal ground which holds, in his view, the whole developmental process.

- Charles Tart, who has pioneered empirical research into altered states of consciousness.

---

1. Michael Daniels points out that James is the first person known to have used the word 'transpersonal' in a 1905 Harvard course syllabus (Daniels, 2005: 17)

2. Rowan (2005: 30) notes that Jung used the word 'transpersonal' in his essay 'The structure of the unconscious' published in France in 1916 (Jung, 1943, para. 454). He did not, however, use it in the same way as later transpersonal theorists, as became clear in a revised version of the essay published in 1943 (ibid., para. 103) in which he equates the transpersonal with the collective unconscious.

3. Assagioli had a close relationship with, and had been deeply influenced by, both Abraham Maslow (1968, 1969) and Victor Frankl (Frankl, 1963). He was based in Italy rather than the USA and immediately embraced the term 'transpersonal' as more accessible than the term 'spiritual', which he had previously used in his work (Rowan, 2005: 11). He was also a member of the editorial board of the *Journal for Transpersonal Psychology* from its foundation until his death in 1974.

- Ken Wilber, the current leading theorist of transpersonal psychology (who now calls his approach 'integral' rather than transpersonal). Wilber, in a series of works from 1977 to today, has sought to chart the evolution of consciousness, integrating philosophies and psychologies of East and West, and the relationship between science and spirituality. His work has developed through five distinct stages and reflects different emphases in each of the stages (Daniels, 1996–2005).

It is also important to recognise the shift in scientific understanding which took place in the mid-twentieth century from the mechanistic 'Newtonian–Cartesian' world-view. This had informed both psychoanalytic and behaviourist attempts to make psychology scientific in the early decades of the twentieth century. By the late 1960s, the impact of Einstein's relativity theory and the emergence of quantum physics was permeating both professional and popular consciousness and enabling scientific investigation of a less rigid, quantifiable kind.

The term 'transpersonal' was chosen by its founders so that research and clinical work with states of consciousness experienced as 'transcendent' (connecting the individual with a sense of reality experienced as originating from more than the individual mind alone) could be investigated and cultivated outside of any specific religious or spiritual tradition. Very rapidly the intentions of this small group of serious researchers and clinicians to establish a fourth, more comprehensive, framework for psychology were disrupted by a 'bandwagon effect'; for a period, from the 1970s into the mid-80s, it seemed that any and every non-rational practice seeking wider legitimacy hitched itself to the transpersonal bandwagon.

The founders of transpersonal psychology wanted altered and non-ordinary states of consciousness acknowledged and investigated rather than automatically pathologised and dismissed. They were committed to serious research on states of consciousness and experiences rejected by mainstream psychology and to broadening clinical practice so that people experiencing altered states of consciousness were not automatically labelled psychotic. They did not, however, intend to open the door to approaches subject to far-fetched claims for self-transformation: unresearched and unsubstantiated by a wider community of transpersonal researchers and practitioners.

By the mid 1980s in the USA, the work of scholars and practitioners such as Roger Walsh, Frances Vaughan, Stanislav Grof, Charles Tart and Ken Wilber provided transpersonal psychology with theoretical frameworks and grounded clinical practice. The emphasis by then was on seeking to develop a distinct theory and practice informed by new developments in more mainstream fields of psychology and psychotherapy. Most fundamental was the recognition that exploring non-ordinary states of consciousness and cultivating meditative spiritual practices could not replace work at the 'basement' of the psyche around early egoic wounding and disturbed interpersonal functioning.

In the UK, transpersonal psychology was pioneered by Ian Gordon-Brown and Barbara Somers. The Centre for Transpersonal Psychology was established in 1973, seeking to integrate Assagioli's (1975) psychosynthesis models with Jungian depth psychology. A second transpersonal training organisation, The Centre for Counselling and Psychotherapy, was established in 1984. Psychosynthesis is the best known approach to transpersonal psychology in the UK, with centres in London established by Joan and Roger Evans and Diana Whitmore in the 1970s, and by Chris Robertson in the1980s.[4] These centres, though small in terms of the numbers of practitioners graduating from them, have led to the emergence of a distinctively British transpersonal tradition, heavily influenced by psychosynthesis. A Buddhist-influenced training centre, Karuna, was established in 1980s in Devon by Maura Sills, and other smaller training and professional development organisations have also been established in various parts of the UK. A Consciousness and Transpersonal Psychology Research Unit, undertaking research on transpersonal psychology, has also been established at Liverpool John Moores University, co-directed by Brian Lancaster and Michael Daniels.

In recent years, there have been important developments in both psychoanalytic (Eigen, 1998; Schermer, 2003) and humanistic theory and practice (Rowan, 2001). Petruska Clarkson (2002, 2003) and John Rowan (2001, 2005) in particular have played influential bridging roles between transpersonal thought and practice and other therapeutic traditions. In person-centred therapy, for example, a growing group of practitioners have developed concepts and practice related to the phenomena of presence, co-presence and synergy in client work (see Moore & Purton, 2006). John Heron (1998) has charted a person-centred approach to the transpersonal and to spiritual enquiry. The work of Caroline and David Brazier and the Amida Trust (Brazier, 1995; Brazier, 2003) has, significantly, added a Buddhist perspective to transpersonal literature. These developments point to an emerging climate in relational therapies, where old barriers between modalities are loosening and space is emerging for transpersonal experience to be validated and explored in the therapeutic relationship.

POSITION OF THE THERAPIST AND CLIENT

Early transpersonal practitioners often widened humanistic frameworks with a potpourri of experiential exercises derived from Eastern spiritualities, and a bewildering array of 'new age' approaches to cultivating spiritual consciousness. There was also confusion between the role of the therapist in facilitating the inner process of the client and the role of a spiritual teacher or director. In the early days of transpersonal psychology these roles were often intentionally blurred because spiritual experiences were seen as an essential component in realising human potential. There was little or no recognition of the impact of transference on the therapeutic relationship. The residues of this approach can still be seen today in the way some transpersonal practitioners describe their work and in a number of transpersonal psychology e-groups on the internet. Psychosynthesis was the most significant transpersonal

4. The Institute of Psychosynthesis (www.psychosynthesis.org), founded by Joan and Roger Evans, was established in 1973. The Psychosynthesis and Education Trust (www.psychosynthesis.edu) became a training centre directed by Diana Whitmore in 1980. Re-Vision Centre for Integrative Psychosynthesis (www.re-vision.org.uk) was established by Chris Robertson in 1988.

psychology to take a more grounded approach. Assagioli, who died in 1974, was clear that the transpersonal practitioner was to work through the relationship established with the client (whether the client was an individual or a group). He was also clear that the roles of therapist and spiritual teacher/director needed to be clearly differentiated. Influenced by Martin Buber (1987), and in the context of his own belief that life is essentially a journey to the realisation of a person's intrinsically spiritual nature, Assagioli (1975) viewed the 'I-Thou' relationship as a vital aspect of work with psychological distress.

The work of a range of transpersonal therapists and writers since the 1980s has contributed to a shift in the emphasis of transpersonal practice to one of recognising the need to balance 'height' and 'depth' in psychological work (Cortwright, 1997). The legacy of the push to 'instant enlightenment' in the late 1960s and 70s has been a recognition that many clients who are drawn to transpersonal experiences lack a 'good enough' container at the level of personality to deal with the challenges of living. They therefore seek to 'fly' to the spiritual to split off from the pain of damaged bonds in infancy and childhood. The work of Grof, with his emphasis on working with spiritual crisis and spiritual emergency has been particularly important in this respect. As transpersonal psychology has 'come of age', the centrality of relationship to the therapeutic process has been increasingly emphasised within all the approaches.

PSYCHOLOGICAL FACTORS IN THE RELATIONSHIP

In considering how transpersonal approaches address therapeutic change, Bryan Wittine suggests that transpersonal psychotherapy affirms:

a) the need for healing/growth on all levels of the spectrum of identity – egoic, existential, and transpersonal

b) the therapist's unfolding awareness of the Self, or deep centre of Being, and his or her spiritual perspective on life as central to the therapeutic process

c) the process of awakening from a lesser to a greater identity

d) the healing, restorative nature of inner awareness and intuition

e) the transformative potential in the therapeutic relationship not only for the client but for the therapist as well. (Wittine, 1993: 166)

Ken Wilber has made a series of distinctions between levels of psychological development which are now generally accepted in most transpersonal approaches.

- the pre-personal level: the stage of ego development and developmental disturbances in attachment, bonding and infancy;

- the personal level: the emergence of the sense of the separate self, or 'I', who acts from choice and inner authority in the world and who experiences existential issues of meaning, values and purpose in life.

121

- the transpersonal level: the sense that 'I' exists within a larger, interconnected whole. In early transpersonal work this was often conceptualised as an opening to the Higher Self represented as a transcendent source of universal wisdom. More recently, as Self (with a capital S) to illustrate Self-realisation as a developmental process and inner presence (Wilber, 1990).

The concept of 'bifocal vision' (Whitmore, 2004: 78) provides a helpful overview of the process of therapeutic change at the core of the practice of most contemporary transpersonal therapists. Bifocal vision requires the therapist to be holding two directions simultaneously. In one direction are the symptoms causing distress to the client and requiring empathic exploration through the medium of the therapeutic relationship. In the other direction is emergent possibility for growth and development. By therapist and client struggling together through the symptom, a deeper and more authentic expression of self emerges as the client starts to access a deeper relationship with the ground of their being, however this is conceptualised.

Elizabeth Wilde McCormick suggests the image of the 'vessel' of the therapist's awareness to describe the essence of the psychological dynamics between therapist and client in transpersonal therapy. The vital core of this vessel is:

> that it will withstand the struggles and fragmentation of personality, and difficult transferences will be able to bear the chill winds or suffocating cloaks of the past, and the fiery rages when the heat is on. This vessel holds the potential for fantasy – how I might have been, how it could be; for illumination, change, for healing, for transformation and the growth for love; for the ever present possibility of coming home to one's self and recognising it as such. (Wilde McCormick, 2000: 24)

THERAPEUTIC INTERVENTIONS

Frances Vaughan (Walsh & Vaughan, 1993: 60) makes a distinction between the context, content and process of transpersonal therapy.

- The context is established by the beliefs and values of the therapist.
- The content consists of the client's experience.
- The process is the encounter between therapist and client through which healing occurs.

Transpersonal approaches, irrespective of their different emphases, clearly recognise that *relationship* is at the heart of the therapeutic process. While there is a whole 'toolkit' of techniques, some specifically developed within a transpersonal framework, others integrated from other modalities, it is relationship not technique which constructs the 'safe ground' for deep work at pre-personal, personal and transpersonal levels.

Transpersonal practitioners differ in the aspects they choose to emphasise and in the value they place on techniques in therapy; in particular, whether transpersonal qualities can be 'evoked' through specific techniques. Whitmore summarises a range of techniques commonly used by transpersonal therapists to specifically explore and evoke the client's emerging potential and impulse for creative self-expression. These are:

- Cultivation of inner dialogue: the purpose of this technique is to guide the client in connecting with archetypes which hold deeper (arguably universal) potential for wisdom, meaning and regeneration.

- Evoking and developing desired qualities: the cultivation of transpersonal qualities (e.g. love, truth, beauty, wholeness, interconnectedness) which the client identifies as being of value in incorporating insights gained through therapy into their everyday life.

- Meditation: meditative techniques can be utilised to evoke a relaxed, purposeful and focused atmosphere to encourage a deepening of transpersonal perception (Whitmore, 2004: 138–142).

Whitmore emphasises how vital it is that techniques are not used as a substitute for relationship in therapy. The transpersonal therapist needs to develop the subtle skill of knowing when to 'stay with' the client's process (in what may be very painful and despairing places) and when a technique may be of value in opening the client further to their own deeper wisdom. In this sense, timing is everything. If a technique is introduced because the therapist finds the process of staying with the client's material too much to bear, it is likely to be of little value to the client, and may actually reopen their wound.

There is an increasing emphasis in transpersonal practice on minimising the use of techniques altogether (Wellings & McCormick, 2000). From this perspective, most clients who enter transpersonal therapy are holding deep fracturing and wounding at early egoic levels of their psyche (Firman & Gila, 1997, 2002). With clients where the ground for transpersonal work has been built, there is also a view, particularly from Buddhist-influenced practitioners, that the 'transpersonal' emerges within the 'inner knowing' that there is a deeper wisdom which can be accessed through mindful presence (Welwood, 2000). Seeking to 'evoke' transpersonal qualities or experiences may well take the client out of the here and now 'moment' with the therapist.

Working with 'shadow energies' in the therapeutic relationship (Wellings & McCormick, 2000) has become an increasingly important issue for transpersonal therapists. It is now more widely appreciated that shadow energies can erupt at any stage of development, and are characterised by the individual projecting onto others the 'bad' which is unbearable for the 'good' individual/group/organisation to acknowledge as also existing within themselves. Shadow work also reconnects transpersonal practitioners with some of the most profound insights from the Jungian and psychoanalytic traditions.

CULTURAL CONTEXTS, POWER AND CONCEPTUALISATION OF INDIVIDUAL DIFFERENCES

The theories influencing transpersonal work do draw on spiritual and philosophical traditions from many cultures, but they have primarily been developed by white males in the West. This should not devalue the important and pioneering work that has been done: women and non-white people have had a voice and played a role in the development of transpersonal psychology. The aspiration to a universal applicability for transpersonal psychology can only, however, be effectively met when the theory and practice has engaged with power, inequality and diversity more fundamentally than has been done to date. The origins of transpersonal psychology lie in the liberal values of West Coast USA in the late 1960s. There has been a tendency to assume that all people, women and men, black and white, gay and heterosexual, disabled and able bodied are of equal value; thus, they are considered without recognition of wounds of oppression and structural discrimination. This has been a useful corrective to the pathologisation and devaluation in earlier generations of psychology and psychoanalysis. The downside is that there is insufficient emphasis on the legacy and continued reality of discrimination and on the internalisation of wounds of oppression in the psyche. Transpersonal psychologies have, by and large, contributed little to these debates.

There has also been an absence of recognition of the impact of class on people's lives, or attempts to engage with the sorts of psychological distress that impacts on the everyday lives of people living in poverty. This imbalance reflects the reality that transpersonal therapy is largely privately practised in the UK and the USA with relatively affluent people. Whilst Wilber and Grof, writing from very different perspectives, have sought to link personal growth and development with the broader issues of the state of the world and the planet, these perspectives have not been integrated into most transpersonal theory and practice.

Wilber has brought together cross-disciplinary scholarship in order to demonstrate that human development is ultimately a process of consciousness development. It occurs in stages that both go beyond (transcend) and include (incorporate) previous stages of development. At any stage, we can have a 'state' of consciousness (non-ordinary experience) which connects us to the ultimate oneness which Wilber holds is the true nature of reality (what he calls 'one taste'). But we then immediately translate this back into the level of development and cultural meanings that have been reached both individually and collectively. He argues that transpersonal theory has ignored the stages of development and focused too much on states of consciousness alone. He calls this perspective integral post-metaphysics (Wilber, 2006: 231–74) and argues that it is essential to recognise the relational and intersubjective nature of all interpretations of reality if transpersonal approaches are to make an effective contribution to the complexity of social and cultural development in the world today.

Jorge Ferrer uses the image of an ocean with many shores (Ferrer, 2002: 133–57) to argue that the key developmental task facing human beings is one of coming into relationship with a multiplicity of different 'shores' (spiritualities, philosophies, world-views) which co-exist in the one 'ocean' (the Great Mystery at the heart of life). The core realisation is that the universe is in an ongoing process of development which we, as human beings, co-create through the way we act. For Ferrer, the challenge facing transpersonal practitioners is that of cultivating deeper levels of communication, dialogue and relationship. This challenge contains important implications for how transpersonal psychology addresses power, cultural difference and diversity. Cultivating relational qualities alongside recognition of developmental differences requires a clearer understanding of culture, power and diversity by transpersonal psychology. While the therapeutic process, of necessity, works with individuals and small groups, the state of life on the planet has from the start been a key concern of transpersonal practitioners. The interdependent nature of the life process means there can be no simple cut-off between self, others and nature. Given the perilous state of the planet at this time, perhaps the major contribution of transpersonal practitioners may be to make some contribution to a shift in consciousness from human beings living mainly as 'skin encapsulated egos' to interdependent beings on an interdependent planet in an interdependent cosmos.

STRENGTHS AND WEAKNESSES

Transpersonal therapy overtly deals with non-ordinary states of consciousness and spirituality in whatever forms they may arise in the therapeutic relationship. The therapist will not deny or pathologise spiritual phenomena or experiences that are outside everyday consciousness. There is a space to explore spirituality and non-ordinary experience phenomenologically and as an energy or presence both for the individual client and in the relationship between client and therapist. There is also space to explore the extent to which spiritual beliefs may be a form of retreat or escape from pain in the individual and/or in the culture. An additional strength in transpersonal psychology is the willingness of the therapist to be co-present with the client and jointly explore experiences that may be non-rational or seem 'crazed' in mainstream culture. Transpersonal therapists focus on being as fully present as possible, psychologically, to meet the client in the therapeutic encounter. There is a willingness to go with the client into any part of their being or experience, with no need to retain an objective theoretical stance. This willingness to join with the other in this way creates an energetic synergy.

Challenges which may be made to transpersonal practice can be summarised as:

1. Different expectations on both sides in the therapeutic encounter not addressed at the start of the therapy create a block in the development of the therapeutic relationship.

2. The possible adherence of the therapist to a road-map approach to development is not congruent with the client's frame of reference.

3. A transpersonal practitioner working at an explicitly spiritual level in a context where transpersonal aspirations are being used by the client to avoid the pain which brought them to therapy in the first place.

4. Linked to this (point 3), by focusing on techniques that encourage the client to look at spiritual dimensions *before* addressing unconscious dynamics and other psychological patterns, there may be an avoidance of early egoic wounding.

5. Certain sorts of transpersonal therapy may encourage 'magical thinking' rather than facing the reality of the situation.

6. In such a wide and, in some ways, all-embracing field many divergent groups may be considered transpersonal. It is therefore hard for the client to know exactly what sort of therapy they will receive when they go to a transpersonal therapist.

At a conceptual level transpersonal psychologies can be criticised for:

1. Not being grounded sufficiently to enable therapists to work with serious levels of psychological disturbance.

2. Providing theoretical maps of uncharted territory with little or no empirical basis in reality.

3. Being insufficiently attentive to the different experiences of gender and cultural difference in relation to transpersonal experience.

Further work is needed in the research of practice, the development of theory, and the training and supervision of therapists, to ensure transpersonal therapists are equipped for these challenges.

RESEARCH EVIDENCE

The founders of transpersonal psychology were clear that they had evidence for the existence of states of consciousness which, if understood and integrated, can have a transformative effect. They chose the word 'transpersonal' specifically because they wanted to investigate these states of consciousness with a spirit of enquiry rather than appealing to faith concepts to explain them. Most subsequent transpersonal psychology has conflated the words 'transpersonal' and 'spiritual', and has tended to assume the reality of spiritual states of consciousness with reference to Eastern or Western meditative or contemplative traditions; this potentially raises questions about the relationship between transpersonal psychology and religious and spiritual practice. In the broader field of transpersonal studies there is, however, a significant and growing body of research which seeks to explore and make meaning of transpersonal experience without reference to spiritual states. This body of work is, in turn, influencing transpersonal therapeutic practice. The nature of transpersonal enquiry means that scientific enquiry is usually hermeneutic.

This means that it:

> focuses upon explicating the human meaning of transpersonal phenomena ... knowledge of brain processes cannot explain the irreducible phenomenological

qualities of the experiences themselves, nor their meaning and significance to the person. (Daniels, 2005: 15)

Daniels (ibid.: 24) summarises some of the key areas of substantive transpersonal enquiry.

- Extensive research on altered states of consciousness and into the physiological and psychological effects of meditation.
- The attempt to define the nature and role of transpersonal psychology more carefully, including its relationship to other disciplines.
- The development of epistemologies and research methodologies more appropriate to its normative agenda and subject matter.
- The creation of intelligible theoretical models of transpersonal states, processes and events.
- Working to develop effective methods and practice guidelines for people seeking to explore the transpersonal.
- The development of transpersonal approaches to psychotherapy, counselling and psychiatry.

Wilber (1995, 1996, 2000, 2006) has made a serious and rigorous attempt to demonstrate that transpersonal explanations are not only experientially but also philosophically and scientifically (in the hermeneutic sense) sustainable. The integral framework he has developed – the all-quadrant, all-level (AQAL) model – is gaining acceptance in terms of its explanatory value to scholars outside the transpersonal and integral field. Grof (1985, 1993, 2000) has developed an extensive body of clinical research findings from several thousand of the patients he has worked with both in his early work with the clinical use of psychedelics and, for the past twenty years, through holotropic breathwork. These research findings provide an impressive body of clinical material demonstrating both the reality of transpersonal states and the value for clients in integrating pre-personal, personal and transpersonal realms of consciousness.

Brian Lancaster (2004) has undertaken significant research on the study of consciousness, seeking to demonstrate that neurophysiological, cognitive and neuropsychological explanations alone cannot account for the nature of spiritual-mystical experiences. He seeks to demonstrate that recent work in neuroscience suggests that consciousness is dependent on re-entrant neural pathways that influence the function of ascending neural fibres. The re-entrant system seeks to impose meaning on incoming information, culminating in the construction of the 'I' as the indexing system of the mind. True creativity is identified with the unbinding of the constraints that the 'I' imposes, which has significant parallels in spiritual and mystical literature (Lancaster, 2007).

Empirical research into the impact on clients of transpersonal counselling and psychotherapy has, however, been limited. Like all therapeutic modalities, weighing the balance between the therapeutic relationship itself and the specific transpersonal orientation is a complex matter. Grof's reports on the outcomes of work with patients in a transpersonal therapeutic context still remain the most comprehensive. There is, however, a field of clients and former clients of transpersonal therapists who do testify to the value they found in working with a therapist holding a transpersonal context. It is clearly an important research task to develop a solid evidential base around the effectiveness of different modes of transpersonal therapy in relation to the lives of clients who are recipients of it.

NEW DEVELOPMENTS IN THE APPROACH

Transpersonal psychology has found a place alongside other therapeutic modalities. There has been a mushrooming of interest in making space for spiritual experience in psychoanalysis (Eigen, 1998; Epstein, 1998), in person-centred psychotherapy (Thorne, 1991) and in humanistic therapy more generally (West, 2000). Jungian psychotherapy has always worked explicitly with spiritual concerns (Jung, 1933). There has been a growth in interest and significance of Buddhist-influenced psychologies in clinical practice (Wellings & McCormick, 2005; Welwood, 2000). A valid consideration is whether it is unhelpful to continue to use the 'transpersonal' label with its diversity of meaning. An increasing number (although still a minority) of psychological researchers and practitioners are open to working with spiritual and other non-ordinary states of consciousness within the therapeutic modality that they practise. Equally, transpersonal practitioners now generally stress the importance of the therapeutic relationship in their work rather than seeking to evoke specifically transpersonal or spiritual insights, unless a client explicitly seeks to work with them.

At the same time, a body of experience and clinical work has developed under the transpersonal framework. At its best, transpersonal therapists do, and have, opened new ground in the capacity to work across levels of pre-personal, personal and transpersonal development, without collapsing these levels into each other. Rowan (2005) makes a strong argument for the continued value of a specifically transpersonal orientation. He makes the case for the inclusion of the transpersonal as a dimension of all therapy, if the therapist is to deal with the client as a whole and present person. He also considers that it is possible to specialise in a transpersonal approach to specific states of consciousness that are appropriate to that approach. He argues that training in a specifically transpersonal approach allows the therapist to be more creative, adaptable and wide-ranging than any other counselling and psychotherapy modality.

A further question at the cutting edge of current transpersonal discussion is to what extent human development is based on universal stages that all individuals and societies must pass through. Although Wilber provides extensive evidence in his writings for this developmental perspective, it remains highly controversial. Experienced therapeutic practitioners generally find that the psyche is messy and disorganised; it is harder in clinical practice to divide it into neat developmental stages than when it is presented in a table in a book. Wilber accepts that although transpersonal states can occur at any level of development, they are interpreted back at the level of development the individual has reached. Grof and many other transpersonal psychotherapists argue that they have worked with many clients whose opening to spiritual or transpersonal states has moved and sometimes transformed their lives.

An issue present at the foundation of transpersonal psychology and resurfacing again in recent transpersonal writing (see Daniels, 2005) is whether holding a transpersonal context necessarily requires a spiritual explanation as opposed to a material explanation for transpersonal experience.

Wilber, Grof and the majority of transpersonal practitioners hold that, once the transpersonal is authentically experienced, it self-evidently leads to a spiritual understanding of the nature of reality. Daniels (2005) holds that it is important to welcome into the transpersonal field all those who have a felt sense of life being 'more than' material reality alone. He holds that the space for dialogue with different perspectives is essential for transpersonal practice. Transpersonal work should provide space for people to experience and to make sense for themselves of the 'mystery' at the heart of life. The skill of the therapist lies in holding the space for the client to engage, when the moment is right, with the mystery of that life journey. This reinforces the principle that relationship is at the heart of transpersonal therapy.

SUMMARY

This chapter has attempted to take the reader on a journey through the history of transpersonal psychology. It has sought to illustrate that, from the start, transpersonal practitioners have been growing and evolving themselves and in their work. The excessive optimism and avoidance of shadow energies of the early days (as well as some of the wildness and innovative creativity) has been replaced with a more grounded and deeper appreciation of both the light and dark aspects of human consciousness. There has been a developing awareness of the value of working creatively with difference both within the transpersonal field and with other therapeutic modalities. As a result, a rich and distinct contribution to therapeutic practice has been made by transpersonal counsellors and psychotherapists, with increasingly profound emphasis on the personal awareness of the therapist and the relationship itself.

REFERENCES

Assagioli, R (1975) *Psychosynthesis*. Wellingborough: Turnstone Press.

Brazier, C (2003) *Buddhist Psychology*. London: Constable & Robinson.

Brazier, D (1995) *Zen Therapy*. London: Constable & Robinson.

British Psychological Society (n.d), Transpersonal Psychology Section. <www.transpersonalpsych ology.org.uk> [Accessed 29 February 2008].

Buber, M (1987) *I and Thou*. Edinburgh: T & T Clark (Original work published 1933).

Clarkson, P (2002) *The Transpersonal Relationship in Psychotherapy*. London: Whurr.

Clarkson, P (2003) *The Therapeutic Relationship* (2nd edn). London: Whurr.

Cortwright, B (1997) *Psychotherapy and Spirit: Theory and practice in transpersonal psychotherapy*. Albany, NY: Suny.

Daniels, M (1996–2005) Introduction to Transpersonal Psychology. <http://www.mdani.demon.co.uk/trans/tranintro.htm> [Accessed 29 February 2008].

Daniels, M (2005) *Shadow, Self, Spirit: Essays in transpersonal psychology*. Exeter: Imprint Academic.

Eigen, M (1998) *The Psychoanalytic Mystic*. New York/London: Free Association Books.

Epstein, M (1998) *Going to Pieces without Falling Apart*. London: Thorsons.

Frankl, VE (1963) *Man's Search for Meaning: An introduction to logotherapy*. Boston, MA: Beacon Press.

Ferrer, JN (2002) *Revisioning Transpersonal Theory: A participatory vision of human spirituality*. Albany, NY: State University of New York Press.

Firman, J & Gila, A (1997) *The Primal Wound: A transpersonal view of trauma, addiction and growth*. Albany, NY: Suny.

Firman, J & Gila, A (2002) *Psychosynthesis: A psychology of the spirit*. Albany, NY: Suny.

Grof, S (1985) *Beyond the Brain: Birth, death and transcendence in psychotherapy*. Albany, NY: Suny.

Grof, S (1993) *The Holotropic Mind*. San Francisco, CA: Harper.

Grof, S (2000) *Psychology of the Future: Lessons from modern consciousness research*. Albany, NY: Suny.

Hastings, A (1999) Transpersonal psychology: The fourth force. In D Moss (Ed) *Humanistic and Transpersonal Psychology* (pp. 192–208). Westport, CT: Greenwood Press.

Heron, J (1998) *Sacred Science: Person-centred inquiry into the spiritual and the subtle*. Ross-on-Wye: PCCS Books.

Huxley, A (1942) *The Perennial Philosophy*. New York: Harper Brothers.

James, W (1986) *The Varieties of Religious Experience*. London: Penguin. (Original work published 1902)

Jung, CG (1933) *Modern Man in Search of a Soul*. New York: Harcourt Brace.

Jung, CG (1943) The structure of the unconscious. In *Collected Works. Vol. 7* (paras. 103 & 454) London: Routledge & Kegan Paul.

Lancaster, B (2004) *Approaches to Consciousness: The marriage of science and mysticism*. London: Palgrave Macmillan.

Lancaster, B (2007) The Unbound Mind: A neurocognitive approach to consciousness and creativity. Keynote presentation to Second International Conference on Consciousness, Theatre, Literature and the Arts, Aberystwyth, Wales.

Maslow, AH (1968). *Toward a Psychology of Being* (2nd edn). New York: Van Nostrand Rienhold.

Maslow, AH (1969) Theory Z. *Journal of Transpersonal Psychology, 1* (2), 31–47.

Moore, J & Purton, C (Eds) (2006) *Spirituality and Counselling: Experiential and theoretical perspectives.* Ross-on-Wye: PCCS Books.

Rowan, J (2001) *Ordinary Ecstasy: The dialectics of humanistic psychology* (3rd edn). London: Routledge.

Rowan, J (2005) *The Transpersonal* (2nd edn). London: Routledge.

Schermer, V (2003) *Spirit and Psyche: A new paradigm for psychology, psychoanalysis, and psychotherapy.* London/New York: Jessica Kingsley.

Sutich, A (1969) Some considerations regarding transpersonal psychology. *Journal of Transpersonal Psychology, 1* (1), 11–20.

Thorne, B (1991) *Person-Centred Counselling: Therapeutic and spiritual dimensions.* London: Whurr.

Walsh, R & Vaughan, F (Eds) (1993) *Paths Beyond Ego.* New York: JP Tarcher/Putnam.

Wellings, N & McCormick, E (2000) *Transpersonal Psychotherapy.* London/New York: Continuum.

Wellings, N & McCormick, E (2005) *Nothing to Lose: Psychotherapy, Buddhism and living life.* New York/London: Continuum.

Welwood, J (2000) *Toward a Psychology of Awakening.* Boston/London: Shambhala.

West, W (2000) *Psychotherapy and Spirituality.* London: Sage.

Wilber, K (1990) *Eye to Eye.* Boston/Shaftesbury: Shambhala.

Wilber, K (1995) *Sex, Ecology, Spirituality: The spirit of evolution.* Boston/London: Shambhala.

Wilber, K (1996) *A Brief History of Everything.* Dublin: Gill & Macmillan.

Wilber, K (2000) *Integral Psychology: Consciousness, spirit, psychology, therapy*. Boston/London: Shambhala.

Wilber, K (2006) *Integral Spirituality.* Boston/London: Shambhala.

Wilde McCormick, E (2000) The therapeutic relationship. In N Wellings & E McCormick *Transpersonal Psychotherapy* (pp. 20–51). London/New York: Continuum.

Whitmore, D (2004) *Psychosynthesis Counselling in Action* (3rd edn). London: Sage.

Wittine, B (1993) Assumptions of transpersonal psychotherapy. In R Walsh & F Vaughan (Eds) *Paths Beyond Ego* (pp. 165–71). New York: JP Tarcher/Putnam.

Chapter 11

THE THERAPEUTIC RELATIONSHIP
A RESEARCH INQUIRY

Jerold D. Bozarth
Noriko Motomasa

Research in psychotherapy has consistently raised the issue that the therapeutic relationship is a primary factor contributing to psychotherapy outcome. The relative importance of common factors, client expectancy, client extra-therapeutic change and technique, has been debated for over six decades (Lambert & Barley, 2002).

It was, arguably, not until the advent of humanistic psychotherapies that the relationship was identified as the curative factor in and of itself. Jesse Taft (1933), an associate of Otto Rank, was one of the first to discuss the dynamics of a controlled relationship. Later, the theory of client-centred therapy (Rogers, 1942, 1951, 1959) and the hypothesis of the necessary and sufficient conditions of therapeutic personality change (Rogers, 1957) cast a particular relationship as the curative factor.

More recently, there has been a compendium of studies that focus on relationships in therapy. Although our investigation concludes that the therapeutic relationship is, indeed, a variable related to positive therapeutic outcome and transcends therapeutic approaches, the nature of this concept is clouded by different underlying assumptions. For example, Gelso and Hayes (1998) extended the psychotherapy relationship from the theoretical formulations of Gelso and Carter (1985) in an examination of the components of relationships and their development in different systems, and what this meant in practice. They attempt to provide a balanced position that does not favour particular types of psychotherapy. However, their examination is contaminated with psychoanalytic bias when they define the psychotherapy relationship as:

1. the working alliance
2. the 'unrealistic' relationship in psychotherapy (transference and countertransference)
3. the 'real' relationship.

Although the importance of the relationship as a major contributor to psychotherapy outcome has come to the forefront, research reviewers often interpret the relationship as variables that the therapist can insert for the benefit of the client.

PROCESS OF INQUIRY

Our inquiry involved the following process: first, two different paradigms of psychotherapy are considered in determining the nature of the therapeutic relationship, one based on reactivity and the other on actualisation.

Second, an examination of research reviewed by the American Psychological Association Task Force on Supported Therapy Relationships (The ESR Task Force) (Norcross, 2001, 2002) provides a base for identifying appropriate quantitative (and a few rigorous qualitative) research studies. Most of these studies were published in the United States, and computer search engines did not identify studies outside the US that might have changed the ESR Task Force conclusions. The conclusions of the task force are considered as a reflection of the current views of most research on the therapeutic relationship. These conclusions have had significant influence on managed care and insurance company decisions in the US and influenced the direction of treatment approaches. The findings provide support for decision-making rationale in other countries as well.

Third, additional quantitative studies from 2002 to 2006 are searched through OCLC FirstSearch and EBSCO. This search did not result in additional studies that we considered significantly different from those reviewed by the ESR Task Force.

FUNDAMENTAL ASSUMPTIONS OF PSYCHOTHERAPY

Two paradigms of psychotherapy affect most research inquiry. The direction and conclusions of research on the therapeutic relationship are related to these two paradigms.

THE REACTIVE PARADIGM

The reactive view is that humans are primarily reactive either to external stimuli (e.g. behavioural) that reinforce behaviour, or they are reactive to internal stimuli identified as inner motivations (e.g. psychoanalytic). Cognitive behavioural theories constitute both external and internal reactive stimuli. The therapist's task is to guide the client towards ways to deal with the 'stimuli'.

THE ACTUALISING PARADIGM

This therapeutic paradigm assumes that individuals have an innate constructive tendency wherein the individual has the potential to actuate his or her psychological healing process (Rogers, 1959). Rogers (1957) postulated a particular relationship that is considered to be necessary and sufficient regardless of the therapeutic approach being utilised. He considered specific therapeutic approaches relevant only to the extent that certain psychological conditions are perceived by the client.

OPERATIONAL DEFINITIONS OF THE THERAPEUTIC RELATIONSHIP

The aims of the ESR committee provide us with a frame for examining the therapeutic relationship.

The ESR Task Force had dual aims for their project. These aims were to:

- identify elements of effective therapy relationships

- determine efficacious (this term is used by research investigators to refer to effective approaches that are believed to be supported by true research designs)[1] methods of customising or tailoring therapy to the individual patient on the basis of his or her non-diagnostic (referring to variables that are not in the psychiatric diagnostic manuals) characteristics.

These dual objectives attempt to address both the generality and the particularity of the therapy relationship (Norcross, 2002: 6).

The therapeutic relationship includes 'the traditional features of the therapy relationship; the alliance in individual therapy and cohesion in group therapy, and, for example, the Rogerian facilitative conditions – empathy, positive regard, and genuineness' (Norcross, 2001: 348). Second, the ESR Task Force defines the therapeutic relationship as the matching of specific 'elements' in order 'to tailor that relationship to the particulars of the specific patient' (Norcross, 2002: 6). For example, it might be determined that an African-American male therapist would be best for a particular client who has certain characteristics.

PARADIGMATIC ASSUMPTIONS

Research inquiry on the therapeutic relationship most often continues the reactive model by assuming that the therapist is the expert. For example, the therapist determines the type of relationship that should be offered to clients in much the same way that the therapist might identify particular techniques that are determined to be most helpful for a client. The ESR Task Force exemplifies this approach. Their assessment rests on only one paradigm of psychotherapy; i.e. the reactive paradigm.

The reactive paradigm is clearly manifested by the second aim of the ESR Task Force (i.e. tailoring the relationship to the client). The elements of the relationship become part and parcel of the reactive model. Thus, the elements are, necessarily, dependent on 'methods of customising' the client–therapist interaction. The ESR Task Force readily admits this formulation as it is pointed out that: 'The task force work tends to be 'therapist-centric' in minimising the client's relational contribution and self-healing process' (Norcross, 2001: 351).

Moreover, the first aim of the task force, to identify elements in therapy relationships, is affected by the dismissal of much of the research on common factors (Norcross, 2002) and dismissal of Rogers' postulate of the necessary and sufficient conditions for

---

1. A 'true research design' is the 'gold standard' of experimental design. It means that all the groups in the research are randomly selected.

therapeutic personality change. Fewer than 25 per cent of over three decades of studies on Rogers' 'necessary and sufficient' conditions were reviewed by the ESR Task Force. This is a problem because the extensive studies were about core conditions of personality changes in therapy relationships across various theoretical orientations. Thus, those studies should be thoroughly reviewed. Norcross offers a rationale for not including additional studies when he states:

> More fundamentally, we have moved past simplified notions of a limited and invariant set of necessary relationship conditions. Monolithic theories of change and one-size-fits-all therapy relationships are out; tailoring the therapy to the unique patient is in. (2002: 12)

However, Norcross' statement misses the point that the notion of the conditions is not monolithic but facilitates the client's personal way of tailoring her/his own therapy. To satisfy the conditions, therapists naturally attend each individual's frame of reference and specific client resources – far from one-size-fits-all.

The ESR Task Force acknowledges that client characteristics are stronger predictors of outcome than tailored techniques, but seem to be unaware of the actualising paradigm that intentionally embeds the client's frame of reference and 'extra-therapeutic' client resources. As well, the ESR Task Force glosses over the research finding that general elements of therapy relationships are more supported than customising elements, that is common factors (e.g. congruence, empathy, and acceptance) are more potent than specific factors (Cornelius-White, 2002).

ELEMENTS OF THE THERAPEUTIC RELATIONSHIP

The critical question for most investigators of the therapeutic relationship is related to the tailoring of the therapy relationship to an individual. The classic question was posed nearly forty years ago: 'What treatment, by whom, is most effective for this individual with that specific problem, and under which set of circumstances?' (Paul, 1967:111).

Amongst the customisation of the therapy relationship are a host of elements that are reported in the ESR Task Force report (see specific references in Norcross, 2001, 2002). These elements include resistance; functional impairment and coping style; stages of change; anaclitic/sociotropic and introjective/autonomous dimensions; expectations and preferences; assimilation of problematic experiences; attachment style; religions and spirituality; cultural and demographic diversity; and personality disorders.

Our review does not examine the above elements. Many of the areas investigated appear to us to be a stretch even with the tailoring of therapy to the individual patient. As noted by Paul's question, the basis for this eclectic determination is that different clients and different problems require different treatment. Likewise, it is implicitly as well as explicitly suggested that different relationships are to be determined for different clients with different problems.

An overview of the general elements considered to be relevant to the relationship is also delineated in the ESR Task Force committee report (see chapters in Norcross, 2002). These include: the alliance; cohesion in group psychotherapy; empathy; goal consensus and collaboration; positive regard; feedback; congruence; repairing alliance ruptures; self-disclosure; the management of countertransference; and relational interpretations.

The ESR Task Force (Norcross, 2001, 2002) offers a thorough review of the available research in these areas in the last decades up to 2001. However, many of the elements appear to us to be more related to particular theoretical positions rather than to clarification of the nature of the therapeutic relationship. The attempt to include most theoretical positions is well intended but, in our view, also misleading, due to the adherence of all of these positions to the reactive psychotherapeutic paradigm.

Our review includes 'empathy', 'unconditional positive regard', and 'congruence', which are central in Rogers' postulate of the 'Necessary and Sufficient Conditions of Therapeutic Personality Change' (Rogers, 1957). We examine 'the alliance' separately as an important sample element in the reactive paradigm, which is often presented as a synonym of the therapeutic relationship.

Although 'feedback' and 'self-disclosure' are also reported as being promising by the ESR Task Force, we consider these two elements to be specific behavioural areas of action. The other elements included in the ESR Task Force committee report are, in our view, more aligned with theoretical foundations of the reactive and therapist-driven view of the therapeutic relationship. Thus, we chose to not discuss the other elements in this paper.

THE THERAPEUTIC ALLIANCE

Therapeutic alliance is examined due to the consistent representation in recent reviews on the therapeutic relationship. Our view is that the therapeutic alliance is only important as a separate variable within the context of the reactive paradigm of therapy. It is simply part and parcel of the relationship in the context of the actualising paradigm.

The generic term, 'alliance' (also periodically referred to as 'the therapeutic alliance' and/or 'the working alliance') has slithered into being identified as one of the therapeutic ingredients shared across different theoretical orientations (Elliott, 2001; Smith & Glass, 1977; Wampold, 2001). One review concludes that 'the strongest evidence linking process to outcome concerns the therapeutic bond or alliance, reflecting more than 1,000 process-outcome findings' (Orlinsky, Grawe & Parks, 1994: 360). A later review (Horvath & Bedi, 2002) refers to a total of 2,055 research publications in reviews and electronic database searches between 1977 and 2000, and they note: 'The therapeutic relationship in general, and the alliance in particular, is the quintessential common ground shared by most psychotherapies' (p. 37). They further refer to the surge of interest in common factors as emanating from the impact of Rogers' theory of therapy and of the interest of psychodynamic and experiential theories on curative dynamics of the therapist-client interaction.

The alliance refers to 'the quality and strength of the collaborative relationship between client and therapist in therapy' (Horvath & Bedi, 2002: 41) and 'the quality of the alliance is an important element in successful, effective therapy' (ibid.: 61). In more direct terms, the more the therapist and client collaborate in therapy, the more likely that the outcome will be positive.

The meaning of collaboration, however, distinguishes the reactive and actualising paradigms from each other. These authors conclude that it is the therapist's role to assess 'the client's relational capacities, preferences, and evaluation of the quality of the relationship' (p. 60) as the therapist progressively negotiates the important and urgent challenge of 'the quality of the relationship' (ibid.) with the client. It is in this sense that the alliance must be forged first, 'including a collaborative agreement about the important strategies to be deployed as a part of the therapeutic work, before therapeutically sound interventions can be usefully implemented' (p. 60). The directive role of the therapist is held in place by the reactive paradigm. The increasing attention to the 'therapeutic alliance' results in a deflection of attention to critical elements of the therapeutic relationship, such as congruence, empathy, and unconditional positive regard. Over a dozen years ago, Sexton and Whiston (1994) did a comprehensive review of the 'counseling relationship'. Their view concurred with another review that exclaims: 'it is only the counselling relationship that has consistently been found to contribute to the success of the therapeutic process' (Orlinsky & Howard, 1986: 7).

Nevertheless, Sexton and Whiston (1994) shift away from the relationship as they convert the notion of 'relationship' to the notion of the 'therapeutic alliance'. The subtle shift is characteristic of most research reviews. The relationship is related to alliance and, in fact, converted to 'alliance' and defined as 'client noncompliance with treatment plans'. The 'therapeutic relationship' is not only founded on psychoanalytic assumptions of the model by Gelso and Carter (1985) but is replete with reference to studies by behaviourally oriented researchers. This has, in essence, become the model for investigating the therapeutic relationship. It is 'a stance of therapist expertise and method to dysfunctional treatment, even when the relationship is the focus of discussion' (Bozarth, 1998: 165).

THE NECESSARY AND SUFFICIENT CONDITIONS OF CARL ROGERS

Rogers (1957) was quite clear in his integration statement that he was *not* referring to one form of therapy. He was referring to 'conditions which apply to any situation in which constructive personality change occurs, whether we are thinking of classical psychoanalysis, or any of its modern offshoots, or Adlerian psychotherapy, or any other' (Rogers, 1959: 230). He further hypothesised 'that effective psychotherapy of any sort produces similar changes in personality and behaviour, and that a single set of preconditions is necessary' (Rogers, 1959: 231). Patterson (1985) has specifically referred to Rogers' conditions as 'the therapeutic relationship' while presenting the conditions as a universal form of therapy.

The specific formulation set forth by Rogers is delineated in Chapter 4 of this book. The formulation includes three of the conditions that are therapist conditions and usually considered general elements in research reviews (see Norcross, 2002). These conditions are therapist attitudes specifically labelled 'congruence', 'empathic understanding' and 'unconditional positive regard'.

CONGRUENCE

One review (Klein, Kolden, Michels & Chisholm-Stockard, 2002) succinctly summarises research on congruence. The authors review the results of 77 studies that depict a positive relationship in 34 per cent of the studies. They 'conclude that the evidence is likely to be more strongly supportive than appears at first glance of a positive relation between congruence/genuineness and psychotherapy outcome' (ibid.: 209). Similar observations were made by Patterson (1984).

Even in this otherwise balanced review, the bias of the reactive assumption of therapy shows itself when the authors summarise with a conclusion derived from two articles by behavioural researchers (Lampropoulos, 2000; Lazarus, 1993). These two articles (both lacking in their research data base) lead the authors (Klein et al., 2002) to conclude that therapist effectiveness requires 'tailoring of the congruence style according to the needs and expectations in order to maintain effectiveness' (Klein et al., 2002). Our view is that they would have been more accurate to maintain their conclusion in the preliminary summary of the report where they contend: 'that there is both empirical and theoretical justification for congruence as a central component of a more complex conception of the therapy relationship' (Klein et al., 2001: 399).

The central component of congruence is succinctly defined by Rogers as 'the therapist's symbolization of his own experience in the relationship [being] accurate' (Rogers, 1959: 214). Rogers emphasises the importance of the wholeness of the therapist but concludes that 'part of the congruence of the therapist must be the experience of unconditional positive regard and the experience of empathic understanding' (ibid.: 215).

EMPATHIC UNDERSTANDING

Empathy has been given considerable attention as a therapeutic construct that stands alone. Rogers and colleagues submit empathy as a mainstay in therapy during the 1940s and 50s. With the advent of Rogers' (1957) 'integration statement' (Bozarth, 1998), research on empathy, congruence and unconditional positive regard continued for over three decades (Bozarth, Zimring & Tausch, 2002).

Empathy was the foundation of the Human Resource or Interpersonal Skills training programmes, popular during the 1960s and 70s (Carkhuff, 1969). A plethora of studies reporting positive results related to empathic understanding were reported in the counselling field. However, these studies are not usually identified, or not significantly noted, in research reviews of psychotherapy. Chapters in several major books dealing with empathy include few, if any, references to these studies (see Bozarth, Zimring & Tausch, 2002; Bohart & Greenberg, 1997; Cain & Seeman, 2002; Haugh & Merry, 2001; Norcross, 2002). Part of the reason for neglecting these studies may be that the interpersonal skills programmes changed to more behaviourally oriented activities that clouded the effects of empathy on outcome (Cormier & Cormier, 1991; Egan, 1975). Synthesis of the relation of empathy to psychotherapy outcome depicts empathy as accounting for nearly ten per cent of outcome variance (Bohart, Elliott, Greenberg & Watson, 2002; Greenberg, Elliott, Watson & Bohart, 2001). This compares to the two to eight per cent that accounted for technique interventions (Wampold, 2001). Greenberg et al. (2001) conclude that the most consistent evidence 'is that clients' perceptions of feeling understood by their therapists relate to outcome' (p. 383).

Bohart et al. (2002) point to empathy as a significant contribution to outcome but also provide another example of the influence of the fundamental assumption that the client is a reacting rather than an actualising individual. They speculate that types of empathic responses can be determined by therapists as they 'continually engage in process diagnoses to determine when and how to communicate empathic understanding and at what level to focus their empathic responses from one moment to the next' (ibid.: 102).

The actualising assumption of therapy rests on the client's process, not the therapist's assessment. Rogers' (1957, 1959) hypotheses are the most notable example, since they solely focus on the client's internal frame of reference. Rogers (1959) defines empathy in the following manner:

- Empathy (or empathic understanding) – 'to perceive the internal frame of reference of another with accuracy, and with the emotional components and meanings which pertain thereto, as if one were the other person, but without ever losing the "as if" condition' (p. 210).

In a re-formulation of this definition, Rogers (1975: 4) emphasises empathy as a process rather than a state. Rogers (Rogers & Russell, 2002) continued his postulate that the therapist's experiencing of unconditional positive regard and empathic understanding towards the client allowed and encouraged the client toward their own experiencing process. Rogers' (1959, 1975) definitions are central to many operatinal definitions of empathy in research studies.

UNCONDITIONAL POSITIVE REGARD

In client-centred therapy, unconditional positive regard is the factor that frees the client from 'conditions of worth' (Rogers, 1959: 224). Freed from the conditions of worth, the client no longer denies or distorts experiences and feelings that do not fit her self-structure. The client moves towards more constructive behaviour. One specific definition of unconditional positive regard is the following:

- Unconditional Positive Regard (UPR) – 'to perceive oneself as receiving positive regard is to perceive that of one's self-experiences none can be discriminated by the other individuals as more or less worthy of positive regard' (ibid.: 208).

Research reviews on UPR include delineation by Watson and Steckley (2001), Farber and Lane (2001), and Bozarth, Zimring and Tausch (2002). These reviews range from moderately to strongly supportive. However, studies of UPR seldom focus only on UPR. Most of the studies involve, and should involve, empathic understanding embedded in congruence. Like the reviews of empathy, support for the client's perception of unconditional positive regard is unequivocally supported (Cornelius-White, 2002). Rogers' (1957, 1959) sixth condition specifically emphasises that it is the client's perception of the conditions that is important.

OVERALL RESEARCH ON EMPATHY, UNCONDITIONAL POSITIVE REGARD AND CONGRUENCE

The reviews for the ESR Task Force (e.g. in Norcross, 2001, 2002) are positive, although skewed by their dedication to the reactive psychotherapeutic paradigm. One review in the ESR Task Force report further clarifies the importance of the therapeutic relationship and psychotherapy (Lambert & Barley, 2001, 2002). Their general conclusion is that 'decades of research indicate that the provision of therapy is an interpersonal process in which a main curative component is the nature of the therapeutic relationship' (2001: 357). Patterson (1984), in a review of reviews, concludes that 'research on the effectiveness of the relationship over a wide range of client conditions or problems provides a basis for a therapy which does not depend on identifying specific causal identifying factors' (p. 438).

THE SCIENTIFIC INQUIRY OF THE THERAPEUTIC RELATIONSHIP

It seems somewhat perplexing that adherents to Paul's question (what treatment, by whom, is most effective for this individual with that specific problem, and under which set of circumstances?) consider it to be the 'standard scientific question' after nearly 40 years of failure to specify different treatment for different clients with different problems. One examination of the research methodology concludes that 'the compelling question of what aspects of therapy work for what kinds of problems when practiced by what kinds of therapists for what kinds of patients is probably empirically unanswerable, because it is methodologically unsolvable' (Kish & Kroll, 1980: 406). Patterson (1989) points out that with only five classes of variables, each with ten levels, the result would include so many cells that the attempt would be unrealistic.

Patterson (e.g. Patterson, 1974, 1985; Patterson & Hidore, 1997) is the most prolific author, apart from Rogers, on the actualising paradigm of psychotherapy. Likewise, Bozarth and Motomasa (2005) conclude:

> [T]hat the common factors are embedded in the client/therapist relationship and the client's self-determination and own resources are the major contributors to therapeutic effectiveness. Client-centered principles have been integral parts of these factors and at the forefront in the exploration of common therapeutic factors. (p. 296)

RESEARCH CONCLUSIONS ON THE THERAPEUTIC RELATIONSHIP

Research on the therapeutic relationship reveals the extensive influence of the relationship on successful therapy. Research based on the reactive paradigm of therapy identifies a host of relationship variables that influence outcome. The reactive paradigm assumes that the most effective variables are to be determined by the therapist's assessment. The actualising paradigm is founded on the freeing of the client from societal conditions. In short, the relationship contributes significantly more to successful therapy than technique or strategy regardless of which paradigm is being considered.

Our review suggests that the premise of therapy as a reactive paradigm guides most research reviews. What seems to be the most accepted definition appears adequate although vague: 'The relationship is the feelings and attitudes that therapist and client have toward one another, and the manner in which these are expressed' (Gelso & Carter, 1985). The definition becomes problematic when the aims are embedded in therapist expertise combined with presumptions about determining just how the therapist might 'tailor-make' the relationship to meet client needs. Consequently, the operational definition becomes one that ignores the assumption of the actualising individual and establishes the reactive paradigm as the only realistic approach.

The 'aims' of inquiry in the actualising paradigm are no longer those of identifying elements of effective therapy relationships and determining efficacious methods of customising tailor-made therapy. Rather, the aims are to create an environment of freedom. This environment is identified by Rogers' (1957) postulate of the 'necessary and sufficient conditions for therapeutic personality change'.

The conditions of congruence, unconditional positive regard, and empathic understanding postulated by Rogers are not 'elements' to be tailored to the client. Instead they are attitudes that facilitate the relationship through the client's development of increased unconditional positive self-regard. The relationship frees the client to move toward constructive ways of living.

SUMMARY

Research on the therapeutic relationship was reviewed with a focus on research identified by the American Psychological Association Task Force Committee on Empirically Supported Relationships.

Our analysis concludes: (1) that there is strong influence of the empathic, congruent and unconditional relationship, as perceived by the client, on successful therapy; and (2) that existing reviews of research are overwhelmingly biased toward one paradigm of psychotherapy: namely, the paradigm of reactive psychotherapy predicated largely on behavioural and psychoanalytic concepts under the auspices of 'integration'. Orlinsky (2006), in a candid discussion of psychotherapy research, comments that 'the dominant research paradigm seriously distorts the real nature of persons and of psychotherapy (as I see them)' (p. 2). Orlinsky expresses the hope for a different paradigm of research to examine the 'realities' of therapy.

The reactive psychotherapeutic paradigm demands definitions of 'elements' that involve therapist expertise of 'tailor-making' the relationship to apply to individual clients. Within its context, the actualising paradigm has been dismissed. Nevertheless, over three decades of research generated by Rogers' (1957) article, congruence, unconditional positive regard and empathy were identified as core conditions of therapeutic personality change. The actualising paradigm views each individual client as a unique being and intentionally utilises the client's frame of reference and specific client resources. It is vital to review the actualising paradigm when examining the therapeutic relationship.

REFERENCES

Bohart, AC, Elliott, R, Greenberg, LS & Watson, JC (2002) Empathy. In JC Norcross (Ed) *Psychotherapist Relationships that Work: Therapist contributions and responsiveness to patients* (pp. 89–108). Oxford: University Press.

Bohart, AC & Greenberg, LS (1997) Empathy: Where are we and where do we go from here? In AC Bohart & LS Greenberg (Eds) *Empathy Reconsidered: New directions in psychotherapy* (pp. 419–50). Washington, DC: American Psychological Association.

Bozarth, JD (1998) *Person-Centered Therapy: A revolutionary paradigm.* Ross-on-Wye: PCCS Books.

Bozarth, JD & Motomasa, N (2005) Searching for the core: The interface of client-centered principles with other therapies. In S Joseph & R Worsley (Eds) *Person-Centred Psychopathology: A positive psychology of mental health* (pp. 293–309). Ross-on-Wye: PCCS Books.

Bozarth, JD, Zimring, F & Tausch, R (2002) Client-centered therapy: Evolution of a revolution. In D Cain & J Seeman (Eds) *Handbook of Humanistic Psychotherapy: Research and practice* (pp. 147–88). Washington, DC: American Psychological Association.

Cain, D & Seeman, J (Eds) (2002) *Handbook of Humanistic Psychotherapy: Research and practice.* Washington, DC: American Psychological Association.

Carkhuff, RR (1969) *Helping and Human Relations: A primer for lay and professional helpers. Vol. 1. Selection and training.* New York: Holt, Rinehart, & Winston.

Cormier, WH & Cormier, A (1991) *Interviewing Strategies for Helpers.* Belmont, CA: Brooks/Cole.

Cornelius-White, JH (2002) The phoenix of empirically supported therapy relationships: The overlooked person-centered basis. *Psychotherapy, 3,* 219–21.

Egan, G (1975) *The Skilled Helper: A model for systematic helping and interpersonal relating.* Belmont, CA: Wadsworth.

Elliott, R (2001) Research on the effectiveness of humanistic therapies: A meta-analysis. In D Cain & J Seeman (Eds) *Handbook of Humanistic Psychotherapy: Research and practice* (pp. 57–82). Washington, DC: American Psychological Association.

Farber, BA & Lane, J (2001) Positive regard. In JC Norcross (Ed) Empirically supported therapy relationships: Summary of the Division 29 Task Force [Special issue]. *Psychotherapy, 38* (4), 390–95.

Gelso, CJ & Carter, JA (1985) The relationship in counseling and psychotherapy: Components, consequences, and theoretical antecedents. *The Counseling Psychologist, 13,* 155–243.

Gelso, CJ & Hayes, JA (1998) *The Psychotherapy Relationship: Theory, research, and practice.* New York: Wiley.

Greenberg, LS, Elliott, R, Watson, JC & Bohart, AC (2001) Empathy. In JC Norcross (Ed) Empirically supported therapy relationships: Summary of the Division 29 Task Force [Special issue]. *Psychotherapy, 38* (4), 380–4.

Haugh, S & Merry, T (Eds) (2001) *Rogers' Therapeutic Conditions: Evolution, theory and practice. Vol 2: Empathy.* Ross-on-Wye: PCCS Books.

Horvath, AO & Bedi, RP (2002) The Alliance. In JC Norcross (Ed) *Psychotherapist Relationships that Work: Therapist contributions and responsiveness to patients* (pp. 37–70). Oxford: University Press.

Kish, J & Kroll, J (1980) Meaningfulness vs. effectiveness. *Psychotherapy: Theory, research and practice, 17,* 401–13.

Klien, MH, Kolden, GG, Michels, JL & Chisholm-Stockard, S (2001) Congruence or genuineness. In JC Norcross (Ed) Empirically supported therapy relationships: Summary of the Division 29 Task Force [Special issue]. *Psychotherapy, 38* (4), 396–400.

Klien, MH, Kolden, GG, Michels, JL & Chisholm-Stockard, S (2002) Congruence. In JC Norcross (Ed) *Psychotherapist Relationships that Work: Therapist contributions and responsiveness to patients.* (pp. 195–215). Oxford: University Press.

Lambert, MJ & Barley, DE (2001) Research summary on the therapeutic relationship and psychotherapy outcome. In JC Norcross (Ed) Empirically supported therapy relationships: Summary of the Division 29 Task Force [Special issue]. *Psychotherapy, 38* (4), 357–61.

Lambert, MJ & Barley, DE (2002) Research summary on the therapeutic relationship and psychotherapy outcome. In JC Norcross (Ed) *Psychotherapist Relationships that Work: Therapist contributions and responsiveness to patients* (pp. 17–32). Oxford: University Press.

Lampropoulos, GK (2000) Evolving psychotherapy integration: Eclectic selection and prescriptive applications of common factors in therapy. *Psychotherapy, 37,* 285–97.

Lazarus, AA (1993) Tailoring the therapeutic relationship or being an authentic chameleon. *Psychotherapy, 30,* 404–7.

Norcross, JC (Ed) (2001) Empirically supported therapy relationships: Summary of the Division 29 Task Force [Special issue]. *Psychotherapy, 38* (4).

Norcross, JC (Ed) (2002) *Psychotherapist Relationships that Work: Therapist contributions and responsiveness to patients.* Oxford: University Press.

Orlinsky, DE (2006) Comments on the state of psychotherapy research (as I see it). *Psychotherapy Bulletin, 41,* 3.

Orlinsky, DE, Grawe, K & Parks, BK (1994) Process and outcome in Psychotherapy – noch einmal. In SL Garfield & AE Bergin (Eds) *Handbook of Psychotherapy and Behavioral Change: An empirical analysis* (4th edn) (pp. 270–376). New York: John Wiley & Sons.

Orlinsky, DE & Howard, KJ (1986) Process and outcome in psychotherapy. In SL Garfield & AE Bergin (Eds) *Handbook of Psychotherapy and Behavioral Change: An empirical analysis* (3rd edn). New York: John Wiley & Sons.

Patterson, CH (1974) *Relationship Counseling and Psychotherapy.* New York: Harper & Row.

Patterson, CH (1984) Empathy, warmth and genuineness in psychotherapy: A review of reviews. *Psychotherapy, 21,* 431–8.

Patterson, CH (1985) *The Therapeutic Relationship: Foundations for an eclectic psychotherapy.* Monterey, CA: Brooks/Cole.

Patterson, CH (1989) Eclecticism in psychotherapy: Is integration possible? *Psychotherapy, 26,* 157–61.

Patterson, CH & Hidore, S (1997) *Successful Psychotherapy: A caring, loving relationship.* Northvale, NJ: Jason Aronson Inc.

Paul, GL (1967) Strategy of outcome research in psychotherapy. *Journal of Consulting Psychology, 31,* 109–19.

Rogers, CR (1942) *Counseling and Psychotherapy.* Boston: Houghton Mifflin.

Rogers, CR (1951) *Client-Centered Therapy.* Boston: Houghton Mifflin.

Rogers, CR (1957) The necessary and sufficient conditions of personality change. *Journal of Counseling Psychology, 21,* 95–103.

Rogers, CR (1959) A theory of therapy, personality, and interpersonal relationships as developed in the client-centered framework. In S Koch (Ed) *Psychology: A study of science. Vol 3: Formulations of the person and the social context* (pp. 184–256). New York: McGraw-Hill.

Rogers, CR (1975) An unappreciated way of being. *The Counseling Psychologist, 5* (2), 2–10.

Rogers, CR & Russell, DE (2002) *Carl Rogers: The quiet revolutionary. An oral history.* Roseville, CA: Penmarin Books.

Sexton, TL & Whiston, SC (1994) The status of the counseling relationship: An empirical review: Theoretical implications and research directions. *The Counseling Psychologist, 22* (1), 6–78.

Smith, MB & Glass, GV (1977) Meta-analysis of psychotherapy outcome studies. *American Psychologist, 32,* 752–60.

Taft, J (1933) *The Dynamics of Therapy in a Controlled Relationship.* New York: Macmillan.

Wampold, BE (2001) *The Great Psychotherapy Debate: Models, methods, and findings.* Mahwah, NJ: Lawrence Erlbaum.

Watson, JC & Steckley, P (2001) Potentiating growth: An examination of the research on unconditional positive regard. In J Bozarth & P Wilkins (Eds) *Rogers' Therapeutic Conditions: Evolution, theory and practice. Vol 3: Unconditional positive regard* (pp. 180–97). Ross-on Wye: PCCS Books.

CHAPTER 12

IN AND OUT OF THE MAINSTREAM
THERAPY IN ITS SOCIAL AND POLITICAL CONTEXT

NICK TOTTON

INTRODUCTION

Throughout this chapter, I am going to be considering the therapeutic relationship in two ways. I will be looking at some aspects of the complex set of interlocking contexts within which therapy (by which I mean both psychotherapy and counselling, throughout) is situated, and which define how it is understood by both practitioner and client. I will also be looking at some of the social and political *wounds* which both client and therapist bring to the situation, and which condition the relationship they form with each other.

I hope to show three things in particular: firstly, that both therapy as a process, and a satisfying therapeutic outcome, are tied firmly to the social and political context in which the therapy takes place; secondly, that therapists and counsellors exercise political agency in their work, whether or not they are aware of it; and thirdly, that conscious or unconscious support from the therapist for mainstream cultural positions – at the expense of the positions of the client – can be both wounding and damaging. An unconscious assumption that mainstream views are 'natural' makes it all too easy not only to pathologise wounds (a danger for all therapists) but to pathologise difference itself. I have listed these three themes sequentially, but in what follows they will be found to be firmly braided together, a braid which runs through everything I have to say.

POLITICAL DISSOCIATION

Like all human activity, therapy takes place in a cultural space which gives it the meaning it has (Erving Goffman's work is helpful here: Goffman, 1997). This is, after all, very odd behaviour: two people sitting in a room together while one of them does most of the talking (often in quite unusual styles) about whatever comes to mind, and the other person responds in *extremely* unusual ways that don't always have any obvious bearing on what has been said by the first person. It is validated by a social context which says that it is called 'psychotherapy' or 'counselling', that it has certain appropriate functions and significances, and that it is socially acceptable and useful. There are also other, simultaneously present, contexts which operate to put the activity of therapy in question, to contest the ways in which it becomes privileged. Some of these contexts are explicitly

145

political and may suggest, for instance, that therapy can be understood as oppressive and reactionary (Guattari, 1984; Hillman & Ventura, 1993; Masson, 1990) or, alternatively, as progressive and liberating (Reich, 1983; Rogers, 1978. For both these contexts see also Totton, 2000).

Interestingly, though, the discourse of therapy itself often tends to ignore *all* of these contexts and to speak as if therapy happens in a social and political vacuum (Samuels, 2006). If the client brings material from wider social and political situations, the therapist might speak in such a way as to strip the material of this context – to reinterpret it as purely personal and autobiographical in meaning. For example, if the client speaks of their opposition to the Iraq invasion, the therapist might respond by speaking of the client's childhood experience of violence, or their need to oppose authority. The client talks about the government and the therapist makes a reference to the client's mother. The client talks about the scars made by a working-class upbringing, and the therapist replies (as someone reported to me recently), 'When are you going to stop letting that define you?'

Although this kind of response can on occasion be bracing or even liberating, I suggest that there is actually something rather mad, or at least dissociated, about its habitual use. It privileges one or two very specific frames (on which the therapist happens to be expert): that of the nuclear family, and that of individual agency. Like several other common therapeutic strategies (Totton, 2006a), it wrong-foots and disempowers the client, seemingly implying that political engagement itself is intrinsically mad, a misunderstanding of what, in the therapeutic context, matters. An alternative point of view is that such engagement is, as Andrew Samuels has suggested (1993: 57–8; 2001: 16–20), a normal human capacity, a specifically 'political energy' which expresses itself in different styles and with different degrees of strength in each of us. At the very least, the politics-avoidant response implies that therapy has nothing to say about politics or society – that therapy is somehow uniquely and wholly apolitical, or even asocial.

I believe that this is far from the truth. As we have already seen, therapy always operates within a political and social context, or set of contexts, which gives it meaning as a human activity. More than that, therapy always expresses a political position, because it always and inevitably has a view on *how human beings should be* and so carries a vision of how we could achieve this desired state (Totton, 2005). However, these visions and positions are often unconscious and implicit; and I will argue that this can be dangerous.

Taking a view on how people should be seems to me an intrinsic part of our interaction with our clients. There are many forms of therapy which aim explicitly at cure and adjustment; the underlying assumption being that people *should* be healthy and well-adjusted – and, of course, each therapy and each practitioner has their own definitions of what 'healthy' or 'well-adjusted' looks like. Each believes that their clients should adjust to whatever aspects of life they themselves see as acceptable, as natural, whilst tacitly assuming that other less acceptable aspects should be resisted. The point, though less obvious, is no less true for more 'permissive' styles of therapy, which make it their goal to support the client in their authentic, spontaneous growth. Apart from the subtle difficulty of establishing which features of the work represent the client's authenticity, and which their resistance to it, this goal is itself no less a political one than the goal of adjustment: it is founded on a belief that people *should* be authentic, spontaneous and growthful.

The goals of therapy, then, are always ultimately frameable as social and political goals. The line which many theorists attempt to draw between individual and social territories is not a real one: what we want for our clients, we necessarily in some sense want for society. And also, as therapists, we are always needing to navigate within society as it is now constituted: many positions we take within the consulting room are also positions about what goes on outside it.

As an extreme example of the impossibility of 'apolitical' therapy, take the situation which Juan Pablo Jimenez describes in Chile under Pinochet. The opposition would frequently call for general strikes or stoppages in protest against the regime; almost all organisations, including the medical association, would agree to join in.

> On such days there is no public transport, colleges and universities close their doors and many doctors do not work. Some patients announce that they will not come for treatment. Others distinguish social protests from the act of being psychoanalysed.
>
> The analyst, for his [sic] part, may decide not to work and thus show his patients a political position, or to work, which some patients will construe as clear evidence of sympathy with the government. He may decide to work with some and not with others, thus introducing a degree of splitting into his daily work. In any case, on some of these days, at certain times, it may actually be dangerous to pass through certain parts of the city. Inevitably, any decision taken by the analyst will, depending on the patient, have repercussions on the transference, and may need to be analysed with the patient. However, this is also not easy. At the time of the socialist government, I knew of a training analysis that was broken off because the analyst and the candidate got into a violent political argument. (Jimenez, 1989: 501)

This is an extreme example of a situation in which *any* move or non-move on the part of the therapist will be interpreted as — and therefore become — an explicit political stance. But aren't we all in this situation all the time? If the client mentions a current political issue, we have several choices: for example, we can ignore them; we can comment from our own perspective; we can say something like 'You obviously feel strongly about that'; we can make an interpretation in terms of what we know of their personal history; we can employ the all-purpose therapeutic 'Mmm-hmmm'; or we can produce some combination of these responses. However, *none* of these are neutral: they all convey some degree or other of more-or-less nuanced approval or disapproval, certainly of the client's introduction of this theme, but surely therefore, by implication, of the theme itself and the client's relationship to it.

I would go further. If a client arrives on the day of the Iraq invasion, for example, without any major personal issue to discuss, and yet *does not mention the invasion,* then I suggest that it would be in line with usual therapeutic behaviour to point out this omission, and to ask about it. Is the client so politically autistic as to have not noticed the event? Do they perhaps feel that we would not approve of their mentioning it? Or are they trying to avoid what they see as a potential row with us over our differing views? All of these possibilities are therapeutically interesting, to say the least. If we do not feel that to mention the omission would be appropriate, then what is it about political territory that seals it off so definitively from the therapeutic?

There are many issues and problems clients bring which, it can be argued, are insoluble and indeed incomprehensible without a social frame of reference. The working-class client's sense of shame and inadequacy; the female client's anxieties around weight and appearance; the black, or gay or lesbian client's experience of exclusion; the poor client's envy and alienation – does it really make sense to address these feelings therapeutically without considering the social factors which help to create and maintain them? (For therapeutic discussion of each of these, in the same order, see Kearney, 1996; Sennett & Cobb, 1977; Orbach,1998; Lago & Haugh, 2006; Davies & Charles, 1996.) Lynne Layton has written of what she calls the 'normative unconscious': the ensemble of mainstream understandings of how people should be which very often remains below the surface of awareness (Layton, 2004, 2006: for different approaches to this issue see Kearney, 1996, and Mindell, 1995). If, for instance, we support the female client just mentioned in her sense that she should work hard to be slim and attractive to men, then we may be failing to analyse our own normative unconscious beliefs and the way in which they collude with the client's beliefs.

This sort of example raises difficult questions about power in the therapeutic relationship, and the dangers of imposing our own views on the client. However, this danger is hardwired into the therapy situation. Ultimately, there is no neutrality; what generally passes for 'neutrality' is a conservative acceptance of the status quo (Totton, 2005, 2006a). If therapists do not acknowledge that (a) they operate in a social and political context, and (b) they are *agents* in that context, then they will be misleading themselves and their clients.

DIFFERENCE, POWER AND RANK

Again, like all human activity, therapy occurs within a framework of sameness and difference. The two participants, each being human, are attuned to many dimensions in which they can perceive each other as *similar,* and many others in which they can perceive *differences* between self and other. Both of these perceptions – 'they are different from me' and 'they are similar to me' – can be helpful to or destructive of the therapeutic relationship in quite complex ways. For example, if held by the therapist, 'they are similar to me' can generate an empathic, supportive response; it can also lead to collusive attitudes, or to illusory assumptions that the client means and feels the same things that the therapist believes *he or she* would mean and feel in the same situation. 'They are different from me' can stimulate curiosity and open-mindedness; it can also produce incomprehension and hostility.

Experiences of difference in social interaction are a potent source of the emotional wounds which people bring to therapy. They can also easily be re-enacted and reinforced in the therapeutic relationship. Information is technically defined as 'difference which make a difference' (Bateson, 1973: 428ff). I want to look at some of the sorts of difference that make a difference to relationships between people, and to consider what sorts of information we take from them. Much of this information is about comparative *rank*.

Arnold Mindell, one of the few leading psychotherapists currently addressing social and political issues in their work, describes rank as 'the sum of a person's privileges' (Mindell, 1995: 28). 'Whether you earned or inherited your rank, it organizes much of your communication behavior' (ibid.: 42). In this society, very few differences are neutral with respect to power and rank. Gender, sexuality, class, ethnicity, income, age, disability – all these carry with them enormous implications for perceived and experienced rank and for actual power (power often comes with rank, but not always; think of the Queen, for example). These issues have traditionally been referred to in terms of 'majority' and 'minority' groups; however, the disempowered group is not always a minority, either in a specific context or in the world as a whole – for example, there are more females than males in the world, but males are a universally empowered group. Therefore I prefer to use Mindell's terms (1995: 30) and speak of 'mainstream' and 'non-mainstream' groups.

A key feature of mainstream culture and values is that they tend to be invisible to their holders (Mindell, 1995: 37). For someone who identifies with the mainstream, their values are simply how things *are* – reflected back to them constantly from the media, and from every authoritative pronouncement. Well-known examples of this include the assumption that everyone is male, white and heterosexual unless specified otherwise; the assumption that representative democracy combined with advanced capitalism is the preferred system for everyone in the world; and the assumption that being 'reasonable' is always a good thing.

Rank is both *perceived* and *experienced*; and how we experience our own rank may not be the same as how another person perceives it. This is particularly true with regard to 'mainstream' rank – the sort of automatic bonus of power and authority which goes with being white, male, middle class, etc. A white, male, middle-class therapist may quite sincerely assert that he claims no superiority of rank over a female, working-class person of colour, who is his client. But if he is unable to recognise the social *reality* that he has far higher rank than her, and to attend to the ways in which this affects her perception of him and vice versa, then the therapeutic relationship will be damaged from the start. 'Rank is a drug. The more you have, the less aware you are of how it affects others negatively' (Mindell, 1995: 49).

In other words, rank is subject to the phenomenon of the invisible mainstream. In the above summary I may well have left out one or more dimensions of difference which, for you the reader, are deeply significant in terms of rank. If so, this is probably a dimension to which, at this particular moment, I am pretty much blind, and I apologise for this. Similar blindnesses occur in the therapy room, and it is enormously important that therapists are open to being educated by their clients in dimensions of rank of which they have not previously been conscious – and to apologising for the hurt which their unconsciousness might create.

It is also important to realise that some therapists are themselves carrying wounds relating to rank, which may negatively affect their work with certain clients: black therapist with white client; working-class therapist with middle-class client; female therapist with male client – all need the therapist's extra awareness and work on themselves in order to refrain from persecuting their 'higher-rank' clients. Most often, however, the therapist's challenge is to be aware of their own higher rank. Besides the acquired or inherited rank which the therapist brings to their occupation, there is also the rank that attaches to the role of therapist itself.

Psychotherapists and, to a somewhat lesser extent, counsellors, are generally perceived as skilled professionals, with some of the same authority as doctors or lawyers. They are also widely credited with a specific, uncanny and somewhat frightening ability to 'see right through' people and straight to their deepest secrets. Besides these perceptions, therapy is undoubtedly a middle-class occupation, whatever the self-perception of individual practitioners, and therapists are in fact very often white and middle class. The steadily increasing length and cost of therapy trainings is likely to increase the distance between the median rank of therapists and of their clients.

This distance of rank in itself translates into various sorts of social power – most fundamentally, *the power to define the situation*, to say whose perception is accurate and whose is distorted, who is 'sick' and who is 'well'. The different contexts in which practitioners work will have a large effect on this: someone working in a GP practice will commonly and naturally be perceived as a member of the medical profession whose statements represent some sort of objective medical authority, and this is even more likely to be the case when the practitioner works in a mental hospital.

EXPECTATIONS AND MISUNDERSTANDINGS

Differences of setting, cultural background, and rank-related dimensions such as gender, ethnicity, class, sexuality, age, etc. will all tend to set up different expectations of the therapist on the part of the client. Most obviously, someone who identifies with (as they perceive it) a group who are relatively disadvantaged compared with the therapist, will approach the therapist with some blend of wariness, deference, hostility and appeasement. Of course, we all approach our therapists with some blend of these qualities! – but this aspect of the relationship will be amplified by differences of rank, as it will be by more 'authoritative' settings, institutional or opulent, as the case may be.

Similarly, therapists will have certain expectations of the client that are influenced by setting, rank, and differences of *therapeutic culture*. By this I mean whatever network of therapy or counselling they are plugged into – largely as a result of their training, but also through choices and connections they have made since then. As a simple example, many therapists expect their clients to sit down and talk! This may not be immediately apparent to clients whose cultures (based on family, class, ethnicity or whatever) have different expectations, and the client who, for example, strides around the room 'shouting' (i.e. speaking in a louder register than the therapist is accustomed to) may well get a negative reaction.

As Mindell has pointed out (1995: 202ff), the communication style of the mainstream (white, Western, middle-class) culture can be characterised as *cool* and *linear*. That is, mainstream individuals tend to speak one at a time, and stick to the subject; they may get angry, but they generally keep this within bounds, and strive for reason and articulacy. Some non-mainstream cultures, however, tend to use *hot* and *non-linear* communication styles, where emotions bubble up freely and the conversation circles around rather than following a straight line.

Neither of these styles is 'right' or 'wrong', 'better' or 'worse' than the other; each has strengths and weaknesses, each is more useful at certain times. But the great majority of therapists are trained and expert in the cool, linear style, and perhaps puzzled and deskilled (and therefore defensive) when faced with hotter and less linear ways of talking. A minority of therapists, conversely, have been trained in 'growth movement' approaches which equally privilege a 'hot', emotive, 'right brain' style; and they will tend to characterise cool communication as 'being stuck in your head'.

The ideal, then, would be for a practitioner to have a range which allows them to accept, respond to and join in whatever communication style the client offers – and in due course, perhaps, to introduce the possibility of using other styles for particular purposes. But even when one is aware of the issues and consciously open to other styles, one can easily be misled by one's expectations. I had a client who was white, but brought up in the Caribbean, and partially identified as black; his accent was a startling jumble, and his communication style was non-linear to the extent that I didn't receive this information about his background for several sessions, and was tentatively considering him rather disturbed! Once he told me about his history, many things fell into place: 'seeing' him as Afro-Caribbean, I could 'hear' him in a way that made sense to me. But should I have needed that information in order to accept him on his own terms? Many families, or even individuals, have idiosyncratic styles and cultures which work for them.

Probably most practitioners would agree that it is the 'naïve clients', those without previous knowledge of therapy or counselling, with whom clashes of expectation can become most challenging. The BBC comedy series about therapy, *Help*, portrays this very well: one new client starts to sit in the chair of the therapist, who gently intervenes, 'That's my chair'. 'But aren't they all your chairs?' asks the puzzled client. And of course there are many symbolic ways in which a client can try to 'sit in the therapist's chair', before they have learnt the unspoken etiquette of the relationship. But perhaps something creative has been lost once the client is house-trained to 'do therapy' properly – that is, in the style to which the therapist has become accustomed. Remember, we do not have to spell out our expectations in order to let our clients know how they should behave. In the heightened atmosphere of the therapy room, the least shift of intonation, the smallest pause or silence, every statement or action of the client we choose to respond to or let pass, all very effectively convey our preferences – even when we do not intend it. The same is true for our values and beliefs (Totton, 2006a: 89ff).

SOCIETY'S EXPECTATIONS

The public identity of psychotherapy is complex and ambivalent, reflecting some of the deep contradictions in society itself. Yet therapy is alertly responsive to the demands society makes on it – sometimes mediated through the employment market, sometimes expressed in the media, sometimes discerned in the agendas of our clients – so that it tends to absorb these contradictions into its own self-understanding (Totton, 2006b).

One place where we can see this happening is around the idea of 'cure': something which therapy cannot provide, but which most clients are nevertheless seeking, either openly or covertly. And society as a whole tends to look to psychotherapy for 'cures' to problems which it is unable or unwilling to resolve – for example, child sexual abuse, or antisocial behaviour; in both cases, the authoritarian response is punishment, the liberal response, to call on therapists or counsellors for help. Neither group is prepared to look at the deep cultural, economic and political issues involved. Just as individual clients often hope to be cured without having to change, so we are asked to cure deep social problems without addressing their causes.

While therapy is often expected to perform individual and social miracles, it is also feared and distrusted, for several reasons: its zeroing-in on what is concealed; its insistence that the causes of human behaviour are complex rather than simple; its mainly positive attitude towards emotions and desires; and its emphasis (still popularly believed in, though not always present) on sexuality. We get called 'shrinks', 'the-rapist', and 'trick-cyclists', and teased about how much money we make from other people's misery. Going to a therapist is widely seen as a combination of major surgery and visiting a prostitute: it may sometimes be unavoidable, but should be done as fast as possible, and certainly without becoming *dependent*. The deep suspicion of therapists' power to do harm emerges most clearly in the repeated moral panics (Pearson, 1983) about psychotherapists as abusers, whether by general incompetence, by creating False Memory Syndrome, or by having sex with their clients.

The issue of dependency has become a major theme of clients in the past few years (Totton, 2006c). At initial meetings, people show an increased reluctance to commit themselves to ongoing weekly psychotherapy – a reluctance which is often based on a fear of becoming dependent. Their hope, it seems, is to have as little therapy as possible, for as short a time as possible, so that they can escape before dependency arises. Depending on a therapist is assumed to be a bad thing, a self-evidently good reason for avoiding long-term therapy. Very often, they mention how friends and family talked of the dangers of depending on a therapist.

The largest context for these attitudes is the ever-increasing value which our society puts on independence, autonomy, self-sufficiency. (For the next twenty years the number of households in Britain is expected to rise by around 200,000 a year, of which 150,000 will be due to an increase in single people living alone (Seager, 2006).) What is striking, though, is how many therapists have adopted anti-dependency beliefs – despite the traditional, and I believe well-founded, therapeutic view that depending on others is not only intrinsic to human existence but also a valuable and satisfying aspect of it, and that one of therapy's important functions is to offer an experience of safe dependency.

Some anti-dependency therapists are led to this view by a critique of power imbalances in the therapeutic relationship (e.g. Bates & House, 2003). A much larger number are practitioners of brief and solution-focused therapies; here the arguments about benefit are inextricable from practical issues, financial constraints and pressures which militate against long-term intensive therapy. If you are only offering six or twelve sessions, dependency is indeed an undesirable development; and a skilled therapist will manage the work so as to avoid it – sometimes in opposition to the client's process.

POWER AND ECONOMICS

Some of the arguments around dependency seem to me to be justifications of the unavoidable. Public and private providers – National Health Service (NHS), managed care, the voluntary sector – all find the expense and long time scale of 'traditional' therapies unacceptable, partly because, in our 'independent' culture, people are unwilling to pay higher taxes to fund such processes. So by a shadowy and over-determined set of negotiations, a virtue is made of necessity.

This is just one example of the pervasive influence of economics on the practice of therapy. Often, ideology is refracted *through* economics: ideological constraints get translated into economic ones, and are then recreated as a theory of good practice. Besides short-term therapy, several other features of public and voluntary provision fall into this category. For example, clients using these avenues to therapy seldom or never have any choice about which form of therapy they receive, or which individual they see. The reasons for this are basically practical – to allow efficient management of time and resources – but they are accompanied by a theoretical picture that makes different practitioners and different therapies more or less interchangeable.

This is just part of a much wider move towards an expertise-based, 'outcome-focused' version of therapy, which I have argued elsewhere is a distorted and reductionist one (Totton, 2005). We are in a cleft stick here: the expense of private therapy means that, in David Pilgrim's words, 'personal growth is reserved for the rich' (Pilgrim, 1992: 233) – yet when therapy is offered within the NHS and by voluntary sector organisations, while on the one hand it becomes available to many more people, on the other hand it is shorn of many of its most valuable features, indeed in some ways turned into a different activity altogether. (Paradoxically, some of the most complex clients are seen by some of the least experienced practitioners – volunteer trainees.) Obviously enough, the NHS and charitable funders require evidence of 'effectiveness'. Yet to define effectiveness for therapy in the same way that we define it for medicine is to undermine the activity of therapy entirely. And therapists who are trained in this approach will create a wholly different relationship with their clients – who, if they cannot afford private therapy, may in any case be more deferential and authority-accepting.

CONCLUSION

A great deal more could be said about therapy in its social and political context, and how these impact the therapeutic relationship. I have tried to indicate what seem to me to be the central issues, without over-egging the pudding. The crucial issue for me is to demonstrate that there *are* such contexts, and that they *do* impact the relationship. To assume otherwise, it seems to me, is, among other things, to infantilise the therapeutic relationship, treating it as something that happens without reference to the rest of the world. This, of course, is not actually true even of the mother–infant dyad, which is very much affected by the set of understandings about childrearing within which it exists. But there has been a very strong tendency in therapy to 'privatise' both the therapy pair, and the childrearing pair, the latter so often used as a governing metaphor for therapy.

Two individuals who meet for therapy bring with them complex histories as social and political beings. They will recognise and misrecognise each other in ways that are, among many other things, socially and politically inflected. And they will carry traces of social and political projects of many kinds. The attempt to exclude all of this material from the relationship is both hopeless and pointless.

In the 1960s, two psychoanalysts who tried to analyse a young woman member of the West African Dogon tribe, in order to investigate differences or similarities in psychic structure from Westerners, came up against a tricky obstacle. 'It was practically impossible to speak to her alone. A whole group of women continuously took part in everything that occurred within the analytic situation' (Morgenthaler & Parin, 1964: 446). However:

> Contrary to what might have been expected, the supervisory group exercised no sort of prohibitive function. Rather, it encouraged the young woman and even the analyst to make their relationship to each other more intense and more intimate. It was not long before they revealed the content of her wishes by making open demands, in words and gestures, for a sexual relationship. (Morgenthaler & Parin, 1964: 447)

In our individualistic culture, this is not a problem we frequently encounter – or not in such a concrete form. However, does any interaction truly take place 'alone', and outside the supportive or obstructive influences of the larger social group? Although the literal absence of the social group is a fundamental condition of therapy, its symbolic presence and profound effect is an equally fundamental fact. We need to recognise and explore its implications.

REFERENCES

Bates, Y & House, R (Eds) (2003) *Ethically Challenged Professions: Enabling innovation and diversity in psychotherapy and counselling.* Ross-on-Wye: PCCS Books.

Bateson, G (1973) *Steps to an Ecology of Mind.* London: Paladin.

Davies, D & Charles, N (1996) *Pink Therapy: Guide for counsellors working with lesbian, gay and bisexual clients*. Maidenhead: Open University Press.

Goffman, E (1997) *The Goffman Reader*. Oxford: Blackwell.

Guattari, F (1984) *Molecular Revolution: Psychiatry and politics*. Harmondsworth: Penguin.

Hillman, J & Ventura, M (1993) *We've Had 100 Years of Psychotherapy – and the world's getting worse*. San Francisco, CA: HarperCollins.

Jimenez, JP (1989) Some reflections on the practice of psychoanalysis in Chile today – from the point of view of the relationship between psychoanalysis and society. *International Review of Psycho-Analysis, 16*, 493–504.

Kearney, A (1996) *Counselling, Class and Politics*. Ross-on-Wye: PCCS Books.

Lago, C & Haugh, S (2006) White counsellor racial identity: The unacknowledged, unknown, unaware aspect of self in relationship. In G Proctor, M Cooper, P Sanders & B Malcolm, (Eds) *Politicizing the Person-Centred Approach: An agenda for social change*. Ross-on-Wye: PCCS Books.

Layton, L (2004) A fork in the royal road: On defining the unconscious and its stakes for social theory. *Psychoanalysis, Culture and Society, 9* (1), 33–51.

Layton, L (2006) Attacks on linking: The unconscious pull to dissociate individuals from their social context. In L Layton, NC Hollander & S Gutwill (Eds) *Psychoanalysis, Class and Politics: Encounters in the clinical setting* (pp. 107–17). Hove: Routledge.

Masson, J (1990) *Against Therapy*. London: Fontana.

Mindell, A (1995) *Sitting in the Fire: Large group transformation using conflict and diversity.* Portland, OR: Lao Tse Press.

Morgenthaler, F & Parin, P (1964) Typical forms of transference among West Africans. *International Journal of Psycho-Analysis, 45*, 446–9.

Orbach, S (1998) *Fat is a Feminist Issue*. London: Arrow.

Pearson, G (1983) *Hooligan: A history of respectable fears*. London: Macmillan.

Pilgrim, D (1992) Psychotherapy and political evasions. In W Dryden & C Feltham (Eds) *Psychotherapy and its Discontents* (pp. 225–43). Milton Keynes: Open University Press.

Reich, W (1983) *The Function of the Orgasm*. London: Condor.

Rogers, CR (1978) *Carl Rogers on Personal Power: Inner strength and its revolutionary impact*. London: Constable.

Samuels, A (1993) *The Political Psyche*. London: Routledge.

Samuels, A (2001) *Politics on the Couch: Citizenship and the internal life*. London: Profile Books.

Samuels, A (2006) Working directly with political, cultural, and social material in the therapy session. In L Layton, NC Hollander & S Gutwill (Eds) *Psychoanalysis, Class and Politics: Encounters in the clinical setting* (pp. 11–28). Hove: Routledge.

Seager, A (2006) Homes crisis feared as households projected to rise by nearly a quarter. *The Guardian*. March 15.

Sennett, R & Cobb, J (1977) *The Hidden Injuries of Class*. Cambridge: Cambridge University Press.

Totton, N (2000) *Psychotherapy and Politics*. London: Sage.

Totton, N (2005) Can psychotherapy help make a better future? *Psychotherapy and Politics International, 3* (2), 83–95.

Totton, N (2006a) Power in the therapeutic relationship. In N Totton (Ed) *The Politics of Psychotherapy* (pp. 83–93) Maidenhead: Open University Press.

Totton, N (2006b) The institutions of psychotherapy. In N Totton (Ed) *The Politics of Psychotherapy* (pp. 108–120). Maidenhead: Open University Press.

Totton, N (2006c) In defence of dependency. *Therapy Today, 17* (5), 18–21.

CHAPTER 13

A JAPANESE PERSPECTIVE

YUKISHIGE NAKATA

BACKGROUND

It has been more than 50 years since the idea of psychotherapy and counselling was introduced into Japan. Carl Rogers' theories (1959, 1961) became known to Japanese psychologists after World War II, and they began to realise that there was a helping profession conducted not by psychiatrists, but psychologists. Clinical psychology gradually gained public acknowledgement, and the licensing system for certified clinical psychologists was established in 1988. During the developmental process of a psychotherapy system, various problems were noted as increasing in the educational field, such as non-school-attending students, serious bullying that was causing suicides and, in the occupational mental health field, problems such as non-working depressed workers. The professions of counsellor and psychotherapist became popular. More and more people became aware that there were (and are) psychotherapists in counselling offices, psychiatric hospitals, schools and other such places.

However, the notion of psychotherapy has not yet permeated into Japan's cultural or emotional climate. Psychotherapy is still an 'imported culture' in Japan and Japanese therapists have not yet developed the ideas in a more appropriate direction. Many books on psychotherapy are imported from Western countries and translated into Japanese. Most Japanese therapists are still following Western thoughts and they neither digest nor sublimate Western ideas into Japanese ones. Indeed, many therapists simply apply Western theories to their practice – and this is in vain. From the client's perspective, there appears to be a great deal of difference between Western countries and Japan with regard to how people feel and receive psychotherapy.

Many Japanese psychotherapists think that Japan is behind Western countries, so they import and follow Western ideas in order to 'catch up'. They still regard it as important to invite Western therapists to Japanese conferences, and to translate Western psychotherapy books. It was certainly important for Japan to learn the basic principles of psychotherapy practice and there are still, of course, new Western ideas and books valuable to Japanese practice, but now the Japanese must explore what kind of ideas should be learned from other cultures and, in order to do that, Japanese psychotherapists need to have an understanding of how the many imported Western ideas affect Japanese practice. In other words, they need to be able to judge if and in what way the Western ideas help or interfere with their practice.

This chapter is intended to reflect clinical work in Japan from a cultural viewpoint that has not been mentioned much in the literature of counselling and psychotherapy. I will discuss the difference between Japan and the West: a difference that is rooted in the different sense of interpersonal attitudes. I hope it will give another perspective to practitioners both in European and non-European regions by showing how deeply clinical work is affected by culture in one particular Asian country.

Firstly, I will describe my personal experience of a large international encounter group, because it will give, I believe, a good example of the cultural differences. Next, I will discuss two phenomena that are often seen in Japanese life; and lastly, relate the discussion to several clinical issues.

PERSONAL EXPERIENCE OF AN INTERNATIONAL ENCOUNTER GROUP

I was amazed by how expressive foreign people were in a certain international encounter groups held in the United States. If I remember correctly, there were about 60 to 80 members from all around the world; most of them seemed to be Western.

The Westerners talked very assertively and behaved expressively. I could not fully follow them because of the speed of their English but, to me, their talk often sounded as if they were fighting – even though I knew they weren't, I was surprised at how forcefully they tried to express themselves. This might happen in Japan several hours after a group has begun but this was right from the start.

For most Japanese, such an expressive attitude would be too intense and it would be very unlikely to occur in an encounter group consisting of only Japanese. I am not the only person who feels this way – many Japanese have a similar impression. For example, just a short time ago I had my graduate students watch a film called *The Steel Shutter* (1973), a documentary concerning one of the peace projects that Rogers undertook in his later career. In this instance, Rogers and his colleague were filmed facilitating a group of people from Northern Ireland who were on conflicting sides. My students' impression of the film was that it was not focused on a dialogue of peace but rather on the group members' strong will to express themselves. The students said that such communication would be very unlikely in Japan. A Japanese encounter group is occupied with silence in various stages because, rather than concentrating on expressing themselves, members first pay attention to how others are responding to the new situation. A theory of encounter group process (Murayama & Nojima, 1977) often cited in Japan, presents seven stages of group development, the first of which is 'puzzlement and exploration' where the group is, initially, frequently occupied with silence.

This is true not only of encounter groups but also other social situations. For example, Japanese students (high school and college) do not speak up in class, even though teachers encourage them to do so. When a teacher invites, 'Any questions, comments, whatever?', it is often silence that occupies the classroom. Many native English teachers come to Japan and discover this phenomenon. Even students of English conversation may not easily speak up. The teachers know from the students' positive facial expressions that they are not harbouring negative feelings, but they do wonder what they are thinking. There are, of course, a small percentage of Japanese who believe that they need to express themselves and do actually try. However, this silence in the classroom happens often in Japan, with Japanese as well as foreign teachers.

All these group and educational experiences suggest that the Japanese tend to hide their opinions and watch the surrounding interpersonal situation carefully before starting to talk about themselves. This can lead to several clinical viewpoints discussed below.

CHARACTERISTICS OF JAPANESE INTERPERSONAL PHENOMENA

1. THE SENSE OF 'I'

As the above suggests, Japanese people do not want to be different or to have a separate existence from others, especially in the first stage of an encounter or in a strange situation. They choose to quietly observe others' response to a social situation and, because they pay a great deal of attention to others' opinion of them, they cannot risk exposure before having assessed the situation; they believe it safer not to draw attention to themselves by voicing an opinion and see this as the best way of maintaining a safe and inclusive position within a group.

However, this is less straightforward than it sounds. It is often actually quite difficult to judge whether the person is truly hesitant about standing out. When a person recognises that they are not the only one in a group wanting to assert their opinion, they begin to raise their hand, but if they are then totally ignored they are dissatisfied. Even though they have not yet voiced their feelings, they want others to recognise their real, unexpressed wish. It is not just psychotherapists but people in interpersonal situations in general in Japan who are required to notice these very delicate non-verbal signs.

So it is frequently hard for the Japanese to say 'I think' or 'I have a question' because this highlights a clear self, different from others. Interestingly, in everyday conversation among the Japanese, terms for 'I' are quite often omitted. If someone says the Japanese terms for 'I' in every sentence in a conversation, it sounds very strange. This seems to suggest that in Japanese culture there is a tendency to erase the perceived 'I'. I should point out that there are many Japanese terms referring to 'I' and they are used very distinctly depending on the situation. This implies that 'I' changes from situation to situation in Japan and that the Japanese do not have an unchangeable fixed self – not at least in the Western sense. If a Japanese person does not have a grasp of the vocabulary of differential 'I' terms, it is difficult to adapt him or herself to society.

2. CLOSENESS

According to Kawai (1976), a Japanese Jungian, the fundamental principle of being in Western countries is 'separation', where people are required to live as individuals, separately from others. In Japan, the fundamental principle of being is 'containing', where people are required to live together like children held in a mother's palm. In Western countries distinct individuality is valued most whilst in Japan more value is placed on *not* being different. Kawai illustrates examples from many contexts and offers a very good analysis.

I suggest that separation/containing can be discussed from the viewpoint of closeness between people. For example, it is quite normal in Japan for a young child to sleep in the same room with their parents. On the other hand, young Western children have to go to bed alone, separated from their parents at night. For me, as one Japanese man, Western children seem to be forced to abandon their dependency and their wish to be together with their parents and, instead, to establish autonomy at a very young age. It has been my experience that there is often an argument between married couples of Japanese and Western cultures. A Japanese parent argues that their child should sleep with them but the Western parent asserts to the contrary. In the United States, most college students leave their parents and live on their own, even if they are in the same town. It is quite normal and very usual for Japanese college students to commute from their parents' home. Closeness between parents and children is accepted as natural in Japan and a child does not have to disregard their dependency if it is not extreme. This Japanese way of being, this closeness, might mean that the relationship between a client and therapist in Japan could be much closer than that in Western countries.

PSYCHOTHERAPEUTIC ISSUES

1. VERBALISATION

There are many Japanese who choose not to go to a counselling or therapy centre, even though they know such places exist and even when counselling is free (for example, in educational centres run by the local government) they are still hesitant. Sometimes, understandably, this is because they are afraid of being considered 'crazy' by their neighbours – but this seems not to be the only reason.

For Japanese clients with the sense of 'I', discussed above, it is perhaps difficult to verbally express themselves to a psychotherapist – even though they realise that this is their opportunity to do so, they are not good at it; some have been 'trained' for so long to hide themselves and to observe others, their own opinions have become lost, almost unreachable.

There was once a discussion between two Japanese therapists, both specialising in intrapersonal techniques, such as focusing (Gendlin, 1981) and visual image therapy. One of them was trained in the United States, the other in Japan. The Japanese-trained therapist said, '[Japanese] clients will recover without verbalising so much.' The US trained therapist responded, 'But, they [US therapists] cannot believe that.' This example shows clearly the difference between Japanese and American therapists as to the recognition of the non-role (or role) of verbalisation.

2. 'FUTOKOU' AND 'HIKIKOMORI'

One of the problems that Japanese psychotherapists spend much time working with is 'futokou' students. There are many students, from elementary to high school level (aged from six to eighteen), who though enrolled, do not go to school. Even though Futokou students may be called 'school-refusals', they do not necessarily refuse school: some wish to go but are incapable of doing so. When asked why they do not or cannot attend, they are either unable to respond or they give an answer that proves to be untrue. Many of them don't even know themselves why they don't go to school. This is where psychotherapy is difficult for them; even when parents or teachers try to 'force' them to go to school, most still don't go, or if they go on the day, they choose to be absent after that.

It has been more than 40 years since the school-refusal problems first occurred and the cause is still unknown. Some cases are related to child abuse but many are not. Some students are not succeeding at school but many excellent students also stop going. If they go to a psychiatrist, some are prescribed medication and do not take it. In short, a typical futokou student is a well-behaved, well-graded, non-antisocial and non-psychotic child who does not know themselves why they cannot go to school. They seem to have a psychological problem, are referred to a clinical psychologist, and long-term counselling begins.

Another symptom is 'hikikomori', a Japanese term meaning 'social withdrawal'. It is the phenomenon of adolescents and young adults who continually stay at home, withdrawn, uninvolved in any social or work-based activity. The young person 'chooses' to be isolated to the extent that, even though they stay with and are financially supported by their parents, they remain in their own room, hardly exchanging a word except when going to the bathroom or kitchen. They do not have clear vision for their life; they just live alone with a feeling of oppression. Like futokou students, they do not go out, even if pressured. They are referred to clinical psychologists but as they usually insist on staying at home, in many cases, psychologists cannot work with them. Self-help or support groups are available and these do seem to be more effective than individual psychotherapy, but the percentage attending such groups is still small. On the whole, futokou and hikikomori are considered to be psychological but not psychotic syndromes that generally do not respond well to medication.

One characteristic that appears common in these two conditions is lack of verbalisation. Typically, hikikomori students scarcely talk to anybody and futokou students verbalise little, especially when asked 'Is there any reason why you do not go to school?' or 'How do you feel about it?' This makes clinical work very difficult. The other common characteristic is that they hide, or fail to have an awareness of themselves, what they are and what they intend to become in the future. Some people might interpret this as a failure to establish identity, which, according to Erikson (1959), is a young person's developmental task. However, I argue that in Japan it should not be simply interpreted that way. Erikson's theory was developed in a culture in which high value is placed on the creation of a distinct self and self-expression. The mixture of an unclear sense of 'I' and poor verbalisation in these symptoms is deeply rooted in Japanese psychological climate.

I have selected these two syndromes because of their interest to Western readers. When I went to Europe to participate in a conference and talked to some Europeans about these two conditions, they found the symptoms very mysterious. I found something interesting in their responses. Some of the Europeans said to me, 'If it was my son, I wouldn't accept it. I'd give him a strong talking to instead – even though I'm a psychotherapist and know that acceptance and listening are important! I'd say "get out of my house!" if he didn't find a job.' Of course, Japanese parents also give their children a strong push, but it just doesn't work. In my clinical experience with these people, I have come to see that in many cases they are trying very hard to express their own existence by remaining non-verbal and unsocial. Being isolated might be the only way to keep their identity. It is their desperate struggle to keep their own space so a parent's persuasion, such as the European would suggest, does not affect them. On the contrary it makes them more withdrawn.

3. ACTING OUT

Acting out, in the psychoanalytic context, is an action expressed by behaviour rather than verbalisation. So a psychotherapy textbook, particularly psychodynamic, will emphasise the importance of getting clients to verbalise the feeling contained in the acted-out behaviour. However, as I have pointed out, it is very natural for a Japanese person not to be verbally expressive. Hence, some type of what might be called 'acting out behaviour' is natural in Japanese culture: for example, giving a present – if a client brings a present to a therapist after coming back from trip, in Japanese culture it is usually accepted. In this way, the therapist may fail to encourage the client to verbalise what they are trying to convey by bringing a present, even though they (the therapist) knows that acting-out behaviour (such as bringing a present) contains a wish for the therapist to understand the client's unconscious desire. But, whilst psychoanalysis aims to lead the client towards insight, the Japanese frequently want others to understand their feelings without any verbalisation on their part – so psychoanalytic thought and Japanese custom come into conflict. Doi (1978) pointed out that there is a so-called 'Amae' feeling at the core of Japanese culture. This is the dependency a very young child has for its mother that in Japanese people persists into adult life towards parents, friends, teachers and others. Such a wish for others to understand them without verbalising is another form of Amae and to some extent is accepted in Japanese culture. When Japanese culture sees such acting-out behaviour as familiar, can the psychoanalytic theory of acting out maintain a therapeutic effect in Japan? So I argue that although psychoanalytical theory on acting-out is correct, it has to be dealt with differently depending on the culture.

4. EMPATHY

There is a technical issue, often discussed, related to empathy and its communication as described by Rogers. Japanese therapists tend to convey, not empathic understanding, but compassion. They tend to say, 'I feel the same way too' rather than, for instance, 'Am I right in saying that you feel anger?'

One of the issues to discuss here may be that of translation. It is not just 'good' or 'bad' translation that matters. Rather, it is whether the Japanese language has a vocabulary compatible with the English for 'communicating empathy', a phrase that can be found in English psychotherapeutic literature generally. Given that empathy is an internal feeling attitude, nobody can be sure if there is a perfectly matching vocabulary, even if the definition of the word is clearly stated in English. The next question becomes, 'Do the Japanese really understand what the English word "empathy" means or what Rogers, for example, tried to describe by the term "empathy"?'

The other issue is that *compassion* seems to be communicated between two people on the same side – each in each other's world. *Empathy* seems to be between two people on different sides – one enters the world of the other. In a society of such interpersonal closeness as Japan, compassion is much more naturally communicated than empathy. Even experienced Japanese therapists tend to respond with compassion rather than empathy. Empathic responses are not used very often in everyday life in Japan, but people are helped psychologically with compassionate responses. So the question is which to use: a thought-to-be therapeutically effective response (empathy) or a culturally natural response (compassion), especially when the two concepts are so different. There is no research on the different effects of empathy and compassion in Japan and Japanese practitioners need to give it more thought.

5. FELT SENSE

In Japan, high value is placed on understanding others without asking. It is considered insensitive or impolite to ask others directly what they think, feel or want. Japanese people pay attention to what is going on in a place, what others are thinking, what they are expected to do and how the whole situation is feeling. They try to understand others and the surrounding situation with a non-verbal feeling quality.

There is an important concept of 'felt sense' in focusing, a phenomenon and technique discovered and developed by Gendlin (1981). The felt sense is an internal, bodily sense which is not yet verbalised but felt somehow around the body, and it contains implicit meaning. The technique of focusing facilitates the person to get a meaning out of the felt sense. Gendlin writes, in the preface to the Japanese edition of his book *Focusing* (ibid.) that people feel about each other more carefully in Japan than in the United States. His observation is very true.

At the same time, I see many Japanese people who find it difficult to get a grip of the felt sense, especially when they are beginning to learn to focus with such instructions as 'pay attention to how your body feels' or 'how is it felt in your body?' or 'ask your body'. The Japanese have long learned to pay attention to the feeling about the others in their situation in life so they do it almost unconsciously. If they are asked to consciously pay attention with emphasis on the 'body', their naturally learned method of feeling ceases to function. For the Japanese, the 'body' in a focusing context might not be what they have learned to pay attention to. This seems to imply that the Japanese term for body, *karada*, and the English term 'body' are conceptually very different and beyond the issue of translation.

162

This reminds me that the Japanese language has very many words using the Chinese letter 'qi 気'. This qi means an air of life, energy and nature that floats through body and surrounding environment. China has had more than a 4,000 year history of dealing with qi. Their traditional medical system is based on qi, which has recently made great progress with the incorporation of Western medicine. Japan had already learned much from China long before its doors were finally opened to Western countries a hundred or so years ago. So the Japanese are very familiar with the concept of qi. Japanese people with their rich history and experience of feeling qi, have learned a method of automatically attending to themselves and their surroundings since early childhood. It is an unconsciously operating attitude. As I indicated above, the Japanese do not verbalise much, so their ability to watch and feel carefully has tended to become refined.

As yet, if what the Japanese have learned to feel is the same as the 'felt sense' of Gendlin's focusing has not been explored, research needs to be conducted to clarify this idea. But more importantly, almost thirty years have passed since focusing was introduced into Japan, so Japanese psychotherapists should consider how to utilise the Japanese traditional feeling ability. Here, I am highlighting the possibility that psychotherapeutic concepts – in this instance, the felt sense and focusing – need to be reconsidered and re-conceptualised within Japanese culture instead of just 'catching up with' Western thinking.

PERSONIFICATION

Personification is thinking of or representing something as having human qualities. I see much more personification in Western psychotherapeutic thinking than in Japanese. For instance, Mearns and Thorne (2000) explain a therapeutic method of working with 'configurations' in the context of client-centred therapy. A configuration is a symbolised part of the person that they feel they have inside, and they give it another name as if it were a different person. Yoshimi Ito, one of the leading Japanese researchers of person-centred and experiential therapy, is now working on publishing a Japanese translation of the book, *Person-Centred Therapy Today*, by Mearns and Thorne (2000). I am the translator of Chapter VI which covers the nature of configurations. The translation for this was hard work because the phenomenon which Mearns calls 'configurations' is so unfamiliar to the Japanese experientially, even though it is understandable cognitively. Another example of internal personification is multiple personality disorder – this is not often seen in Japanese society to the extent it is illustrated in Western books. Imaginary companions are not so often observed in Japanese people either.

There are many other examples that relate to therapeutic theory and practice that are linked to the above. Freud's theory also has such personified concepts. The relation between the 'superego', 'ego' and 'id' is described and conceptualised like interpersonal relationship. For example, in Freud's theory, 'defence' and 'resistance' are the concepts that are associated with combat. There are focusing techniques called 'acknowledgement', invented by Cornell (1994), one of which is saying 'hello' to a felt sense. This can be thought of as personification of felt sense. Many Japanese find it somewhat strange to

163

do, because it is a deeply unnatural approach. Many Japanese people also feel hesitant toward the Gestalt's empty-chair technique and role play in psychodrama because they appear so artificial. Other Western psychotherapeutic concepts and practices also seem to be difficult to assimilate into Japanese culture.

DISCUSSION

I can present two interpersonal characteristics unique to the Japanese: 'we-feeling' and 'non-verbalisation'.

WE-FEELING

Japanese culture gives much more respect to non-verbal communication and accepts 'togetherness' as compared to Western culture. This makes psychotherapy for Japanese very different from that for Westerners. To the Japanese, psychotherapy seems based too much on individuality, something which may be entirely natural for Westerners. Japanese clients are similar to Western clients in that they come to therapy for solutions to their problems, however, the quality of relationship they seek as the basis for psychotherapy is very different. Japanese clients tend to expect to have 'we-feeling' with therapists. This dyes Western clinical theories a different colour. For instance, Mahler's separation-individuation theory (1975) has an assumption that it is normal development for human beings to leave their parents and live by themselves when they grow up. It is true that Japanese adults also become capable of taking care of themselves, but the emphasis is not on separation but on bond. The Japanese letter for human beings is '人'. It means that human beings live, survive or exist by helping each other. The letter is originally Chinese so it is not only in Japan but also China (and some other Asian countries) that the concept for human beings is this way.

There is much less personification of symptoms and therapy techniques in Japan than in Western countries. As I indicated above, in the sense of 'I' the Japanese do not have such a fixed self as Westerners. The sense of self changes as the term referring to 'I' changes, depending on the situation. So Japanese have much more flexibility to change their 'self' than Westerners. Consequently, Japanese people do not need personification to expand their selves' possibilities. As noted above, Erikson theorised (1959) that it is an adolescent's developmental task to establish an identity and I have to point out that this theory was born in Western culture. It is a hard developmental task because the young person has to exclude all other possibilities in order to have one identity. Those excluded possibilities might need to come into the self structure of the Westerner in a form of personification.

In Japan, people do not have so much pressure to create an identity as in the West; on the contrary, they need to keep 'we-feeling' instead. So, what does the 'we' in 'we-feeling' mean? I remember speaking, in English, with an American colleague at the university. He asked me, 'what do you mean by the "we", you often use?' Then I found out with surprise that, unconsciously, I meant many things by 'we'. I then asked my Japanese graduate students the same question. All of them became aware, also with surprise, that they frequently use the term 'we' unconsciously. The students and I realised that the Japanese meant friends, colleagues and the whole Japanese society by 'we'. This suggests that the Japanese usage of the term 'we' refers not necessarily to a fixed entity but to a vague image and feeling of togetherness. The feeling of togetherness is maintained by the use of 'we' and supports the Japanese psychologically.

This seems to be analogous to the difference between Western and Japanese religion. In Western countries, religion is based on a person-to-God relationship, which is a one-to-one relationship. In Japan, there are several hundred gods in nature surrounding people (Yamaori, 1999). These religious conceptions influence the interpersonal relationship in both worlds. While Western culture emphasises person-to-person interaction, the Japanese culture sees people as part of nature. Hence 'we' for 'we-feeling' can expand to surrounding nature.

NON-VERBALISATION

Because the Japanese verbalise so much less than Western people, they are amazed at Western expressiveness. In psychotherapy, it takes time for Japanese clients to realise it is their right to express their concern; it also takes time for them to be able to verbalise what they want to say.

Some clients do not know what they want to say. They seek 'we-feeling' and 'togetherness' in the therapy situation and they try to achieve it by not having their say. In other words, their attention is focused on the relationship with the therapist, so that when they focus on their own mind they find nothing to say. Of course, this can be an individual client's psychological theme to explore in psychotherapy. However, this is something that can be said about the Japanese in general. If they are asked to say something, they first explore what is OK to say here, not what they think of the issue. From a developmental viewpoint verbal communication is seen as being at a more advanced stage than non-verbal communication. In comparing the different cultures, Japanese culture places value on non-verbal levels of communication, whilst Western culture places value on verbal levels of communication. But it is clear in thinking of the 'felt sense' that if you verbalise less, you feel more. In the field of psychotherapy, one of the more recent innovations has been that of paying attention to the wisdom of the body. There are many non-verbal therapies, such as relaxation techniques, image therapy, focusing, body-awareness, invented in Western countries. This suggests that Western culture is now beginning to realise the importance of non-verbal feeling.

It is fortunate for the Japanese people to hold a non-verbal culture: if they can find and develop the possibility of non-verbal communication in psychotherapy, it might make some contribution to Western countries and make psychotherapy really grounded in Japan's climate.

INTEGRATION OF CULTURE AND PSYCHOTHERAPY

I have been criticising the Japanese tendency to just follow Western ideas without reference to Japanese culture, but this is something that has long been nourished in the country's history. Japan has always tried to catch up with other countries – China, Europe, and now the USA – and this attitude has made a great contribution to Japan's progress. However, now that the country has imported so many Western ideas, Japanese psychotherapists have to be able to think for themselves about what is really right for the Japanese. The attitude of independent thinking is the one idea that Japanese therapists have not yet learned from the West. They have to fully utilise their traditionally-accumulated ability of feeling in order to judge whether or not each theory or technique from the West fits the Japanese.

As for me, I too was a follower of Western thought but I gradually became aware that I was ignoring, repressing or abandoning my own feelings and ideas when I simply applied Western thought to my practice – and these are feelings and ideas that I have nourished for such a long time. Then I remembered that Rogers said, '*Experience is, for me, the highest authority.* The touchstone of validity is my own experience. No other person's ideas, and none of my own ideas, are as authoritative as my experience' (1961: 23). I realised that my trying to ignore, repress or abandon my own feelings and ideas was the exact opposite of Rogers' remark, even though I am a person-centred psychotherapist. Since then, I have become free from person-centred (and even Rogers') thoughts. Instead of following foreign ideas, I always check my feelings about theory, technique and anything else, in order to explore what is right for me, in my culture.

As a result of the discussion above, I present a perspective on psychotherapy theory and technique that is 'culture-near' or 'culture-distant'. I have discussed several examples of Western ideas above that are 'culture-distant'. It is not simply a case of saying that 'culture-distant' ideas are ineffective. Judging from the fact that many Japanese are helped by psychotherapy, which is culture-distant, it is clear they can be effective. But there are also many other Japanese who feel something strange towards such culture-distant therapies. It seems to depend on the client – this may or may not be true – it might be the outcome of a culture-distant therapy. This will be an important research topic: to compare culture-near therapy and culture-distant therapy in terms of outcome.

What then might be culture-near psychotherapy in Japan? One way of finding a clue for this is to study how people dealt with psychological problems before the idea of psychotherapy or counselling was introduced. In Japan, there was no tradition of confidential consultation such as counselling and psychotherapy. One of the traditional systems in Japan was that the helper was a Buddhist monk or psychic reader. People got together in a religious room and each one consulted the helper in turn; other people could listen, it was not confidential and was even shared with the others in the room. I suppose that the place might have occasionally been host to a spontaneously created encounter group (and as a matter of fact, this system is still working in some places of Japan). The exception was the tea room, where confidentiality was maintained. In a tea room, the helper was a tea master who was in a lower class than 'busho', the highest leader of Samurais in the area, but in the tea room (and only in the tea room) they were supposed to be on the same level. However, a tea room was not available to most people: it was only available to small number of upper-class people like busho.

This implies that even though there are many Japanese who are helped by psychotherapy in a confidential setting, there might be many who could be helped by 'unconfidential' sharing of their experience with others. This might be called not 'psychotherapy' but a 'group approach'. However, as I have already pointed out, the Japanese are familiar with non-verbal 'we-feeling' rather than person-to-person verbal communication. So the concept of a group will be different if it is adopted as a more formal helping system. It would be pointless to try to raise group cohesion by verbal self-expression because group cohesion is almost certainly already there. It is easy for the Japanese to be emotionally together because they share 'we-feeling'.

To finish this chapter, a last question comes to mind. Do Western theories and techniques really fit Western people? They are culture-near ideas to the Westerners so would supposedly fit them. However, considering the fact that many Japanese people are helped with culture-distant Western psychotherapy, might there not be Westerners who can be helped with culture-distant helping systems? Are there Westerners who feel it too much of a burden to establish identity? If this is true, there may be a vast field for the Western psychotherapist to explore.

REFERENCES

Cornell, A (1994) *Focusing Guide's Manual* (Trans J Bester) (3rd edn). Berkeley, CA: Focusing Resources.

Doi, T (1978) *Anatomy of Dependence.* Tokyo: Kodansha International.

Erikson, EH (1959) *Identity and the Life Cycle.* New York: International Universities Press.

Gendlin, ET (1981) *Focusing.* New York: Bantam Books.

Kawai, H (1976) *Pathology in Japan Femaleness Society.* (in Japanese). Chuo-Koron-sha.

Mahler, M (1975) *The Psychological Birth of the Human Infant.* New York: Basic Books.

Mearns, D & Thorne, B (2000) *Person-Centred Therapy Today.* London: Sage.

Murayama, S & Nojima, K (1977) Developmental stages of encounter-group process. *Research Bulletin (Educational Psychology) of the Faculty of Education, Kyushu University, 21* (2), 77–84, (in Japanese).

Rogers, CR (1959) A theory of therapy, personality, and interpersonal relationships, as developed in the client-centred framework. In S Koch (Ed) *Psychology: A study of a science. Vol. 3 Formulations of the person and the social context* (pp. 184–256). New York: McGraw-Hill.

Rogers, CR (1961) *On Becoming a Person: A therapist's view of psychotherapy.* London: Constable.

Rogers, CR, McGaw, WH Jr & McGaw, AP (Directors) (1973) *The Steel Shutter.* La Jolla, CA, Center for the Studies of the Person. [Motion picture].

Yamaori, T (1999) *The Power of Religion: Where will the Japanese psych go?* (in Japanese), PHP Research Institute, Inc.

CHAPTER 14

INTERCONNECTIONS BETWEEN PRIVILEGE AND OPPRESSION

KAY MCFARLANE

In writing this chapter I wanted to explore an area that I have been pondering a lot recently. Namely, the implications to therapeutic work of the interconnections between the various groups to which we belong, particularly regarding experiences of privilege and oppression. For example, how do my class privileges impact my gendered oppression and my ethnicity-related privileges? How does my non-disability relate to my age, class and sexuality? By exploring the interrelationships between the various groups to which we belong, this chapter could be described as illustrating one aspect of working with the cultural, political, and social in therapy sessions. In this way it links closely to Nick Totton's chapter (this book, Chapter 12) in which he establishes the importance of contextualising psychotherapy and counselling and incorporating the social and political dimensions of life into therapy practice. For a long time I have considered this to be fundamental to psychotherapy and counselling, more important in fact, than any particular theoretical orientation. I fervently believe this and I have established this premise as central to my teaching in counselling and psychotherapy. I am therefore dissatisfied with myself and very curious as to why I still do not routinely and explicitly make this central to my psychotherapy work with clients. In this chapter I include a brief exploration of this avoidance, as I believe that paying attention to the difficulty can be fruitful in identifying new ways forward, as well as recalling approaches previously used.

In writing this chapter, I draw on experiences and ideas more than theory. I use the terms 'therapy', 'psychotherapy' and 'counselling' interchangeably as I believe the points I make are relevant to all therapeutic practice. Similarly, I mainly refer to the groups to which we belong, but at times I also refer to the roles we live and to elements of our identity/identities. These various terms are culturally embedded and are not necessarily completely interchangeable. However, I deliberately use them all as I believe that the experience of advantage or disadvantage is intrinsic to our existence, so is relevant to all of these terms. To protect anonymity I create composite examples – intertwining and adapting elements of my own therapy, supervision and teaching practice, with illustrations from literature and peer discussion.

First, I introduce the premise on which I base my thoughts about interacting groups to which we belong, that is, the centrality of social, cultural, and political contexts. I then scan recent ideas about advantage and disadvantage depending on the groups to which we belong. Finally, I briefly consider why it might seem difficult to consistently address these themes, whilst suggesting ways to 'work with' or 'move beyond' the omission to work therapeutically with the significance of our social and cultural existence. If you are reading this chapter and you haven't thought a lot yet about your interconnecting group memberships, I have a suggestion. Each time an illustration is outlined, you could identify examples from your own life. This might help you decide how significant the notions of interrelating identities are, in your view.

SOCIAL, CULTURAL AND POLITICAL CONTEXT

It seems that some therapists/counsellors still believe that anti-oppressive practice or working with diversity is relevant to them only if they themselves or some of their particular clients belong to minority groups. Specific literature or training is then often sought. Of course issues of diversity, oppression and privilege are central to all of us – we all have an age, ethnicity, gender etc., which is significant personally, culturally, socially, politically. We all exist in relation to the world and to each other (in close proximity or at a distance, individually or in groups), so that issues of power and difference are always in relation to someone else. If one person, or group, is oppressed, then someone else or another group is (knowingly or unknowingly) oppressing them, and yet another group is (knowingly or unknowingly) colluding with the oppression. If I have a privilege, it might be at the expense of someone else; the fact that I have a particular privilege might mean that someone else cannot have it or it might mean that they too could have it if things were organised differently. A recent example of this dynamic is buying my first house, a privilege not enjoyed by everyone in the world due to social, environmental, cultural, political, structural factors.

For me, in/equality, in/justice, identity, difference and power form the foundation of all therapeutic work. I believe it is, therefore, necessary to explore how therapists and clients exist in relation to structures, institutions, cultures, and contexts. A great deal has been written about how therapy tends to over-individualise – it focuses on the client's own thoughts, feelings, behaviour, needs and wishes without taking account of social contexts and dynamics that influence or are influenced by the client. Unless we are attending to contexts, we are perpetuating existing power inequalities and forms of oppression (Kearney, 1996). This is graphically illustrated by Owusu-Bempah and Howitt (2000), who suggest that psychological practice that focuses only on the individual is like giving a drowning person mouth to mouth resuscitation – under water. One central purpose of therapy is to understand 'self' better, we only partially understand ourselves if we do not recognise the contexts, structures and organisations that we create, participate in, perpetuate and/or challenge. (For a fuller account of the importance of bringing the social and political into the therapy room see Chapter 12, this volume.) I will finish this section by referring to a simple model from the arena of social work that makes this contextual focus most tangible for me. I often refer to literature and research from the field of social work as I find that it is more grounded in and more explicit about social

Fig. 1

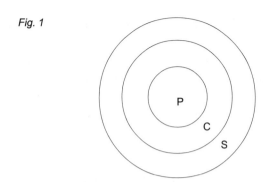

and political contexts than the literature of counselling and psychotherapy.
Thompson (1997) reminds us of three levels of our existence: personal, cultural and structural. He portrays these as three concentric circles

> P refers to the *personal* or *psychological*; it is the individual level of thoughts, feelings, attitudes and actions. It also refers to *practice*, individual workers interacting with individual clients, and *prejudice*, the inflexibility of mind which stands in the way of fair and non-judgemental practice. C refers to the *cultural* level of shared ways of seeing, thinking and doing. It relates to the *commonalities* – values and patterns of thought and behaviour, an assumed consensus about what is right and what is normal; it produces conformity to social norms, and *comic* humour acts as a vehicle for transmitting and reinforcing this culture. S refers to the structural level, the network of *social divisions*; it also relates to the ways in which oppression and discrimination are institutionalised and thus *'sewn in'* to the fabric of society. It denotes the wider level of *social forces*, the *socio-political* dimension of interlocking patterns of power and influence. (p. 20)

This simplified model is a very useful way to summarise my view of the purpose and practice of therapy both to students and sometimes to clients. I often add dotted lines and two-way arrows to emphasise how each level is not ultimately separable from the others.

Fig. 2

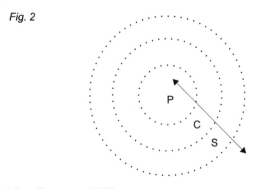

(Adapted from Thompson, 1997)

170

ADVANTAGED AND DISADVANTAGED IDENTITIES

Each of us is embedded in a structural, cultural, and political existence; the groups to which we belong, and each aspect of our identity, has structural, cultural and political significance. Who we are is never socially neutral. For example, whatever our age, as well as having personal meaning, it has structural implication; it permits or prevents us legally (voting, retiring, drinking). It also has cultural significance; others may assume that we are young and disrespectful or old and dependent. Our age affects our social status; we are advantaged and/or disadvantaged by our age. Other group memberships might be significant in additional or different ways. For example, our sexuality means we are part of a minority or majority, mainstream or not mainstream; our ethnicity means that we are privileged in some ways and/or oppressed in some ways. Until recently, writers have tended, more often than not, to focus on one or two groups or elements of identity, such as age or race. This simplistic focus can be useful for raising awareness or deepening our understanding of the significances and nuances of one aspect of who we are. For example, a white person who has never explored their whiteness could spend time focusing specifically on ethnicity in all its complexities and contexts. However, perpetually isolating aspects of identity is also deficient. Having increased understanding of their whiteness, they would need to investigate how their ethnicity relates to other elements of their identity such as gender, age, sexuality, dis/ability and class.

At the social level of analysis, Burman (2004) reminds us of writers who assert that 'mutually exclusive categorizations' (p. 299) lead to divisions between people/groups that severely hinder coalition (Bondi, 1993; Spelman, 1988). McDonald and Coleman (1999) discuss the notion of 'divide and rule' (Freire, 1996) in which the more privileged in society maintain their status by allowing or encouraging the less privileged to be in conflict with other disadvantaged groups. It seems that conceiving people as having one-dimensional identities does serve the interests of those who are considerably advantaged. More recently there has been increased interest in exploring how various elements of our identity or roles interrelate (Atkinson, 2001; Constantine, 2002; Croteau et al., 2002). Construing ourselves as multi-identitied, multi-faceted or multi-grouped, helps dislodge the prevailing Western notion of a contained, unified, independent self. Exploring the relationships between the groups to which we belong makes it easier to think and talk as if we are 'beings in process' or as if self is in flux rather than a complete or static entity. Moreover, exploring multiple identities aids 'an analysis of multiple oppressions' (Zerbe Enns et al., 2004: 415). Burman (2004) points out that by acknowledging the 'intersectionality' between 'various dimensions of difference' (p. 297), forms of oppression could be more thoroughly scrutinised. 'Racisms, for example, can be analysed as gender-specific in their forms (and also classed and endowed with sexuality') (p. 299).

Most of the literature that now expounds multiple identities focuses primarily on oppression, very little attends to privilege or advantage. If we really want to understand ourselves, I believe we need to discover how belonging to a particular group disadvantages *and* advantages us and how the various elements of who we are interconnect. How does the advantaged and disadvantaged experience of each group membership or element of identity interact with the others? It is impossible to imagine that each element of our identity or each group to which we belong will be entirely privileged or entirely oppressed. Of course, existence is much more complex than that. We need to explore how we might be oppressed whilst oppressing others; how we might even be advantaged in some ways by our experience of oppression, and how we are diminished through sustaining our privilege at the expense of others. So *each* group membership or element of identity needs to be explored for the ways in which it is advantaged *and* disadvantaged. For example, I am structurally advantaged in so many ways because I am white; at the same time, because I am white I believe I have a limited sense of myself as an embodied spiritual being: my way of perceiving the world is limited. If I accept prevailing social notions about race, I will continue with a skewed perception of my group's impact on the world. I will also lose out on the opportunity to recognise what I personally achieve and what is actually the lived benefit of my ethnicity.

In addition to examining particular elements of our individual identity in isolation, it is vital to explore the interplay between our various identities in order to avoid perceiving our clients or ourselves as merely 'oppressed' or 'privileged'. For example, we can be disadvantaged through direct discrimination *and* through the experience of being privileged. Such distinctions are well worth examining. There is clearly disadvantage in not experiencing a privilege or through being oppressed – for example, a white, middle-class, disabled male client finding it very hard to find employment in the financial world in spite of having high-level qualifications. Privilege itself has its downsides – for example, a middle-class, non-disabled, heterosexual woman valuing independence may not understand the subtleties of dependence and so experience limiting relationships. Conversely, as a result of experiencing oppression, some people can gain status or credibility. There can be advantage in the spiritual gain (Mindell, 1995) or moral and political currency (Kincheloe, 1999) acquired through surviving oppression.

As Croteau et al. (2002) remind us, whilst some elements of our identity can be hidden, others are immediately visible so there is less choice about whether and how to reveal them. Often, 'visibility' relates to the dominance of a particular element of identity, or group membership: others may see only that particular part of you – or it seems as if that element mediates all the others (a client talks of her colleagues seeing her as a walking/talking emblem of Islam). Robinson (1999) claims that dominance of one particular element of a person's identity can emerge because it is different from the mainstream or from the 'norm'.

> [W]hen an identity status deviates from a normative standard, it tends to dominate and thus render invisible other equally viable components of a person's identity. One layer of identity can then function as a primary-status trait, overriding other core dimensions of personhood due to the stigmatising act of categorization. (p. 75)

And, according to Robinson, belonging to a highly valued group can mediate other less valued aspects of identity: for example, a middle-class man claimed a greater confidence in telling people he was gay once he had climbed the career ladder and achieved more status (and money). On the other hand, through qualitative research, Croteau et al. (2002) identified various ways that experience of oppression due to one element of identity can affect another, privileged, element of identity. One of the participants in this research, a white female working at director's level, described how, within her organisation, she was only consulted on interpersonal issues needing a 'nurturing' perspective – her 'woman's perspective' was seen as different (and less valuable than) a 'professional perspective'. There are many ways and reasons that a particular element of identity or group membership may become more prominent, and it is important to understand how this happens. It is also important to explore other elements of identity that may be neglected. For example, facilitating a client to recognise the significance of his whiteness and heterosexuality enables him to understand others' reactions to him and to have a clearer grasp of his strength and confidence, or vulnerability.

Whilst all identities are always present and relevant in some way, their prominence may shift; whether or not we perceive several interlocking group memberships or identities, or several elements of one identity, the divisions or borders between each can be very permeable or seemingly impermeable. There may be quite fixed divisions between two particular elements: a person might never reveal to others or refer to their sexual identity in family contexts, even though it is always relevant. Some elements of identity might be so closely connected that they overlap or merge – a person habitually and exclusively perceiving their sexuality through their gender, for example. One reason for therapists and clients to explore the divisions between these interacting identities is to check whether firm, impermeable divisions are useful; or whether the divisions are too permeable and what degree of permeability is appropriate in various contexts. As an illustration of this: one client found increased freedom and hope through experimenting with her various roles in her community, at work and at university. These roles had previously been out of awareness but she experimented by noticing and then emphasising the process of her selection of these roles. As a result, she understood more about how she related with others as well as the beliefs and values underlying some of her relationships.

In their research, Pittinsky, Shih and Ambady (1999) consider the negative and facilitative impact of stereotypes on people's multiple identities. They noted that:

> stereotype-relevant social contexts prompt an implicit reorientation of an individual's affect across his or her many identities. This suggests that the experience of being the target of common stereotypes is a good deal more complex than has been examined. (p. 514)

These researchers examined how the interconnections between group memberships are impacted by stereotypes and prejudices in various social contexts, including the therapy room. What happens for the client, for example, if he or she experiences stereotypical responses towards different aspects of their identity, i.e. a disabled working-class woman seen as fragile and dependent, or a white male seen as rational and authoritative? On the other hand, what happens for a client faced with stereotypes in conflict: what are the consequences of being expected to be a strong and dependable middle-class male and, at the same time, needing help, as a disabled person?

Understanding how stereotypes and social interactions in general impact our interconnecting identities can help challenge internalised negative messages. This is explored by Croteau et al. (2002) who suggest that experiencing oppression ourselves increases our understanding of others. At the same time, understanding our interacting disadvantaged and advantaged identities could lead to a realisation of the ways we might oppress others as a result of experiencing oppression ourselves. Kincheloe (1999) describes how, as a result of economic oppression, some white people accuse different ethnic communities of eroding white identity, and subsequently develop racist world-views. Freire (1996) describes how the experience of oppression structures and shapes our thinking, so that the oppressed can become the oppressor. McDonald and Coleman (1999) use the phrase 'internalised oppressor' to describe this.

Of course, the interconnections depend on context. We may experience gendered power and status in one place and gendered discrimination in another. The interconnections are also fluid and changing. Social norms shift, some aspects of identity (such as age and sexuality) alter over time. This perhaps inevitably renders exploration and understanding over-simple – perhaps we can only ever glimpse a snapshot. However, despite these difficulties and limitations, it is still worth doing it is better for therapists and clients to work towards understanding the complexities and layers of their existence than to disregard them. If we do not attend to the structural and cultural dimensions of life in therapy, we are surely hindering clients' awareness; we are letting clients down as well as colluding with existing power inequalities. I am not suggesting that the role of therapy is always to formulate ways to combat oppressive social dynamics (although it might become so at some points with some clients). I am suggesting that it is the role of therapy to help people better understand themselves *in relationship*. I believe this can only be done if the world – including structures, political occurrences, cultural and social dynamics – is actively explored in sessions as an elemental part of the life that we shape and are shaped by. Of course, central to this endeavour is the understanding of the interconnecting group memberships.

DIFFICULTIES OF WORKING IN SESSIONS

The implications to therapy practice of the above notions are of course countless; in particular, the amount of work the therapist needs to do for themselves, and the relationship between the therapist and client, considering the interconnecting privileges and oppressions of their group memberships. In my teaching, I use theory, activities and discussion to establish this shift in focus between and across social, political, structural, personal and cultural levels, including paying attention to the students disadvantaged and advantaged interrelating identities or group memberships. For example, I envisage a continuum – between privilege and oppression or advantage and disadvantage – along which we all move, over time, even moment by moment, dependent on the various groups we belong to. I invite students to position themselves on the continuum in the various groups to which they belong or the various elements of their identity. Through discussion or creative-therapy techniques we then explore the patterns of group memberships or interconnections between the group memberships or identities. Depending on the therapeutic orientation, such activities can also be used effectively with clients in a therapy setting. This seems obvious. However, despite my commitment to this, I still find I do not consistently make explicit such a focus with clients. There are numerous reasons for this, and I am sure other people who also overlook this focus, or who find it difficult, have their own. Some of my obstacles are my own experiences of oppression and privilege, my cultural context, my prejudices, my feelings, and the clients' expectations of therapy. There are definitely some I have not yet identified and others that I probably never will. Nevertheless, I am hoping that by identifying and understanding the difficulties a little more, I will be able to identify additional relevant strategies in future.

MY EXPERIENCE OF PRIVILEGE AND OPPRESSION

I am part of several majority and privileged groups, so I live with a sense of myself (and my values) as being 'neutral'. It is hard to see the social structures and cultures creating and being created by some of my groups when it is all so taken for granted. For example, I continually need to increase my awareness of my ethnicity because 'whiteness makes itself invisible precisely by asserting its normalcy' (Frankenberg, 1997: 6).

Effort and time is needed to de-centre my experience, beliefs and values and to understand that these are just versions of life; they are not 'normal'. When some, or all, of our group memberships are minority groups, disadvantaged, less socially or politically powerful, it is less likely that we will experience our beliefs and ways of living as 'taken for granted': living in relation to a majority culture, we are constantly aware of how the mainstream operates and how our own values and lifestyles differ. In some ways, my own lived oppressions and privileges, advantages and disadvantages makes it difficult to sustain a social and political focus in therapy settings. In my own life, I know that at times I operate from a stance of 'I am not entitled to ...'. Through schooling and therapy training I have been encouraged to view this as a personal issue/weakness rather than as partially developed through group membership of my gender and influences relating to class. Conversely, I still often overlook the structural, cultural privilege that underpins my personal achievements. Both personal struggles and achievements have been a part of agreeing to write this chapter and buy my first house. Yet overcoming the personal struggles can easily disguise the privilege that makes both these events possible. Some achievements take a lot of hard work, anguish and overcoming of hurdles. As a result, it can be hard to perceive the advantage or privilege that has contributed to the success (see McIntosh, 1998). In fact, identifying the social privileges inherent in an achievement can feel like being undermined or being robbed of the satisfaction of the success.

Moreover, my own lack of awareness of my privilege and oppression can sometimes hinder my capacity to facilitate my clients' exploration. As I continue to develop my understanding about the various elements of my identity or group memberships, I continue to learn to de-centre my own dominating culture and to illuminate the subjugated memberships so that I can see them alongside and in relation to others. All this learning, in my view, is vital to being a psychotherapist. It involves reading, dialogue with others, focused development activities, noticing more in everyday life, and consciously taking the opportunity to learn from other peoples' reactions to me. For example, on occasions I have found it very useful to ask someone I am working with what it is like for them that I have been privileged in a way they have not, and to express to them how it is for me. A particular way of thinking that I find relevant, perhaps central, for myself and for my work with clients, relates to social-constructionist psychotherapeutic orientations. For one example, see Simon and Whitfield (2000), who describe the use of a hypothetical audience, encouraging the client to consider community, shared understandings, values and challenges. At the same time, I find it vital to incorporate attention to physical and emotional existence as well as cognitive experiencing – this could be described as phenomenological focusing.

MY CULTURAL CONTEXT

Seeing the various elements of our identity as separate and independent of each other, or seeing other people as a one-dimensional identity, fits the more Westernised idea of self. I was born and raised in a Western culture in which the emphasis is on an independent, self-contained idea of an individual self. In many Eastern cultures on the other hand, group identity takes precedence over an individual identity. Although this East/West distinction is vastly oversimplified here, the point remains pertinent that, as a result of the more individualistic stance of the culture I am part of, I am less likely to discern my communities, my groups, or the communities or groups in which a client is constructed/ immersed. It is therefore harder for me to perceive the interacting group memberships or elements of identity. This individual focus of my culture closely relates to the education system through which I have grown up. The schooling, higher education, and even the psychotherapy training that I received, did not encourage political critique generally (Kearney, 1996) nor, in particular, the social significance of identity or interacting identities. I have had to come, later in life, to these ideas of socially and structurally creating and created people. I am still in the process of training myself (in a way) to actually perceive us all as situated, embedded in community, social structures and cultures.

I propose that one of the purposes of therapy is to support clients to perceive the social, structural and cultural influences and influencing. How else can anyone understand themselves and others? In the initial sessions with a client, I often describe how I approach psychotherapeutic work. In the same way that I inform clients that I consider the relationship between us as a central part of the therapeutic work, I also usually let them know that, to me, the cultural, community and social dimensions of life are central. This enables them to decide whether this stance fits with their world-view and it also creates a framework and reference for our subsequent attention to the social, cultural self. Stating these views about therapy also gives clients who are far more socially and structurally aware than I am, the chance to decide if there is anything I can offer them. Occasionally, it has seemed relevant to actually draw the model described above (Thompson, 1997) as a visual way of conveying my stance to clients. Where appropriate, this can also be a starting point for clients to explicitly examine their social and political existence, as can using life-spirals or life-circles in which clients select one or maybe two particular elements of their identity or group membership and chart the influences or issues at structural and cultural, as well as personal levels (Thompson, 1997). It can be useful to just explore one element in this way, but the format can also be used to trace connections between various elements of identity or group memberships, to discover where they connect (or seem not to), to experiment with developing connections and to speculate about what could be gained from seeing or creating connections.

The idea of our group membership being significant because it is created and *creates*, is an important point to establish with clients. If we do not do this we run the risk of thinking of the self as merely irrevocably shaped by the community or society from which we come. Clearly, we can withstand, convert or defeat internalised oppression, challenge accepted norms, resist social pressures and recognise our privileges. Sometimes it is useful to help clients identify or remember ways they have already done this individually or through group membership. More than a decade after leaving home and coming out to his parents, a client was finally able to 'be himself' when visiting them, rather than talking and behaving in a way that 'real men' do. Exploring how this change occurred helped him to identify how internalised messages had lingered, how these had diminished, and how he used informal and formal support to help disarm them.

MY PREJUDICES

Of course my prejudices can also get in the way of facilitating clients to explore the interconnections between elements of their identity. My prejudices about therapy, about particular groups or the client in front of me, all limit my imagination or confidence to interact in certain ways or on certain subjects. I am not as likely to see or encourage connections if I am making assumptions. Rigid thinking does not facilitate fluid engagement with the person sitting in front of me and their social and cultural existence. If I feel resentment and disrespect (in or out of my awareness) towards a new client's accent, I am immediately perceiving group membership in a particular way, before exploring the client's relationship to either their own group, or to mine. So, as well as being aware of my own prejudices, I need to find ways of discussing the impact of these prejudices with my clients. We need to prepare the ground for such discussion by exploring their experience of prejudice; what they are alert to in their interactions with people; how they might let me know if they experience my prejudiced or rigid thinking, and what response they might then expect from me.

MY FEELINGS

A range of feelings gets in my way of attending to clients' interconnecting group membership: feeling overwhelmed, feeling fear, feeling shame. More positively experienced feelings, such as the desire for harmony and comfort, can also interrupt my attention.

Sometimes, when I am thinking or talking about the social and structural significance of our lives, the complexity is overwhelming for me; everything connects to everything and I sometimes feel that I cannot move or think in any direction because I will be oppressing or overlooking. I am stumped by the fact that everything needs scrutiny; all aspects of life are up for challenge. This can be exhausting, frightening and demotivating. It can stop me in my tracks and lead to inertia. At these times it can help to stay in that inertia, to find out more about it. At other times, I usefully remind myself that examining everything is neither sustainable nor possible and is never-ending. Thus, I can proceed slowly, a little at a time. Sometimes, I tell myself that staying stuck or not moving will perpetuate the oppression or inequality anyway, so it might be better to be making an effort and getting it wrong rather than giving up completely. This process relates closely to shame – that debilitating feeling when I get something wrong, offend someone or discover another bigoted belief or feeling, previously unrecognised. Learning to tolerate the shame rather than avoiding it makes a big difference when working with issues of privilege or oppression. The consequence of this is that in my teaching and my work with clients, instead of playing safe or always giving in to the desire for comfort, harmony or warmth, I need to continue to develop my capacity to tolerate discomfort and conflict.

CLIENTS' EXPECTATIONS OF THERAPY

I am not suggesting that we attend to every group membership interconnection with a client or to all elements and nuances of interconnections between privilege and oppression. If we did there would be little time to do anything else. What about the issues that the client comes to therapy to address?

We owe it to clients to raise some of these relevant dimensions even if they do not want to explore them. Surely our role is to draw attention to *all* of who we are, not simply to gaze at the internal or personal dimensions of being human. If we believe a client is not attending to their thinking or feeling, we might not insist on exploring it but we would usually point out the oversight or avoidance. Our existence is social, cultural and political, as well as personal; so whatever the client's reason for coming to therapy, the social, cultural and political dimensions are relevant to some degree and in some way. If the remit of psychotherapy is to support clients to increase their awareness of themselves, their issues and their ways of relating, then are we not doing them a disservice if we do not attend to social and political dimensions? Increasing awareness of these dimensions is simply part of increasing awareness generally.

One way of doing this in the therapy setting is to select a particular event or scenario that the client is talking about or working on and look at the 'position' of all the elements of the client's identity at that moment or in that situation – like taking a snapshot of the pattern of their identities. This might involve looking at each element's prominence or invisibility in the client's own perception, envisaging the perception of other people, looking at how the various elements relate to each other at that moment, exploring whether one group membership could inform or influence another, or considering if overlooked elements could usefully be brought forth.

This chapter highlights the age-old proposition that difficulties or problems are often actually opportunities. Writing this has given me a chance to draw together my haphazard thoughts and has served to remind me to attend to the social, political and cultural dimensions of existence in my own work with clients. Now I'm really curious about whether, having written it, I will do so more consistently.

REFERENCES

Atkinson, E (2001) Deconstructing boundaries: Out on the inside? *International Journal of Qualitative Studies in Education, 14* (3), 307–16.

Bondi, L (1993) Locating identity politics. In M Keith & S Pile (Eds) *Place and the Politics of Identity* (pp. 84–101). London: Routledge.

Burman, E (2004) From difference to intersectionality: Challenges and resources. *European Journal of Psychotherapy, Counselling and Health, 6* (4), 293–308.

Constantine, M (2002) The intersection of race, ethnicity, gender and social class in counseling: Examining selves in cultural contexts. *Journal of Multicultural Counseling and Development, 30,* 210–15.

Croteau, J, Talbot, D, Lance, T & Evans, N (2002) A qualitative study of the interplay between privilege and oppression. *Journal of Multicultural Counseling and Development, 30,* 239–58.

Frankenberg, R (1997) Local whitenesses, localizing whiteness. In R Frankenberg (Ed) *Displacing Whiteness: Essays in social and cultural criticism* (pp. 147–52). London: Duke University Press.

Freire, P (1996) *Pedagogy of the Oppressed.* London: Penguin.

Kearney, A (1996) *Counselling, Class and Politics: Undeclared influences in therapy.* Ross-on-Wye: PCCS Books.

Kincheloe, J (1999) The struggle to define and reinvent whiteness: A pedagogical analysis. *College Literature, 26* (3), 162–94.

McDonald, P & Coleman, M (1999) Deconstructing hierarchies of oppression and adopting a 'multiple model' approach to anti-oppressive practice. *Social Work Education, 18* (1), 19–33.

McIntosh, P (1998) White privilege: Unpacking the invisible knapsack. In M McGoldrick (Ed) *Re-visioning Family Therapy: Race culture and gender in clinical practice.* New York: Guilford Press.

Mindell, A (1995) *Sitting in the Fire.* Portland, OR: Lao Tse Press.

Owusu-Bempah, K & Howitt, D (2000) *Psychology beyond Western Perspectives.* Leicester: BPS Books.

Pittinsky, T, Shih, M & Ambady, N (1999) Identity adaptiveness: Affect across multiple identities. *Journal of Social Issues, 55* (3), 503–18.

Robinson, T (1999) The intersections of dominant discourses across race, gender and other identities. *Journal of Counseling and Development, 17,* 73–9.

Simon, G & Whitfield, G (2000) Social constructionist and systemic therapy. In D Davies & C Neal (Eds) *Therapetuic Perspectives on Working with Lesbian, Gay and Bisexual Clients* (pp. 144–62). Buckingham: Open University Press.

Spelman, E (1988) Gender and race: The ampersand problems in feminist thought. In E Spelman (Ed) *Inessential Women* (pp. 114–32). New York: Beacon Press.

Thompson, N (1997) *Anti-Discriminatory Practice* (2nd edn). Basingstoke: Macmillan.

Zerbe Enns, C, Sinacore, A, Ancis, J & Phillips, J (2004) Toward integrating feminist and multicultural pedagogies. *Journal of Multicultural Counseling and Development, 32*, 414–27.

CHAPTER 15

THE GROUND OF OUR RELATING
MARTIN BUBER'S *I AND THOU*

RICHARD WORSLEY

> There are moments of silent depth in which you look on the world order fully present. Then in its very flight the note will be heard; but the ordered world is its indistinguishable score. These moments are immortal, and most transitory of all; no content may be secured from them, but their power invades the creation and the knowledge of man. (Buber, 1958: 47)

The sentences in the above quotation from Buber's *I and Thou,* immortal and transitory, seem to contradict each other. The first sentence hints of permanence, that which never dies. The second, tastes of life's passing quality, slipping out of existence moment by moment. For Martin Buber (1878–1965), human relationships have both these qualities. Our ability to relate at depth is always returning to the superficial. Yet, when we relate at depth, Buber claims, we echo something of universal significance, something which cannot decay.

Why should therapists get to know Buber's work? Buber has had a huge influence upon modern thinking. He is a philosopher of immense importance, particularly in the continental tradition (Schilpp & Friedman, 1967). He is one of the most powerful Jewish thinkers and theologians of our age. He has made a huge impact upon therapeutic thinking (Crossley, 1996). Buber met with Carl Rogers in a famous dialogue chaired by the greatest of Buber scholars, Maurice Friedman (Kirschenbaum & Henderson, 1990). In their dialogue, they immediately recognised in each other a depth of mutual understanding, both stunning and intriguing. Even today, Buber provides some of the most interesting challenges to, as well as affirmations of, therapeutic thinking. In short, Buber is crucial to seeing what therapists of all persuasions might mean by 'relating'. He invites us to understand in a fresh, challenging way the nature of relationships that heal. He does so at a time in the history of therapy when the relationship is becoming central to all major modalities.

We are coming to recognise, in general, that it is crucial to meet the client at a relational depth (Mearns & Cooper, 2005). The Austrian person-centred scholar, Peter Schmid, has an increasing impact upon our thinking about meeting the client as the Other, and of being the Other for the client (Schmid, 1998, *inter alia*). In this, he uses the thought of Martin Buber alongside that of his fellow Jewish philosopher, Emmanuel Levinas. All practitioners need to explore the depth or groundedness of relating, according to their own theoretical approach. My own practice is person-centred/experiential, so I relate this to Carl Rogers' thinking. However, I have enough acquaintance with Object Relations theory and practice to see that many schools of counselling and psychotherapy have a common heritage in the work of Buber.

While Martin Buber's thought is largely congruent with Rogers' insights, I have come to believe that Buber invites us to develop Rogers' thinking, finding in the intersubjective (in that space between people where contact and relating happen) new ways of understanding what it is to be human and to find wholeness. This is not an easy idea for all person-centred therapists. Sometimes it is tempting to take refuge in what I think of as a Rogers-fundamentalism. However, the person-centred movement will grow and change just as every individual must. Martin Buber's way of thinking encourages us to change the way we think and feel, to reconceptualise what it is to relate to another human being.

In this chapter, I will offer a brief introduction to Martin Buber, the person and scholar, and then set his thought in the context of the therapeutic relationship. I will then open up some of the key themes from *I and Thou*, interweaving Buber's thought with its impact upon our understanding of relating. Buber is not only a philosopher of immense importance – one perhaps still underestimated by academic philosophers – but is beautifully accessible. Much of his key thinking sits in one short book. He writes more as a poet. We therefore need to absorb his words and allow them to create in us recognitions of what we already half know. His words are beautiful. In teaching counselling over a number of years, I experienced so many students finding their way of practice subtly changed and enriched by a poetic love of Buber's *I and Thou*.

However, I guess that Buber also warrants a health warning. He is not only a poet and philosopher, but also a mystic. We need not so much to understand, in a technical-critical mode, what he says, but rather to absorb, although not uncritically, something of his vision. As a mystic, Buber challenges the limitations of our view of life. He tries to open up gateways to the beyond. One-third of his *I and Thou* is explicitly religious. Do not be put off if this is not your life-view. However, the reader will need to learn to 'translate' this aspect of Buber into his or her own language or world-view. In spite of what Crossley (1996: 10) says, this aspect of Buber's thought cannot be merely discarded. It conditions how he sees the world, and what he strives to point to for us. Notwithstanding this, Buber is just as powerful from a secular stance as a religious one.

WHO WAS MARTIN BUBER?

During the early years of the twentieth century, European Judaism was undergoing a rebirth as both a cultural and a religious movement. This rebirth came to a cataclysmic end with the coming to power of the Nazis, and died as a possibility for the time being in the concentration camps. Yet, for a small number of years, this revival was led by Martin Buber.

Buber was a scholar of Judaism but also a philosopher. He is still valued for both his religious and his secular thinking. He came out of the Hasidic tradition: Hasidism is a medieval mystical strand in Jewish spirituality, in which direct access to God is particularly to be prized. To understand something of the feel of Hasidism, a good starting place is Chaim Potok's (1974) novel, *My Name is Asher Lev*. It is important to see Buber's roots in Hasidism in order to get the feel of *I and Thou* as a work that is mystical in its aspiration.

Yet, perhaps the most formative moment in Buber's life brought him into conflict with aspects of his Hasidic background. One evening, Buber had been at a religious meeting of what might be called a fervent or revivalist flavour. He came home entranced by his experience. Shortly after arriving home, a young man visited him. Buber welcomed him in and listened to him for a while before sending him on his way. He was aware that the impact of the religious meeting had clouded his interest in this strange young man. A few days later, Buber learned that he had committed suicide.

Buber was profoundly shocked by his own failure to give real attention to the young man. He experienced a deep change in his way of being. He determined that human relating was to be the key to living, for it had been in failing to relate that Buber had contributed to the end of a human life. As I have said above, Buber's religious language and feeling can seem difficult. It cannot be merely discarded as if Buber's God can be subtracted from *I and Thou* without loss. Rather it must be translated. We can do this with a thought-experiment. What is the highest, most transcendent quality of being alive, of being human, in which you can believe? Then, Buber's *I–Thou* is to be modelled on that.

BUT WHY SHOULD I BE INTERESTED?

Here is one of Buber's *Tales of the Hasidim*, for it is in his early work that he began to learn the power of relating:

> When young Rabbi Eleazar of Koznitz, Rabbi Moshe's son, was a guest in the house of Rabbi Naftali of Roptchitz, he once cast a surprised glance at the window, where the curtains had been drawn. When the host asked him the cause of his surprise, he said: 'If you want people to look in, then why draw the curtains? And if you do not want them to, why the window?'
>
> 'And what explanation have you found for this?' asked Rabbi Naftali.
>
> 'When you want someone you love to look in,' said the young rabbi, 'you draw aside the curtain.' (Buber, 1948: 177)

The Hasidic tradition had already within it the concept that love involves a disclosure of our selves to others in mutuality. On this tradition Buber was to build his philosophy. The image of a meeting as the drawing aside of a curtain is powerful. In its spirit, I can ask: What do you want to disclose to your clients in your invitation that they might love you?

These words sound scandalous. Most counsellors are rightly very careful about disclosing anything to the client, if by 'disclose' we mean the telling of personal information or experience. All too often this can just get in the way. 'Love', too, is a word that is only just finding its way back into counselling vocabulary. However, Buber encourages us to acknowledge that there is far more to any relationship than the deliberate words and actions of either party (see the quotation at the head of this chapter). Consider for a moment the person who facilitates a personal development group. After a while the group may come to a keen appreciation of what that person is like, even though she may have said very little about herself. Who we are, our way of being, discloses itself at the heart of relating. It does not rely upon disclosing *facts*. Self-disclosure is more like a leaking around the edges of all that we do and do not do. Relating cannot be reduced to deeds and words. Our love, our *agape*, for our clients will out. Relating is deeper than we often allow. Buber challenges us to discover afresh its depths.

So far, this might seem quite uncontroversial. I suggest that a taking seriously of Buber's thinking will challenge the heart of our work. Why? The core conditions of therapy – empathy, congruence and unconditional regard (Rogers, 1957) – are the bedrock of all approaches to therapy. In the early days of practising, there is a tendency for therapists to see these three conditions in rigid form. Yet Rogers' proposal of the core conditions is not at all rigid. I may strive to be empathic, but I do not always know what it *is* to be empathic. Indeed, in his later life, Rogers became intensely irritated with the notion that empathy, or even the whole of the approach, was about the reflection of feelings (Rogers, 1986). The core conditions cannot be reduced to particular acts or words.

Rogers, like Buber, invites us to consider what it is to be a human being in relationship. Buber's primary category for this is the I–Thou quality of relating, while Rogers subsists in the therapeutic conditions. They do not contradict but elaborate on each other.

Firstly, though, I want to flag up a number of other important overlaps between Buber and all therapists who work from a relational and, in particular, a phenomenological base. This will include almost all humanistic therapists and a good number of psychodynamic therapists, while cognitive behavioural therapists are now paying a lot more attention than previously to the relational stance:

1. Phenomenology is a philosophy developed in the early twentieth century by the German thinker, Edmund Husserl. It is hugely influential to this day in philosophy and theology. Husserl's work is best summarised for therapists by Spinelli (2005). The key point of phenomenology is that we cannot know with certainty any particular object (or person). All we have is the structure and texture of our sense impressions and our consequent interpretation of these. However, by paying careful attention to ourselves, we can develop an *as-if* version of the thing or person we are engaging with. Buber offers an account of relating which is strictly phenomenological.

2. Relational therapy was based on the question: What is it to be human? Buber offers a reply that is existential. It has depth. It is worth living by. I am struck by the fact that Buber, of all thinkers, is unashamedly rooted in faith in God and yet has the ability to contact and to inspire those who do not share that faith (Crossley, 1996: 10).

3. The spirituality of counselling has, over the last two decades, become a matter of hot debate (Moore & Purton, 2006). Buber's depth and curious universality is an ideal place from which to explore this field.

4. Over the same two decades, humanistic and psychodynamic therapies have been far more engaged with what is sometimes referred to as intersubjectivity (Crossley, 1996) and sometimes as the dialogical nature of therapy (Mearns & Cooper, 2005). In brief, this means that the therapeutic conversation should be seen more as a holistic engagement with another person. I suggest that all therapeutic approaches, without exception, need to learn further about engaging in encounter, with its risks, its warmth, its self-disclosure. This is as true for the professedly relational therapies, such as the person-centred approach, as it is for the more technically orientated modalities. Buber helps us think through what risks are worth taking. How can I be a 'Thou' to your 'I' and vice versa?

THE INTRIGUING QUESTION OF CONFIRMATION

One of the key themes of Rogers' dialogue with Buber (Kirschenbaum & Henderson, 1990) centred upon the concept of acceptance or unconditional positive regard. I have read the dialogue on many occasions and still feel unsure whether Buber and Rogers ever understood each other fully. Rogers noted that Buber also believed that meeting involved acceptance. Buber objected that he and Rogers meant different things by 'acceptance'. From his perspective, Rogers accepts the person *just as they are*, but Buber intends to accept that person *with all of their potentialities*. This he terms 'confirmation of the other' (Buber, 1961). (I am not sure that Rogers agreed to this difference between them.) What is Buber saying and why? He is observing that in a relationship one person may perceive and believe in potentialities, possibilities, in the other, that the other does not yet either see or trust. These are to be expressed. I suspect that the underlying reason for this is in the nature of the I–Thou relationship: there is a sufficient interpenetration of being, so that we see the other's soul. Put too strongly, this can seem quirky, but Buber is surely not wholly wrong in this?

If Buber is right, then my idea of congruence shifts. I need to be prepared to express my appreciation of the client's potential in life. This will sometimes go markedly beyond the client's self-trust. In so doing, some might object, I have left the client's frame of reference. I have even set my face against their self-concept. This can be a valid objection, but it does not hold *in principle*. Rather, how and when we confirm the client in their potential is a matter of therapeutic wisdom and judgement. It remains ever in the room as a possibility. An appreciation of Buber leads me to be challenged in my way of being present with the client.

READING BUBER'S *I AND THOU*

Reading Buber is not easy. He is a poet as well as a philosopher. In the following account, I want to combine some understanding of what he says with a sense of how he gives structure and texture to his ideas. I want the reader to feel the passion and density of his thinking, and so be prepared to read further into *I and Thou*. In the space of this chapter it is not possible to give a comprehensive reading of Buber's most important work, however compact it is. I will focus upon the two main concepts of I–Thou and of I–It. Let us begin with the opening words of the book.

> To Man the world is twofold, in accordance with his two-fold attitude.
> The attitude of Man is twofold, in accordance with the twofold nature of the primary words which he speaks. (Buber, 1958: 15)

These opening words of *I and Thou* have, tucked within their dense structure, the roots of Buber's whole approach to human existence. The heart of being human is in relating. We see the world as twofold – other people and objects. That is the basis of our existing. There is nothing more 'real' than our own attitudes, which define our construing of the world. I am, because of my basic attitude to the world. I come into being because first I 'see' the world in a particular way. I 'see' thus by using two primary words: I–Thou and I–It. Buber uses the idea of a primary word to mark up the fact that the I–Thou is not a joining together of two, pre-existing entities, but rather it is in the I–Thou relationship that the individual comes to be. It is primary. When I say 'I–Thou', I relate with my whole being to the other who also shares in the wholeness of being. I intuit the humanness of others. When I say 'I–It', I construe the other as an object, a *thing*.

We live with the illusion, bequeathed by Descartes' view of being human as being a thinking self or soul, that first of all I am 'I'. Yet, before I am 'I', I need to speak the primary words 'I–Thou': I must address the other. This is how we are by virtue of being human; it is also how we grow from the womb to become mature people. We come into being as individuals by being first of all in relation to others. The 'saying' of I–Thou can be a silent attitude, not necessarily a literal speaking. This attitude defines our being. We exist, because always we may meet the other as Thou. We become, we develop when we come to see and address the other as 'Thou'.

As I read the opening pages of *I and Thou*, I am dizzied by the unfamiliar that is demanded of me. No longer is the 'I' the starting point that I fondly imagine. I come into being only in the saying of 'I–Thou' and 'I–It'. The 'I' that I took myself to be does not exist in and of itself. It is always part of an act of relating that comes before or rather gives birth to my own existing. To exist *is* to be open to the other as I–Thou. Relating is both ontologically and developmentally prior to my being (ontology is the study of being itself). To read Buber adequately is to feel the startle of this uprooting of familiar thought patterns.

I–Thou has to be spoken with my whole being; I–It can never be so spoken. The I–Thou has no *object*, for it does not reduce the other to objectivity: a thing. Thus, the way I encounter the other defines my being human. To reside in I–It is to be less than present with my whole being. Buber invites me to let go of the radical complacency of the belief that I can relate in the way that I walk or sing. To speak 'Thou' demands my whole being. The very depth of this experience stretches language. Buber invites me to intuit, if I can, what it is to be present with my whole being. If I listen to my experiencing, my being, I will discover what it is that is definingly human – that I can only find in meeting the other as one like myself.

I–It is not, as it were, morally inferior. It is simply different. We need to be as I–It to encounter most of the world. If there were no I–It, there would be no tools, no science, and no experience.

I am startled again by Buber's word 'experience'. I am so used to hearing the word as intensely personal – *my* experience, *your* experience. For Buber, experience is of the I–It; for whenever I know what I experience, I render it an object. Experience is at arm's length. It does not live until it is embraced in or gives way to the Thou, the encounter, the dialogue.

We must not make the error of believing merely that we say 'Thou' to people and 'It' to objects. It is about the quality of relating. Buber puts forward a case for encountering a tree as Thou, I think, with some whimsy. To a tree I may say *Thou* 'when I have been seized with the power of exclusiveness' (Buber, 1958: 20). This claim has perhaps been open to more criticism and misunderstanding than anything else that Buber has said. Understanding it is crucial. It is so tempting for me to read that a tree may be a Thou as some sort of nature mysticism. It is not. There is no quasi-personal aspect of the *tree*. It is in us, our attitude, that the I–Thou subsists. People and trees are very different in their surface properties. These differences persist. Buber invites us to make a radical intuitive leap to see what he means. The other, the tree, can be over against me and not an object for me. The relating contains the other. Buber offers a metaphor: 'prayer is not in time, but time in prayer' (Buber, 1958: 22). This is a mischievous metaphor for, again, it could lead us to a sort of mysticism. It should not. When I conceive of prayer as an activity, then I do it now or then. It is a thought-about object of my experience. I reduce it to an 'It'. I can say: 'Praying doesn't much appeal to me today.' However, in praying, the act-as-relating comes to include within it all time, for it encounters eternity. Buber means this quite literally. In the saying of 'Thou', the quality of being towards God, a person or a tree has more in common, each with the other, than do any of them with making an object of a person, God or a tree.

In struggling to help us make the intuitive leap to I–Thou, Buber draws near to his view of authenticity. All real living is a meeting, a dialogue, even a silent dialogue. Another metaphor for authentic being is art:

> To produce is to draw forth, to invent is to find, to shape is to discover. In bodying forth, I disclose. (Buber, 1958: 23)

I am reminded of the story of the child taken by her father to see a sculptor at work. On the first visit, there is a large block of stone and some tools. The child is fascinated. On the second visit there is, appearing from the block of stone, a lion: 'But, Daddy, how did she know that the lion was in there?' We smile, but the child's question makes perfect sense. The sculptor knew the lion was there because she met the lion. As stone became lion, so the sculptor disclosed herself.

In authentic being as I–Thou, all that is of the 'It' is displaced. When I desire, I image forth to myself the object of my desire – a girl, a promotion, a bottle of wine, whatever. It is as if my desire dreams in the I–It. Yet, within the I–Thou, I desire the other with a directness that, for the time being, stops me from objectifying what I desire; for in the I–Thou, the other is part of the primacy of being with the I. I can feel a closeness to another, to Thou, which is forgetful of all but the immediacy of relating. Meeting is direct. It blesses. It is of the spaceless, timeless present. It is immortal and transitory.

Yet I–Thou slips continually into I–It as I lose the engagedness of relating. The Other becomes an object of my experience, an It. Even so, the sliding away from relating can reconstitute itself time and again in the Thou. What force can reconstitute the I–It as I–Thou?

Love is near the heart of I–Thou intimacy. Love is *between* the I and the Thou. It does not cling to the I, having Thou as its content. Thus, when I say 'I love you', the surface grammar is deceptive. 'I' seems to be the subject and 'you' the object. But if the surface grammar were the truth, then the beloved other would have become objectified as an It. Love is inherent in the relating. I do not possess the one I love.

In love, all aspects of the other are open to acceptance. The good and the bad, the beautiful and the ugly, each may become engaged in acceptant loving: 'set free they step forth in their singleness and confront [the lover] as Thou' (Buber, 1958: 29). Authentic loving is in offering an unconditionality that invites each aspect of the other to be uniquely present. Judgement in the most literal sense – discrimination between objects – is set aside to permit the other to be a Thou for us.

BUBER AND THERAPEUTIC RELATING

I feel tempted simply to write that once you have grasped the meaning of I–Thou at a deep level, that is sufficient. For some people it may be. For others, it is useful to reflect again upon the practice of relating. Thus, I want to offer two complementary ways of thinking about Buber and the therapeutic relationship. The first is about the whole relationship; the second about relating in terms of the therapist's attitude.

My relationship to any other person is about my fundamental attitude, my life-stance. I may *think* that I am implementing the core conditions, but if I persist in seeing the client as an It, then I am not in a good enough relationship with her. This example can prove to be an interesting problem for therapists under pressure. The trainee therapist on placement, for instance, will frequently feel a deep irritation with the client who does not show up. 'How dare they when I need my hours for the course!' It is necessary at that point to recognise the process, legitimate within us, of our own need, and then, taking a deep breath, move back to the client as an autonomous Thou. The I–Thou relationship is thus an attitude-based condition. Look again at the curious claim of Buber that I can have an I–Thou relationship with a tree. As argued above, this is not nature mysticism, but rather to do with the attitude of the human party. Attitude matters. I want now to think about the saying of *Thou*.

The Oxford philosopher, J.L. Austin, observes that much of our speech is performative (Austin, 1961). That is to say, we perform action through speech itself. Performative utterance is often exemplified with wording such as, 'With this ring I thee wed'. That is to say the contract of marriage is performed in the words themselves. This sort of contractual performative speech is by its very nature interpersonal. I contend that there are also intrapersonal performative speech acts. That it to say, when we speak to ourselves we change ourselves, our fundamental attitude. When I say *Thou*, I change my attitude to the client.

On a number of occasions, I recall having clients whom I found very difficult, either because I felt a background fear of them, or because I felt a persistent and significant anger towards them. For me, this is rarely about a mere withholding of acceptance. It is about something genuinely difficult being in the room. Yet, to live in fear or rejection of the client will not do. I can face the specific issues, if I can get to them, but whether or not they dissolve, I need to shift my attitude, my felt sense of who this person is for me. I suggest that, silently, and deep within me, I utter a *Thou*. Of course, this is not magic. The word in itself has no effect. I want to tap into my understanding at the imaginative depth of Martin Buber's work and life. The *Thou* forms itself. It speaks itself from within. I am changed. The client becomes for me more fully a person. This is not a mystical process but simply the internal, felt sense of *Thou*, with all of its cognitive and emotional meaning, becoming more fully present to me.

Yet, for some people, this level of generalisation is not helpful. A more methodical approach to relating is useful.

BUBER AND THE PRACTICE OF RELATING

As we grow in experience we aim to become more fluent, more genuine in implementing a therapeutic relationship. We tend to become more idiosyncratic, more distinctive in our style of work. There is, however, a risk to this. Sometimes, I am confronted with a client with whom I am ill at ease. At other times, the volume of work becomes a major pressure. On both these occasions I can feel a shift in my practice. 'Idiosyncratic' might be the word. Yet, this is likely to be an undesirable shift. How, then, can I learn to let go and just be with a client, while still monitoring myself against the distortions of internal or external pressures?

I want to begin by recalling that Buber stated that the I–Thou always slips back into the I–It. This is inevitable. Moreover, the I–It is not immoral: it is merely a state of being in an objectifying relationship with the client. I suggest, therefore, that when I think about the client in a quiet, reflective moment, or talk about her in supervision, I am in the I–It to some degree. There is nothing wrong with this. Yet, it does imply that when I am in the client's presence I will need to be as spontaneously engaged as possible, open both to the client's process and to my own. This is why difficult clients can stretch our relating. The challenge of the client who I am afraid of or angry with can (rightly) drive me away from spontaneity into thinking hard about what is happening. Yet, at best, I am present in such a way that only a small part of my immediate awareness is detached and monitoring. Almost all of me is so closely caught up in being with the client that I am forgetful of myself. It should not be *all* of me, for that is to let go of one sort of responsibility towards the client. Empathy and congruence each, in turn, become absorbing moments in my felt process.

Similarly, I am present to the other in a way that asserts within me her being there as an ethical demand. I am responsible – not in the sense of rescuing the client or being accountable even for the success of her therapy – but, rather, in a holding of her within my focus because of her unlimited worth as a fellow human being.

Her Thou is not possessed by me. It is not an extension of my ego. She is different from me. This aspect of Thou-ness frees me to be genuinely and deeply puzzled by her. 'When you describe this, try as I may, I do not at all grasp how it really is for you.' I do not need to feign competence. To be committed to relating at depth is, then, not a stern summons to heightened and intimidating competence. It gives permission to face honestly the chasm that can separate and unite the I and the Thou.

As I seize the client's Thou-ness as of infinite value to me, so I have to be available as infinitely valuable to her. Thus, I must care for myself. Beyond this, I must value what I feel and, after due consideration, be prepared to trust what I feel and share that with her. The more she is a Thou for me, the more I find I can take risks that seem to bear fruit for the client. My client's Thou-ness redeems my timidity of congruence.

When she is self-deprecating, negative about her whole being, not only do I strive to appreciate her, but I can confirm her. In Buber's terminology, this means that I actively stretch out within myself for all of her genuine potentialities. From time to time, I am willing to express these. I risk having a wider vision than the client about who she might be or become. I need, in doing this, to monitor that I am not idealising the client. Always, I must check that my hope and care is rooted in reality and not in my own denial of the client's limitations.

In case this sounds to some a little over-reaching, I am conscious that in the face of her Thou, I want to experience an 'aimless' and guileless trust in her. She is over against me and not an appendage of my therapeutic persona. She is herself and, in her, I have my being. I trust whom she might become and I strive to trust (and I find this trickier) how she might change me as we meet in a transitory and yet immortal moment.

The power of Buber's thought is that, beyond its concepts, its poetry enlivens and nourishes the imagination, and I feel freed into new ways of thinking and experiencing relationship. It must not be an uncritical excuse for mere eccentricity but, in my own work, I have found it to be a challenge to the stale, the portrayed and the self-conscious. Above all, it calls me back to the underlying truth that how I relate, how close I come to I–Thou, is an ethical calling.

REFERENCES

Austin, JL (1961) *How to Do Things with Words.* Oxford: Oxford University Press.

Buber, M (1948) *Tales of the Hasidim: Later masters.* (Trans Olga Marx) New York: Schocken.

Buber, M (1958) *I and Thou.* (Trans R Gregor Smith) Edinburgh: T & T Clark.

Buber, M (1961) *Between Man and Man.* (Trans R Gregor Smith) London: Collins, Fontana.

Crossley, N (1996) *Intersubjectivity: The fabric of social becoming.* London: Sage.

Kirschenbaum, H & Henderson, VL (Eds) (1990) Martin Buber. In *Carl Rogers: Dialogues* (pp. 41–63). London: Constable.

Mearns, D & Cooper, M (2005) *Working at Relational Depth in Counselling and Psychotherapy.* London: Sage.

Moore, J & Purton, C (2006) *Spirituality and Counselling.* Ross-on-Wye: PCCS Books.

Potok, C (1974) *My Name is Asher Lev.* Harmondsworth: Penguin.

Proctor, G, Cooper, M, Sanders, P & Malcolm, B (Eds) (2006) *Politicizing the Person-Centred Approach: An agenda for social change.* Ross-on-Wye: PCCS Books.

Rogers, CR (1957) The necessary and sufficient conditions of therapeutic personality change. *Journal of Consulting Psychology, 21* (2), 95–103.

Rogers, CR (1986) Reflection of feelings. *Person-Centered Review, 1* (4), 375–7.

Schilpp, PA & Friedman, M (Eds) (1967) *The Philosophy of Martin Buber.* La Salle, IL: Open Court; Cambridge, UK: Cambridge University Press.

Schmid, PF (1998) Face-to-face: The art of encounter. In B Thorne & E Lambers (Eds) *Person-Centred Therapy: A European perspective* (pp. 74–90). London: Sage.

Spinelli, E (2005) *The Interpreted World: An introduction to phenomenological psychology* (2nd edn). London: Sage.

CHAPTER 16

SPIRITUAL DIMENSIONS

WILLIAM WEST

Out beyond ideas of wrongdoing and rightdoing,
there is a field. I'll meet you there.
(Rumi, 1999: 36)

In this chapter, I will argue that we should take spirituality seriously and recognise its rightful place at the heart of the therapeutic encounter. This involves a willingness to accept spirituality within the therapist, within the client, and within the therapeutic encounter. I realise immediately that some readers will be troubled by this notion. I hope in the course of exploring this topic it will become apparent that spirituality is a word attached to beliefs and to experiences that are common to most people and that the words like 'spiritual', 'mystical' or 'religious' should not lead us to avoid discussing this dimension of human experience.

I write from my own experience, from my own therapy, training and research, from my work with clients, supervisees, trainers and researchees. I also write, and draw on implicitly, my own spiritual journeying, from my early upbringing in a post-war Christian society, my time in my thirties exploring meditation and healing, and my 'coming home' to Quakers at the time of the first Gulf War. For the last twenty-five years, the spiritual dimension has been real to me; sometimes very close, sometimes frustratingly far away, but always of tremendous importance to me, and very linked to my development as a therapist since 1982.

I think in the current climate of Islamophobia and with the word 'crusade' being bandied about post-9/11, the honouring of spirituality in all its glories and the recognition of its shadow side is probably the most important task facing us today. Indeed, if we did this in the right spirit, we would also, I believe, be likely to find the best response to climate change and world hunger.

In this context and spirit, I offer these reflections on the spiritual dimension in the therapeutic encounter.

WHAT IS SPIRITUALITY AND WHY IS IT IMPORTANT FOR SOME CLIENTS?

When I was ill, I certainly learned VERY quickly to keep the spiritual side of myself separate from the rest of myself whenever I met with any of the 'professionals'.
(Counselling client, in Jenkins, 2006: 80)

Most of the world's population hold a religious view of life. Even in Britain, which is a secular society (or at least appears so), the vast majority of the population believe in God and value their spirituality, whatever they mean by this word (Hay & Hunt, 2000). So a secular stance, which is still the dominant narrative within counselling and psychotherapy and psychology, is different from most people's values and beliefs. This is of overwhelming importance to a profession that values the client's perspective and which places a high premium on accurate empathy.

It is not a question of whether spirituality is important to any one therapist, or theoretical model, or school of therapy. Spirituality is important to most clients. If we then begin to consider how little spirituality is explored in therapist training and continuing professional development, the residual negative view of religion and spirituality that remains in our profession, and how problematic it can become in supervision (West, 2000b, 2003), then the conclusion I come to is that we are short-changing our clients. Many counsellors simply lack the competence to work well with their clients' spirituality.

Spirituality is as much part of clients' lives as is their gender, sexuality and ethnicity. Therapist training courses do address issues relating to gender, sexuality and ethnicity, but training can and does occur without a focus on spirituality and religion. Sometimes, religion is explored as part of 'difference' or 'diversity' and then the focus is usually on religion and ethnic minorities. The religion and spirituality of the white majority is not usually considered. This lack of preparedness to work with client issues of religion and spirituality is a profoundly ethical issue – it is simply unethical to be so ill-equipped to do such work.

So what is spirituality? Before I offer some thoughts on this, I think it is important to remember that it is the client's view of spirituality and its relevance to their lives that is the key feature in counselling – rather than our own. I have found some profoundly spiritual people who have no religious faith at all and who do not discuss their experiences in spiritual terms but who describe occurrences that most of us connect with the word 'spiritual'. For example, some people talk of spiritual experiences in terms of 'energies'. In other words, calling an experience 'spiritual' is a choice we make that has all kinds of implications; it gives us a vocabulary within which to talk about such experiences and has several potential frames for understanding the phenomenon.

It is also worth realising that, in Britain, there has been a big decline in Christian church attendance in recent years (see Bruce, 1995, for statistics) and a similar if less sharp decline in attendance at synagogues, so that many people's sense of themselves as being spiritual is divorced from organised religion.

Drawing on definitions and discussions of what spirituality is, particularly in a therapeutic context (for example, Elkins et al., 1988; Rowan, 2005; Swinton, 2001; Jenkins, 2006), the following features are appropriate, I believe, in defining spirituality:

- it is rooted in human experiencing rather than abstract theology
- it is embodied
- it involves linking with other people and the universe at large
- it involves non-ordinary consciousness
- active engagement with spirituality tends to make people more altruistic, less materialistic and more environmentally aware
- it deals with the meaning that people make of their lives
- it faces suffering and its causes
- it relates to God/gods/goddesses/ultimate reality
- it often uses the words 'soul' or 'higher self'
- techniques such as prayer, meditation, contemplation, mindfulness, yoga and Tai Chi are often used as spiritual practices.

Any clients actively exploring their spirituality are likely to resonate with many of the above features and may have issues arising from them and from residual childhood and adult interactions with organised religion.

WORKING WITH RELIGIOUS CONTENT

I do not believe that therapists need to be reluctant to work with issues arising from their clients' spiritual or religious beliefs. Because I am not a woman, that has not stopped me working therapeutically with women, nor stopped me seeking therapeutic help from women. So why, for instance, should I refuse to work with a client who is a Buddhist and who may well raise issues relating to their Buddhism in the course of their therapy with me. If I was profoundly ignorant of Buddhism, that would be different. I think I owe it to my religiously minded clients to have some working knowledge of their faith tradition. There are some excellent resources available to guide us (for example, Richards & Bergin, 2000). I have no time for counsellors who insist that their clients should teach them about their religion (or culture). I accept we need to hear the clients' view but my understanding of Buddhism has enabled me to challenge unhealthy thinking in Buddhist clients. For example, one client felt that he could not return to his Buddhist teacher because he felt so bad about his sexual practices. I asked him 'Is compassion not a central teaching to Buddhism?' 'Yes, of course.' 'Surely your teacher will have a compassionate response to your behaviour?'

I have worked similarly with very devout Christians who suffer extreme guilt about 'sins' they have committed and who clearly feel unforgiven. Yet the central teaching of

Christianity, emphasised in the Lord's Prayer, is of forgiveness. ('Forgive us our trespasses as we forgive those that trespass against us.') Crucially, the person seeking forgiveness must first offer that same forgiveness to anyone they feel wronged by. And the forgiveness they seek is granted by God, not necessarily by the person they have wronged. This process has profound healing implications for Christians.

There are, of course, dangers in pushing someone towards an act of forgiveness they are not ready to make, but that is a different issue to someone feeling unforgiveness. Seemingly mild 'sins' can have disproportionate consequences. The issue of sin and its role in our post-Christian culture is worth further reflection outside the scope of this chapter (see, for example, West, 2004; Richards & Bergin, 2000).

I think the two examples above create a powerful case, but such work needs careful reflection and excellent supervision from someone willing to accept this way of working with clients' religious beliefs.

Of the various studies around this issue (well summarised in Richards & Bergin, 2005) one of the most interesting is that of Propst et al. (1992) who, in the USA, researched 59 Christian clients suffering from depression. The clients were assigned to three differing forms of group therapy: the group offered cognitive behaviour therapy (CBT) (which used religious imagery) and the group offered pastoral counselling had better outcomes (i.e. less depression) than the group offered standard CBT or the waiting-list group. Incidentally, the therapists using CBT and religious imagery were not all religious themselves, proving that it is possible for a therapist to work with a client's spiritual and religious beliefs without sharing that faith or even having a faith.

TRAINING THERAPISTS

The message there [in the professional development group] was that a lot of counsellors had anti-religious feelings ... So I suppose there too there is a message being given that it is not okay to talk about your spirituality ... certainly never in my [counsellor] training have we talked about religion. (Counsellor, in Jenkins, 2006)

In recent years in Britain there have been huge changes in religious affiliation and attendance at religious services. Many people have given up on Christianity, many more are actively pursuing New Age spiritualities or becoming Buddhists, and paganism is one of the fastest growing religions (Davie, 1994; West, 2000a). It also seems to me that counselling has many of the hallmarks of a religion (or at least a substitute for religion), not least, the evangelism of some counsellors!

However, despite these caveats, I do hold that a broad span of religious beliefs and of the main faith groups would seems to be a useful and, above all, respectful part of therapist training. This could be enhanced by inviting counsellors in training to share with their colleagues, where appropriate, something of their personal religious experiences and practices as a way of developing therapist understanding. Such an approach to learning is commonly used on many therapist training courses for other aspects of students' lives.

In conclusion, with regard to training, I would reiterate in summary form an agenda for change that I first put forward in West (2000a) and revised in West (2004):

- the inclusion of a substantial training around spiritual issues in basic counsellor and psychotherapist training courses with BACP and UKCP support
- specialist post-training CPD courses on working with spirituality to update existing therapists
- such packages would include: religion, spirituality and culture in Britain today; Wilber (1996) and other psychospiritual maps; spiritual experiences; diagnostic issues; spiritual countertransference; pastoral care and referrals; and spiritual interventions in therapy
- further development of theories, maps and sense-making around spirituality and therapy (see for instance, Jenkins, 2006)
- further research into the religiosity of therapists and their attitude to spirituality; therapist use of spiritual interventions; outcomes of spiritual interventions
- personal development work around therapists' own spirituality
- considering spirituality in a postmodern post-Christian context.

THERAPISTS' SPIRITUAL LIVES

I am not the first (see Tart & Deikman,1991) to recognise that the practice of being a therapist is essentially spiritual, very akin to mindfulness. For example, the careful focus on one's inner life and reaction to the client, the attempt to be very much in the 'here and now', the careful consideration of the client's experiencing, the offering of regard and empathy. So, after years of such practice, it is not surprising to see counsellors having spiritual development and spiritual experiences. Rowan (2005) regards therapists' spirituality as so crucial that he thinks all counsellors have a spiritual practice. It is tempting to agree but I don't think we can or should insist on this. I would insist, however, that therapists carefully explore their own attitudes to religion and spirituality and make more effort to inform themselves about such issues.

WORKING ACROSS RELIGIONS AND CULTURAL ISSUES

Firstly, it is helpful to acknowledge that on a micro-cultural level, every therapy session is a cross-cultural experience. This is because there will always be significant differences across many key aspects, such as age, gender, sexuality, class, race, religion etc. Indeed, it is important therapists don't assume, just because they share some cultural background with a particular client, that they inevitably use language the same way, that words have the same subtleties of meaning, and that a similar view of the world is shared.

Where there is a macro-difference of religion or culture, it is useful to consider why the client has chosen to come to us for therapy rather than someone from their own background. This can have a variety of possible meanings:

- the client may not trust that confidentiality will be maintained if they seek counsel from within their own minority community or faith
- the client might well wish to explore life outside of their cultural box or faith
- the counsellor may be seen as a representative of the dominant culture who will, therefore, be able to support and advise the client to find their place within society.

PRACTITIONERS' STANCE AROUND RELIGION AND SPIRITUALITY

There is no need to insist on therapists holding any spiritual or religious beliefs. Although it might be important for a religiously minded client to investigate the belief system of her or his therapist, Propst et al. (1992), in their research into the use of religious imagery with depressed, religious clients, found that CBT practitioners who were non-believing, were able to work very effectively using religious imagery with Christian clients. This echoes Wyatt's view:

> When I am clear about my faith and comfortable with it – whatever it looks like – then that is good. I know what I think. I know what I believe and I know what I do not believe. I know what my values are, or I know that I don't know. Then, when I am like that, I can listen to clients. (Wyatt, 2002: 182)

Likewise, religious practitioners who work within appropriate boundaries with non-believing clients should not face difficulties around spiritual and religious issues. In fact, this must be a common experience for many therapists. As ever, any challenges or dilemmas that arise for such therapists can be explored within supervision. What is clearly unacceptable is any sense of evangelism on the part of the therapist. I have found that some therapists with a strong religious background have shied away from supporting their clients' exploration of spiritual issues in their counselling for fear of being seen to be evangelical. This is a shame and is also short-changing the clients.

What also concerns me is how successful clients, who have clearly benefited from counselling, often then go on to train as therapists. These situations feel a bit evangelical. So instead of the client taking on the religious faith of their therapist they take on their therapeutic faith instead. How many of such clients are stuck in unresolved countertransference? In what ways is counselling a narcissistic substitute for religion?

FUNDAMENTALISM

The problem with fundamentalism is that it is selective. I would dearly love fundamentalist Christians to take Jesus' teachings to heart by loving their neighbours as themselves, turning the other cheek, walking the extra mile and, of course, obeying the commandment 'Thou shall not to kill'. This fundamentalism is of course a human psychological trait. I see the same splits in socialism and communism as I do in Christianity and Islam. I also see this same human tendency to be fundamental and to split in the therapy world, with all the differing schools in competition, each claiming to be the most effective. Then, within the broad stream of approaches, we have the many varieties of each approach. So in the person-centred world, some schools insist on Rogers from his Chicago days, others like his more spiritual Californian days, and there are strong feelings between such groupings.

The one thing that comes out of research, despite what those driven by the evidence-based practice 'what works for whom?' approach, is that the therapeutic alliance is the largest factor in successful outcome. Or, to put it another way, 'to advocate empirically supported therapies as preferable or superior to other treatments would be premature' (Lambert & Ogles, 2004: 180).

It is my experience that fundamentalist religious believers do not tend to present themselves to non-religiously based counsellors unless or until they have some crisis in their lives that includes their faith community in some way. At this point, it can be a real challenge (especially to a prejudiced counsellor) to *hear* the client's story, particularly that their religious faith was 'good and healthy' and that they wish to hold on to it. The careful listening, working with and shifting through these clients' experiences can be a real challenge but, in principle, no different to any other client's story of the realisation that it is maybe time to move on.

THE PLACE OF THE SPIRITUAL IN THERAPY

I hold that spirituality is always present in some form in any therapeutic encounter, whether in the foreground or background. If it is never discussed, the question arises – assuming it is there, how are you avoiding it? If it is in the client's life, it will be in the counselling encounter. What does it mean to the client to dismiss it so?

On the other hand, spirituality can be brought to the foreground as a way of avoiding other less comfortable issues. Also, a profound historical shadow hangs over spirituality: the persecution of witches, the Spanish Inquisition, the Crusades, and so on. There are those who feel that the Catholic Church, for example, has a lot to answer for with its opposition to condoms at a time of spreading HIV infection. The current conflict around gay vicars in the Church of England seems unbelievable to those of us committed to sexual equality. It is possible that therapists might ignore their anger with religion and fake forgiveness with a kind of pseudo, saint-like behaviour. Working with client's spirituality in a therapeutic relationship requires all their skills.

USE OF RELIGIOUS AND SPIRITUAL PRACTICES IN THE THERAPEUTIC
RELATIONSHIP

One of the surprises to emerge from Peter Gubi's research (2002) into prayer and counselling was the number of counsellors praying for their clients. Gubi surveyed just over half of BACP-accredited practitioners and 43 per cent (247) replied. Of his respondents, 59 per cent had used prayer covertly with clients and 12 per cent had used it overtly with Christian clients. Only 24 per cent of those who used prayer had ever discussed it in supervision. Given that many counsellors are spiritually or religiously minded perhaps this use of prayer should not be surprising but, of course, since it is does not fit with the largely secular models of therapy, perhaps it is also not surprising to find that such use of prayer is often not taken to supervision. We can rail against this all we like but it has become clear to me that counsellors will persist in carrying on doing what they think is right for their clients whether it is using touch, healing or prayer, and if they think their supervisors will not approve of such interventions then they will not disclose them (further explored in West, 2003). Unless we video or audiotape counselling sessions as a routine activity, we have no effective way of controlling what in Gubi's (2002) memorable phrase 'goes on behind closed doors'.

The persistence of such practices could be an invitation for all of us to pause for thought. If seasoned practitioners are using prayer, touch or healing on a regular basis, then to merely say, 'This is wrong, this is unacceptable' is not likely to change their behaviour. It also flies in the face of the research evidence referred to above and of the gut instinct of these practitioners. We need a serious, informed debate about a practice by therapists that is regarded as taboo and we need appropriate supervision around such innovations in practice.

ISSUES OF POWER, CULTURE AND DIVERSITY

One way in which therapy deals with difficult topics like spirituality, religion, race, class etc. is to lump them all under the phrase 'diversity'. This can serve to treat the white, heterosexual, largely female majority as the norm and for training to focus on the diversity from this norm. Consequently, challenging questions about growing up in a post-Christian culture are not addressed. One of the reasons this occurs is the pain, anger and disappointment many of us have in relation to organised religion.

It takes a brave or foolish soul to cross barriers of gender, race and culture but therapists do it all the time. It is important to reflect on why any one client has come to us for therapy. Why has this woman chosen to work with me, a man? Why has this second-generation Asian woman come to see me? There are reasons here that could be of crucial importance. For example, a woman might consult me because she needs a man to hear her story. Or a person from an ethnic minority might seek a white therapist because they don't trust someone from their own ethnic background to maintain confidentiality. Or they might feel that I, as a white man, will offer an understanding of white culture that will prove helpful to them. These expectations may not be true or realistic but they may well be present.

We have to think further and consider the impact of counselling on society and on community life. We have taken a human activity and turned it into a speciality that is taught in colleges and universities. In the process, we have undermined traditional forms of helping and listening. Instead of sharing our problems with our partners, we confide in our therapists and wonder why we feel increasingly distanced from each other.

Modern Western counselling and psychotherapy plays a similar role to that of Christianity in the days of the British Empire. The English-speaking world has globalised therapy. Every modern city in the world now seems to have its UK or US-trained therapists. The destructive impact of the missionaries on traditional religion and traditional healers is now being repeated by Western trained therapists.

However, traditional methods do not die out: they mutate, they become New Age and fashionable. So, many spiritually minded people in Britain turn to Tai Chi, Buddhist meditation, mindfulness and Yoga. People attend courses about Native American medicine, including sweat-lodges and shamanism. The old ways of spiritual healing still continue within the white majority, even if mostly held up to ridicule.

MODELS

There are two very important models that can help our thinking around counselling and spirituality, Wilber's (1996) and Assagioli's different models of human spiritual development, both discussed elsewhere in this book (see Shiers & Paul: 117–31) help us to think about the spiritual context in which our work with clients can be located. There are some caveats:

1. Humans are not as neat and tidy as these fascinating diagrams and models.

2. Changing stages in Wilber's model, or contacting the Higher Self or Soul in Assagioli's model can be frightening, life changing, making people fear for their mental health. However, putting clients' experiences into this sort of broader context can have a tremendous grounding impact on them.

3. Wilber's model has been criticised as being too linear, too hierarchical and patriarchal. A lot depends on the spirit in which it is used. John Rowan (2005) has made particularly creative use of Wilber. There is always the danger of too rigid an application of any model. Wilber's model does rely on the notion that each stage contains the earlier stages. This may not be true, and it does give his model a hierarchical flavour.

4. We need to remember that the map is not the territory. Do Assagioli and Wilber help us understand and support our clients? We should use these models with discernment.

Wilber's model does three important things:

- It distinguishes between the pre-personal and the transpersonal – which neatly deals with Freud's critique of religion as being based on the pre-personal.
- It helps us think of the varieties of religious states and experiences.
- It brings together common threads from a number of spiritual traditions showing the collective shared wisdom inherent in such traditions.

Chris Jenkins' research (2006) into clients' experience of having their spirituality denied resulted in him developing a useful model of therapists' use of spirituality, bringing together Richards and Bergin's (2000, 2005) seminal views on spiritual interventions in therapy, Clarkson's five types of therapeutic relationships (2003) and my own writings on therapists being spiritually inspired (West, 2000a, 2004). Again, Jenkins' model enables us to think about where and how we locate our work in relation to spirituality.

Jenkins suggests that Clarkson's (2003) five types of therapeutic relationship – working alliance, transference/countertransference, reparative, person to person and transpersonal – provide an embracing framework for any therapeutic work, and this can include working with spirituality. Within this frame, he situates the theistic approach of Richards and Bergin (2005) that focuses on possible spiritual interventions to pursue with spiritually minded clients. Overlapping with the Richards and Bergin approach, Jenkins situates my own work – encouraging intuition, spiritual moments, insights and encounters within therapy. Jenkins argues that any of us working with clients and their spirituality can be located somewhere within this model.

CONCLUSION

I am profoundly convinced that we can only do our best work as therapists from a position of deep self-knowledge. This has to include what other people will call the 'spiritual'. This may not be a word we use or are comfortable with, but we owe it to our clients to have explored this area of human experience. I have attempted in this chapter to consider this vexed question of spirituality and therapy and to raise some of the key issues. Thankfully there are now many good sources of relevant literature and training but the key factor remains the individual therapist's willingness to do their own journeying.

REFERENCES

Bruce, S (1995) *Religion in Modern Britain.* Oxford: Oxford University Press.

Clarkson, P (2003) *The Therapeutic Relationship* (2nd edn.). London: Whurr.

Davie, G (1994) *Religion in Britain since 1945.* Oxford: Blackwell.

Elkins, DN, Hedstrom, JL, Hughes, LL, Leaf, JA & Saunders, C (1988) Toward a humanistic-phenomenological spirituality. *Journal of Humanistic Psychology, 28* (4), 5–18.

Gubi, P (2002) Practice behind closed doors: Challenging the taboo of prayer. In 'Mainstream Counselling Culture'. Paper presented at the Annual Conference of the Society for Psychotherapy Research (International), Santa Barbara, CA, June.

Hay, D & Hunt, K (2000) Understanding the Spirituality of People who Don't Go to Church. Centre for the Study of Human Relations Research Report. Nottingham: University of Nottingham.

Jenkins, C (2006) A voice denied. PhD thesis, School of Education, University of Manchester.

Lambert, MJ & Ogles, BM (2004) The efficacy and effectiveness of psychotherapy. In M J Lambert (Ed) *Bergin & Garfield's Handbook of Psychotherapy and Behaviour Change,* (pp. 139–93). New York: Wiley.

Propst, LR, Ostrom, R, Watkins, P, Dean, T & Mashburn, D (1992) Comparative efficacy of religious and non-religious cognitive behavioral therapy for the treatment of clinical depression in religious individuals. *Journal of Consulting and Clinical Psychology, 60,* 94–103.

Richards, PS & Bergin, AE (Eds) (2000) *Handbook of Psychotherapy and Religious Diversity.* Washington, DC: American Psychological Association.

Richards, PS & Bergin, AE (Eds) (2005) *A Spiritual Strategy for Counseling and Psychotherapy.* Washington, DC: American Psychological Association.

Rowan, J (2005) *The Transpersonal: Spirituality in sychotherapy and counselling* (2nd edn). London: Routledge.

Rumi, J (1999) *The Essential Rumi* (Trans C Barks). London: Penguin.

Swinton, J (2001) *Spirituality and Mental Health Care: Rediscovering a 'forgotten' dimension.* London: Jessica Kingsley.

Tart, CT & Deikman, AJ (1991) Mindfulness, spiritual seeking and psychotherapy. *Journal of Transpersonal Psychology, 23* (1), 29–52.

West, W (2000a) *Psychotherapy and Spirituality: Crossing the line between therapy and religion.* London: Sage.

West, W (2000b) Supervision difficulties and dilemmas for counsellors and psychotherapists around healing and spirituality. In B Lawton & C Feltham (Eds) *Taking Supervision Forward: Dilemmas, insights and trends.* London: Sage.

West, W (2003) The culture of psychotherapy supervision. *Counselling and Psychotherapy Research, 3* (2), 123–7.

West, W (2004) *Spiritual Issues in Therapy: Relating experience to practice.* Basingstoke: Palgrave Macmillan.

Wilber, K (1996) *The Atman Project.* Wheaton, IL: Quest.

Wyatt, J (2002) 'Confronting the Almighty God'? A study of how psychodynamic counsellors respond to clients' expressions of religious faith. *Counselling Psychotherapy Research, 2* (3), 177–83.

ACKNOWLEDGEMENTS

My thanks to Stephen Paul for inviting me to write this chapter and for the help of the following people in developing my thinking, practice and teaching on the questions around spirituality and therapy: Linda Ankrah, Allen Bergin, Dee Brown, Fenia Christodoulidi, Peter Gubi, Henry Hollanders, Chris Jenkins, Pittu Laungani, Roy Moodley, David Orlinsky, Abdullah Popoola, John Rowan, Mike Sivori, David Smith, Dori Yusef.

CHAPTER 17

TOUCH AND THE
THERAPEUTIC RELATIONSHIP
SHIFTING A PARADIGM

ANDREA UPHOFF

Being physically connected the way we are, it's kind of rewiring my brain.
(Audrey Niffenegger, *The Time Traveler's Wife*)

This quote stems from a recent and popular novel. Reading it, I was struck by what Henry is saying to his wife Clare; his physical relationship to her has changed the structure of his brain. Certainly current advances in the fields of neuroscience (Schore, 1994; Grawe, 2004) and biochemistry (Pert, 1998) substantiate Henry's experience. They show the brain to be dependent on experience of relationships for maturation – a maturation influenced at a biochemical level through sensory information including touch. The brain maintains plasticity throughout the lifespan, allowing modification of neuronal connections depending on new experience and use. This has implications for the psychotherapeutic relationship.

What makes a relationship therapeutic per se – and where, specifically, the issue of touch fits in with the psychotherapeutic relationship – have been topics that have interested me for a number of years. It began with a small research study into the effects of person-centred counselling and reflexology delivered concommitently over the same period (Trousdell & Uphoff-Chmielnik, 1997). The results of this qualitative study indicated that those clients receiving both therapies moved to a significantly more positive psychological posture and physical well-being within a shorter time span than expected.

Piece by piece, a jigsaw of evidence has come together, creating a picture of theory which, I believe, could offer a rationale for touch within the psychotherapeutic relationship. For the purpose of exploring touch within the therapeutic context, I define 'touch' as that which is not intended to stimulate or elicit sexual feelings, nor is it regarded culturally as sexual. I am not intending to consider the topic of systematised touch as utilised in massage, nor the techniques utilised as part of body psychotherapy. My focus is turned toward a much more opaque area – the place of tactility in the ordinarily more verbal everyday practice of psychotherapy.

Prior to the emergence of psychoanalysis, it was accepted wisdom that touch would be a part of psychiatric treatment. The 'laying on of hands' inherited from longstanding shamanic and religious practice was integral to healing relationships, including those that proposed to heal the mind. This stance was gradually eroded, or disappeared entirely as psychoanalysis evolved, later to resurface within the humanistic movement. Hunter and Struve (1998) and Smith, Clance and Imes (1998) provide a comprehensive history and review of the current status of the role of touch in various therapeutic schools, where a range of opinions prevail. Despite strong allegiances to one stance or the other, Tune's research (2001) shows that touch does, in fact, occur across all orientations in psychotherapy, but is not generally shared with colleagues or supervisors. It seems practitioners feel as if they need to hide this part of their relationship – that it might not stand up to peer/supervisor scrutiny.

From the late 1980s onwards, neurosciences (by this I mean all disciplines that study structure and function of the nervous system, including psychology/psychotherapy) have delivered new and exciting information about the development and activities of the human brain. In turn, this has highlighted primary relationships as the foundation to self-organisation and emotional/physiological regulation and has confirmed many of the earlier suppositions of theorists such as Winnicott (1958), Bowlby (1969) and Bion (1991). An optimal or 'good enough' primary relationship, a relationship in which things are more right than wrong, is multi-modal in its communication: child and caregiver[1] act, react and interact utilising all the senses, including touch. Stern writes, 'The ultimate magic of attachment is touch. And this magic enters through the skin' (1990: 99). We now know that interaction which conveys love, intimacy, safety and well-being contributes to the structure of the brain and builds the substrate for future cognition, feelings and behaviour (Schore, 1994; Grawe, 2004). Added to this is the knowledge that 'brain' or 'mind' is a 'bodymind'[2] phenomena and is not only located in the actual organ (Pert, 1998).

The results of interdisciplinary research show that in spite of structure created through early impressions, the brain retains plasticity and the potential to reorganise itself well into old age. Through new uses and new experiences, growth and change can be initiated (Grawe, 2004; Hüther, 2004). In my opinion, we are still a long way from a true neuropsychotherapy: a therapy in which interventions are aimed at a particular part of the brain in order to give an impulse for change. However, I do believe we can begin to use the current information as a framework to examine different facets of our psychotherapeutic practice. For what has become clear is that activating emotion through the process of relationship is advantageous to that growth/change. As Hüther metaphorically puts it, the relationship, 'must get "under the skin"' and be an 'encounter at "eye-level"', meaning a mutual encounter, if something is to be changed in the brain (2004: 244–5, author's translation).

It is astonishing that in psychological circles, the physiology of human touch is often ignored, despite research that evidences the physical and physiological value that touch has for human beings, as well as its healing qualities. Beginning at the start of the twentieth century with Spitz's observations of institutionalised children wasting away due to lack of touch; to Harlow's research with primates in the 1950s and 60s; to

---

1. I use the terms 'parent', 'caregiver' and 'mother' interchangeably and the term 'primary relationship' as synonymous with a relationship to any of these.
2. The bodymind network is regarded by Pert (1998) as mind, spirit and emotions unified with the physical body.

Montagu's seminal work in the 1970s; the developmental necessity and healing qualities of touch have been well documented. Skin-to-skin contact is reported to lower blood pressure, reduce stress and stimulate the body's hormones (Bergman, 2005) and these are the keys to bonding and to promoting well-being and contentment. It would therefore seem that touch is a perfect method of making contact and communicating in our ever more depersonalised Western world.

Repair of relationship has long been seen as a fundamental tenet of many forms of psychotherapy. To strengthen this view, people from a number of disciplines and schools are now writing and evidencing the importance of the primary relationship (in which touch is a primary source of communication) in the shaping of the brain (van der Kolk, 1987; Schore, 1994; Hüther, 1998; Siegel, 1999). All except a few brave souls (Fosshage, 2000; LaTorre, 2000; Rothschild, 2002), however, seem to be successfully skirting the issue of touch within the psychotherapeutic context, expressing through their very avoidance an ambivalence towards more integrative thinking and approach. It is my contention that, if we wish to develop our understanding of the psychotherapeutic relationship in its entirety, we need to look closely at current research on touch in psychotherapy, as well as at the primary relationship and the role of touch within it, before considering both in relation to current psychotherapeutic practice.

RESEARCH – WHAT DOES IT TELL US?

Research on touch in psychotherapy is scant and often contradictory in its outcomes, and has done little to alleviate the controversy. For example, in 2004, Stenzel and Rupert collected evidence from 470 participants of mixed gender and diverse theoretical orientations and reported that the psychotherapists indicating the highest rates of non-erotic touch identified as humanistic, whilst those indicating the lowest rates identified as psychodynamic. In addition, Stenzel and Rupert (2004) discovered a number of socially stereotypical behaviours occurring in psychotherapeutic practice in regard to non-erotic touch; the handshake being the most prominent and accepted example endorsed by more than half of the mixed gender participants, although predominantly used more by male participants than female – a gender role stereotype.

They also noted some other interesting gender patterns emerging: female therapists are more likely to touch female clients, and touch is generally more likely to occur in female/female dyads than in male/female or male/male dyads. They noted that this is a reflection of society and Western culture at large, where considerable research suggests that overall touch between women is more prevalent than touch between men. Their research also indicated that female therapists were less likely to touch male clients, again reflecting the general findings that women are more likely than men to be the recipients of touch, and minimising the possibility of sexualisation in mixed gender dyads. In their conclusion, Stenzel and Rupert seem to take comfort from these findings, feeling that non-erotic touch is safely tucked into social norms, theoretical considerations and professional training experience. It could be considered a shortcoming of their research that they avoid the issues of cultural diversity, status and power inherent in these stereotypical responses.

In contrast, Dupree and Reddick (2001) conducted an earlier study via questionnaire to investigate whether or not gender, theoretical orientation or academic training of the psychotherapist are related to attitudes about, and usage of, safe non-erotic touch. The results showed that no significant gender differences were found, except that male therapists showed more caution in using touch. They regarded a handshake as acceptable before and after a session, but commented that most therapists use touch too much. Surprisingly, there was no difference between therapeutic orientations regarding attitude on the use of non-erotic touch – with one exception: those identifying as 'humanistic' were more apt than others to endorse the statement 'I wish we had more training or discussion of the use of touch in therapy', possibly confirming an idea that touch is a useful contribution to therapy, but at the same time conveying an insecurity about how it could be contributed. Generally, therapists involved in this study reported a lack of training on the topic, and that what little training they did receive discouraged the use of touch. Dupree and Reddick (ibid.) came to the conclusion that therapist gender, theoretical orientation, or academic training had only a limited impact on whether the clinician uses touch. Touch was in the main regarded by the respondents as unnecessary to effective psychotherapy and perhaps even inappropriate.

At the opposite end of the spectrum there are researchers who recognise touch as developmentally important, enabling movement towards verbalisation of feelings (see Goodman & Teicher, 1988). After a series of studies, Fagan and Silverthorn concluded that 'the ability to understand emotional communication from others as communicated by touch is an important component of mental health' and further, 'therapists who assume the responsibility to help people become better adjusted and more emotionally stable should be able to help their patients translate touch into *understandable messages*' (1998: 72) (italics added).

It seems that those working from a base of attachment theory (Bowlby, 1969; Ainsworth, 1977) are more easily able to recognise the benefits of multi-modal work and touch, particularly with children. Hughes writes that 'The therapeutic stance of holding the child is often the most important intervention in the therapeutic process' (1997: 103). The Keys Attachment Centre in Lancashire, England, anchors physical holding firmly within its therapeutic concept. Here, children and young people can experience safe physical holding as a means of creating relationships and dealing with trauma. Research at the centre (Fearnley & Howe, 2003) shows that this aspect of therapy is positively evaluated by recipients. It is interesting to note that cultural norms are reflected yet again. It is culturally more acceptable to touch a child than another adult (Cowen, Weissberg & Lotyczeuski, 1983). Others who have researched touch and examined the pros and cons of touch with adults tend to err on the side of caution, transmitting ambivalence to the practitioner. Examples are Horton et al. (1995) who, in one of the very few studies into touch from a client perspective, found that touch was generally experienced as positive. Even so, they advocate caution in its use, despite the positive outcome. Shaw (2003) notes this and suggests that as the profession remains confused on this issue, we need to develop a framework to actively work with somatic phenomena, but without *necessarily* bringing touch into it. This communicates Shaw's own ambivalence, thereby perpetuating the cycle of confusion.

Lyall (1997) posited that the absence of nurturing touch in psychotherapy is, in part, due to the patriarchal nature of our culture and its emphasis on verbal communication. Leijssen (2006) concurs, adding that the Anglo-Saxon culture has developed a fear of intimacy and is afraid to be touched at any level. Many researchers (e.g. Stenzel & Rupert, 2004; Dupree & Reddick, 2001) omit to mention that psychotherapy is itself a cultural practice and, just as a dominating culture may not consciously experience that culture (Lago, 2006), it is probable that many psychotherapists unquestioningly live these societal norms and values acculturated into their profession and status.

From an ethical standpoint, the controversy of touch in the psychotherapeutic relationship seems to revolve around the potential for harm and exploitation. The progressive move towards litigation in Western societies has led most therapists to insure themselves against malpractice. Further, therapists seem extremely uncomfortable even when their clients touch them on their own initiative, and the profession is imbued with fear. In the US, ethical and legal concerns have led organisations, such as the American Psychological Association (APA), to develop rules and guidelines that, whilst not prohibiting touch absolutely, do seem to reinforce a view of all touch as sexual in nature and to create an atmosphere of suspicion around it. British literature also reflects this great concern about sexual misconduct and sexualised touch by therapists (Russell, 1993). Research to date on the use of touch in psychotherapy has tended to focus on the negative effects of touch and, more specifically, the issue of sexual exploitation. Relevant research documents from both sides of the Atlantic support the case that these abuses do occur (Russell, 1993; Kertay & Reviere, 1998). However, attempts to prove a connection between non-erotic touch and sexual misconduct per se have not been successful. Research available does not lead to the conclusion that touch in psychotherapy is routinely sexualised, nor that it has anything to do with therapists' practice of using or not using bodily ways of working (Milakovich, 1998). Further, it is not proven that, where sexual contact has occurred, it is the component of touch in isolation which has caused damage to the client, as opposed to other variables, such as power abuse. Acknowledging such concerns is legitimate; it does not, however, correlate that touch becomes problematical in the therapeutic relationship.

I would strongly suggest that our practice evolves against a background of culturally and professionally imbued regulatory processes designed to control outcomes and maintain the prevailing power relationships of our environment, even those of our therapist–client relationships; choices are limited to what is condoned by strong political lobbies such as those promoting professional regulation, as well as health services and insurance companies. In what I see as a response to some of these anxieties, there have been attempts to define what type of touch is acceptable, when and with whom (Smith, 1998: 36–51; Hunter & Struve, 1998: 127–56). Even with the best of intentions, this kind of adherence to rules is colluding in the inadvertent suppression of a meaningful dialogue and does nothing to contribute to a creative process in psychotherapy. All these apparent 'safety nets' might not guarantee our safety, or that of our clients, but what they do guarantee is a wooden relationship. I do not believe that this is a way forward for the enlightened psychotherapist.

CONNECTING MIND AND BODY

We began before words, and we will end beyond them.
(Ben Okri, *Birds of Heaven*)

Smith (1998) posits that it is separatist thinking which makes it difficult to envisage touch (the physical) as a legitimate part of psychotherapy (the mental). Certainly Descartes' legacy of a division between mind and body has made it inherently difficult to explain interactions between the two. The Cartesian idea of a disembodied mind has skewed our perspective to look only in one direction or the other – to body or mind – a dichotomy reflected in our language (Young, 1994: 4–8). In contrast, Seeman offers a useful organic matrix in which to ground multidisciplinary theories holistically and locate a rationale for touch in the psychotherapeutic relationship. His Human-System Model (Seeman, 2001: 624) of health is based on concepts of connectedness and communication. The model organises complex structures and simultaneously accounts for their underlying connectedness, a critical feature of human system structure. The system has a vertical dimension of personal subsystems; biochemical, physiological, perceptual, precognitive, cognitive, moving into the interpersonal, person-environmental and interpersonal-ecological. A horizontal dimension indicates the passage of time, continuity and development of the person. Both dimensions have bi-directional influence on each of the subsystems, indicating their transactional nature and connectedness, e.g. something affecting the biochemical level will inevitably change something throughout the system; something in the past or anticipation of the future will effect the present. Emotion covers the breadth and depth of all subsystems because, Seeman argues, 'An emotion might begin with a particular perception or with an interpersonal event, transfer rapidly to the biochemical and physiological subsystems, engage then with a cognitive response, and circle back to a revised interpersonal response' (ibid.: 625). Emotion activates multiple responses; skeletomuscular, autonomic and endocrinal activity, a subjective feeling state, and an urge to respond to the situation in a particular way (Smith & Kirby, 2000, cited in Seeman 2001: 626).

Seeman's model provides a framework within which the research of biochemist Pert (1998) and neuroscientist Schore (1994) fit coherently. Pert gives an explanation of how peptides, or 'information substances', function and intercommunicate within the bodymind network, while Schore (1994) illustrates the role of the primary relationship in regulating biochemistry to create the structure of the brain. Using these theories it is possible to see how the psychotherapeutic relationship might repair an experience of a less than satisfactory primary relationship, and to begin to surmise why touch may be so important in reparation. Pert (1998) presents her thesis, firmly lodged in scientific enquiry, that chemicals internal to the body, neuropeptides and their receptors, are the biological underpinnings of awareness, activating emotions and influencing how we experience and respond to the world. These biochemical messengers communicate information and direct a number of conscious and unconscious processes at any given moment. Further, they link neural, endocrine and immune systems into one vast communicative web, providing information that is constantly mobile and adaptive, held in one giant feedback loop.

Schore (1994), delivering a psychoneurobiological basis for attachment theory (Bowlby, 1969), sees self-regulation as the essential organising principle of all living organisms. He has based his research on the way in which the brain of the infant is psychobiologically regulated through the medium of its primary caregiver. Research indicates that the increasingly complex self-regulatory structural systems are located in the right hemispheric prefrontal cortex. These are not made at birth and do not arise spontaneously but are formed postnatally, in the process of social contact. The prefrontal cortex is a nodal point of multimodal input, including touch, from all sensory areas of the bodymind. In the caregiver–baby dyad, it is the external caregiver who acts as regulator for the experience-dependent development of the baby's nervous system, particularly during the intense period of growth during the first two years of life. Social environment exerts influence on the homeostatic regulation of the baby's psychobiological system through creation of 'reciprocal mutual influences' between mother and baby. Meanwhile, they are also shaping the maturation of structural connections within the areas of the brain which mediate socio-affective functions. In short: the physical development of a child's brain is dependent on experiences with the outside world, and it is the primary caregiver who is the regulator of those experiences.

Good-enough mothers provide a variety of modulated and stimulating affective experiences which facilitate growth of brain connections and contribute to self-regulatory functions in the child through brain-to-brain interaction. The mother's right hemisphere (responsible for expressing and processing of emotional information and non-verbal communication) is specifically engaged in psychobiological attunement[3] with output from the child's right hemisphere. As this matures it becomes dominant in processing visual information such as recognising the mother's face. One doesn't have to be a scientist to observe how mother and baby 'lock' into each other's gaze much in the same way as lovers. This 'snapshot' of mother's face and multimodal interactions, including touch, give the impulse for neuropeptide production and release of a high level of opiates in the child's developing brain. The baby simultaneously creates another 'snapshot' of its internal

---

3. Elsewhere (Uphoff-Chmielnik, 1999), I sought to expand on Stern's (1985) concept of attunement, differentiate between attunement and empathy, and establish attunement as the baseline for the latter. Attunement is based on the caregiver's 'reading' of the infant's inner state. The caregiver is not empathising as it is generally understood, not 'stepping into the baby's shoes', but literally 'reading' the infant, determining what the momentary emotions and needs are, and responding in an immediate, interactive and multimodal way to confirm, or 'playback' that she is receiving the information, that she is attuned to the rhythm of the baby.

state, connecting the two as pleasurable. Schore (1994) regards these neuropeptides as biochemically responsible for the pleasurable qualities in our social interactions, social affect and attachment. What it amounts to is a merging of two network systems into one connected circuit, mutual psychobiological regulation within the unit mother–child, each influencing the other's bodymind system in 'a fusion which gives rise to something new at the fulcrum of human life' (Barrett-Lennard, 2006). It is exactly this communication on all levels which Seeman's meta-theory defines as pivotal to human system function, because it is what holds the connectedness together and makes the system work bi-directionally and coherently across the whole spectrum of subsystems.

During critical periods of right hemispheric growth, various attunements and misattunements (Stern, 1985) which emphasise positive and negative emotional experiences within the relationship, imprint themselves on the prefrontal cortex (Schore, 1994). Prolonged episodes of negative, stressful misattunements cause chaotic biochemical release of stress hormones. One of these negative interactions might happen in the form of overstimulation. Think of a child being tickled: it starts off as a pleasant experience, but if the adult does not realise when the level of tolerance has been reached, it becomes something the child cannot escape – pain and powerlessness are the consequences, as well as, possibly, a wish to avoid this type of play in future as too demanding and painful. In extreme cases of continuous misattunements, the formed circuits break off into smaller, disconnected sections (Schore, 1996), perhaps resulting in an experience similar to the following: Fiona is an opera singer, activating the right side of her brain constantly in her work. It would seem her early negative experiences have been 'filed away'. She describes her embodied experience of herself: 'When I feel into the right side of my body [left brain], I am energised, critical, rebellious. I am either explosive or the "whistler" [mimes whistling in a 'don't care' attitude]. When I am in the left side of my body [right brain], I feel quiet, battered, a dark cloud comes over me [head down, hair over her face, cowed]. That implodes, I am ashamed.'

It is now well documented that memories, stress, trauma, and deprivation create imprints in the body which affect the unique mental, emotional, and physical personality of human beings (Pert, 1998; van der Kolk, 1994; and Rothschild, 2002 give detailed biochemical descriptions of how this takes place). Early experiences of being with a stressful and psychobiologically dysregulating person who prompts misattunements (like our tickling parent) but does not aid their repair (stop and calm the child), are also incorporated into long-term memory as an interactive representation, which is generalised: a working model of the 'self-misattuned-with-a-dysregulating-other' (Stern, 1985). These representations are stored in memory, but largely outside conscious awareness, as a template for further interactions. This explains the intergenerational aspect of dysfunction. Inefficient caregivers who are unable to regulate the physiology underlying emotion cause defective neurobiological patterns which become instrumental in insecure attachment functions – psychobiological alterations to the experience-dependent regulatory system are thus shaped. According to Schore (1996), impairment of the prefrontal system indicates an enduring susceptibility to psychiatric disorder later in life.

Stern (1985), Schore (1994), Pert (1998), Seeman (2001) and also Grawe (2004), coming from their different viewpoints and disciplines, albeit using different words, all agree on the most important point: dysfunction and psychopathology are the result of impeded access to one's own experiential data – the dysfunction of organismic connectedness and communication on some or all levels of Seeman's Human-System Model.

WHAT THIS MEANS FOR PRACTITIONERS GENERALLY

Having established that psychological and structural damage can be caused through dysregulated, misattuned relationships, we might pause to consider Mearns and Cooper who ask, 'if damage is caused through relationship, cannot healing be too?' (2005: 1). They suggest that close interpersonal engagement, such as that of in-depth relational encounters in therapy, may be a critical element of therapeutic success, and Schore supports this view on the basis of research (Schore, 2003). Effective functioning is when intrapersonal and interpersonal features of communication (feedback loops) are without, or have minimal disturbance: organismic connectedness and integration are the result. The task of psychotherapy is to help the client explore ways of communicating with self and other, maximising organismic connectedness and integration. Where a connection cannot be felt, or is felt at the 'edge of awareness', it becomes the work of the therapist to tentatively facilitate the client's naming of experience, enhancing clarification by linking Seeman's personal subsystems of precognitive with cognitive experience. Gendlin (1978) based his concept of focusing, working with felt sense, on this precognitive level of implicit knowledge being made explicit. Prouty's Pre-Therapy is also based on symbolisation of precognitive or facilitated understanding of condensed symbolisation (Prouty, 1994, 1998). Touch must be considered a crucial element in symbolisation because physical contact corroborates information received through other modalities. For example, our eyes may tell us that a cushion is soft but only skin contact can verify that information.

It is the primary caregiver's accurate symbolisation of the baby's experience that constitutes the basis for empathy and empathic understanding: transferring right brain polysemantic felt senses into monosemantic left brain words (Warner, 2006), thus aiding corpus callosum development (neural pathways connecting the right and left hemispheres of the brain). If this does not take place satisfactorily, clients are apt not to be able to name their experience accurately or are not able to experience the feelings they are naming. Misattunements may have altered or even changed experience, leaving a person unable to evaluate their own internal states. For some, there has been gross trauma where nothing has been named and nothing has been shared. For example, a client came to therapy because she had periods of extreme dizziness. She had been thoroughly examined and no organic cause could be found. During therapy and with empathic following of her experience, she began a process of renaming; the feeling she was describing progressed from 'dizziness', to being an 'alteration in perception', to feeling 'sick' in her stomach, to being downright scared. As a child she had had no recognition of her fear, consequently she was feeling something unnamed. The only symbolisation she could find to give this feeling was 'dizzy'. She was not able to use a verbal mechanism congruently to describe affective states because these were initially unrepresented in her brain – the imprint was missing – so processing these representations became the work of the therapist.

Pert (1998) highlights the importance of skin as a nodal point or so-called 'hot spot' at which the system can be entered and the bodymind network influenced, activating molecular stimulation through touch, rather than words. This triggers changes in the non-material mind of emotional feeling and mood, increasing physical and mental well-being. I have come to think of all our senses as 'entry points' (Seeman, 2001) of contact, connection and communication, that present a powerful contribution when combined. I surmise that a combination of touch with words, the symbolisation of what is currently happening, is another powerful contribution to the therapeutic relationship and a way that gives meaning to Pert's ideas of how one vital bodymind system may in fact 'ignite' a psychobiological response in another person, substantiating Seeman's bidirectional influence at the interpersonal level.

According to Sunderland (2006), those who grow up with little or no communication through touch become adults with 'troubled bodies' – having taken on board subliminal messages that their bodies are untouchable. This, possibly, opens the door to psychosomatic conditions, or even Alexthymia, a condition in which there is the absence of a bridge connecting thought with feeling, but in which the body may display very disturbing symptoms (McDougall, 1986). What indeed are we communicating as therapists, contributing to this process, if we withhold physical contact, restrain ourselves from this most basic of all communication? For those who regard themselves as unlovable and undesirable, we fail to provide unconditional positive regard, one of the six necessary conditions proposed by Rogers (1957) for therapeutic personality change. Furthermore, Schore's (1994) explanation of brain development tells us that dysfunction in a person's right prefrontal cortex, where empathic perception and understanding of other people's feeling states is 'wired', could hinder a person's capacity to give or receive empathy.

THE MEANING OF DISCOVERY

The sheer volume of material connected with the topic of psychotherapy when taking neuroscientific and biochemical information into consideration substantiates Grawe's (2004) fear that the dedication required to take command of the intricacies of theory and its implications for practice, means that psychotherapists will not use this new knowledge actively, rather only as a way of rationalising current theories of psychotherapy. He envisions a future where psychotherapists not only analyse psychological patterning and interactions, but actively diagnose and treat particular parts of the brain with specific interventions targeted at, for example, an overactive and therefore hypertrophied amygdala (hypothetical case, Frau H., Grawe, 2004: 29–38).

As with all new knowledge, alongside the enhancements to practice, there are inherent dangers. In Grawe's standpoint I sense a danger of a new kind of reductionism and determinism, a danger of targeting an organ or organic functioning through psychotherapy, rather than a whole-person communication, and therefore a return to a dualism based on soma instead of psyche. Caution is required lest we be drawn to definitive diagnoses and labelling. Inevitably, there will arise the question of what to do about those who appear to the experts to need treatment but do not desire it. How do we ensure that we are not acting upon cultural imprints that go beyond the individual and that we maintain that 'people have the right, desire, and ability to determine what is best for them and how they will achieve it' (Cain, 2001: 5)?

And what does all this mean to us, the psychotherapists? Touch remains, despite new knowledge, a complicated and multifaceted issue which only highlights the need for personal development on behalf of therapists, and for increased training and research. This approach is encouraged by Smith (1998) and others (Kertay & Reviere, 1998) who have suggested that practitioner attitudes and personal comfort with physical contact are important factors in the decision to use touch. Experience, won through more reflection and discussion, encourages a willingness to engage in physical contact with clients (Stenzel & Rupert, 2004). Crucially, we need to be aware of our own stress responses and how we respond when client narrative and experiencing is too painful for us. Grawe (2004) encourages therapists to activate new neuronal patterns in themselves by practicing that which they do not naturally bring to the relationship; a particular form of body language or tone of voice which stimulates attachment. This may indicate a need to stimulate right-brain functioning through imagery, art, dance, and singing, or self-development opportunities that explicitly include the body.

Training courses of all orientations need to be more focused on the relationship and review entrenched views on touch. It can no longer be deemed acceptable to say to students of counselling, as Casemore does, 'Do not touch your client, even if they ask you to' (2001: 115). Instead, more time and in-depth work must be dedicated to theoretical, ethical and experiential aspects of physical contact. Research is, of course, not a neutral endeavour and it would be folly to try to generalise anything on the basis of research to date. The one thing all researchers, without exception, seem to agree upon is that more research is needed. Up to now, research has emphasised therapists' use of touch in sessions and only a few have studied clients' experience. Now is the time to be proactive in inviting the client into the research process and examine their experience of touch in sessions. In particular, more research on age and ethnicity in connection with touch in psychotherapy is needed.

May I impress upon the reader that this chapter is not a treatise for laissez-faire and indiscriminate tactility. Rather an impulse to think about touch in a more positive way, to consider it as a dimension of the therapeutic relationship and not as a taboo. It cannot be useful to scrap ethical debate, but it is necessary that we take up the challenge of reflection in a constructive way and question continuously the very foundations from which our ethics arise, personally, culturally and professionally. It is my hope that, in this way, touch may be restored as a significant and healthy dimension of the therapeutic relationship.

REFERENCES

Ainsworth, MDS (1977) Social development in the first year of life: Maternal influences on infant–mother attachment. In JM Tanner (Ed) *Developments in Psychiatric Research* (pp. 1–20). London: Hodder & Stoughton.

Barrett-Lennard, GT (2006) Human relationship: Linkage or life form? *Person-Centered & Experiential Psychotherapies, 6* (3), 183–95.

Bergman, N (2005) More than a cuddle: Skin-to-skin contact is key. *The Practising Midwife, 8* (9), 44.

Bion, WR (1991) *Learning from Experience.* London: Karnac. (Original work published 1962)

Bowlby, J (1969) *Attachment.* London: Hogarth Press and The Institute of Psychoanalysis.

Cain, DJ (2001) Defining characteristics, history, and evolution of humanistic psychotherapies. In DJ Cain & J Seeman (Eds) *Humanistic Psychotherapies: Handbook of research and practice* (pp. 3–54). Washington, DC: American Psychological Association.

Casemore, R (2001) Managing boundaries: It's the little things that count. In R Casemore (Ed) *Surviving Complaints against Counsellors and Psychotherapists* (pp. 111–20). Ross-on-Wye: PCCS Books.

Cowen, EL, Weissberg, RP & Lotyczeuski, BS (1983) Physical contact in helping interactions with young children. *Journal of Consulting and Clinical Psychology, 51,* 132–8.

Dupree, JL & Reddick, LT (2001) Predictors of clinical use of non-erotic touch in psychotherapy. Available from <http://www.humboldt.edu/~chem_dpt/Poster01/index.html> [Accessed 14 October 2007].

Fagan, J & Silverthorn, AS (1998) Research on communication by touch. In E Smith, P, Clance & S Imes (Eds) *Touch in Psychotherapy: Theory, research and practice* (pp. 59–73). New York: Guilford Press.

Fearnley, S & Howe, D (2003) Disorders of attachment in adopted and fostered children: Recognition and treatment. *Clinical Child Psychology and Psychiatry, 8* (3), 369–87.

Fosshage, JL (2000) The meanings of touch in psychoanalysis: A time for reassessment. *Psychoanalytic Inquiry, 20* (1), 21–43.

Gendlin, ET (1978) *Focusing.* New York: Bantam.

Goodman, M & Teicher, A (1988) To touch or not to touch. *Psychotherapy, 25* (4), 492–500.

Grawe, K (2004) *Neuropsychotherapie.* Göttingen: Hofgrebe.

Horton, JA, Clance, PR, Sterk-Elifson, C & Emshoff, J (1995) Touch in psychotherapy: A survey of patients' experiences. *Psychotherapy, 32* (3), 443–57.

Hughes, DA (1997) *Facilitating Developmental Attachment: The road to emotional recovery and behavioral change in foster and adopted children.* New York: Aronson.

Hunter, M & Struve, J (1998) *The Ethical Use of Touch in Psychotherapy.* London: Sage.

Hüther, G (1998) Stress and the adaptive self-organization of neuronal connectivity during early childhood. *International Journal of Devlopemental Neuroscience, 16,* 297–306.

Hüther, G (2004) Psychotherapie und Beratung kann die Plastizität des Gehirns nutzen. *Gesprächspsychotherapie und Personzentrierte Beratung, 4,* 243–5.

Kertay, L & Reviere, SL (1998) Touch in context. In E Smith, P Clance & S Imes (Eds) *Touch in Psychotherapy: Theory, research and practice* (pp. 16–35). New York: Guilford Press.

Lago, C (2006) Whiteness, 'difference' and diversity: A significant silence in person-centred therapy?' Presentation at 7th World Conference for Person-Centered and Experiential Psychotherapy and Counseling. July, Potsdam, Germany.

LaTorre, MA (2000) Touch and psychotherapy. *Perspectives in Psychiatric Care, 36* (3), 105–6.

Leijssen, M (2006) Validation of the body in psychotherapy. *Journal of Humanistic Psychology, 46* (2), 126–46.

Lyall, M (1997) The pastoral counselling relationship: A touching place? *Contact Pastoral Monographs, 7.*

McDougall, J (1986) *Theatres of the Mind.* London: Free Association Books.

Mearns, D & Cooper, M (2005) *Working at Relational Depth in Counselling and Psychotherapy.* London: Sage.

Milakovich, J (1998) Differences between therapists who touch and those who do not. In E Smith, P Clance & S Imes (Eds) *Touch in Psychotherapy: Theory, research and practice* (pp. 74–92). New York: Guilford Press.

Pert, C (1998) *Molecules of Emotion.* London: Simon & Schuster.

Prouty, G (1994) *Theoretical Evolutions in Person-Centered/Experiential Therapy.* Newport, CT: Praeger.

Prouty, G (1998) Pre-therapy and the pre-expressive self. *Person-Centred Practice, 6* (2), 80–8.

Rogers, CR (1957) The necessary and sufficient conditions of therapeutic personality change. *Journal of Consulting Psychology, 21,* 95–103. Reprinted in H Kirschenbaum & VL Henderson (Eds) (1990) *The Carl Rogers Reader* (pp. 219–35). London: Constable.

Rothschild, B (2002) *The Body Remembers.* New York: Norton & Co.

Russell, J (1993) *Out of Bounds.* London: Sage.

Schore, AN (1994) *Affect Regulation and the Origin of the Self.* Hillsdale, NJ: Lawrence Earlbaum.

Schore, AN (1996) The experience-dependent maturation of a regulatory system in the orbital prefrontal cortex and the origin of developmental psychopathology. *Development and Psychopathology, 8,* 59–87.

Schore, AN (2003) *Affect Regulation and the Repair of the Self.* New York: Norton.

Seeman, J (2001) Looking back, looking ahead: A synthesis. In DJ Cain & J Seeman (Eds) *Humanistic Psychotherapies: Handbook of research and practice* (pp. 617–51). Washington, DC: American Psychological Association.

Shaw, R (2003) *The Embodied Psychotherapist.* Hove: Brunner-Routledge.

Siegel, DJ (1999) *The Developing Mind.* New York: Guilford Press.

Smith, EWL (1998) A taxonomy and ethics of touch in psychotherapy. In E Smith, P Clance & S Imes (Eds) *Touch in Psychotherapy: Theory, research and practice* (pp. 36–51). New York: Guilford Press.

Smith, EWL, Clance, P & Imes, S (1998) (Eds) *Touch in Psychotherapy: Theory, research and practice.* New York: Guildford Press.

Stenzel, CL & Rupert, PA (2004) Psychologists' use of touch in individual psychotherapy. *Psychotherapy, 4* (3), 332–45.

Stern, DN (1985) *The Interpersonal World of the Infant.* New York: Basic Books.

Stern, DN (1990) *Diary of a Baby.* New York: Basic Books.

Sunderland, M (2006) *The Science of Parenting.* London: Dorling Kindersley.

Trousdell, P & Uphoff-Chmielnik, A (1997) Making connections. User perceptions of the effects of reflexology and counselling. An evaluation of a complementary health care project at Worthing Mind Report, Worthing Mind.

Tune, D (2001) Is touch a valid therapeutic intervention? *Counselling and Psychotherapy Research, 1* (3), 167–76. Rugby: British Association for Counselling and Psychotherapy.

Uphoff-Chmielnik, A (1999) An exploration into touch in search of a rationale for its use within

and as an adjunct to psychotherapy, with an emphasis on a person-centred model; or Beware
– Here There Be Tiggers! Unpublished MA dissertation, City University, London.

Van der Kolk, BA (1987) *Psychological Trauma*. Washington, DC: American Psychiatric Press.

Van der Kolk, BA (1994) The body keeps the score. *Harvard Review of Psychiatry, 1,* 253–65.

Warner, MS (2006) Everyday process/schizophrenic process – A path to understanding the
functioning of brains and minds. Presentation at 7th World Conference for Person-Centered
and Experiential Psychotherapy and Counseling. July, Potsdam, Germany.

Winnicott, DW (1958) *Through Paediatrics to Psychoanalysis: Collected papers.* London: Tavistock.
Republished (1987) Karnac Books.

Young, RM (1994) *Mental Space.* London: Process Press.

CHAPTER 18

THE THERAPEUTIC RELATIONSHIP IN CREATIVE ARTS PSYCHOTHERAPY

JENNY STACEY

The woman emptied the basket of materials onto the cold floor, and began to sift and sort them. She wanted to create a cloak, a garment to conceal and reveal, to protect and excite. A layer between the inner world and the outer. She began with the blue velvet, her background, the context on which everything would be attached.

In this chapter, I will explore important principles within creative arts psychotherapy, some key theoretical concepts, and then use these ideas to examine the therapeutic relationship. I will begin with some of the context and historical details of the arts therapies, the development of the profession in this country, and then focus more specifically on working with individuals relationally as a creative arts therapist. For the purposes of this chapter, I will use the generic term 'creative arts therapist' to indicate my own desire for dialogue and relationship between all areas of creative arts therapies, such as art, drama, dance, music and all related activities.

BACKGROUND TO THE APPROACH

Karkou and Sanderson's (2006) exploration of the historical development of the arts therapies in the twentieth century is helpful in understanding the wide range of ideas that coexist under the arts therapies mantle. These writers show the different theoretical and practice-based concepts and elements coming from humanistic psychotherapy, psychoanalysis, arts education, mental health, views of creativity and the arts. I will briefly describe some of these foundations, to illustrate the links and differences that abound within the field of arts therapy. It is important to realise that the theoretical orientation of the training courses influences how the creative arts therapist comes to understand and emphasise particular aspects of the therapeutic relationship. Additionally, all therapy schools need to be aware of the cultural bias inherent in the theories they support. Sapriel and Palumbo (2001) point out that:

> Our theories help us to see clearly, but can also obscure what does not fit. Often in our professional training, therapeutic theories or developmental models are presented as if they describe universal givens, and the ethnic or cultural biases underlying these theories are rarely addressed. (p. 86)

THE HUMANISTIC SCHOOL

The humanistic school has been a particularly strong influence in the development of the creative arts therapies, and many practitioners today place themselves ideologically and theoretically within this framework. Here, the purpose of therapy is for the client to 'become' himself or herself, to self-actualise (Maslow, 1998). The client is seen as an expert regarding their own needs and growth, and the therapist works alongside the client to facilitate this process. The therapist sees the whole person as significant and is interested in the client's body data and non-verbal communication, as well as verbal information. In other words, the therapist is as interested in how the client moves and sits, where they focus their gaze, whether they hold their breath or breathe shallowly, as in the content of what the client says and how they say it.

Humanistic psychotherapy places importance on the therapeutic relationship as a means through which the client becomes more aware of her relationship patterns and emphasises what is happening between the client and therapist in the here and now of the session. The therapist brings all their available skills to the session whilst striving to keep the relationship between themselves and the client as 'horizontal' as possible, with regard to differences in power and knowledge. Each main school within humanistic psychotherapy teaches its counselling or psychotherapy students expertise in how to 'be with' their clients; for example, in person-centred counselling and psychotherapy (Rogers, 1961), through using the core conditions of empathy, unconditional positive regard and congruence; in Gestalt psychotherapy, through practising inclusion, confirmation and presence as aspects of the dialogic relationship (Hycner, 1993). Creative arts therapists have additional skills to bring to this ideological home and use the arts to establish and develop the therapeutic relationship. The therapist might do this by actively engaging in the arts process themselves, for example by playing a role directed by the client, or by being alongside the client and facilitating him or her to engage with the arts medium.

THE PSYCHOANALYTIC SCHOOL

The concept of the unconscious is central to many creative arts therapists, who believe that the arts enable material from the unconscious to be manifest in the conscious world, either within what is produced through the creative process or in the creative process itself. For some arts therapists, Jung's (1964) theoretical ideas and experiences about the healing aspects of the unconscious and active imagination are significant here. Change is seen as coming about through the exploration and transformation of material evoked by the client's relationship to the therapist (and vice versa) and the client's relationship to the arts. Psychoanalysis and the psychodynamic theories provide the original therapeutic backdrop to these ideas (see Chapter 3 this volume) and they focus on working with transference material in the therapeutic relationship. In other words, the client (and therapist) transfer feelings and emotions from the past into the here and now of the therapeutic relationship. Though each theorist in the psychodynamic school understands the transference through her or his own particular theoretical lens, there is a belief that, through the transference, unconscious feelings, thoughts, fantasies and ways of behaving from the past become manifest in the therapeutic relationship. Thus, transference is a mobilising force for change and creative arts therapy allows access to this material (Schaverien, 1992).

THE ARTS

The transformational and healing aspect of the arts has been known throughout the history of all cultures and has been studied by social anthropologists, historians and artists. Each culture defines what is artistic, and it is fascinating to consider how this definition alters over time, depending on the wider environmental conditions, for example changes in the economic, religious and political climate. At the beginning of the twentieth century, artists from all disciplines (dance, drama and visual arts) began to use different methods of emphasising the importance of emotions and self-expression, and this provided valuable inspiration for the emergent arts therapies. For example, Iljine developed Therapeutic Theatre in the Soviet Union (Jones, 1996) and Duncan's revolutionary shift in dance to natural movement (Karkou & Sanderson, 2006).

THE ARTS IN HEALTH AND EDUCATION

Following the Second World War, the wave of energy and curiosity about psychological well-being and how to achieve this signified the beginning of the humanistic movement. There was similar excitement and interest about the impact of the arts on emotional and physical health. Artists were to be found working and volunteering with occupational therapists using the arts in the UK National Health Service. Community artists were employed to bring the arts into neighbourhoods by working on projects with local people. Likewise, within the education system, many teachers and support workers emphasised the therapeutic value of the arts. From the 1970s, education became more child-centred, especially at primary level and the social and emotional well-being of the child became a focus in which creativity and self-expression were important. Inspirational teachers could ignite the creativity in their students, and some of these teachers went on to become creative arts therapists.

However, as the educational and political agenda has changed over the decades, so has the importance of creativity and the arts in education. Over the last twenty-five years, education has shifted to emphasise the monitoring and evaluation of schools' performance in terms of pupils' educational progress and whether schools provide value for money. SATS (Standard Assessments Tests), league tables and OFSTED (Office for Standards in Education) ensure that schools focus their attention and efforts on meeting government targets and policies. Arts education has been drawn into this culture; for example, it has altered its focus and now concentrates upon developing skills and improving aesthetic quality.

THE PROFESSION OF ARTS THERAPISTS

From these eclectic beginnings, like-minded people came together, and over the last 40 years different art therapy disciplines have developed their own professional bodies. In this country, there are four separate associations: the British Association of Art Therapists (BAAT), the British Association for Dramatherapists (BADth), the Association of Professional Music Therapists (APMT) and the Association for Dance Movement Therapy UK (ADMT UK). These were all set up from the 1960s onwards. Currently, trained arts therapists are registered as part of the Health Professions Council (HPC), an organisation which regulates and monitors health professionals training and services in this country. The separate associations share similarities and common beliefs, which makes it possible for the term 'arts therapist' to be used. One of these commonalities is an agreement about the importance of the therapeutic relationship in working with individual clients and groups. Likewise, the training of arts therapists is at postgraduate level, and all the associations have professional structures for their members; for example, codes of ethics, supervision, therapy and continuing professional development requirements.

However, as indicated above, within each association there are variations in academic emphasis, depending on the theoretical foundations of the training establishments. Similarly, though some arts therapists welcome the strength that comes from a united voice, others prefer each association to retain its own individual presence and expertise within its own discipline.

One strand of this debate about retaining separate disciplines concerns those who believe that it is essential for the therapist to be proficient in the art medium they have selected and who use this as a criteria for entry to training. Once trained, the therapist would use that art form as the main modality for the work with a client. An alternative stance is where the therapist is trained in a range of arts, emphasising the idea that imagination expresses multi-layered and multi-sensorial experiences; thus, the therapist is able to move between the different art media, depending on the individual needs of the client in that moment. For example, the client may begin a session orally and then explore, kinaesthetically, movement and dance. In Britain, the Institute for Arts in Therapy and Education (IATE) has developed an integrative arts psychotherapy training where all the different art forms are represented, for example, drama, music, body work, art, poetry, clay, puppets, movement and dance. IATE's beginnings were in education and psychotherapy – reflected in its membership of the United Kingdom Chartered Psychotherapists (UKCP). Other countries have developed training courses that work with a wide range of arts, emphasising the similarities in the arts media rather than the differences (McNiff, 1992; Levine, 1997). Recent publications in this country regarding the arts therapies (Karkou & Sanderson, 2006; Jones, 2005) suggest that there is movement here towards union. Both books discuss the debates for separate identity and differences in approach, as well as describing the overarching connections.

THE ROLE OF THE ARTS

Where to begin with the objects on the blue? Everything is beside her, ready. She picks up some stones, smooth and weighty, and places them with care, as the other looks on.

It is not only arts therapies that use creative methods in counselling and therapeutic practice – and looking at the role of the arts, it is helpful to think of a continuum with talking therapies at one end, the creative arts therapist at the other and, between them, variable degrees of verbal or arts interventions. Nearer one end of the continuum, a therapist might use an exercise as a tool to help the client gain a different view. For example, whilst most of the therapy session would be verbal, the therapist could invite the client to use pebbles to show the relationships within their extended family. Nearer the other end of the continuum, a music therapist might engage in some musical improvisation with their client, then perhaps, play to the client, attuning with his or her emotional state.

Each arts therapy school (or even each arts therapist) will find a place along the continuum that fits with their own theoretical beliefs and relates to the needs of the individual client or group situation. Obviously, during the process of therapy, or indeed one session, the role of the arts may alter: for example, following a period of creativity with a drama therapist, a client spends some time reflecting and discussing what they did and the implications for their relationship with their son.

KEY ELEMENTS

Now she touches the feathers, collected from the riverside, left by the preening geese before they flew to the sun. She takes the golden thread and sews them round to make the collar, as soft as down, as sleek and sharp as arrows.

CREATIVITY AND PLAY

Within arts therapies, creativity and play are two very important concepts. For Jones (2006) creativity is the core process of all the arts therapies:

> A client creates something in an arts therapy session, or there is the intention or resistance to creating something. Whether art work is being created or not, the act of creation through an art form is always immanent or present. (Jones, 2006: 248)

From the psychotherapeutic literature, Winnicott (1971) has much of interest to say to the creative arts therapist about creativity, play and the relationship between the internal and the outside world. He says creativity 'refers to a colouring of the whole attitude to external reality' (p. 65). He sees creativity as integral to being fully alive and the creative impulse as indicative of mental health. For him, in play, the imagination reaches out from inside the child into 'the space between' internal and external reality, which he calls a 'potential space' (Winnicott, 1971). In psychological ill-health, where this creative impulse has not been met in a 'good enough' way by the other person, the child, to protect itself, develops a 'false' or 'caretaker self' that complies to the demands of the outside world and, thus, the child may lose touch with its true creative self. For Winnicott, the therapist's role is to help the child or adult rediscover their creativity by (re)learning how to play. This happens in the play space where both the client and therapist 'reside'. From his work as a paediatrician, Winnicott believed strongly that the therapist was always involved. Levine (1997) observed of Winnicott that he 'is always playing with the child, even when he is merely present. That is, he never becomes a disinterested observer, outside the field of play. Rather the therapeutic space is understood as a playground' (p. 32). Winnicott's views are important to the creative arts therapist as they emphasise both the importance of play *and* the therapeutic relationship. By being held in the safe therapeutic space by the therapeutic relationship and rediscovering creativity and play through the arts, internal material can be embodied and projected into the outside world. This links to other theoretical ideas about play. Play is seen as the symbolic transformation of experience and, whilst playing, a child is making sense of their world (Cattanch, 1992). Within the safe world of play, which is both real and not real, the child can process difficult feelings and material through indirect expression. For example, within the metaphor of stories, intense feelings can be expressed, dilemmas and solutions shown and enacted (Sunderland, 2000).

These ideas resonate with creative arts therapists who facilitate adult clients to rediscover their creativity and how to play – processes which can lead to change. Initially, the therapist may be helping the client to work through introjects or messages that block access to their creativity, for example: 'I'm no good at Art.' 'I never sing. At school I was always told to stand with the growlers at the back.'

IMAGE AND METAPHOR

Linking with the ideas above, a client may play with different art materials to produce an image. This may reveal unconscious material where the arts act as a bridge to the unconscious. Many clients experience this way of working as liberating, as they allow the image to come 'without trying'. Alternatively, a client may consciously think of an image and then use different art forms to explore it. Schaverien (1992) (who would describe herself as an 'analytical art psychotherapist') is helpful here in describing how the unconscious material manifests in the art image. She makes a distinction between the 'diagrammatic' and the 'embodied' image. For her, the client creates the diagrammatic image from a conscious position, even though it might reveal unconscious material. The embodied image is one where unconscious material is revealed: 'it is as if the intensity of the pre-conscious or unconscious mental image is articulated in the pictured forms' (ibid.: 87). Creating an image can unblock a client and make tangible feelings and memories that have no verbal form. These may be pre-verbal feelings, for example, or difficult and destructive feelings that the client struggles to recognise. Using the arts, the client is able to explore internal feelings externally and come to a greater awareness of herself. The client may reflect on what she has created, making associations with it, or look at the creative experience of making the image – in other words, both the content and process are valued. Within the therapy, the client may wish to play out scenes from the past and find different endings that were not possible before. She may wish to stay with the metaphor in her work and thus allow information to be safely revealed. The arts provide a safe container where the client can begin the process of ownership, integration or transformation.

THE THERAPEUTIC RELATIONSHIP

She unravels the wool and then, with sharp stabbing movements, cuts it and cuts it into a hundred pieces. She gazes at the tangle of threads and then slowly and lovingly rescues each one. She knows each strand has a place on the cloak. And the other looks on.

All arts therapists would see the relationship between the therapist and client as crucial for change to occur. Mirroring current ideas from all the counselling and psychotherapeutic literature, the therapist would need to create a safe holding environment in which the client can explore their process. To do this, again in line with most other therapeutic schools, the therapist would assess the client and establish a working alliance with them (Clarkson, 1995). This would be done by negotiating therapeutic frame issues (Grey, 1994) and would include consideration of the aims of the therapy, the agreements for meeting and the role of the arts. Some clients would be aware of and have chosen to work with the specific arts discipline of the therapist, whilst others would need to be 'introduced' to the arts and this would be done within the assessment period. The arts can be important in establishing the therapeutic relationship, as well as being a place where aspects and dynamics of the relationship can be revealed. In the assessment period, the therapist would be attending to the quality of contact between the client and therapist, i.e. how the client relates to the therapist, how the client relates to the therapeutic space and how the client relates to the arts medium.

As a creative arts therapist, I would be looking at the ways in which the client uses the art materials made available to her. I would notice how she regards the materials, how she makes her choices and how these choices vary over time. I would notice how she 'is' in her body. As she works with a projected image, I would be noticing how she comes into contact with the clay, what colours she chooses when painting and which puppets are called into dialogue. This information I would 'hold lightly', as within my school of therapy I do not interpret my client's material; rather my job is to help the client gain more awareness of her 'way of being' in relation to herself, the outside world, other people and the creative process. However, these initial observations will hold much of the material that the therapy may need to address. This initial stage, where the working alliance is established, echoes the stage in counselling practice where the client tells his story, although this information is expressed with the arts.

The therapist's role here is to attune to the client's process and, in addition to what I am noticing about the client, I will be using my 'self as instrument' (Perls et al., 1951) and monitoring the important data of my own reactions and responses to the client.

To get a sense of the dynamics between the therapeutic relationship and the role of the arts, imagine a triangle with the client at one point, the therapist at another and the creative arts at the third. The lines joining each of these points indicate the different relationships that are present: the relationship between the client and therapist; the relationship of the client to the art material and the relationship of the therapist to the arts. At any particular moment, one of these relationships will be where the energy is focused, whilst the others, though still present, will be more in the background. The concept of figure and ground (Perls et al., 1951) from Gestalt therapy is useful here as a way of understanding how the attention and energy can shift to highlight and bring into the foreground another aspect of the triangle.

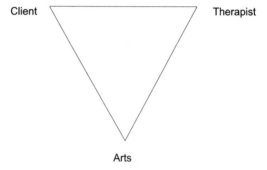

TRANSFERENCE IN THE THERAPEUTIC RELATIONSHIP

Within the therapeutic relationship, the transference can be contained in the arts image, and the client can communicate aspects of the therapeutic relationship through the arts, either consciously or unconsciously:

Jane is using the sand tray with small figures. The sand tray is between the therapist and client. Jane moves all the sand to the side of the tray next to her, revealing the blue bottom of the sand tray nearest to her therapist. In this part, she places a five-headed monster whom she says lives alone at the bottom of the sea. All the other creatures that live on the land are happy and have no idea that the monster is alive. A rabbit goes down to the sea shore and is eaten by the monster, who burps contentedly once the rabbit is swallowed. The monster decides that it will eat all the rabbits on the shore.

Jane looks up and smiles at the therapist and says 'The End'.

This is a powerful and rich communication. What the therapist does at this point will link to her theoretical perspective of what is happening here. Is Jane telling the therapist how lonely she feels in the therapeutic relationship? Or how angry she feels with the therapist? The therapist might decide to stay in metaphor and ask 'How does the monster feel now?' She might ask more about the rabbit. She might focus on the way the sand is positioned in relation to the therapist and client, noticing that Jane's side of the tray is full. She might comment on Jane's smile. Or ask Jane if she feels she needs to be alone in her anger and if this matches her past experience.

One way of understanding this would be that the client is enacting the transference: identifying with the monster, and seeing the therapist as the uncaring/unknowing other. The relationships are being contained and yet 'acted out' within the story. It is as though, in her story, the client unconsciously illustrates how she feels within the therapeutic relationship. She feels 'her monster part' is unseen by the therapist, and within the metaphor of the story she can allow this aspect of herself to appear.

ISSUES OF SAFETY

It is important for the client to feel safe enough to take risks with the arts, and it is the combination of the therapeutic relationship and the 'holding' of the client in the therapeutic space that allows this to happen. In gestalt terms, Perls (1965) would suggest 'experiments' to his clients; he called this a 'safe emergency', risking being different to gain more awareness. In gestalt terminology, the therapist would grade the experiment to provide just enough risk for the exploration to happen. It is with this attitude that the creative arts therapist would invite the client to discover more about him or herself using the arts.

As a dramatherapist, I would invite my client to look around the room and create a 'safe place' for herself using any of the materials available. This would provide a place for the client to return to if at anytime she felt the need for more safety. In this, the arts therapist is also drawing on the work of Bowlby in enabling the client to find or create a 'secure base' (Bowlby, 1998; Karen, 1994). The physical movement from one area of the room would change the client's sense of security and provide important information about how the client relates to the environment.

One client may grab the arms of the chair she is sitting in, saying 'This is my safe space', whilst another might spend much of the session creating her safe space in a corner of the room with cushions, fabrics, shells, soft toys and imaginary dragons to guard the entrance.

Clients also use the space to create scenes they wish to explore using furniture and props within the room and by placing cushions to represent other people/things that they might wish to return to later in their story. This might, for example, be a client's description of a real life situation ('Last night at the pub'), a dream or a fictitious landscape. Once the scene was set, I might ask the client where she would like to begin by inviting her to notice what attracts her interest and energy as she looks at what she has created. The client might then embody the role she has decided to explore by physically shaping the character with her body and noticing how she feels in that position.

Some clients find the world of miniature figures contained within a sand tray a more accessible way of attending to issues than using the space in the room described above. Once the client has placed the objects in the tray, the therapist encourages her to notice her different emotions in relation to each object. The therapist invites the client to see where she wishes to focus, and to speak as if she were one of the figures, for example, the 'man with no face'.

From this contained and distanced position (see below) the client can tell the story of what she has created in the sand tray whilst, if appropriate, having the option to explore aspects physically, i.e. to become more embodied (for example, I might say: 'Show me how the lion would stand ... what sound would he make?')

An important concept in creative arts therapy is *distancing*: by projecting aspects of self into the art form, the client immediately not only gains some distance from it but also gains a different perspective as she is both artist and audience – she has created the image, and the painting, sculpture or sand tray is *in* the world to be seen and worked with. Aspects of self can be safely shown by the puppets or by 'becoming' Lady Macbeth, for example. In dramatherapy this concept is known as *dramatic distance* and recognises that, within the safety of the role, the client is free to reveal aspects of themselves – the role allows the client permission to explore. Once the client has de-roled, they may have greater insight into their own process and, thus, more choices.

THE CREATIVE PROCESS AND CHANGE

In the arts therapies, the creative process is emphasised more than the finished product. This stance means that each person can bring their creative self to the therapeutic relationship without fear of judgement or a sense that they are 'not artistic'. This is in line with the holistic nature of the humanistic school of psychotherapy where all aspects of the self are acknowledged. Change can occur at different points of the therapeutic process with the arts. Throughout the process there is an emphasis on inner material being expressed in the outer world and the way in which that process or product affects the client's inner world. I have numbered these areas of change for illustration:

1. the process of using the arts
2. projection of inner material (whether unconscious or conscious)
3. exploration of the material: gaining a different perspective
4. where the client gains insight

Shabana has been coming to therapy for some months. She has recently visited an osteopath for her neck and back pain. She had been discussing her stooped posture and had been made aware of her constant habit of tensing her shoulder muscles. When she arrives at therapy she wants to explore this further. At this point, the therapist might have worked with the body, but decides to work with a projected image, as here the arts allow a distance from the experienced body pain.

Hilary suggests that she uses paint and Shabana takes a large piece of paper and collects some red paint. With wide sweeps of her arm, she paints two large red spirals to show the pain in her shoulder blades. (1) When she has finished, Hilary asks Shabana how the red spirals feel and then invites her to talk as if she were a red spiral.

SHABANA: I am tense and I am hurting. I want you to know how much you make me work. More, more, more. There's always more to do. Let me stop. Let me rest. You're like a slave driver. *(2) Having explored this, Hilary invites Shabana to move positions and speak as if she were the 'slave driver'.*

As the conversation continues between the slave driver and the pain, Shabana becomes aware that the tension in her shoulders is a protective stance. (3) She is always ready for fight or flight.

SHABANA: Sometimes when I've thought about the pain in my shoulders I've realised – if I had wings they would grow from this exact same place.

She reaches out for another piece of paper and draws some large wings. She cuts them out and places them over the red spirals.

SHABANA: They're like angel wings: my guardian angel wings. They could be soft and warm and hold the pain and tell my shoulders they don't have to work so hard.
HILARY: Tell them that directly. Speak as if you are the wings.

As Shabana begins to do this she starts to cry. (4)

Later, Hilary asks Shabana to check if there is anything the wings might want to say to the slave driver, or to see how she would like to finish this experiment. Shabana holds the wings over the painting again and says:

I just need to remember they are there.

This example illustrates that, through this experiment, the client gains more awareness into her process. The arts allow her to express her pain creatively in a projected image. Through the image, feelings that have been held in her body can be represented outside herself. Thus, the client is distanced from the pain and gains a different perspective. The paper provides a boundaried space that contains the pain and the dialogue enables her to go deeper into her intrapsychic world, to come into contact with other feelings that have been buried and out of awareness. She brings a thought from the past into the here and now of the session, which she extends creatively in order to allow a more nurturing aspect of herself to be experienced.

It might be that the image also illustrates the transference in the therapeutic relationship. Does the client feel the therapist 'drives' her, or could the therapist be represented by the 'wings'?

FINAL THOUGHTS

At last it was complete. The woman sat back and sighed as she gazed upon her work. She noticed something she might like to change, but for now the overwhelming feelings was of contentment.

This chapter has described some of the ways a creative arts therapist works with clients, the role of the arts in the therapeutic process and the significance of the therapeutic relationship. In therapy, the client sets out on a journey into the unknown accompanied by the therapist and, here, the arts provide the means of transport. Historically, the arts therapies have their roots firmly in bringing creative work to people on the edges of mainstream society who often have little overt power; for example, people in prisons, hospitals and schools, people who have learning, emotional and behavioural difficulties, and physical and sensory differences. In this approach, the art form itself is a means of contact and empowerment, allowing so much communication to occur without words. As a society, there is a need for creativity, play and the imagination to have more space to flourish. For all ages, so much of daily life is focused on task and outcome. Creative arts therapists provide one way for this to happen, and the challenge is for their voice, dance, music and movement to be heard.

REFERENCES

Bowlby, J (1998) *A Secure Base: Clinical application of attachment theory.* London: Routledge.

Cattanch, A (1992) *Play Therapy with Abused Children.* Philadelphia, PA: Jessica Kingsley.

Clarkson, P (1995) *The Therapeutic Relationship.* London: Whurr.

Grey, A (1994) *An Introduction to the Therapeutic Frame.* London/New York: Routledge.

Hycner, R (1993) *Between Person and Person: Toward a dialogical psychotherapy.* New York: The Gestalt Journal Press.

Jones, P (1996) *Drama as Therapy: Theatre as living.* East Sussex: Brunner-Routledge.

Jones, P (2006) *The Arts Therapies: A revolution in healthcare.* East Sussex: Brunner-Routledge.

Jung, CG (1964) *Man and His Symbols.* London: Aldus Books.

Karen, R (1994) *Becoming Attached: First relationships and how they shape our capacity to love.* Oxford: University Press.

Karkou, V & Sanderson, P (2006) *Arts Therapies.* Oxford: Churchill Livingstone.

Levine, SK (1997) *Poiesis: The language of psychology and the speech of the soul.* Philadelphia, PA: Jessica Kingsley.

Maslow, AH (1998) *Toward a Psychology of Being* (3rd edn). New York: Wiley & Sons.

McNiff, S (1992) *Art as Medicine.* Boston, MA: Shambhala Publications.

Perls, F (1965) *Three Approaches to Psychotherapy. Part 2, Frederick Perls (Gestalt Therapy)* [DVD]. Corona del Mar, CA: Psychological & Educational Films.

Perls, F, Hefferline, R & Goodman, P (1951) *Gestalt Therapy: Excitement and growth in the human personality.* New York: The Julian Press.

Rogers CR (1961) *On Becoming a Person: A therapist's view of psychotherapy.* New York: Houghton Mifflin.

Sapriel, L (1995) Infant research, mutual regulation and field theory. *British Gestalt Journal, 4* (1), 50–2.

Sapriel, L (1998) Can gestalt therapy, self-psychology and intersubjectivity be integrated? *British Gestalt Journal, 7* (1), 33–44.

Sapriel, L & Palumbo, D (2001) Psyche and culture. *British Gestalt Journal, 10* (2), 86–96.

Schaverien, J (1992) *The Revealing Image.* London: Jessica Kingsley.

Sunderland, M (2000) *Using Story Telling as a Therapeutic Tool with Children.* Oxford: Winslow Press.

Winnicott, D (1971) *Playing and Reality.* Harmondsworth: Penguin.

CHAPTER 19

THE RELATIONSHIP IN GROUP THERAPY

STEPHEN PAUL

INTRODUCTION

Group therapy, in general, developed from around the turn of the twentieth century and was initially the only psychological therapy available to those unable to afford individual psychiatric or psychoanalytic support. It further developed as a therapy in its own right during the Second World War, mainly in response to the large numbers of traumatised war veterans needing intensive support. The 1950s and 1960s saw the formation of therapeutic schools and a proliferation of group therapy continued during the 1960s and1970s. Now, at the beginning of the twenty-first century, the main approaches to group therapy are psychoanalytic, existential-humanistic, cognitive-behavioural and interpersonal.[1] In this chapter, I will examine the place of the therapeutic relationship in these approaches, the social-psychological research into leadership and group dynamics, and relevant research into group therapy. I will consider anti-oppressive practice and make proposals for the future development of group therapists in the modern era.

DEVELOPMENT OF GROUP THERAPY

As with most schools of therapy, it is important to consider the context for development. Modern group work was initiated in the US in 1905 by Joseph Pratt, a physician working with tuberculosis sufferers, who started an outpatient programme for groups of patients unable to afford individual treatment. Pratt used encouragement and support as well as practical information to help patients deal with their illnesses, and the psychotherapeutic nature of these groups became evident when he realised the benefits of a mutually supportive group to its members.

At the end of the First World War, Cody Marsh, who worked with the chronically mentally ill, developed these group methods with his patients. He was one of the first psychiatrists to realise the therapeutic value of the psychiatric hospital. At around the

---

1. There are a number of current texts which detail the main approaches to group therapy practice: notably Shaffer & Galinsky (1989), Corey (1995), Aveline & Dryden (1988) and Yalom (2005).

same time, Edward Lazell worked with groups of mentally disturbed soldiers using a didactic-instructional approach. He taught his students about Freudian theory in relation to their conditions and recognised the value of socialisation for patients who were perceived as isolated. He was one of the first to theorise about group treatment.

In the 1920s, therapists started using group approaches with patients suffering from neurotic disorders and also in institutional settings, such as hospitals and asylums. Wender (1936) observed transference in groups and Schilder (1936) encouraged free association. Burrow (1927), an American psychoanalyst who coined the term group 'analysis', noted that when in groups, individuals conformed to what they thought was acceptable behaviour, and that maintaining these social images impeded spontaneity and caused isolation.

Around the same time, in Europe, Jacob Moreno (1958), who introduced the term 'group psychotherapy', was developing psychodrama, a form of role play which enabled large-group participants to re-enact past experiences and resolve repressed feelings. Adler (1958) developed a model of group work which focused on the social and interactional empowerment of the individual. In the 1930s, Samuel Slavson (1943) developed activity group therapy with children using creative activities such as art and play to encourage children to express repressed feelings. He developed his group therapy into a more structured group interview which enabled children to verbalise their feelings.

As many people left Austria and Germany in the 1930s, new ideas were developed in Britain and North America. Melanie Klein (Segal, 1964) settled in London and was central in the development of the object relations theory which influenced Bion (1959) in his development of group analysis. Foulkes (1964) worked under the neurologist Kurt Goldstein alongside Fritz Perls (Perls, Hefferline & Goodman, 1959), the founder of gestalt therapy. Goldstein (1939) considered that individual neurones always functioned as part of a network. Foulkes developed the theory that the individual is a nodal point within the network of relationships within any group. He postulated that psychoanalysis should view all the relationships the individual is involved in and that there are no rigid delineations between the individual and the environment, the inner and the outer. Alexander Wolf (Wolf & Schwartz, 1962), a psychiatrist and psychoanalyst, after experimenting with working with his patients in groups, continued to focus on group work and played an important role in developing group therapy with traumatised war veterans.

Kurt Lewin (1947), a social psychologist, founded 'T' Groups (experiential training groups); he also developed field theory, a conceptual model of group forces which proposed that the *force field* of a group contained both *restraining forces* pushing the individual away from the goal and *driving forces,* driving the individual towards the goal. If these forces were equal, then no movement would take place. Lewin proposed that it was easier to weaken the restraining force than to strengthen the driving force. He also believed that the group as a whole had different qualities to its individual members; that the individuals influenced the group and the group members, creating a gestalt or whole. The group had a tension of its own with each individual member of the group having a vital part in the group process.

231

In Britain, Bion, Foulkes and Ezriel (1952) developed a group-dynamics approach to group psychotherapy which drew on the social psychological theory (particularly the work of Lewin) that the group is a dynamic organism. Lewin's field theory, which emphasised the interconnectedness of individuals, influenced the development of the psychoanalysis of the group and psychoanalysis through the group. T-Group theory is considered to have informed both Bion and Rogers in their own quite different approaches to group therapy.

In the late 1940s, Maxwell Jones (1953) was instrumental in the development of the therapeutic community. The hospital ward or hostel was seen as a group setting in which the promotion of healthy social relationships was encouraged.

Rogers (1951) was a key player in demystifying the patient–therapist relationship, seeing the therapist as a facilitator of personal development. During the 1950s, he created encounter groups as a means of developing psychological growth. The formation of humanistic psychology by Maslow, Rogers and others evolved from the work of Goldstein who stressed self-actualisation as a basic human need. Goldstein criticised the psychoanalytic concept of 'homeostasis' – that is, that the person is a closed system with no potential for growth other than making compensatory adjustments to meet any threat to the personality. He postulated that the desire for change and growth is the healthy result of inner sickness. Maslow (1964) developed the notion of 'synergy', in which an individual has more potential for development in a healthy group than alone. In 1961, with the opening of the Esalen Institute in the US (the first 'growth centre' in a decade), there was a mushrooming interest in personal growth and self-development. The centre offered people the chance to work on themselves outside the orthodox psychiatric fields and it brought worldwide attention to the groupwork approaches of Rogers, Schutz and Perls. Will Schutz (1973) developed the open encounter group, which through the facilitation of openness and honesty, was reported to promote self-understanding and joy in its participants. Fritz Perls developed the gestalt group in which a person is made aware of living in the 'now' and taking responsibility for the self. Encounter and other growth groups proliferated within the humanistic orientation. Some approaches were non-directive and facilitated the development of empathy and group cohesiveness (e.g. Carl Rogers), whilst others (such as Gestalt) were directive and confrontational.

The late 1950s and 1960s saw the development of family therapy (see Slipp, 1993), with the notion that the disturbed family member represented a dysfunctional family unit. Laing (1985), and others in Britain, popularised the therapeutic community approach, based on existential philosophy and family-systems theory as an alternative to psychiatric treatment. Martin Buber (1970), Ludwig Binswanger and Medard Boss (Halling & Carroll, 1999) laid the foundations for the development of existential and experiential group work in which the individual is seen as the source and evaluator of his or her own experience. Therapy focused around authenticity, being open in the here and now. Existentialist thought, with its emphasis on individuality and the search for self-authenticity, was taken up by R.D. Laing who saw that it was not an individual's perception of the world that was at fault but a society that caused the falsification of the self. Yalom (1981) is considered the main contemporary writer on this approach to group work, although his writing on group work theory and practice can now be considered more widely within an interpersonal, relational frame.

The explosion of personal development groups in Britain in the 1970s led to a period of pragmatism in the 1980s in line with social trends. Formal training schools for certain humanistic therapies were opened and many of the fringe approaches were abandoned.

Cognitive and behavioural groups have been mostly developed in mental health settings. Task-focused approaches to groupwork were used commonly from the 1960s onwards based on cognitive and behavioural psychologies. The outcomes of such groups were more measurable quantitatively and thus lent themselves to research. A mushrooming of evidence-based practice research in this field and the development of wide-ranging group approaches for a variety of psychological problems has greatly enhanced the pace of cognitive behaviour therapy (CBT) in health service practice.

In recent times, humanistic approaches can be found in many group-work settings. Gestalt therapy, existential group therapy, person-centred therapy and psychodrama have formed into separate disciplines. Many of the techniques of humanistic therapy are used by group leaders worldwide. Analytic group therapy has developed more relationally and is commonly used by psychotherapists. In the modern era, a more theoretically generic, interpersonal approach to group therapy has also developed (Ratigan & Aveline, 1988; Yalom, 2005). This approach is more often used by therapists of different professional disciplines who work more relationally and are not formally trained within one core-model paradigm.

THE RELATIONSHIP IN PRACTICE

PSYCHOANALYSIS IN GROUPS

Slavson (1943) was one of the main exponents of this approach, which involves the analyst and a small group of up to eight patients. The procedure is similar to individual analysis in that the interaction between the analyst and each patient is central. The main focus of interaction is the transference from the patient to the analyst, working through Oedipal guilt, infantile sexuality and resistances. Free association is encouraged. Wolf started training therapists in group therapy and with an ex-student, Emanuel Schwartz (Wolf & Schwartz, 1962), co-authored books on psychoanalysis in groups. Adherents of this approach favoured the wholesale application of concepts drawn from individual psychoanalytical theory, notably resistance, transference and interpretation, into the group setting. The individual remained the central focus. This approach is more commonly used by classically trained individual therapists where the therapist is an expert and does not engage relationally with group members.

PSYCHOANALYSIS OF THE GROUP

Bion (1959) developed a theory of group processes useful in the understanding of small therapeutic groups. The sole task of the analyst is to interpret the group phenomena. The group learns about its behaviour as the analyst identifies for the group what is happening to the group. The analyst adopts a passive observer role allowing the group to determine its own path. He describes two levels of functioning in a group. At one level is the 'work group', where the group sets about its agreed task at a conscious level. Meanwhile, there is a second, unconscious level of three basic assumption states, where the group impedes its agreed working aims:

1. *Dependency.* The group looks to the leader to resolve all its difficulties, to take charge and to work for the group. When the leader does not step up in this way, the group may challenge the leader or seek to nominate an alternative.

2. *Pairing.* The group focuses on the interaction between two members and fantasises that they will 'give birth' to a solution to the group's problem. However, in order for the group to continue to avoid working, the group supports the pairing in maintaining the status quo.

3. *Fight/flight.* The group takes flight from the issue at hand by taking refuge in alternate activity. Alternatively, the group unites against external forces and so avoids its own internal struggle.

Ezriel (1952), a colleague of Bion, developed a more commonly used psychoanalysis of the group called the 'Tavistock' model. In this approach the focus is on the 'here-and-now' interactions. The therapist interprets the transference relationship of the group to the therapist. Interpretation of this in the here and now produces change. All people experience tension in new groupings and attempt to resolve this by imposing familiar patterns of relationship onto the group. Clearly, as all members attempt to do this, some may be pushed into alien roles. This creates what is known as a 'common group tension'. The patient acts to the therapist in a way he or she believes is required – 'the required relationship' – in order to avoid the emergence of 'the fantasy, unconscious relationship' he or she would love to have with the therapist – 'the avoided relationship'. He or she fears that if this fantasy relationship was expressed it might result in rejection and hurt – 'the calamitous relationship'. For example, a group may, at first, be polite and accepting (the required relationship) in order to avoid being critical and dispassionate (the avoided relationship), which may then result in the group being labelled or even terminated. The therapist takes a passive, neutral role, interpreting the transference, firstly to the group as a whole as it develops its common group structure, and then to individual members. This mode of working demonstrates that the therapist *does* know the content of members' repressed feelings (the avoided relationship) but does not respond by using rejection (the calamitous relationship). This approach may be considered less helpful for a disturbed client group, who may need clearer boundaries and a more active and engaging therapist.

PSYCHOANALYSIS THROUGH THE GROUP

Foulkes (1964), drawing on the work of Lewin, saw the individual as a social animal whose psychological disturbances have their roots in relationships. In new situations, people behave in ways which seek to reduce their anxieties based on self-perceptions they believe to be true. A group has a 'group tension', which is the conflict between individual's needs and the group's needs. As a result of this tension, individuals take up roles. Foulkes dismissed the notion of the 'group mind' as an entity. He further differed from the views of Bion and Ezriel in that he felt that the tool of interpretation was not to be used by the leader alone: group members could also have meaningful insights about co-members. The role of the therapist is as a conductor, making subtle, informing contributions. Foulkes believed in working with the healthy functioning of group members (Lewin's driving forces) enabling the group to move towards maturation and gradually lessening the influence of neurotic forces (restraining forces). The conductor encourages free-floating group discussion. As the culture of the group develops through open personal communications between members, the group matrix is formed. Group members respond in their own subjective ways, sharing their feelings with the group. The open sharing of all feelings creates a resonance in the group, each member resonating to the content. The conductor's role is to identify the underlying cause of the disturbance. This approach has been significantly developed in Britain.

EXISTENTIAL-HUMANISTIC APPROACHES

EXISTENTIAL POSITION

The existential approach places phenomenology and the subjective experience of the individual at its core (Walsh & McElwain, 2002). The freedom of the individual to choose how to respond to life's limitations; the intersubjectivity of living, temporality, acceptance of the givens of life and the focus on authenticity, are all central tenets.

The aim of an existential approach to group therapy can be said to be threefold:

1. enabling members to become authentic with themselves

2. broadening members perspectives on themselves and their environment and

3. enabling members to find meaning for their lives (van Deurzen-Smith, 1990)

The existential therapist emphasises the therapeutic relationship as a focus for corrective emotional experiences and sees therapy as a partnership (Corey, 2003). Change comes from relationship. The therapist works to foster meaningful relationships between group members. The therapist will also work with members in confronting and working through existential life issues, common in some way to all members, and find meaning and authenticity. Yalom, in particular, has done much to bring existential factors into the therapeutic arena and has further developed interpersonal factors, which will be looked at later.

Person-centred

The work of Rogers is central to the development of humanistic group therapy. The place of facilitative factors is seen as central to the development of the therapeutic relationship in the group. Genuineness, unconditional positive regard and empathy are seen as core conditions for the facilitation of the therapeutic process. Towards the end of his life, Rogers (1986) proposed that a further quality, *presence*, was becoming important for him in his work with groups. This quality can be considered to have an energetic or transpersonal dimension. For others (e.g. Natiello,1987), person-centred groupwork enables and facilitates the emergence of personal power. The person-centred group therapist is present in the group, is willing to take part as an equal member of the group and to share their struggles with group issues as appropriate.

Gestalt

Gestalt therapy was developed primarily by Fritz Perls (Perls et al., 1959) in the 1940s and 1950s and has its roots in psychoanalysis – from the work of Freud and ego psychology to Wilhelm Reich (1949) and his notion of 'character armour'. To this was added the insights of Wertheimer's (see King & Wertheimer, 2005) gestalt psychology about perception and the tendency of the individual to complete incomplete gestalts, to form 'wholes' in their perception. Lewin's (1947) field theory and Goldstein's (1939) holistic theory of the organism were important influences on the development of this approach. Gestalt therapy was also influenced by existential philosophy, Buber and I–Thou relatedness, and the work of Moreno. There were additional influences from existentialism, particularly the 'I–Thou' relationship as it applies to therapy, and the notion of personal choice and responsibility. Gestalt group therapy (Hinksman, 1988) aims to enable the individual to become more fully alive, to overcome the blocks and unfinished issues that prevent them from being fully aware and fulfilled in the here and now, and to enable them to take responsibiltiy for their situation. Group members are encouraged to make contact with others in the group, to explore and work through blocks to full contact with self and others. The group is the medium for therapy, as it is the multifaceted 'therapeutic field' that members inhabit. As gestalt theory views the individual self as relational, the individual actualises and fulfils their organismic needs in relation to others. In gestalt therapy, therefore, the group provides a rich and promising environment for development. The main focus of the therapist in this approach is to enable contact. The therapist aims to meet others and work with members around their boundaries and defences at making contact with themselves and other group members. Whilst techniques (e.g. two-chair work) may be used to some degree, technique is seen as a medium for individuals to explore relational contact; the fulfilment of the process being in I–Thou relatedness.

COGNITIVE BEHAVIOURAL THERAPY (CBT)

Similar to analytic therapy, CBT group therapy was originally developed to facilitate the treatment of individuals in groups. Group processes and dynamics were not considered important or helpful to the task in hand. The therapist's role was to assess and treat group members. However, an underlying assumption was that a good therapeutic relationship between therapist and members was developed. Meichenbaum (1985) stressed the importance of a good working relationship in which clients are accepted, understood and liked by the therapist. Lazarus (1986, 1989) indicated the importance of establishing a climate of trust and respect, and found that particular human characteristics are indicated with successful therapists, notably, respect for others, a non-judgemental attitude, warmth, humour, congruence and authenticity. As a key component of CBT approaches is modelling (Bandura, 1986), the behaviour of the therapist is an important element in the CBT process. Rational-emotive therapists focus more on unconditional acceptance of the client, with a focus on confronting group member irrational behaviours, and are less likely to demonstrate unconditional warmth. Ellis (1992) emphasises the use of personal authenticity and appropriate self-disclosure with group members. More recently CBT group therapists have begun to recognise and work with group dynamic processes in their work (White, 2000). Many CBT programmes are psychoeducational and didactic in nature. Within this context, however, the therapeutic relationship is pivotal.

> The non-judgemental attitude and emphasis on responsiveness to patient's needs and desires can be seen to be equivalent to unconditional positive regard, as advocated by Carl Rogers, and the explicitness of therapy can be extended to transparency in all aspects of the therapeutic process. There is also a demystification of both therapeutic content and process together with a clear emphasis on collaboration and respect between the therapist and the patient. (Free, 1999: 8)

INTERPERSONAL GROUP THERAPY

The work of Sullivan and the later prolific contributions of Yalom are important in the development of an interpersonal approach to group therapy. An approach identified by Ratigan & Aveline (1988) is commonly used but with little common, conceptual methodology.

The underlying assumptions are threefold:

1. Existential factors, as exemplified by Yalom (1985, 2005) and including self-determination, choice and responsibility.
2. Interpersonal and social psychology, with the notion that *I define myself through my relations with others,* based on the work of Lewin, Rogers and Buber.
3. Group analytic theory, particularly the contributions of Ezriel (1952). Group members behave normatively (the required relationship), because if they said and did what they really wanted to (the avoided relationship), something terrible would happen (the calamitous relationship).

Sullivan (1953) proposed that personality is developed by social forces not innate or determined in childhood, and that psychopathology is based on maladaptive interpersonal experience. He developed what he called *the theorem of reciprocal emotion*: namely that we gain or suffer as our needs are met in relationships and that we base our perceptions of others on our own (distorted) inner experiences (*parataxic distortions*). These distortions are corrected by consensual validation, comparing our experience with the feedback of others.

Therapy works by *interpersonal learning* (see Yalom's curative factors), the *group as social microcosm* and the *here-and-now focus* of the group.

The therapist works to translate presenting complaints into inter personal symptoms, to activate the here-and-now process and the here-and-now interactions of group members by the use of their own transparency in the group. The therapist will work with the relationships between the members and the therapist; the relationships between the group members themselves; and relationships between group members and the group. The therapist processes individual (intrapsychic), interpersonal and group as a whole phenomena.

Paul and Pelham (2000) articulate a relational paradigm in which they propose that the focus of therapy is relational and that a range of theoretical perspectives can assist the therapist in the task of working with the individual in making sense of her or his social relationships. The therapeutic relationship itself is considered 'central to change' (2000: 110).

SOCIAL PSYCHOLOGY AND GROUP DYNAMICS

Modern group therapies have quite different approaches towards effecting change in their members. Research inspired by social psychologists (see Feld & Radin, 1982) gives insights into the outcomes of interpersonal interaction in ordinary group and social settings. This research is important in that it is not within the realm of group therapy or a theoretical paradigm but indicates important dynamics for individuals in social groups. Key factors that have been found to affect the experiences of individuals in groups are interpersonal attractiveness, attitudes, cohesiveness, conformity and norms. This research can help inform group therapists on typical group phenomena.

INTERPERSONAL ATTRACTIVENESS

People are more likely to be attracted to others with similar attitudes, status and personalities who are positive, empathetic and helpful and who they find physically attractive. The presence of someone a person likes has been shown to reduce stress whilst the presence of someone the person dislikes does not. People are less likely to help or to be influenced by someone they do not like and the amount and quality of communication has been shown to be less. Clients who dislike their interviewer are less likely to return to a helping agency than those who do. A therapist is more likely to evaluate positively a client who is liked by the therapist than one who is not.

ATTITUDES

Studies (e.g. see Feld & Radin, 1982) have shown that people are more likely to change their attitudes with the minimum of inducement. If the external justification or stimulus is minimal, the individual must attribute to him or herself a significant internal justification or motivation. The person therefore makes his/her decision to change without any sense of compulsion. People are also likely to make judgements about others based on their behaviour in one particular situation. Similarly, we tend to attribute others' behaviour to internal disposition factors whilst attributing our own to external situational factors. This is called 'attribution theory' (Heider, 1958). A person will change his or her values when inconsistencies between their stated values (what they say) and their behaviour (what they actually do) are pointed out. Discrepancies between attributed traits and actual traits of group members can be recognised and changed. However, if the group culture is not healthy, attitudes may develop that are not psychologically positive. A group member confronted with attitudes different to their own, and unsupported, may feel justified in withdrawing or playing little part in the group interaction. Another possible outcome is that the group member may choose to act in opposition to their beliefs. When a person experiences conflicting attitudes (dissonance) he or she may adapt them to fit the status quo; this is called 'cognitive dissonance' (Festinger, 1957).

COHESIVENESS

Cohesiveness has been shown to be a major factor in group dynamics (summarised in Secord & Backman, 1964).

A group with high cohesiveness is considered to have the following advantages:

1. the behaviour of group members is under more normative control
2. the group boundary is more defined
3. communication is freer and more efficient
4. members are more likely to report a sense of security and high self-esteem
5. there is a freer and more wide-ranging expression of opinions.

A low-cohesive group performs less effectively and achieves fewer goals than a high-cohesive group. An individual in a group that has low cohesiveness may not benefit to the extent he or she would in a more cohesive group. A new member may be scapegoated or alienated. Alternatively, members of a high-cohesive group may challenge members who threaten the cohesiveness which in itself may be blocking growth.

CONFORMITY

Another effect of group membership is conformity. Many studies have shown the power that group members have to make individuals conform to group norms, even against the individual's personal judgement (e.g. Ash, 1956). Janis (1972) proposes that 'groupthink' takes over and that a group will aim at unanimity at the expense of a realistic approach. There is higher conformity amongst 'like' people, and a person is more likely to conform to group members perceived as more competent or having higher status. An individual's decision making in a group is affected by the desire to protect the self and others in the group, by self-interest and by pressures to conform.

NORMS

Social groups develop their own norms. Groups apply pressure to achieve conformity by rewarding members who conform, by encouraging deviants to conform and by punishing or rejecting members who do not. A group member may receive such negative feedback that he or she may be psychologically damaged and/or may withdraw from interaction within the group to avoid such feedback. Group members who refuse or are unable to conform to group norms are liable to be scapegoated. In fact, minority groups within a therapeutic group are liable to be adversely affected by the experience (Hulse, 1985). The same can be said of sub-groups. A member of a minority in a group may become the object of projections and fantasies by other group members.

Similarly, studies by Fielding and Llewellyn (1986) and others have indicated different dimensions in group participation which affect group relations:

- Intragroup factors
- Intergroup factors
- Interpersonal factors
- Intrapersonal factors

This and similar research can inform the group therapist in their understanding of the behaviour of individuals in groups. Clarkson and Fish (1988) and Tudor (1999) explore the notion of the *client in context*. Every group member brings with them their family, work and social systems, all of which filter and illuminate how they view the therapist and the group.

SOCIAL PSYCHOLOGY AND GROUP LEADERSHIP

The position of group leader is most important in any group. Dies (1985), in a study of short-term group therapies, reports that the facilitating effect of the group leader is important for the success of the group as a whole. Other studies have shown the importance of the leader in facilitating the resolution of resistance and conflict. Bales (1958) shows two roles a successful group leader must fulfil:

1. The instrumental task function – initiating action, keeping members focused on the task, organising the group and emphasising the need to meet original aims.
2. The socio-emotional function – meeting expressed needs of the group, sensitivity to members' feelings, mediating disputes, encouraging and supporting other members, using humour to relieve tension.

Bales (Borgatta, Bales & Couch, 1954) suggested that there is one ideal leader, 'the great man', who incorporates the qualities of both types. This approach supports the notion of the 'born leader' with a specific cluster of personality characteristics. Other researchers suggest that leadership style arises out of the interaction between the demands of the situation and the characteristics of the leader. Fiedler (1967) has shown that the success of leadership style is linked to the specific situation. A leader with a specific leadership style will achieve more favourable results by modifying the situation to fit with his or her predisposition. This is called 'contingency theory'. However, groups pass thorough different stages which require different interventions on the part of the leader. For example, at times of crisis, when group members are under severe stress or when the group dynamic becomes intense and opaque, then directive, authoritarian, leadership is necessary. If the group leader is not skilled to deal with such situations, individual members may again experience distress and even psychological damage.

Adorno (1950) and Milgram (1963) have shown how individuals conform to the wishes of authority figures against their own personal judgement. Groups with directive leaders have been found to propose and discuss fewer alternative solutions than groups with less directive leaders. Furthermore, they are more willing to comply with the leaders' stated preferences. In a therapeutic group, a directive leader may impose his or her values, attitudes or beliefs, which may not be in the best interests of the client. A good leader will develop functionality in both areas. Later studies in leadership have emphasised a more multi-modal and inter-relational leadership approach which is more situation specific (Hersey & Blanchard, 1982).

GROUP PSYCHOTHERAPY RESEARCH

Clearly, research by social psychologists illustrates important factors for therapists to consider in relation to therapy groups. Research into group psychotherapy is much less clear-cut in its findings. Yalom (2005: xiv-xiv) summarises key factors as to why this may be:

- resistance from traditional schools
- lack of funding for long-term research group outcomes
- difficulty in quantification
- difficulty in evaluating interpersonal processes
- focus on appearance of efficiency versus effectiveness.

Yalom goes on to question those approaches which rely on technique and are driven by goals of efficiency rather than effectiveness – for him the 'interactional focus is the engine of group therapy' (Yalom, 2005: xvi). The therapeutic factors developed by Yalom (1975, 1985) have been recognised as a benchmark in group therapy research (Bednar & Kaul, 1994; Burlingame, MacKenzie and Straub, 2004):

- self-disclosure
- self-understanding/insight
- acceptance/sense of belonging/being valued
- learning from interpersonal action
- catharsis
- guidance
- universality
- altruism
- vicarious learning
- instillation of hope

Further studies have sought to focus specifically on core factors. Cohesiveness is now considered as a central factor in therapy-group effectiveness (Bednar & Kaul, 1994). Cohesiveness is identified by Burlingame, Mackenzie and Strauss, in their summary of group therapy research (2004: 683), as 'the therapeutic relationship in group psychotherapy'.

Burlingame et al. further consider that group therapy is blighted with too many models. Meta-summaries of research do concur that group members who experience acceptance, belonging and support, *regardless of therapeutic model*, typically report more improvement (Burlingame, Fuhriman & Johnson, 2002). Attributes such as warmth, openness and empathy have been associated with increased cohesion and better outcomes. Research into person-centred group therapy, not surprisingly, concurs with these outcomes. Page, Weiss and Lietaer (2002), in their summary of research into person-centred group therapy, indicate a significant positive correlation between both therapist- and client-offered conditions of empathy, warmth and genuineness and positive outcomes. Apart from these, it is difficult to quantify other significant findings.

To summarise, therefore, research delineates that there are specific therapeutic factors that are helpful in group therapy. Cohesiveness is central to group therapy and the therapeutic relationship is central to outcome.

ISSUES OF RACE, CULTURE, DIVERSITY AND POWER

Clearly in the group therapeutic milieu, awareness of difference is multiplied by the number of people present and the life-relationships and conditioning they bring with them. Social-psychological research is much more revealing here as to the nature of prejudice and normative behaviour than personality theory or therapeutic models. Such models can be blind to group interactions in their adherence to their defining theories. There is a fine line between working with group processes, working with the psychological material of group members, and protecting the individual rights of all group members. Glassman and Kates (1990) believe that humanistic values per se can be empowering, and propose principles for group work practice.

It is important to enable group members to work through their own psychological issues in relation to others, but not at the expense of others. Given potential transference issues in groups, it is often likely that the presence of one member may stimulate personal material in another.

The place of the group therapist in their own self-awareness and reflexivity, their ability to work in a non-oppressive way, and their ability to separate out group-process issues from the prejudicial behaviour of members, is thus focal. Significant attention needs to be given, both in the training of therapists and their practice, to developing anti-oppressive ethical modalities.

CONSIDERATIONS FOR FUTURE DEVELOPMENTS

Yalom (2005: xiii) has delineated a differentiation between the *front* and *core* of the different modalities: the 'front', including the trappings, language and techniques, and the 'core' comprising the *bare-boned mechanisms of change*. He concludes that change mechanisms across the therapies are very similar (see Paul & Pelham, 2000).

Findings both in social psychological and group therapy research indicate the importance of interpersonal relationships as change mechanisms. Research findings are inconclusive as to which therapy works best for whom: they conclude that generally to have therapy is better than not to have it. There is no evidence that one theoretical paradigm is any better than any other. In consideration of the relationship, the body of accumulated research indicates that a group in which members experience higher levels of cohesiveness, acceptance, warmth and genuineness will lead to better outcomes.

What the great majority of interpersonal group therapists actually do, be they existential-humanistic, psychodynamic or cognitive in orientation, may be quite similar. The emphasis for both the future training of and developing practice in group therapy, needs to focus on both the awareness and actions of the therapist-in-relationship with others. More emphasis needs to be put on the dynamics of the therapeutic relationship and less on complex theory.

REFERENCES

Adler, A (1958) *What Life Should Mean to You.* New York: Capricorn Books.
Adorno, T (1950) *The Authoritarian Personality.* New York: Harper & Row.
Ash, SE (1956) Studies of independence and conformity. A minority of one against a unanimous majority. *Psychological Monographs, 70.*
Aveline, M & Dryden, W (1988) *Group Therapy in Britain.* Milton Keynes: Open University Press.
Bales, RF (1958) Task roles and social roles in problem-solving groups. In EE Maccoby, TM Newcomb & EL Hartley (Eds) *Readings in Social Psychology* (3rd edn) (pp. 437–47). New York: Holt.

Bandura, A (1986) *Social Foundations of Thought and Action: A social cognitive theory*. Englewood Cliffs, NJ: Prentice Hall.

Bednar, RL & Kaul, T (1994) Experiential group research. In AE Bergin & SL Garfield (Eds) *Handbook of Psychotherapy and Behavior Change* (pp. 631–63). New York: John Wiley & Sons.

Borgotta, EF, Bales, RF & Couch, AS (1954) Some findings relevant to the great man theory of leadership. *American Sociological Review, 19* (6), 755–9.

Bion, WR (1959) *Experiences in Groups*. New York: Basic Books.

Buber, M (1970) *I and Thou* (Trans W Kaufmann). New York: Charles Scribner's Sons.

Burlingame, GM, MacKenzie, KR & Strauss B (2004) Small-group treatment: Evidence for effectiveness and mechanisms of change. In MJ Lambert (Ed) *Bergin & Garfield's Handbook of Psychotherapy and Behavior Change* (5th edn) (pp. 697–742). New York: Wiley & Sons.

Burlingame, GM, Fuhriman, A & Johnson, J (2002) Cohesion in group psychotherapy. In J Norcross (Ed) *A Guide to Psychotherapy Relationships that Work* (pp. 71–87). Oxford: Oxford University Press.

Burrow, T (1927) *The Social Basis of Consciousness*. New York: Harcourt Brace & World.

Clarkson, P & Fish, S (1988) Systematic assessment and treatment considerations in TA child psychotherapy. *Transactional Analysis Journal, 18,* 123–52.

Corey, G (1995) *Theory and Practice of Group Counseling* (4th edn). Belmont, CA: Wadsworth.

Corey, G (2003) *Theory and Practice of Group Counseling* (6th edn). Belmont, CA: Wadsworth.

Dies, R (1985) Leadership in short-term group therapy: Manipulation or facilitation? *International Journal of Group Psychotherapy, 35,* 435–55.

Ellis, A (1992) Group rational-emotive and cognitive-behavioral therapy. *International Journal of Group Psychotherapy, 42* (1), 63–80.

Ezriel, H (1950) A psycho-analytic approach to group treatment. *Brit. J. Med. Psychol, 23,* 59–75.

Ezriel, H (1952) Notes on psychoanalytic therapy: II: Interpretation and research. *Psychiatry, 15,* 119–26.

Feld, S & Radin, N (1982) *Social Psychology for Social Work and the Mental Health Professions*. New York: Columbia University Press.

Festinger, L (1957) *A Theory of Cognitive Dissonance*. Stanford, CA: Stanford University Press.

Fiedler, FE (1967) *A Theory of Leadership Effectiveness*. New York: McGraw-Hill.

Fielding, RG & Llewelyn, SP (1986) Applying the social psychology of groups in clinical settings. *British Journal of Psychotherapy, 2* (4), 281–91.

Foulkes, SH (1964) *Therapeutic Group Analysis*. New York: International Universities Press.

Free, ML (1999) *Cognitive Therapy in Groups*. Brisbane: Wiley & Sons.

Glassman, G & Kates, L (1990) *Group Work: A humanistic approach*. Thousand Oaks, CA: Sage.

Goldstein, K (1939) *The Organism: A holistic approach to biology derived from pathological data in man*. New York: American Book Company.

Halling, S & Carroll, A (1999) Existential-phenomenological psychology. In D Moss (Ed) *Humanistic and Transpersonal Psychology* (pp. 94–124). Westport, CT: Greenwood Press.

Heider, F (1958) *The Psychology of Interpersonal Relations*. New York: Wiley & Sons.

Hersey, P & Blanchard, KH (1982) *Management of Organisational Behavior: Utilizing human resources*. Englewood Cliffs, NJ: Prentice Hall.

Hinksman, B (1988) Gestalt group therapy. In M Aveline & W Dryden (Eds) *Group Therapy in Britain* (pp. 65–87). Milton Keynes: Open University Press.

Hulse, D (1985) Overcoming the social-ecological barriers to group effectiveness: Present and future. *Journal for Specialists in Group Work, 10* (2), 92–7.

Janis, IL (1972) *Victims of Groupthink.* Boston, MA: Houghton Mifflin.

Jones, M (1953) *The Therapeutic Community: A new treatment method in psychiatry.* New York: Basic Books.

King, DB & Wertheimer, M (2005) *Max Wertheimer and Gestalt Theory.* New Brunswick, NJ: Transaction.

Laing, RD (1985) *Wisdom, Madness and Folly: The making of a psychiatrist.* London: Macmillan.

Lazarus, AA (1986) Multimodal therapy. In JC Norcross (Ed) *Handbook of Eclectic Therapy* (pp. 65–93). New York: Brunner/Mazel.

Lazarus, AA (1989) Multimodal therapy. In RJ Corsini & D Wedding (Eds) *Current Psychotherapies* (4th edn) (pp. 273–302). Itasca, IL: FE Peacock.

Lewin, K (1947) Frontiers in group dynamics: Concepts, method and reality in social science: Social equilibria and social change. *Human Relations, 1,* 5–41.

Maslow, AH (1964) Synergy in society and the individual. *Journal of Individual Psychology, 20,* 153–64.

Meichenbaum, D (1985) *Stress Inoculation Training.* New York: Pergamon Press.

Milgram, S (1963) Behavioral study of obedience. *Journal of Abnormal and Social Psychology, 67,* 371–8.

Moreno, JL (1958) Fundamental rules and techniques of psychodrama. In JH Masserman & JL Moreno (Eds) *Progress in Psychotherapy* (pp. 86–132). New York: Grune & Stratton.

Natiello, P (1987) The person-centered approach: From theory to practice. *Person-Centered Review, 2* (2), 203–16.

Page, RC, Weiss, JF & Lietaer, G (2002) Humanistic group therapy. In DJ Cain & J Seeman (Eds) *Humanistic Psychotherapies: Handbook of research and practice* (pp. 339–68). Washington, DC: American Psychological Association.

Paul, S & Pelham, G (2000) A relational approach to therapy. In S Palmer & R Woolfe (Eds) *Integrative and Eclectic Counselling and Psychotherapy* (pp. 110–26). London: Sage.

Perls, FS, Hefferline, RF & Goodman, P (1959) *Gestalt Therapy: Excitement and growth in the human personality.* Harmondsworth: Penguin.

Ratigan, B & Aveline, M (1988) Interpersonal group therapy. In M Aveline & W Dryden (Eds) *Group Therapy in Britain* (pp. 45–64). Milton Keynes: Open University Press.

Reich, W (1949) *Character Analysis.* New York: Noonday Press.

Rogers, CR (1951) *Client-Centered Therapy.* Boston, MA: Houghton Mifflin.

Rogers, CR (1970) *Carl Rogers on Encounter Groups.* New York: Harper & Row.

Rogers, CR (1986) Client-centered therapy. In IL Kutash & A Wolf (Eds) *Psychotherapist's Casebook* (pp. 197–208). San Francisco, CA: Jossey-Bass.

Schilder, P (1936) The analysis of ideologies as a psychotherapeutic method. *American Journal of Psychiatry, 93,* 601.

Schutz, W (1973) *Elements of Encounter.* Big Sur, CA: Joy Press.

Secord, PF & Backman, CW (1964) *Social Psychology.* New York: McGraw-Hill.

Segal, H (1964) *An Introduction to the Work of Melanie Klein.* New York: Basic Books.

Shaffer, JBP & Galinsky, SR (1989) *Models of Group Therapy.* Englewood Cliffs, NJ: Prentice Hall.

Slavson, SR (1943) *An Introduction to Group Psychotherapy.* New York: Commonwealth Fund.

Slipp, S (1993) Family therapy and multiple family therapy. In H Kaplan & B Sadock (Eds) *Comprehensive Group Therapy* (pp. 270–82). Baltimore, MD: Williams & Wilkins.

Sullivan, HS (1953) *The Interpersonal Theory of Psychiatry.* London: WW Norton.

Tudor, K (1999) *Group Counselling.* London: Sage.

Van Deurzen-Smith, E (1990) *Existential Therapy.* London: Society for Existential Analysis Publications.

Walsh, RA & McElwain, B (2002) Existential psychotherapies. In DJ Cain & J Seeman (Eds) *Humanistic Psychotherapies: Handbook of research and practice* (pp. 253–78). Washington, DC: American Psychological Association.

Wender, L (1936) The dynamics of group psychotherapy and its application. *Journal of Nervous Mental Disorders, 84,* 55.

White, J (2000) Introduction. In J White & A Freeman (Eds) *Cognitive-Behavioral Group Therapy for Specific Problems and Populations* (pp. 3–28). Washington, DC: American Psychological Association.

Wolf, A & Schwartz, K (1962) *Psychoanalysis in Groups.* New York: Grune & Stratton.

Yalom, ID (1975) *The Theory and Practice of Group Psychotherapy* (2nd edn). New York: Basic Books.

Yalom, ID (1981) *Existential Psychotherapy.* New York: Basic Books.

Yalom, ID (1985) *The Theory and Practice of Group Psychotherapy.* (3rd edn). New York: Basic Books.

Yalom, ID (2005) *The Theory and Practice of Group Psychotherapy.* (5th edn). New York: Basic Books.

Chapter 20

CONCLUSION
IS THE RELATIONSHIP THE THERAPY?

Sheila Haugh
Stephen Paul

It is not unusual for a book such as this, with a number of contributors writing on the same theme, to finish with a conclusion that rounds up the ideas presented and suggests future areas for discussion and research. It is tempting to look at each perspective and attempt to draw together themes common to each orientation. It is tempting to try to recount one consistent narrative describing and detailing what is a therapeutic relationship. But, for the most part, we will resist this temptation. Rather, we will take an opportunity to consider the ideas and thoughts that have arisen while bringing this book together, some more formed and coherent than others. Reading and re-reading each chapter has provoked many ideas and debates between us – some more robust than others. This chapter attempts to explore some of these ideas, a few of which are very tentative and only just forming, others that have a more definite shape.

Before we go further, we would just like to say a little about the research evidence into the therapeutic relationship. As has been noted elsewhere (Bozarth & Motomasa, Paul & Haugh, this volume), research is not a value-free activity. There are a number of factors of which we take particular note. Firstly, researcher allegiance has an effect on the outcome of the research findings themselves. Secondly, the 'gold standard' of research, randomised controlled trials (RCTs), are not always as random as might first appear. Thirdly, the paradigm of the RCT research may not be the most appropriate for research into psychotherapy. Fourthly, whilst a mixed approach to research on the psychotherapeutic relationship (RCTs, causal, quantative and qualitative approaches) might be most preferable, currently this is extremely difficult to implement. Lastly, we would not wish to ignore the possibility that a completely different approach to research may be developed. The sum total of these comments is to say that the research data is not perfect, not exhaustive and not to be relied on as an objective truth. At the same time, when considered judiciously, we can accept findings as a guide and a pointer to future directions of enquiry.

In the introduction we identified a number of themes we would seek to explore and clarify in this book:

- what works in therapy
- how different models view the relationship
- modern developments and trends

- commonalities and differences in different approaches
- how different models work with power and diversity
- to help the practitioner understand different approaches and clarify their own approach.

Hopefully, it is now apparent to the reader that whilst philosophies, theories and approaches to practice may differ across orientations, some key themes have emerged:

- the relationship is significant to therapeutic change in every model of therapy
- there is an increasing focus on relational factors across all models
- for therapeutic change to occur there is clear evidence that positive relational factors must be present regardless of therapeutic model.

The following areas are some of the ideas and thoughts these key themes have provoked.

UNIQUE COMMONALITIES

The phrase 'unique commonalities' is used deliberately to indicate how a therapeutic relationship can be described in a number of different ways, captivate different people at different times and, in this way, is completely unique to those people involved. At the same time, it is clear that there are aspects of this relationship on which all can agree. Rogers' (1957) conditions of empathy, congruence and unconditional positive regard seem to be necessary in some form, even if there is disagreement as to whether or not they are sufficient for therapeutic personality change. All the authors in this book attest to this idea, even if the language used is different. An authentic encounter encompassing all aspects of each person (the personal, cultural and social spheres of their existence) is also valued as being helpful and growth promoting. How this encounter is manifested will be unique to each relationship. It might include touch or it might not: it might include exploration of a spiritual dimension, or it might not. The exact expression of this meeting will not, and cannot, be constrained and determined beforehand. Nor should it be constrained and determined by the inflexible demands of a particular orientation. It must remain idiosyncratic. At the same, a common factor we can acknowledge is that if we are to truly offer ourselves as a useful companion to a person on their (therapeutic) journey, then we need to meet with them openly and truthfully, with profound understanding and respect.

There are interesting questions posed by this position. How do we learn to enter (or rediscover) a relationship authentically, without defences and façades? What is the 'aim' of this activity we call psychotherapy? Feltham (1999), for example, suggests that personal growth is more linked to the arts and religions than to therapy, fulfilment being typically found outside the therapeutic relationship. So, it is interesting to note how the client group for counselling and therapy has widened quite dramatically from the days when Freud worked with young women with 'debilitating symptoms' (Howard, this volume), and Rogers with traumatised servicemen (Rogers & Wallen, 1946). These days, therapists work with people in deep psychic distress, and with those who are experiencing a vague unhappiness or feelings of being unfulfilled. Would something other than therapy be a preferred response for this second group of people? On the other hand, if the relationship is the fundamental factor in therapeutic change and/or personal development, then it will be growthful for all participants (therapist and client), regardless of whether distress is conceptualised as severe mental dis-ease or lack of personal fulfilment. Here we come full circle and return to the importance of the idiosyncratic aspect of the relationship. Whilst we may be able to identify the commonalities, the unique aspects of the relationship are brought to the meeting by the individual participants – the therapist and client.

THE CONTEXT OF THE THERAPEUTIC RELATIONSHIP

One of the most startling aspects of the therapeutic relationship is the dearth of research into its socio-political aspects. We found very little research that considered the relationship between a client and therapist from different social/cultural groups, and/or with different privileges or ranks (see Totton, this volume). We hope that this is an important aspect of the therapeutic relationship for *all* practitioners, although we have yet to be convinced. There are a number of factors that need to be considered in relation to the therapeutic relationship and the socio-political context of the client and therapist.

- Do differences between the therapist and client affect the outcome of psychotherapy?
- Whose account of therapy are we listening to – the therapist or the client?
- Does the (Western) emphasis on the self help or hinder the therapeutic process?

DIFFERENCES BETWEEN THERAPIST AND CLIENT

It can be stated with some confidence that all people are different and relate to each other in different ways. Early parenting experiences, experiences throughout life, the quality of our interpersonal relationships, all affect how we each manage relationships. This is as true of the therapeutic relationship as any other and as true for the therapist as the client. Thus, difference is inherent between the therapist and client and this requires us to face the 'challenge of the otherness of the Other' (Schmid, 2006: 240). In therapy 'we are confronted with the two essential and contradictory phenomena of togetherness and separateness' (ibid.: 248). Most therapists seem comfortable and at ease with the concept of togetherness: the idea that separateness can be transcended. Indeed, many might even claim that separateness *should* be transcended. However, if separateness and difference are ignored we are in danger of missing an exploration of the advantages of difference (for example, we are less likely to make assumptions about the other person if we are aware of our differences) and we are more likely to parallel the oppression in our society and replicate it within the therapeutic relationship. Totton and McFarlane (this volume) both point out the dangers that are present when therapists are not aware of their privilege and rank. McFarlane, in particular, asks the question of why it is so

249

difficult to keep these aspects of our relationship with clients in our awareness. These differences, if unknown and/or unacknowledged, will have a profound effect on the therapeutic relationship and, therefore inevitably, on the outcome of therapy.

Using notions of figure and ground, we need to understand more fully the *ground* of the relationship: that is our cultural and social context, the power we have or are ascribed as having, our expectations, our personal belief systems, our blind spots and so forth. By doing this we are able to engage more freely in the *figure* of the relationship itself.

WHOSE ACCOUNT?

It is clear that clients and therapists often have quite different perspectives on what works in therapy. Despite many practitioner claims to mutuality in the relationship with their clients, very little research has followed this line of enquiry. Too many practitioners describe their relationship with the client as though their (the therapist's) experience is also the client's experience. As Feltham (1999) points out, nearly all accounts of the therapeutic relationship are written by therapists themselves and this may distort our understanding and practice. The fact that therapist self-assessment of high levels of empathy has little relation to the positive outcome of therapy is rather worrying. For, if we are unable to assess the level of empathy experienced by our clients, this is probably true of other aspects of the relationship. It seems that practitioners have less knowledge, understanding and appreciation of the moment-to-moment process of the relationship than they believe.

Our review of research (Paul & Haugh, this volume) has also indicated a real gap between client and therapist perception of change in therapy itself. Further, there is little evidence of research into what researchers refer to as interactive or reciprocal coordination and congruence, what we may call common mutuality in the therapeutic process. Clearly, where this is present, therapeutic outcomes are more favourable, yet studies have been more concerned with therapist variables or client variables as opposed to the dynamics of the interaction as experienced from *both* sides.

WESTERN EMPHASIS ON SELF

Nakata (this volume) suggests that the need to develop a self-identity may be a considerable burden for many people. This is echoed by van Blarikom (2008) when he writes that 'the emphasis on the individual [takes] its toll with vulnerable people' (p. 22). Nakata wonders if Western psychotherapists might find that a more 'we-based' therapy would be a fruitful area of exploration. There is an inherent contradiction in therapy as it is practised in the West: whilst we are becoming clear that it is the relationship that is the curative factor, at the same time it is a relationship where the focus is the selfhood of the client. For most approaches, most of the time, attention to the relationship is in the service of the development of self. This concept of the self and the centrality of the self have little in common with non-Eurocentric psychologies, including Asian and African perspectives, suggesting that the self does not exist as a biological entity or an ontological certainty. Rather, it is a culturally determined phenomenon. This does not mean that the idea (and the experience) of the self should be discarded: cultural awareness and sensitivity should extend to all cultures. At the same time, Western psychology's preoccupation with this notion may well be detrimental to the therapeutic relationship itself and thus caught in an ultimately self-defeating circle. If Western psychotherapists could break free of this conditioning and see beyond their own cultural boundaries, it might deeply enhance the relational, and therefore curative, nature of the therapeutic relationship. After over a century of self-development in Western countries, whereby the individual has been glorified and indulged, and self-awareness more valued than community awareness (or other-awareness), it is ironic that we now find ourselves suggesting that relationships are the catalyst for personal growth. Perhaps this is a counterpoint to the alienation and personal isolation people feel when external conditions of modern Western society do not meet internal needs.

IT IS THE RELATIONSHIP

Research evidence points to the importance of relational factors. As indicated above, meta-studies concur that variations of empathy, warmth and positive regard are central to therapeutic change. Models of therapy and/or techniques may be marginally more effective than other approaches in individual studies. But overall, no school is considered more or less effective than another. These often intangible or seemingly idiosyncratic relational elements of the therapeutic encounter are therefore significant in the dynamics of change.

HOW DIFFERENT MODELS VIEW THE RELATIONSHIP

Typically, classical psychodynamic approaches have viewed the client's phenomenological perspective of, and behaviour in, therapy as symptomatic and indicative of their problem and thus the focus of expert interpretation and interventions. Humanistic approaches have seen the authenticity of the interaction as central to change. In common with psychodynamic practitioners, humanistic therapists have been critiqued as acting as the agents of change and using power or the application of techniques in their practice. The cognitive-behavioural practitioner has been seen more as an educator who teaches strategies to change the life of the client. The transpersonal school, which is less identifiable as 'one' approach, sees the therapist as a guide or catalyst for change. We are reminded of the classic story of the blindfolded men and the elephant. All are clear by their touch in the description of what they are touching. 'It's like a snake.' 'It's a tree trunk.' 'It's a hut on legs.' Each man has his own perspective, but none can describe the creature as it is, nor recognise it as an elephant, and each thinks they have the whole truth of what they are touching.

Given the research findings that indicate common relational factors have more currency than school or techniques, we wonder whether the focus on what may be called 'schoolism' is an outdated methodology. The fact is that the elephant is alive and healthy, even whilst being understood as a snake, a tree trunk or a hut on legs. There is a competitive quality that travels alongside schoolism: one perspective is better than another and vice versa. A significant amount of research energy has been spent on the pursuit of finding out the 'best' approach, with no winner found. Perhaps all modalities have something to offer that is unique and valuable in our understanding of the human condition. It is worth considering whether an approach valuing the needs, problems and context of the individual may be more fruitful than what may be an arcane attempt to fit all problems into one, unisize box.

A UNITARY PARADIGM?

Some theorists have attempted to formulate an explicit unitary model. For example, Clarkson (2003) has proposed that there are five modes within the therapeutic relationship.

Relational Matrix
Working alliance
Transferential
Reparative
Person-to-person
Transpersonal

She suggests they are woven like threads into all aspects of the relationship with any particular mode coming to the fore at one time whilst the others remain in the background, akin to notions of figure and ground. Assagioli (1975) and Wilber (2007) have both created models of human growth and development that incorporate different modalities of therapeutic practice. We question the ultimate accuracy of such a unitary model and are nervous of making such global assertions. Like the blindfolded men and the elephant, all such models or matrixes are by their nature contextualised from the perspective of the writer. On the other hand, they can be helpful in assisting us in moving toward understanding the whole and finding a common language and conceptualistion. Patterson (1974) saw the search for a unitary paradigm as a wasted endeavour, considering the facilitative conditions of 'empathy, warmth, respect, concern, valuing and prizing, openness, honesty, genuineness, transparency, intimacy, self-disclosures, confrontation' as intrinsically humane. He believed that these conditions 'constitute love in the highest sense or *agape*' and thus 'we already have the answer' (1974: 89–90). By this he meant, quite simply, that love is all there is to psychotherapy (Patterson, 1996). If, to some degree, therapy provides support or alleviation for the pain of people who are missing love in their lives (currently or in the past) then perhaps it is not too far-fetched to suggest that a form of love (*agape*) is an *essential* component in the therapeutic relationship itself.

In the same vein, but from a different perspective, Feltham raises concerns about the clinicalisation of therapy and therapeutic relationships, and the impetus to make the therapist the 'expert' healer of the human condition. Clearly, the medicalisation of human distress raises significant problems both for the therapeutic work and the place of therapy in our culture. The manualisation of a cure for human distress, by its very nature, detracts from the therapeutic relationship. It continues an I–It relationship at the cost of a potential I–Thou relationship. Given that the therapeutic relationship and common factors, including variously, empathy, rapport, positive engagement, and authenticity, are central to change, here we have a paradox. 'Treat' the symptom (a medical metaphor even if the treatment is with empathy, rapport and so forth) and we fail the person. Yet we must not ignore the reality of what clients present in therapy and their personal suffering. Perhaps the answer lies in where we position our power in the therapeutic encounter. Who directs the therapy – the therapist or the client?

There is no evidence (see Paul & Haugh, this volume) that an approach founded only on these common factors is any more (or less) fruitful than a manualised or orientation-specific approach. We are not arguing for what may be called an *unorganised eclecticism,* nor indeed are we necessarily arguing for a non-specific approach. In terms of therapist training, for example, is it better to be deeply skilled in one approach or not so deeply skilled in a number of different approaches? What is clear is that any approach that is grounded in a closed model, seeking to prove its superiority and rightness in its interventions and claiming universality, will by its very nature remain closed and unchanging. This may be of service to the therapist in terms of the security of knowing 'what's what' but it will not be in the service of the client. That any individual therapist or approach has access to the sum of all knowledge, even knowledge that is yet to be found, is a patently absurd position. An approach that does not seek to be refreshed and illuminated by the evidence of ongoing research outcomes will become stultified and rigid.

A PHILOSOPHICAL PERSPECTIVE

The four forces of psychology which became the foundations for the current psychological therapies all embraced different philosophical roots. In our consideration of the different conceptualisations of successful psychotherapy it is worth considering whether the differences across orientations may be distilled down to a philosophical stance. Stated like this, it might seem that if the answer is in the affirmative it would be relatively easy to let go of the competiveness across orientations. Each therapist could coolly reconceptualise their perspective as agreement was formed on the 'best' approach to mental dis-ease. However, our philosophical perspective informs our beliefs and ethics and is the basis of how we live our lives. It is not a simple exercise to let go of these deeply held values and ideals, so intimately connected are they to our moral codes and sense of integrity. Nevertheless, can practitioners find a way to truly accept practitioners from other modalities having a unique experience of the same phenomenon? Can we allow that the elephant is just too big for each of us to see all of it and that we are all just seeing a part of it?

From this perspective, we can attempt to describe three approaches to the therapeutic relationship:

• a model-based approach – dictated by a core set of beliefs within that model

- a pragmatic approach – based on what the therapist knows works for them (founded in personal experience as much as on research and a core model)
- a phenomenological approach – based on the encounter, and the uniqueness of the persons in that encounter

Whilst this brings clarity to how the therapeutic relationship is approached and understood, we return to the point made above that it is imperative that we listen more intently to our clients in our endeavour to understand what works in therapy.

In conclusion, it is perhaps apparent that we would answer the question 'is the relationship the therapy?' with a confident 'yes'. It is clear that more research and exploration needs to be undertaken regarding issues relating to difference between client and therapist and the implications regarding the power dynamic of that difference. More examination of the interactive components of therapy is required if we are to move toward understanding what is happening dynamically in the relationship that enables change. At the same time, it is imperative that the person who makes up the other half of the therapeutic relationship, the client, is heard more clearly.

In this modern era we are at a crossroads. We need to bring to our process of understanding the same attitudes we bring to the therapeutic relationship. We approach each new encounter with openness and a willingness to meet the other afresh, not knowing the outcome or how we will behave, but trusting in the unique capacity of the human spirit. Can we move away from old models of understanding and embrace a new dynamic approach to the therapeutic relationship in the same way, with openness and unknowing? This means an open, non-partisan approach to the therapeutic relationship which welcomes surprise and perhaps even radical change.

REFERENCES

Assagioli, R (1975) *Psychosynthesis.* Wellingborough: Turnstone Press.

Clarkson, P (2003) *The Therapeutic Relationship* (2nd edn). London: Whurr.

Feltham, C (1999) Contextualising the therapeutic relationship. In C Feltham (Ed) *Understanding the Counselling Relationship* (pp. 4–32). London: Sage.

Patterson, CH (1974) *Relationship Counseling and Psychotherapy.* New York: Harper & Row.

Patterson, CH (1996) Leona Tyler Award address. *The Counseling Psychologist, 24* (2), 335–47.

Rogers, CR (1957) The necessary and sufficient conditions of therapeutic personality change. *Journal of Consulting Psychology, 21* (2), 95–103.

Rogers, CR & Wallen, JL (1946) *Counseling with Returned Servicemen.* New York: McGraw-Hill.

Schmid, PF (2006) The challenge of the other: Towards dialogical person-centred psychotherapy and counseling. *Person-Centered and Experiential Psychotherapies, 5* (4), 240–54.

Van Blarikom, J (2008) A person-centered approach to borderline personality disorder. *Person-Centered and Experiential Psychotherapies, 7* (1), 20–36.

Wilber, K (2007) *The Integral Vision: A very short introduction to the revolutionary integral approach to life, God, the universe, and everything.* Boston, MA: Shambhala.

CONTRIBUTORS

Jerold D. Bozarth, PhD, learned client-centered therapy from working with chronic psychotic, hospitalised clients. He has published over 300 articles and book chapters and three books, and has consulted with person-centered training programs in Austria, Brazil, Czech Republic, England, Portugal and Slovakia. He is Professor Emeritus of the University of Georgia and a member of the Golden Pantry Coffee Club. (Contact: bozarthj@bellsouth.net)

Toni Gilligan is a gestalt psychotherapist, and a director and faculty member of the Gestalt Centre, London. She has worked as a clinical psychologist in mental health in the National Health Service and in the field of alcohol and drug dependence. She runs training programmes in Motivational Interviewing and is in private practice as a psychotherapist, supervisor and trainer. Her particular interest currently is bringing a gestalt understanding to political life. (Contact: toni.gilligan@which.net)

Sheila Haugh is a senior lecturer in psychotherapy at Leeds Metropolitan University, a UKCP-registered psychotherapist, and a BACP accredited practitioner. Formally Convenor for the British Association for the Person-Centred Approach (BAPCA), she currently serves on the board of the World Association for Person-Centered and Experiential Psychotherapy and Counseling (WAPCEPC). She is course leader for the MA in Client-Centred Psychotherapy and Counselling at Leeds Metropolitan and her interests presently include the development of theory within the classical approach to client-centred psychotherapy. (Contact: s.haugh@leedsmet.ac.uk)

Pam Howard is senior lecturer in counselling and psychotherapy at the University of Brighton. She has lectured on psychoanalysis and psychodynamic theory and practice for the past fourteen years. She was previously the Chief Executive of the UK Council for Psychotherapy and the Chair of the Universities Psychotherapy and Counselling Association. She currently practises as a psychoanalytic psychotherapist in private practice. (Contact: P.Howard@bton.ac.uk)

Noriko Motomasa received her PsyD from the Illinois School of Professional Psychology and completed research on client-centered couple and family therapy with Dr Barbara T. Brodley as her chair. She currently works with individuals suffering from a wide spectrum of difficulties, as a licensed clinical psychologist. (Contact: nmtms15@gmail.com)

Kay McFarlane works as a psychotherapist and lecturer. She has a particular interest in prejudice, identity and anti-oppressive practice. She enjoys working with people on various courses and runs a Postgraduate Certificate in Working with Diversity at Leeds Metropolitan University. Kay loves to dance and has recently discovered the joys of gardening. (Contact: k.mcfarlane@leedsmet.ac.uk)

Yukishige Nakata, PhD, is a professor of clinical psychology at Kansai University, Osaka, Japan, studying person-centered/experiential psychotherapy with Shoji Murayam to graduate level. His current concern is the therapeutic power of communities and the community approach. He lives with his wife and two lovely young daughters. He likes to play classical music on the piano but is too busy with work. His aim for this year is to reduce work and multiply fun! (Contact: Nakata.gm@gmail.com)

Stephen Paul is director of the Centre for Psychological Therapies at Leeds Metropolitan University. He is a psychotherapist with over thirty years of practitioner experience and was previously head of a therapeutic school for children with emotional and behavioural difficulties. He has particular interest and expertise in the areas of existential, humanistic and transpersonal psychologies, client-centred psychotherapy, spirituality and group therapy and has led courses in counselling and psychotherapy since 1992. In his spare time he enjoys the tranquillity of French country life. (Contact: s.paul@leedsmet.ac.uk)

Geoffrey Pelham has worked for many years as a counsellor, psychotherapist and supervisor in private practice. He has also been responsible for the delivery of counselling and psychotherapy courses at Leeds Metropolitan University. Recently, he has become head of coach training at a leading UK coaching provider. Throughout this time, he has been particularly interested in the therapeutic relationship and how this is understood across the various therapeutic traditions. (Contact: g.pelham@yahoo.com)

Professor Ernesto Spinelli is a Fellow of both the British Psychological Society (BPS) and the British Association of Counselling and Psychotherapy (BACP) as well as a UKCP-registered existential psychotherapist. In 1999, he was awarded a Personal Chair as Professor of Psychotherapy, Counselling and Counselling Psychology. In 2000, he received the BPS Counselling Psychology Division Award for Outstanding Contributions to the Advancement of the Profession. His most recent book is *Practising Existential Psychotherapy: The relational world*, which was published by Sage in 2007. (Contact: plex@dircon.co.uk)

Jenny Stacey is a gestalt psychotherapist, dramatherapist and supervisor, and has a private practice in Yorkshire. She delivers courses on the use of the arts in educational and therapeutic settings and works in primary schools as a therapist and trainer where the focus of her work is on creative communication and emotional literacy. She is an organisational consultant and coach. (Contact: jenny.stacey@yahoo.co.uk)

John Shiers is a psychosynthesis psychotherapist, supervisor and trainer. He is also an organisational consultant and is developing a transpersonal training and development agency, Synthesise, in North West England. He has a particular interest in making transpersonal psychology more accessible and available in both therapeutic and organisational settings. (Contact: john.shiers@synthesise.org)

Mike Thomas is Dean of the Faculty of Health and Social Care and Professor of Eating Disorders at the University of Chester. For the last eighteen years he has maintained a clinical caseload working with individuals experiencing complex and enduring eating disorders and delivers seminars and workshops nationally. Mike has a particular interest in working at the schematic level using CBT.

At Leeds Metropolitan University he created the Centre for Eating Disorders, and at the University of Salford he developed the degree programme in CBT. (Contact: m.thomas@chester.ac.uk)

Nick Totton is a body psychotherapist, trainer and supervisor in private practice in Calderdale, West Yorkshire. He runs a post-qualification training in his own modality, Embodied-Relational Therapy. Nick has published several books, including *Psychotherapy and Politics* (Sage), and has edited several others including *The Politics of Psychotherapy: New perspectives* (Open University Press). He edits the journal *Psychotherapy and Politics International*. (Contact: nick@3-c.coop)

Andrea Uphoff is a UKCP-registered psychotherapist and Convenor of BAPCA (British Association for the Person-Centred Approach). She is currently engaged in PhD studies at Regent's College, London, where her dissertation research is focused on client experience of touch in the psychotherapeutic relationship. Andrea works in both England and Germany, dividing her time between the two countries. She has been a practitioner of Sahaj Marg meditation for over ten years. (Contact: uphoffandrea@compuserve.de)

Jane Walford is a psychiatrist, Certified Transactional Analyst, Teaching and Supervising Transactional Analyst and UKCP-registered psychotherapist. Jane is a director of Leeds Psychotherapy Training Institute and is course leader on the MA in Transactional Analysis Psychotherapy course. She is interested in how the therapeutic relationship can be used to facilitate change, and how the relationship between student and tutor can enhance the psychotherapy training process. (Contact: jane.walford2@btinternet.com)

Robin Walford is a Certified Transactional Analyst, a Teaching and Supervising Transactional Analyst, a UKCP-registered psychotherapist and an Anglican priest. Robin is a director of Leeds Psychotherapy Training Institute and also teaches in a wide variety of settings as a visiting trainer. As a psychotherapist his primary focus is on the nature of the relationship between therapist and client. (Contact: robinwalford@lpti.org.uk)

William West, PhD, is a Reader in Counselling Studies at the University of Manchester in Britain where he is Director of the Counselling Studies Programme and where he delights in supervising doctoral students. He is a Fellow and accredited practitioner member of the British Association for Counselling and Psychotherapy. William's key areas of research and publication include: counselling and spirituality, culture, traditional healing, supervision and qualitative research methods. (Contact: william.west@manchester.ac.uk)

Richard Worsley is a university counsellor. He has previously directed a person-centred diploma course. He has interests in client process, group therapy, psychopathology, integration, spirituality and theology, and the philosophy of counselling. In particular, he wants to continue to explore the way the thoughts of Martin Buber and Emmanuel Levinas inform thinking and the experience of relating and encounter in both therapy and interfaith relations. (Contact: richardjworsley@btinternet.com)

INDEX

PERSON-CENTRED PSYCHOPATHOLOGY
A POSITIVE PSYCHOLOGY OF MENTAL HEALTH

EDITED BY STEPHEN JOSEPH AND RICHARD WORSLEY

ISBN 978 1 898059 69 1, pp 375, £22.00

This volume examines the relationship between the Person-Centred Approach and psychopathology and attempts to build bridges between disciplines. Person-centred theory is often misunderstood as superficial and naïve. This book shows it is a theory with real depth—able to confront both the dark side of the human condition as well as the positive aspects—promising to provide the foundation stone for a new psychology of mental health. An international collection of writers discuss psychotic functioning, autism and Asperger syndrome, post-traumatic stress, postnatal depression, and antisocial personality disorder, plus chapters on a carer's perspective, research, person-centred assessment and a critique of the medicalisation of distress.

This book stands for both of us as a learning about, and an assertion of, the human capacity to grow in the face of adversity. We hope that practitioners, trainers, and those in training in the varied mental health professions will also find the learning and the wisdom in this book of value to them. (Joseph & Worsley, Preface)

PERSON-CENTRED PRACTICE
CASE STUDIES IN POSITIVE PSYCHOLOGY

EDITED BY RICHARD WORSLEY AND STEPHEN JOSEPH

ISBN 978 1 898059 95 0, pp 240, £20.00

Person-Centred Practice: Case studies in positive psychology is a follow-up to the best-selling and critically acclaimed *Person-Centred Psychopathology*. It takes forward the work of the previous volume by rooting the theory of that volume in the practice of internationally renowned practitioners and scholars. The book demonstrates that person-centred theory has real depth in its ability to address the distress of challenging client groups by tackling childhood sexual abuse, maternal distress, eating disorders, schizophrenia, long-term depression, and psychosis with learning difficulties.

Editors

Stephen Joseph is Professor of Psychology, Health and Social Care in the Centre for Trauma, Resilience, and Growth (CTRG) at the University of Nottingham. He is a chartered health psychologist, and member of the British Psychological Society's Register of Psychologists, specialising in trauma and adversity from a positive psychology orientation.

Richard Worsley has worked for a number of years as a person-centred counsellor, supervisor and trainer. He is also an Anglican priest. He has particular interests in process in therapy, in spirituality, in philosophy and therapy, and in therapeutic groups. Richard works at the University of Warwick as a staff and student counsellor.

Buy direct for free shipping (in the UK) and permanent discounts from
www.pccs-books.co.uk

THE LIFE AND WORK OF CARL ROGERS

Howard Kirschenbaum

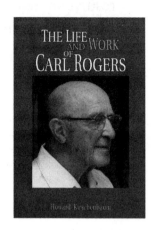

ISBN 978 1 898059 93 6 (cased) £29.00

ISBN 978 1 898059 98 1 (with jacket) £50.00

pp 736

Twenty years after his death, PCCS Books celebrates the life and work of Carl Rogers with the long-awaited second edition of his biography by Howard Kirschenbaum. This completely re-written and re-titled edition includes a more detailed personal and professional history, and a full account of the last decade of Rogers' life. That decade turned out to be one of the most important periods of his career in which he developed peace work all over the world including South Africa and Northern Ireland, culminating in a Nobel Peace Prize nomination just days before his death. Until now this work has not been widely known.

The new edition adds deeper understanding of Rogers' contributions to psychology, the helping professions and society. On a personal level, access to recently revealed private papers tells us much more about Carl Rogers the man than was known to many of his closest associates. Kirschenbaum's own understanding of Carl Rogers, psychotherapy, education, and the human condition has matured over the intervening years. This much-anticipated second edition reflects a wiser and more balanced perspective of his subject. Now fully referenced, this is the life and work of Carl Rogers.

I couldn't put it down. I kept jumping from one part of the book to another and getting absorbed in the close research and the wonderful detail. I know the book took years to research, and now I can see why. Even reading the footnotes is absorbing.
Professor Dave Mearns, University of Strathclyde

Buy direct for free shipping (in the UK) and permanent discounts from
www.pccs-books.co.uk